"A tightly written and original work that brilliantly weaves together global Anabaptist history from Europe to Africa to Asia and across the Americas. *Radicals and Reformers* adds great depth to our collective understanding of Anabaptism across geographies, languages, and cultures."
—**FELIPE HINOJOSA**, John and Nancy Jackson Endowed Chair in Latin America and professor of history at Baylor University

"*Radicals and Reformers* is the first text that truly integrates the history and evolution of Anabaptists and Mennonites across the globe from their origins to present-day realities. Troy Osborne is to be commended for outlining a complex story that balances a people's feats and foibles in equal measure and introduces little-known actors and events to offer new perspectives on familiar tales."
—**MARLENE EPP**, professor emeritus of history and peace and conflict studies at Conrad Grebel University College

"I have been waiting for this book for my entire teaching career. Troy Osborne has synthesized research from the past forty years into an engaging new global narrative that is concise enough for use as an undergraduate college textbook. Employing a transnational approach, Osborne brings the long and complicated sweep of Mennonite history into the twenty-first century. Through explicit discussion of how faith has interacted with culture, modernization, colonialism, indigeneity, and globalization, the book provides rich fodder for discussion of Mennonite reality today."
—**MARY SPRUNGER**, professor of history and program director of history and political science at Eastern Mennonite University

"*Radicals and Reformers* tells the challenging story of Christ-following communities captivated more by the enactment of faithful practices than by the affirmation of key doctrines or the maintenance of enduring institutions. Such a story of concrete discipleship is difficult to tell because it involves a constantly shifting cast of characters and contexts, with persistent disagreements that disrupt as well as energize spiritual renewal. Troy Osborne gives us an expansive and inclusive Anabaptist story, full of both faith and failure, whose coherence arises from radical Christian hope harbored amidst contested communal convictions."
—**GERALD MAST**, professor of communication at Bluffton University

"*Radicals and Reformers* is a gift to undergraduate classrooms—pedagogically flexible with expansive possibilities for drilling down or connecting to other areas of study. Inclusive of a wide range of Anabaptisms, Troy Osborne's focus on the ways that Anabaptist-Mennonites have responded to the realities of their contexts across time and space makes this text particularly relevant to today's academic challenges, as well as those that face the church."
—**ELIZABETH MILLER**, assistant professor of history and director of the Institute for the Study of Global Anabaptism at Goshen College

"Troy Osborne has presented a remarkable work that delves into the Anabaptist movement's history, spanning over five centuries and five continents. It is an excellent resource for anyone seeking a comprehensive understanding of the Anabaptist tradition's past and present. It is highly recommended!"
—**CÉSAR GARCÍA**, general secretary of Mennonite World Conference

"This welcome new study lays out the five hundred-year story of Anabaptism in compelling and sometimes provocative ways. It is the fruit of extensive research and well-balanced analysis. Both scholarly and accessible, the volume brilliantly captures the multivalent tapestry of an evolving tradition that began in Europe and grew to become a global reality."
—**KARL KOOP**, professor of history and theology at Canadian Mennonite University

"The analysis made by the author of this wonderful book takes the reader on a journey through the history, origins, and preservation of the religion and cultural identity of the Anabaptists since late medieval times. At the same time, it invites readers to reflect on the movement's principles and how they endure even in new generations around the world, since they have resisted the influence of other groups or religions and adapted their way of living nowadays."
—**PATRICIA ISLAS SALINAS**, researcher at the Universidad Autónoma de Ciudad Juárez

"Troy Osborne links Anabaptist themes of radical faithfulness and reconciliation with God and humans across five centuries and five continents in one sweeping and accessible narrative. Vivid personal stories illustrate how everyday encounters with a living God embodied in this specific tradition of biblical interpretation and discipleship redirect lives whether in twentieth-century Africa, sixteenth-century Europe, or other places and times this movement has appeared."
—**MARK JANTZEN**, professor of history at Bethel College

RADICALS & REFORMERS

RADICALS & REFORMERS

A Survey of Global Anabaptist History

Troy Osborne

Harrisonburg, Virginia

Herald Press
PO Box 866, Harrisonburg, Virginia 22803
www.HeraldPress.com

Library of Congress Cataloging-in-Publication Data
Names: Osborne, Troy, author.
Title: Radicals and reformers : a survey of global Anabaptist history / Troy Osborne.
Description: Harrisonburg, Virginia : Herald Press, [2024] | Includes bibliographical references and index.
Identifiers: LCCN 2023054561 (print) | LCCN 2023054562 (ebook) | ISBN 9780836199888 (paperback) | ISBN 9781513813325 (hardcover) | ISBN 9781513813332 (ebook)
Subjects: LCSH: Anabaptists—History. | Mennonites—History. | BISAC: RELIGION / Christian Church / History | RELIGION / Christianity / History
Classification: LCC BX4931.3 .O84 2024 (print) | LCC BX4931.3 (ebook) | DDC 284/.3—dc23/eng/20240229
LC record available at https://lccn.loc.gov/2023054561
LC ebook record available at https://lccn.loc.gov/2023054562

Study guides are available for many Herald Press titles at www.HeraldPress.com.

RADICALS AND REFORMERS
© 2024 by Herald Press, Harrisonburg, Virginia 22803. 800-245-7894.
   All rights reserved.
Library of Congress Control Number: 2023054561
International Standard Book Number: 978-0-8361-9988-8 (paperback); 978-1-5138-1332-5 (hardcover); 978-1-5138-1333-2 (ebook)
Printed in United States of America
Cover and interior design by Merrill Miller

All rights reserved. This publication may not be reproduced, stored in a retrieval system, or transmitted in whole or in part, in any form, by any means, electronic, mechanical, photocopying, recording or otherwise without prior permission of the copyright owners.
   Scripture quotations, unless otherwise noted, are from *New Revised Standard Version Bible* Updated Edition. Copyright © 2021 National Council of Churches of Christ in the United States of America. Used by permission. All rights reserved worldwide.

28 27 26   10 9 8 7 6 5 4

Contents

Foreword 9
Introduction 13
1 "Good and Right Order": Late Medieval Christendom 17
2 Repentance and Reform: Radicals in Swiss Lands 42
3 South German Anabaptists: Mysticism and Community of Goods 61
4 Apocalypticism in the North: Melchior, Münster, and the Mennonites 82
5 The Earth Is the Lord's: Seeking the Peace of the City 107
6 Renewal and Revitalization: Seventeenth- and Eighteenth-Century Anabaptists 131
7 Movement and Modernity: The Nineteenth Century 150
8 To the Ends of the Earth: Anabaptist Missions 176
9 Age of Cataclysm: 1914–45 197
10 A Transformational Era: 1945–present 229
11 Continuity and Change: Anabaptists in Africa 243
12 Conversion and Adaptation: Anabaptists in Asia 262
13 Migration and Mission: Latin American Anabaptists 285
14 Renewed Identities and New Realities in the West 305
15 Faith in Changing Times: Evangelism, Anabaptism, and the Old Orders in the Twentieth Century 327
   Conclusion: The Ties That Bind a Global Movement 345
   Notes 348
   Bibliography 361
   Index 379
   The Author 383

Foreword

That Anabaptism could turn half a millennium old would have shocked early Anabaptists, many of whom thought that the end of time was imminent. That so many early Anabaptists were apocalyptic might shock many contemporary Anabaptists.

This historical blind spot, among others, stems from a narrative inherited from mid-twentieth American Mennonitism. In his 1944 essay "The Anabaptist Vision," historian Harold S. Bender emphasized freedom of conscience, the church as a voluntary fellowship of believers, and an ethic of love and nonresistance as key markers of identity. As a rejoinder to hostile Reformation-era accounts that depicted Anabaptists as heretics and fanatics, this narrative was deeply satisfying. William R. Estep's *The Anabaptist Story* (1963) echoed Bender's normative account. He envisioned the Anabaptist attempt to restore the church to what it was before Emperor Constantine as a bright meteor bursting through a dark Catholic sky.

But every generation rewrites history. In the 1970s, a new set of scholars, diving deep into the archives to look at both leaders and ordinary Anabaptists, began to deconstruct this idealized golden age. James Stayer, for example, demonstrated that early Anabaptists held a variety of positions on the sword and violence. Claus-Peter Clasen applied a new social lens of analysis. Werner Packull recovered the mystical and apocalyptic dimensions of early Anabaptism. Collectively, this generation of scholars sought to capture the premodern weirdness of a movement with no single origin, no single authority, and no single theology.

An even younger set of scholars has emerged in a new multicultural moment. Anicka Fast, Felipe Hinojosa, Jaime Prieto, John D. Roth, Masakazu Yamada, and many others have begun narrating the diffusion of an incredibly diverse movement after the sixteenth century. About two-thirds of the over two million baptized believers in eighty-six countries now live in Africa, Asia, and Latin America. The most typical Anabaptist is now an Ethiopian woman, not a man with a bowl cut in Holmes County, Ohio.

In this volume, an absorbing synthesis of scholarship on five hundred years of Anabaptist history over five continents, Troy Osborne captures it all. We're introduced to a stunningly diverse cast of characters. In addition to the usual suspects, we meet Anna Baerg, Edna Ruth Miller Byler, Helena von Freyburg, Daniel Kitamba, Julia Yellow Horse Shoulderblade, Tee Siem Tat, Adolphine Tshiama, and Ibrahim Tunggul Wulung. Yes, Amish cabinetmakers appear in this great crowd of witnesses. But so do Indian matchmakers, a naked man parading through Amsterdam, evangelical church planters in Indonesia, and a zealous baker from Haarlem who believed he was the true Enoch. Menno Simons doesn't appear until page 96 and mostly disappears after page 124. This is an Anabaptist history for a new, globalized, and multicultural era.

Osborne recognizes that there is no such thing as a "naked Anabaptist." We are not disembodied theologies. We are not pure representations of the pure gospel. Faith is always lived out in the clothing of ethnicity, gender, diet, technology, worship styles, and other markers. Sometimes that clothing takes the pleasing shape of mutual aid, costly discipleship, mission, spiritual renewal, and cultural discernment. But it can also take the troubling shapes of violence, inequality, patriarchy, and colonialism.

This critical lens comes with a cost. Bender's Anabaptism offered a center and a more coherent narrative. But there are gains to this lens, too. Osborne's Anabaptism offers more usable pasts for a diverse constituency. As the movement has come full circle in the past century's global swell, it is difficult not to notice, for example, resemblances between the enchanted landscapes of Africa and Latin America and the supernatural terrains of sixteenth-century farmers and fisherfolk in Europe.

Even more importantly, it feels more real and faithful to the complexities of lived experience. What writer and civil rights activist James Baldwin said about America is also true about Anabaptist history: that wherever and whenever humans do life—and seek transcendence—together, it is both terrible and beautiful.

—David R. Swartz, professor of history at Asbury University and author of *Facing West: American Evangelicals in an Age of World Christianity*

Introduction

On January 21, 1525, a group of radical students, former clergy, and peasants baptized one another in a private home in Zürich, Switzerland. By baptizing each other as adults, these young radicals were willing to break with centuries of tradition because they believed that they were reforming the church along biblical lines, and they dedicated themselves to renewing their commitment to scriptural models of faithfulness. As they gathered to pray and read Scripture together—often in secret—they promised to support one another in following Christ, even if it led to suffering or death. While they knew that religious and civic authorities would condemn them for "rebaptizing" one another, they could not have guessed at the remarkable course of events that would lead to a split in the reforming movement, persecution, exile, growth, and centuries later, an Anabaptist movement whose members can be found throughout Asia, Africa, and across the Americas.

This book attempts to tell that remarkable history in an honest way that includes both positive and critical elements of the Anabaptists' stories. I identify as a member of that movement, and I hope that the story that readers encounter in these chapters is an honest account of people who can inspire by their faithfulness as well as instruct from their failures. To find common threads throughout these stories, I have tried to highlight how Anabaptists have nurtured their collective identity through revival, peace, separation, and discipleship within a broader narrative exploring how Anabaptists have adopted or resisted changing contexts.

Anabaptists have been creating a common story since their earliest days, when believers from the north and south of Europe reached out to one another to see whether they shared reforming goals and a common identity. Subsequently, they shared songs and stories with one another, creating an imagined community that stretched from the marshy lands of the Low Countries to the mountains and valleys of the Alps. As Anabaptists spread west across the Atlantic Ocean and east into Ukraine, the story grew with them and continued to connect them to each other. Today, the membership of Mennonite World Conference includes Anabaptists from across the globe, even though members may at times question what connects them to one another. Despite core theological similarities, the differences between Anabaptist practices can seem near total. Throughout the movement's history, churches have written themselves out of the Anabaptist tradition or disagreed about whether other churches truly belonged. While it is easy to focus on the many moments of conflict and exclusion, there are also numerous examples of times when Anabaptists have rewritten their story to include new members.

My hope is that this text will be used by college, university, and seminary students in Canada and the United States, as well as by curious leaders and laity in Anabaptist churches. Instructors may choose to augment this text with primary sources and their own lectures. Given the length of a typical academic term and course syllabi, I have chosen to restrict the scope of the tradition at the cost of some of its rich depth. The narrative and examples of this book should be understood to be illustrations of Anabaptist streams, but not their totality. There are Anabaptist groups whose histories do not receive the attention they deserve, notably the Hutterites, Brethren in Christ, and the Church of the Brethren. I am also aware that Mennonite and Amish history contains many more distinctions, traditions, and countries than can be covered within these pages. To members of those groups, I ask for their forbearance, and I hope that they may still discover patterns or dynamics that reflect their own experiences.

To tell this history, I have relied on the expertise and assistance of many others. I wish to thank the group of readers who looked at my chapters over the years, especially those who met in person at Conrad Grebel University College: Marlene Epp, Mark Jantzen, Karl Koop, Gerald Mast, Jamie Pitts, John Roth, and Mary Sprunger. A generous grant from the Showalter Foundation made it possible to gather these scholars for an invaluable conversation on teaching Mennonite and Anabaptist history. I would also like to thank Maxwell Kennel and Colin Friesen, who helped find materials in the early stages of the writing. Illustrations and indexing were made possible by the support of Conrad Grebel University College's Academic Development and Research Fund.

A synthesis of five hundred years covering five continents would not have been possible without the expertise of many other scholars. I am indebted to the historians who have come before me, especially to the editors and scholars of the Global Mennonite History Series. Special thanks to the students at Eastern Mennonite University, Bethel College, and Canadian Mennonite University, who have engaged some of this material in their courses. Valerie Weaver-Zercher, Laura Leonard Clemens, and Amy Gingerich have provided much needed encouragement and been extraordinarily patient with this book. Finally, I wish to thank my parents and grandparents, who loved to tell me their stories, sparking my interest in a movement that continues to surprise me in archives and in pews.

— ONE —

"Good and Right Order"

Late Medieval Christendom

In the year 1476, an illiterate shepherd named Hans Behem experienced a divine encounter with the virgin Mary while tending his sheep in the hills outside the German town of Niklashausen. In his vision, the mother of God instructed the illiterate shepherd to burn all his excess possessions and begin a life of virtuous poverty. Hans obeyed and began preaching Mary's message to others. Word of Hans Behem's vision spread, attracting throngs of supporters and the curious to the virgin's pilgrimage shrine in Niklashausen. As Hans Behem's popularity surged, his sermons became more radical and critical of the religious and political structures around him. Government informants who heard one of his sermons reported that Hans Behem preached, among other things, that

> the Emperor is a villain, and, along with the pope, is nothing.
> The Emperor gives to the princes, dukes, knights, and servants what he gains through taxes from the common people. Woe to those poor fools.

> The clergy have many benefices [church appointments]; that should not be. They should have no more than is sufficient to maintain themselves. . . .
>
> The fish in the water and the animals in the field shall belong to all. The princes of the world and the church have so much. What should it take for the common people to have enough? It must come to pass that the princes and lords have to work for a day's wage . . . .[1]

Though he came from one of the lowest social rungs of late medieval Europe, Hans Behem commanded spiritual authority by claiming to speak for the virgin Mary and performing miracles. Tens of thousands of pilgrims traveled to Niklashausen to hear his prophecies for themselves. Ultimately, Hans Behem's movement ended after troops captured him and burned him at the stake for heresy on July 1476. Böhm's prophetic movement died with him on the pyre, but his calls for the restructuring of church and society lived on.

Like Hans Behem, disempowered and resentful common men and women found comfort and support in Christianity, despite the perception that church institutions contributed to their suffering. Increasingly, as anticlerical sentiments surged, the hope for a new society included the hope for a renewed and reformed church. Calls for social, political, and religious change among disempowered (and powerful) Europeans continued to build momentum until they burst forth in the Reformations of the sixteenth century.

Modern-day Mennonites, Amish, and Hutterites trace their roots back to sixteenth-century reforming movements in what is now modern-day Switzerland, Germany, and the Low Countries (Belgium, the Netherlands, and northwest Germany). Known by their opponents as Anabaptists, or "rebaptizers" (the prefix *ana-* means "again"), these men and women were, like the peasants who joined Hans Behem, seeking new ways to encounter God outside of the official church structure, which they believed was more concerned with worldly wealth and status than the care of souls. But even before the Protestant Reformation of the 1500s, there were efforts to renew the church and calls for a more just society. To fully grasp the origins of the Anabaptists, it is important to place them in the context of the turbulent religious, economic, and political changes that challenged the authority of the traditional sacred and secular institutions of late medieval Europe.

This chapter will explore how Martin Luther's teachings overturned the church's authority and paved the way for Christians to seek new avenues to encounter God.

The institutions of Christendom

The sixteenth-century Protestant and Catholic Reformations marked the beginning of a period of profound change that unraveled the political and religious institutions that had held western European society together for centuries. The intertwined power of secular and religious authority began in 313 CE, when the Roman emperor Constantine reversed the imperial policy of discrimination and persecution of Christians, and his successors eventually declared Christianity the empire's official religion. In the fifth century, Germanic tribes migrated into Europe, and many of them converted to Christianity. The kings and chieftains of these tribes converted to Christianity with the hope of allying themselves with the church to solidify their power over neighboring tribes and reforge a new Roman empire, this time knit together with the help of the church. Over the next thousand years, the subjects living under these rulers underwent a complex historical process known as Christianization, whereby a new hybrid culture—combining elements of Greco-Roman thought, Germanic traditions, and Christian practices—shaped Europeans into Christians.

The church led the process of Christianization, but it collaborated with secular powers in forging Christendom. The bishop of Rome, known as the pope, was the head of the Catholic Church in western Europe and ran the most sophisticated bureaucracy in medieval Europe. The church was governed by canon law, or the church's laws and regulations, which was enforced by its legal courts. The pope's closest advisers, the College of Cardinals, were the "hinges" (*cardine* in Latin) who opened and closed the doors of power in the church, including the election of the pope.

The church divided its administrative structure into districts called dioceses, each of which was governed by bishops. Bishops, often members of noble or wealthy families, wore purple to indicate that their authority in the church was equal to that of worldly princes, who also wore purple as a sign of their rank. A bishop's main responsibility was to supervise the priests at the parish level, which was the local neighborhood or village church. Called "secular" clergy because they were in the world (*seculum* in Latin), parish priests were the most visible members of the church for common people.

In medieval Europe, many sought to escape the corrupting influences of the world by joining religious orders and taking vows of poverty, chastity, and obedience. Monasteries and convents provided a retreat for these individuals and were run by abbots and abbesses. Members of these orders followed the rule (*regula*) of their founder (such as Saint

Fig. 1.1 Benedict of Nursia, founder of Western monasticism.
Print by Christoffel van Sichem (II), *Heilige Benedictus*, 1648. Rijksmuseum, Amsterdam, RP-P-1905-6478.

Benedict), so they were called regular clergy. Although the monasteries originally formed as retreats from the corrupting influences of the world, pious men and women donated land and money to the monasteries and convents, which grew into powerful institutions over time.

Anabaptism and Monasticism

Several early Anabaptist leaders had already left monastic orders before joining the new movement. For example, after he left the Benedictine order in the 1520s, Michael Sattler, future author of the Schleitheim Confession, joined the Anabaptist movement, where he was an influential leader before his death by burning at the stake in May 1527. Modern scholars have suggested that Sattler's monastic experience shaped his Anabaptist theology and spirituality.[2] This excerpt on discipline from the Rule of Benedict, for example, is very similar to the views laid out in Sattler's Schleitheim Confession, a key statement of Anabaptist principles from 1527.

Rule of Saint Benedict
If any of the community prove rebellious, disobedient, proud, or murmuring, or contemptuously disobey the holy Rule or the commands of the elders, he shall be admonished, according to the precept of our Lord, once and then twice by the seniors in private. If notwithstanding he does not mend his ways, he shall be publicly rebuked. If then he remains incorrigible, and understands how great the penalty is, he shall be excommunicated.[3]

Schleitheim Confession
The ban shall be employed with all those who have given themselves over to the Lord, to walk after [Him] in His commandments; those who have been baptized into the one body of Christ, and let themselves be called brothers or sisters, and still somehow slip and fall into error and sin, being inadvertently overtaken. The same [shall] be warned twice privately and the third time be publicly admonished before the entire congregation according to the command of Christ (Matthew 18).[4]

In the twelfth and thirteenth centuries, new religious orders emerged in response to the increasing wealth and influence of monasteries. These orders sought to revive the monastic tradition of living a committed Christian life, but with a focus on serving the world, especially in towns and cities. Known as friars, their members were like monks, but unlike monks who lived in isolated communities, friars served society and often relied on charity and donations for support. The Carmelites, Franciscans, Dominicans, and Augustinians—all orders within this new stream—gained renown as teachers and preachers. The local priests often resented the intrusion of the interloping friars, whose popular preaching style made them into minor celebrities. Reminding their audiences to prepare themselves for their inevitable deaths, the mendicant preachers admonished their audience to get their spiritual accounts in order and confess their sins.

Most laypeople (non-clergy) experienced Christianity through the rituals of the sacraments, physical signs of God's grace. Since the thirteenth century, the church had practiced seven sacraments—baptism, penance, the eucharist, confirmation, marriage, priestly ordination, and the anointing of the sick. Through these sacraments, the church helped people make their way through the joys and sorrows of this life and prepare their souls for the next.

In the earliest years of Christianity, baptism was given to those who chose to leave their old religion. As Christianity became the dominant religion of western Europe and the former Roman Empire, fewer Christians converted to the religion from paganism—people were born into it. By the seventh and eighth centuries, it had become the universal practice to baptize infants soon after birth, marking the moment of initiation into the church and the local community. Confirmation, received in late childhood, established full membership in the church. The church expected its members to confess their sins at least once a year, fast at the appropriate times, pay tithes, give to charity, have a basic understanding of the Lord's Prayer and perhaps the Apostles' Creed, and take communion during the mass, the liturgy that brought together communities for worship and provided the primary rite for most Europeans.

The eucharist, or communion, was the central moment of medieval Christian worship, as it was believed to provide a direct connection between the communicant and Christ. According to the doctrine of transubstantiation, when during the mass the priest spoke (in Latin) the words of institution, "This is my body," and "This is my blood,"

"Good and Right Order" 23

Fig. 1.2 According to tradition, a vision of Christ as the Man of Sorrows appeared on the altar to Pope Gregory to convince a deacon who doubted the doctrine of transubstantiation. The text at the bottom of the engraving states that whoever recites the Apostles' Creed, the Lord's Prayer, and the Hail Mary before the image will be pardoned twenty thousand years of time in purgatory. Engraving by Israhel van Meckenem, *The Mass of Saint Gregory*, c. 1490/1500. Courtesy of National Gallery of Art, Washington, Rosenwald Collection, 1954.12.91.

the substance of the bread and wine of the eucharist became the physical body and blood of Christ. Whereas the clergy consumed both the wine and the bread, the laity typically received only the bread, which was placed on their tongues by the priest. The sacrament of communion grew so important that some people attended mass at multiple churches on a Sunday morning; others would yell at clergy who misspoke the words and command them to restart the ceremony from the beginning. Despite the importance of the mass and the eucharist, the laity seldom partook in communion. Because it was Christ physically present, the consecrated bread itself became a focus for devotion and was believed to work miracles.[5]

If someone felt remorseful for sinning against God, they could confess their sins (at least once a year) to a priest. Using a confessional manual (originally developed for monks), the parish priest imposed an appropriate penance for the particular sin committed. The penance was not enough to cover all the sins in the believer's spiritual ledger, the church taught, so the penance continued after death in purgatory until God was satisfied. Located above hell and heated by its fires, purgatory was believed to be where most people went before they could enter heaven. Because suffering there was preferable to hell, purgatory was seen as an expression of God's grace and love for humanity.

By the sixteenth century, it was believed that the time required in purgatory would need to be thousands of years. Individuals could shorten the time in purgatory by purchasing indulgences, charters of grace and forgiveness. Originally, the church dispensed indulgences for acts of charity or generosity, but over time, the church allowed people to buy them for themselves or for family members. Partial indulgences for a fixed amount of time could be gained by giving to charity to the church, going on a pilgrimage, giving alms, or performing acts of devotion, like prayer or fasting. Plenary indulgences, much rarer, would remit all of one's penance. A family or guild might also hire a priest to pray for the deceased in the hope of reducing their loved ones' time in purgatory.

Medieval Christianity offered means for believers to navigate their struggles in this world in addition to the world after death. Among the common farmers and fisherfolk of Europe, there was a fundamental belief in supernatural forces that actively intervened in the world.

Fig. 1.3 Having satisfied their penance, people are hoisted from purgatory to heaven thanks to the prayers and alms (alms dede) of the living. Manuscript page reproduced by permission from *The Desert of Religion* (England, first half of fifteenth century). British Library, London, Additional MS 37049, f. 24v.

Some of these forces were beneficial, and others were malicious. The devil, angels, and demons were actively intervening in the world to torment and tempt the faithful. Special objects, like amulets or charms, could keep malevolent forces at bay. Parishioners could also turn to the church's spiritual power to deal with these forces. For example, priests blessed their parishioners' fields, boats, homes, or livestock to increase their abundance.[6] A parishioner could pray to saints—dead holy men and women—who would intervene in the world for them. Shrines—holy sites associated with saints—were locations of notable spiritual power. People would travel on pilgrimages to visit shrines, believing that these were favorable places to connect with God, angels, or saints. Relics, such as a body part or article of clothing associated with a particular saint, were believed to carry sacred power and to spiritually connect the person praying with the saint associated with the relic.

Some practices, such as amulets, were not officially approved by the church, but it is wrong to dismiss them as mere folkloric superstition. For most Christians, sacramental Christianity helped them understand their world and provided a sense of control in it. For its part, the church occasionally tried to trim away and control practices that veered too far from Christian teachings into pseudo-magical practices.[7] But on the eve of the sixteenth century, there were renewed calls to purify Christianity from nonbiblical traditions that had built up over time.

The crisis of authority in the late medieval world

The Anabaptists emerged from within a society where 90 percent of people lived and worked in the countryside. Most northern European villages were small collections of self-sufficient farms that produced barely enough to keep their occupants alive from year to year. Villages were relatively isolated, but the institutions, teachings, and practices of the church linked Europeans together institutionally and culturally. Although there were significant Jewish and Muslim communities living in Europe, most Europeans were Christians who looked to the bishop of Rome, the pope, as their spiritual leader.

In addition to the practice of the sacraments, Christian art, literature, philosophy, and law also helped Europeans make sense of and survive this world and pass through to the next one. Europeans who shared this combination of religious culture and secular authority understood themselves to be part of "the body of Christ," or *corpus Christianum*. This deep connection between political and religious institutions knit this body together into "Christendom," in which there was no separation of sacred and secular authorities, but each structure, in theory, worked together to give order to western European society and culture. Although the unity of Christendom had already begun to unravel by 1500, the Reformations of the sixteenth century permanently shattered the ideal of a religiously, politically, and legally unified Europe.

Looking back from the perspective of the post-Reformation world, historians have tried to make sense of why the late medieval church fractured in the sixteenth century, never to be put together again. Some scholars have argued that the late medieval church was fundamentally flawed in both its institutions and its ideas. These authors describe a church that no longer met the spiritual needs of its members and was incapable of responding to the changing socioeconomic context of late medieval Europe. Other historians have emphasized the ways that Europeans' devotion was stronger than ever. Rather than emphasizing a corrupt and fallen church, these scholars stress that Europeans were demanding more of Christianity and its leaders.

How do we explain these differing perspectives? Scholars who focus on corruption and incompetence in the church have drawn from sources written by sixteenth-century Protestant Reformers who wanted to justify their new movements. There were also many vocal critics of the late medieval church who called for it to reform itself in its "head and members." Just as Hans Behem and other downtrodden peasants hoped for a fairer world, the intellectual and religious elites also wanted meaningful reform. In 1411, King Sigismund, the future Holy Roman Emperor, promised "to bring the affairs of the Holy Church in the Holy Roman Empire into good and right order, to repair justice and the common weal which have been too long suppressed, and to check the ruination of the Holy Church and succor to the Holy Roman Empire."[8] On the other hand, historians who hold up the positive dynamics of the late medieval church have noted that people gave more money to the church, went on pilgrimages, and joined lay religious organizations in greater numbers. Their sources seem to suggest that late medieval Christianity was more vibrant and vigorous than ever.

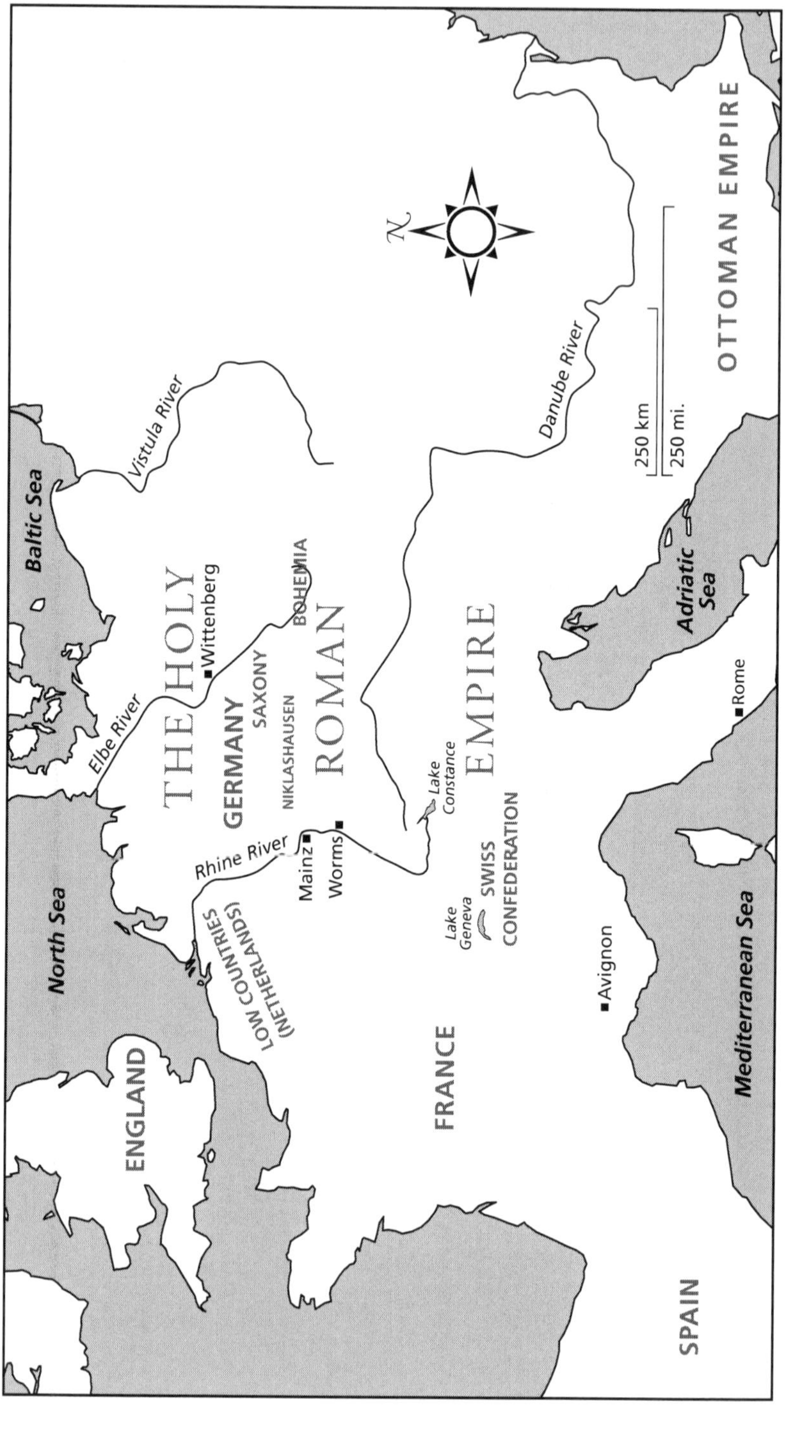
THE HOLY ROMAN EMPIRE
OTTOMAN EMPIRE
Baltic Sea
North Sea
Adriatic Sea
Mediterranean Sea
Vistula River
Elbe River
Rhine River
Danube River
Wittenberg
GERMANY
SAXONY
NIKLASHAUSEN
BOHEMIA
Mainz
Worms
Lake Constance
SWISS CONFEDERATION
Lake Geneva
LOW COUNTRIES (NETHERLANDS)
ENGLAND
FRANCE
SPAIN
Avignon
Rome
N
250 km
250 mi.

Calls for reform

In truth, the late medieval period witnessed both a growing devotion to and dissatisfaction with the official church. The church's success in deepening the religious commitments of its members simultaneously increased people's expectations of what the church should provide for them. When religious institutions or individuals failed to live up to their own standards, the laity or some members of the clergy began to call for reforms of the church in its structure and theology.

It was assumed that any reform of the church would originate from the pope or reform-minded bishops and spread down to the parish level. However, papal authority was severely weakened on the eve of the sixteenth century. The strife between French kings and the papacy over who would control church appointments and finances undercut the pope's spiritual, bureaucratic, and temporal authority. In 1309, Clement V was elected pope, but the French-born pontiff refused to travel to Rome, with its diseases and political intrigues. Instead, he founded a new papal court in the city of Avignon, where the pope could be influenced more easily by the French monarch's wishes instead of Roman ones. After seven popes kept their courts in Avignon, Pope Gregory XI moved the papal seat back to Rome in 1377, but after his death the following year, French cardinals elected a relatively unknown bishop as pope with hopes of returning the papal seat to Avignon. They soon regretted their decision after this new pope, Urban VI, refused to move to Avignon. They then elected a second pope, thereby beginning the Great Schism, or church split, which divided the Western church until 1417.

During the years when there were two, or even three, competing papacies, church leaders, hindered by the lack of clear authority, could not put much effort into reforming the church or addressing heresies spread by, say, John Wycliff in England or Jan Hus in Bohemia. To solve the crisis in papal authority, they convened a council to settle the schism. The resulting doctrine of conciliarism claimed that church authority ultimately rested in a general council outside of papal control. By claiming its superiority to the papacy, the Council of Constance (1414–17) managed to heal the schism. To shore up its power, the council released the document *Sacrosancta* in 1415, which claimed that the council's authority came "immediately from Christ; everyone, of every rank in condition, including the pope himself, is bound to obey it in matters concerning the faith, the abolition of schism, and the Reformation of the Church of God in its head and its members."[9] Conciliarism seemed to raise the possibility of reforming the church by bypassing papal authority. Ultimately, successive popes managed to resist and reduce conciliar authority in the hope of repairing the image and authority of the Roman papacy. Even though it died out, the conciliar movement introduced the new and potentially divisive idea that church authority rested with all its members, not just the papacy.

The humanists go back to the sources

While the church hierarchy was divided by schisms and crises, a new educational paradigm was turning to ancient sources for models to reform individuals and society and foster the birth (or rebirth) of a golden age. As the defining intellectual outlook of the era, humanism rejected medieval theological curriculum for the study of things that made one virtuous: grammar, rhetoric, poetry, history, and ethics. In Italy, humanists studied Greek and Latin in order to immerse themselves in the world and languages of the classical age. The models found in the story and language of the ancient texts, they argued, would cultivate virtue in the hearts and minds of students, who would then reform society and usher in a new age that recaptured the glory and virtue of ancient Greece and Rome

Whereas Italian humanists promoted the Greek and Roman sources for virtuous models, Northern humanists learned Greek and read the New Testament in its original language. To form more virtuous Christians, they published new, authoritative editions of classical and religious sources. The movable-type printing press, with its large print runs of inexpensive books, fed Europe's insatiable desire for devotional reading material. Well-educated urban laity, often educated in humanist schools, were particularly interested in mystic devotional readings that guided them in the imitation of Jesus in daily life.

The former Augustinian canon Erasmus of Rotterdam was a leading Northern humanist who gained international celebrity status through his biting criticisms and calls for church reform. After studying various Bible translations, he published a Greek New Testament in 1516, which would offer scriptural justification for reforming ecclesial excess.

For example, Erasmus's translation of the Greek word *metanoeite* as *respiscite* (repent), instead of *poenitentiam* (to do penance), challenged centuries-old teachings of the church and weakened scriptural support for its penitential system. He also promoted pacifism for all Christians, even rulers. For Erasmus, reading and meditating on the Scriptures

Fig. 1.4 Although he never broke from the Catholic Church, the great humanist Erasmus of Rotterdam is often credited by historians and his peers for laying the foundation for the Reformations. Engraving by Albrecht Dürer, *Portrait of Desiderius Erasmus*, 1526. Metropolitan Museum of Art, New York, Fletcher Fund, 1919, 19.73.120.

was more important than church ceremonies, and the veneration of the saints was less important than praying directly to God. While some humanists expected students of the classics to reform the church, Erasmus believed that secular rulers should lead the reforming process. Erasmus was a severe and relentless critic of the church and inspired vernacular translations of his New Testament, but he did not join any reforming movement, which earned him the scorn of both Catholics and Reformers.

Slipping outside of Rome's control: New devotion, mysticism, and the Hussites

Erasmus's religious views were likely shaped by his education with the Brothers and Sisters of the Common Life, a quasi-monastic communal group whose pious lifestyle challenged the special status of the traditional religious orders. In the fifteenth century, the brothers and sisters formed communities to seek a direct connection with God outside of the church, which they called *devotio moderna* (new devotion), emphasizing private prayer instead of priestly sacraments, as outlined in a key work, *The Imitation of Christ* (1441) by Thomas à Kempis. The *devotio* provided a path for the laity to circumvent the traditional routes of institutional piety by teaching spiritual exercises that they could practice at home, without having to go through clergy or the sacraments. However, it is important not to overdramatize the difference between the *devotio moderna* and traditional Catholic teaching. By the eve of the Reformation, followers of the *devotio* had been integrated into traditional forms of religious orders. Nonetheless, the desire for personal contact with God through unmediated scripture reading would arise again in the Anabaptist movements of the sixteenth century.

In the late Middle Ages, many people filled their hunger for God through mysticism—experiencing the direct and unmediated presence of God. The writings of medieval German mystics Meister Eckhardt and Johannes Tauler as well as the anonymous *Theologica Deutsch* offered individuals paths to understanding and encountering God by detaching themselves from the cares of the world, a process known in German as *Gelassenheit,* or yieldedness. Tauler and the *Theologica Deutsch* refashioned Eckhardt's speculative mysticism, making it accessible to the common person, emphasizing moral principles and individualizing one's union with God. Mysticism's unmediated access to God potentially undermined the authority of the church and its sacraments. While mysticism did not directly challenge the church during the early sixteenth century, it influenced the theology and spirituality of early Anabaptists in southern Germany.

In what is roughly today the modern Czech Republic, Bohemian nationalism mixed with religious reforms to spark the first attempt to formally escape from the papacy's control during this period. In the Bohemian capital of Prague, the priest and professor of philosophy Jan Hus preached a series of reform-focused sermons in the early 1400s. His vision for Bohemian churches to break free from foreign (German) control inspired Czech nobility to back his reforming agenda, which included serving both the bread and the wine to the laity during the mass. Hus traveled to the Council of Constance to defend his reforms, but the council had him arrested and burned at the stake in 1415. Soon thereafter the Hussite churches declared their independence from Rome, taking the eucharistic chalice as the symbol of their movement.

After decades of warfare, the Roman Catholic Church recognized the Bohemian church's independence. A further split soon followed; inspired by Petr Chelčický, the Union of Bohemian Brethren (Unitas Fratrum) broke away from the new Hussite church in 1457. In addition to rejecting beliefs in transubstantiation and a separate priesthood, the Brethren attempted to live out the Sermon on the Mount by refusing to swear an oath or serve in the military—themes that would emerge again in the sixteenth-century Reformations.

The *devotio moderna* and Hus's reforms serve as important reminders that efforts at church reformations were geographically and chronologically wider than the German reforms that began with Martin Luther in 1517. Across Europe, many believed that the day of judgment was quickly approaching. The need for reform grew more urgent as the papacy seemed to take on more characteristics of the prophesied antichrist in many people's eyes. In the east, the troops of the Muslim Ottoman Turks marched seemingly relentlessly north from Constantinople toward the heart of Christendom. Many people grew convinced that the Ottoman troops would dispense God's punishment on unfaithful individuals and communities and inaugurate the end of the world. As the final days drew near, anxious souls expected the arrival of an apocalyptic prophet to announce the beginning of the reign of God.

The Luther affair

The sixteenth-century Reformations that fractured the unity of the Catholic Church arose out of a variety of social forces and criticisms. The various reforming trajectories succeeded because of the intellectual, political, and financial support of countless men and women in cities and villages across Europe. Although multiple social and political causes fueled the movement, scholars of the sixteenth-century Reformations acknowledge the persuasive power of the ideas and personality of one person—Martin Luther, a theology professor from the relatively unknown University of Wittenberg in Germany. Luther's ideas and their promotion in text, song, and image unleashed the pent-up forces and started a series of reformations, including the renewal movements from which Anabaptist groups descend.

Luther came from an upwardly mobile German family. His father, Hans Luther, planned for Martin to become a lawyer and thus sent him to university. But the elder Luther's carefully laid plans for Martin to secure a well-paying legal career unraveled on a stormy night in 1505. Caught in the open countryside during a severe lightning storm, the twenty-one-year-old Luther cried out, "Saint Anne, help me! I will become a monk." After surviving the storm, Luther kept his promise to the saint and joined an Augustinian friary, against the wishes of his father and mother.

Luther thrived in the Augustinian order. He became a priest in 1507, earned a doctor of divinity degree, and began teaching at the University of Wittenberg in 1512. Luther taught biblical studies at the new university, which the ruler of Saxony, Frederick the Wise, had founded a decade before. Luther was a well-liked teacher, and his lectures on Psalms, Romans, Galatians, and Hebrews proved popular with students and laid the foundations of his theological principles. His careful study of Scripture also helped him tackle his own spiritual crisis.

Luther had been a fastidious friar, yet despite regularly fasting, praying, and confessing all his (relatively minor) sins, he never felt as if he had been contrite enough to satisfy God's righteous wrath. If God were truly just and holy, Luther agonized that nothing could be done

"Good and Right Order" 35

Fig. 1.5 Images of Luther in his monk's habit were mass produced to aid the spread of the reformer's message. Engraving by Lucas Cranach the Elder (German, Kronach 1472–1553 Weimar), 1520. Metropolitan Museum of Art, New York, gift of Felix M. Warburg, 1920, 20.64.21.

on earth to cleanse him from sin. However, while reading the epistle to the Romans, Luther rediscovered this verse: "The righteousness of God is revealed through faith for faith; as it is written, 'The one who is righteous will live by faith'" (Romans 1:17). Luther's theological breakthrough rested on his interpretation of God's "righteousness." Fallen humans could never do enough to be saved on their own, but God declares everyone righteous and imputes, or credits, the merits of Christ's sacrifice to sinners. Later in life, Luther reflected on the moment when he became aware that a merciful God justifies people by faith: "Here I felt that I was altogether born again and had entered paradise itself through open gates."[10] Luther believed that there was nothing humans alone could do—fasting, confession, charitable deeds, going to mass—to ever sufficiently deserve salvation. This gave him a deep sense of relief and gratitude for God's merciful love despite humanity's fallenness. It also undercut the theological underpinnings of much of the authority of the Catholic Church.

In 1514, Albrecht of Brandenburg desired to become the bishop of Mainz, thereby adding a third bishopric to his previous ones at Halberstadt and Magdeburg. To secure papal dispensation for holding multiple benefices, he offered to pay Pope Leo X ten thousand ducats in addition to the ten thousand he was already going to pay to secure the office. Albrecht, who lacked sufficient funds to pay the pope right away, took out a large loan from the House of Fugger, the pope's German bankers. To pay back the loan and the pope, Albrecht agreed to dispense plenary indulgences, which the pope had issued to help finance the building of a new basilica of Saint Peter in Rome.

Albrecht commissioned the Dominican friar Johann Tetzel to promote the indulgences. An experienced indulgence agent, Tetzel and his coworkers did not technically sell the indulgences, which were offered for acts of charity or piety. Those who bought indulgences assumed that their donation funded the completion of Saint Peter's Basilica in Rome, but they probably did not realize that half the money went to repay Albrecht's debt. To encourage people to pay as much as possible, Tetzel employed catchy jingles and posters to promote the new indulgence, which grew incredibly popular among Luther's parishioners. When Luther saw the indulgence and learned about Tetzel's marketing techniques, his growing outrage led to his first public protestation.

To challenge these indulgences, Luther wrote ninety-five arguments, or theses, in Latin, which he posted on the church door in Wittenberg in October 1517.[11] Luther contended that buying an indulgence, a simple piece of parchment, could do nothing for one's salvation. The pope, Luther claimed, did not have the authority to release souls from purgatory. Luther's doctrine of grace dispensed with the need for indulgences, or indeed any good deeds, since God justifies sinners on account of their faith, not for their good deeds or their financial donations. Tetzel's catchy ditty "As soon as the coin in the coffer rings / the soul from purgatory springs!" seemed to suggest that one could purchase the forgiveness of sins without any contrition or penance. Luther objected to both the theology and the avarice that the indulgence seemed to represent.

German humanists seized on Luther's ideas and spread them wherever they thought there might be a market. Luther became a hero to the burgeoning reform movement, and added to his fame through his fiery counterblasts against all who challenged him. The humanists'

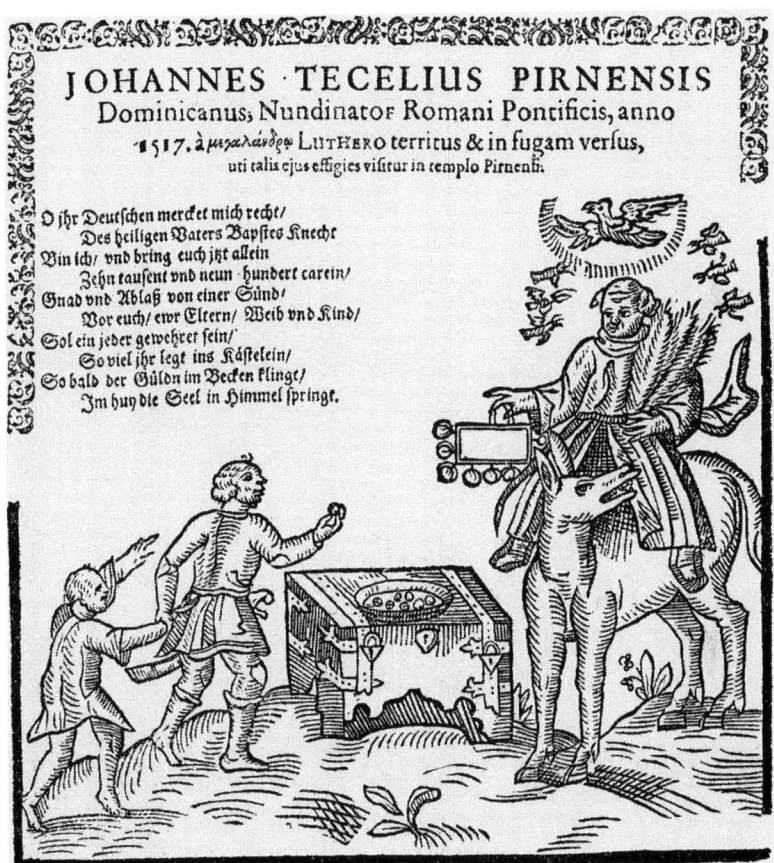

Fig. 1.6 In this woodcut, Johann Tetzel's sermon and jingle promote the efficacy of the plenary indulgence. The seals around indulgence prove its legitimacy, and the poem promises, "As soon as the Gulden in the coffer clings / The soul from purgatory to Heaven springs." Woodcut from INTERFOTO / Alamy Stock Photo.

promotion of Luther in printed pamphlets and booklets created a mythology of Luther as the savior of the church, and the German nation against the machinations of the corrupt Italian church. For the humanists, the obscure monk and professor who challenged the pope himself seemed like a classical hero, even though Luther's arguments had more in common with scholastic theology than they did with humanist writers. As the tone of Luther's and Catholic writers' attacks became more bitter, Luther grew convinced that papal Rome was under the domination of satanic forces, and the possibility of schism grew more likely.

In 1520, Luther published three major treatises that elaborated his agenda for reforming the church. In his declaration on reforming

Fig. 1.7 Luther (in his friar's garb, *center*) outbowls the pope and cardinals (*right*) because his bowling ball is the "Holy Scripture." Woodcut title page adapted from Otto Clemen, *Flugscrhiften aus den ersten Jahren der Reformation*, vol. 3 (Leipzig: R. Haupt, 1907–11). Scan courtesy of Milton Good Library, Conrad Grebel University College, Waterloo.

worship, *The Babylonian Captivity of the Church*, Luther reduced the true sacraments to those found in Scripture: baptism, penance, and communion. In *An Address to the Christian Nobility of the German*, he declared that all Christians (but especially secular rulers) were obligated and had the authority to reform the church. In *The Freedom of a Christian*, Luther wrote that good deeds spring naturally out of gratitude for God's boundless love and mercy in justifying sinners, despite their sins. Luther was convinced that the renewal of Christian life required secular leaders, not religious ones, to reform the church in order that the message of "salvation by faith" could be freely proclaimed to everyone.

Luther's three powerful treatises and his understanding of "salvation by faith" directly challenged and dismantled the authority of the church. Initially, the papal court ignored what it thought to be an obscure theological controversy at a backwater university. However, Luther's rising popularity at a time when the pope desperately needed to unite the German princes in potential war against the advancing Ottoman Turks forced the papal courts to condemn Luther and his teachings. In June 1520, the papal decree *Exsurge Domine* ("Rise up, O Lord") ordered Luther to recant his heresies. When a copy of the declaration arrived in Wittenberg, Luther and his students burned it, along with a copy of the canon law. The following January, the church excommunicated Luther, which only emboldened him further in his criticism of the papacy.

Soon, the secular powers began to take sides in these theological disputes. The newly elected Holy Roman Emperor Charles V wanted to preserve the unity of his vast territory, one of the largest empires in the history of western Europe. The young ruler called the princes and urban delegates of the Holy Roman Empire to assemble at the Diet (general assembly) of Worms in April 1521. Charles summoned Luther to defend himself and his writings. At Worms, Luther acknowledged the charges leveled against him, but when he was directly challenged to answer yes or no to whether he would recant, he requested a day's adjournment to consider his answer. The next day, Luther stood before the gathered might of the imperial throne and German princes and said, "Unless I am convinced by the testimony of the Scriptures or by clear reason . . . , I am bound by the scriptures I have quoted and my conscience is captive to the Word of God. I cannot and I will not retract anything, since it is neither safe nor right to go against conscience. I cannot do otherwise, here I stand, may God help me. Amen."[12]

Even though they took different trajectories and had different agendas, nearly all future reforming movements built on Luther's appeal to the authority of individual reason and Scripture to supersede the authority of church and state. This emboldened many of those who desired to reform the church and Christian life to begin their own reforms in ways that Luther may not have initially envisioned. After the Diet of Worms, Luther went into hiding in Frederick of Saxony's Wartburg Castle to translate the Bible into German. During his yearlong absence, his followers were left on their own to discern how to convert Luther's theological propositions into concrete reforms. Luther's critique and manifestos gave them the authority to reform the church in ways that Luther would never have imagined.

Looking forward: Church renewal and reform

The pleas for reforming the church and its members had sounded before the sixteenth century, and there would continue to be calls for reform after the events now referred to as "the Reformation." It was in Luther's emphasis on the authority of Scripture and the individual's conscience that the people of late medieval Europe found ideas that would allow them to reform the church and relate to God without waiting for the intervention of the church hierarchy. Those who hoped to renew or reform the church would draw from a variety of spiritual and intellectual resources to support their challenges to existing structures. In the coming centuries, when Christians, including Anabaptists, called for the reform and renewal of Christianity, they might call upon Pietism, evangelicalism, Pentecostalism, reason, or the use of history as the key to reigniting a fire among believers. Regardless of their approach, it's clear that reformers throughout history believed that rightly reforming the church was a matter of existential importance to avoid divine judgment in this world or the next.

This sense that Christianity had fallen away from its best ideals, and that people can lead movements of reform to renew the church, continues to echo in the modern era. One example can be found in the South Korean Anabaptist churches. In the early 1990s, Lee Yoon

Shik and other Korean Christians looked for alternatives to militaristic Korean churches. They prayed and studied the Bible, asking, "What is the nature of the New Testament Church and how can we bring that church into our lives?" They eventually concluded that the Anabaptist understanding of the free church of adult believers was "as close as they could get to the New Testament Church." In 1996, they formed Jesus Village Church, the first Anabaptist church in Korea.[13]

— TWO —

Repentance and Reform

Radicals in Swiss Lands

In 1523, alert passersby may have noticed a stream of visitors coming and going from Andreas Castelberger's home in Zürich, Switzerland. In the small city of roughly six thousand residents, Castelberger's work as a bookseller allowed him to meet anyone who was interested in purchasing the ideas of religious reform. The previous year, he had begun a Bible study where people could gather to read the Scriptures and share their visions for reforming the church. Members of the Castelberger circle came from a variety of backgrounds and included men like "Heini Aberli, a baker; Hans Ockenfuss, a seamster; Lorenz Hochrütiner, a weaver; Wolf Ininger, a cabinetmaker; Bartlime Pfister and Claus Hottinger."[1] At these meetings, artisans and peasants joined with an increasingly radical group of young reformers who had been aggressively calling for the renewal of Zürich's religious institutions. These urban reformers, trained in the sophisticated humanism of Europe's leading universities, had also heard of the rising grievances of rural men and women. In the coming years, many of those who gathered around the Scriptures in Castelberger's house went on to play major roles in the radical reforming movement in Zürich and neighboring

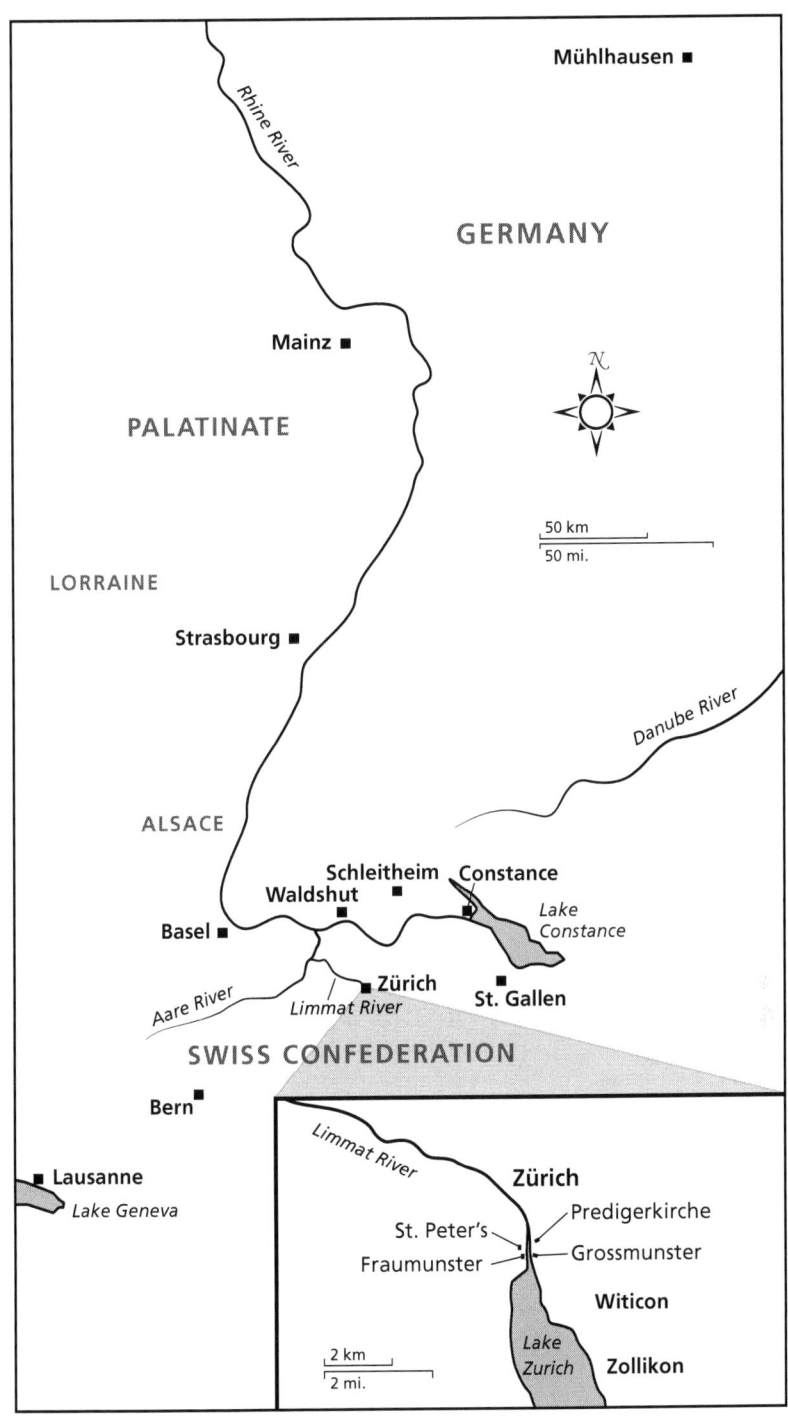

communities. Drawing on the Scriptures as the only authority for reform, they advocated the need for only adults to receive baptism, since only adults could decide to repent and follow Christ. They referred to each other as the Brethren, but their critics ridiculed them as rebaptizers, or Anabaptists.

Scholars have studied the early days of radical renewal in Zürich more than any other group of sixteenth-century Anabaptists. Hoping to find a normative vision to renew the twentieth-century church, Mennonite historians tried to trace a peaceable strain of Anabaptism back to those first Swiss radicals. They sifted through the writings of the group's leaders for the "essence" of Anabaptism to carry over into the modern world. Historian Harold S. Bender, for example, located the origins of all Anabaptists in Zürich, among the "sober-minded and peace-loving paragons of Christian virtue."[2] Since the 1970s, however, the quest for a normative Anabaptism has lost its hold on the scholarly imagination. As historians began to listen to the voices of ordinary Anabaptists, they identified a movement with multiple origins that professed a variety of fluid (and sometimes muddied) goals.

In the exhilarating days of 1524 and 1525, Swiss radicals remained convinced that the Bible, not city council proclamations or papal decrees, was the only guide for reforming the church. However, many of the beliefs of the Anabaptist agenda would not stabilize until they had been forged in the fires of public disputations, mission, and persecution.

Urban reform

The actors and ideas that made up Zürich's radical reforms demonstrate the range of reforming agendas that converged to form Swiss Anabaptism. The leading reformer, Ulrich Zwingli, and his circle attempted to reform the church at the citywide level. For civic reformers like Zwingli, the entire city *was* the congregation, and it was the sacred duty of political and church leaders to renew and reform the quality of their subjects' religious life. At the same time, in the rural outskirts of Zürich, long-standing resentment simmered over the tithes that flowed from the villages to the city without any local control. For the peasantry, the reforming ideas they learned from Castelberger's books provided a new language with which they could voice their age-old grievances.

Zürich was ripe for reform, and leading the cause was Zwingli, a popular preacher who had studied at some of the finest universities in Europe. When he was called to preach in Zürich in 1519, he established a humanist gathering, or sodality, to study ways to renew the church according to Scripture and the ancient church authorities. In 1520, Conrad Grebel joined Zwingli's study group, whose members also included future Anabaptists Felix Manz, the educated son of a canon, and Simon Stumpf, who had already earned a reputation as a radical agitator for calling for the destruction of images and preaching against tithes.

Bible studies became crucial hearths for the Anabaptist movement. Initially, Zwingli's sodality focused on reading the Bible in the original Greek, but they soon switched to discussing it in the vernacular. For the Zürichers, the doctrine of *sola scriptura* (Scripture alone) meant not only that the Bible was the only authority, but that it was accessible to all readers and hearers, even those without a sophisticated education. They believed that anyone who was prepared by the Spirit could interpret the Scriptures with confidence. In a spirit of Christian equality, Castelberger's group of peasants and craftspeople believed that they could use the Scriptures as skillfully as the clergy and scholars in Zwingli's group. With this confidence in their own authority, these men and women with little education also scoured the biblical texts to learn what they said about charging interest on loans, paying tithes, images in churches, war, and infant baptism. Rural and urban people alike believed that the key to reforming the church was to read and engage Scripture directly in order to encounter Christ and discern the model of the early church.[3]

The Affair of the Sausages

The first step on the way to reforming the Zürich church was an unexpected one. On March 9, 1522, during Lent, members of Zwingli's sodality met in the home of the printer Christoph Froschauer, where they cooked and ate sausages. The simple act violated the traditional prohibition against eating meat during Lent. Zwingli refrained from this first act of reforming disobedience, but he defended it from the pulpit on March 23, arguing that fasting was a personal choice. What was important was whether people believed in Christ, not what foods they ate. Thus, the first step to reform in Switzerland came with the eating of sausages.

Zwingli began to preach against fast-keeping, monastic vows, clerical celibacy, indulgences, and the use of images. His followers were not afraid to confront the church head-on, even disrupting the services of monks and scorning their veneration of the saints. Zwingli himself went so far as to interrupt the sermon of a Franciscan friar. When the magistrates disapproved these disorderly provocations, Conrad Grebel, an educated humanist and member of a prominent Zürich family, was undeterred. He warned, "If my lords do not allow the Gospel to advance, they will be destroyed," and slammed the door on his way out of the service.[4]

On January 29, 1523, Zürich's Great Council held the first of its reforming disputations to decide whether they would follow Zwingli's reforms or the bishop of Constance's traditional views. The representatives of the bishop of Constance asserted the authority of the Catholic Church, whereas Zwingli argued that "the Scriptures are so much the same everywhere . . . every diligent reader, insofar as he approaches with humble heart, will decide by means of the Scriptures, taught by the spirit of God, until he attains the truth."[5] In other words, the Bible was the ultimate authority, and its truths were accessible to those who let the Spirit guide them.

Using both persuasion and provocation, Zwingli and his followers convinced the city leaders to reform the church in accordance with Scripture alone. The council subsequently commanded Zwingli and all the city's preachers to "preach nothing but what can be proved by the holy Gospel and pure divine Scriptures."[6] From then on, Zwingli and the city council would turn to the Scriptures as the ultimate authority. However, the same view of Scripture would also open Zwingli to accusations by some of his followers that he did not follow scriptural commands closely enough when it was not politically expedient.

The reform splinters

These initial reforms inspired peasant men and women in the villages outside Zürich, and they eagerly anticipated a time when the city's reforming agenda would address their long-standing grievances against unfair tithes. When rural parishes tithed to the Zürich Grossmünster, the main Zürich church, those funds were often earmarked to monasteries and chapter houses instead of serving the communities who gave them. Many villages resented this practice, blaming it for the poor quality of rural priests. As the pressure to reform the churches intensified, the tithe began to symbolize all that was wrong with the church. In 1523, Castelberger's group declared that those who had more than they needed were worse than a poor person who stole to feed his children. Simon Stumpf, pastor of the village of Höngg, preached that the tithe did not have to be paid at all. These rural reformers understood themselves to be echoing Zwingli's break from papal control.

With a similar spirit, the rural communities hoped to take charge of their own parish administration. In December 1522, the parishioners in Witikon had declared Wilhelm Reublin their pastor without going through the proper channels in Zürich. In April 1523, both Reublin and Hans Brötli, another member of the Manz-Grebel circle, were some of the first priests to be married openly. Reublin preached in neighboring villages against the tithe and called for priests, monks, and nuns to marry, as he had. Priests in other villages, inspired by Reublin, "now instructed and informed by the holy Gospel that the tithe was nothing," apart from charity that should be given to the poor. In his sermons, Reublin reprimanded peasants for their deference to "stinking" patricians, mayors, and bailiffs. These bold words and actions of the rural parishes and the critiques of the city aristocracy threatened the gains that Zwingli had achieved in Zürich. The city magistrates could work with Zwingli in implementing gradual changes, but they could not condone the more radical reforms of Reublin, Simon Stumpf, or urban provocateurs like Grebel and Manz. In response to pressure from his own circle, in June 1523, Zwingli defended the city government's right to collect tithes, an act that widened the growing division among his supporters.

Zwingli's decision to side with the city council regarding the tithe led some of his friends and followers to doubt his desire for true reform. Between September and November of 1523, they started to reform the church's use of images without waiting for the approval of Zwingli or the council. Lorenz Hochrütiner and Claus Hottinger (both of whom also took part in the sausage affair) tore down a large crucifix at a crossroads outside the city. Hottinger claimed that he wanted to sell the wood and distribute the profits to the city poor. In the village of Zollikon, Reublin encouraged iconoclasm—the removal and destruction of religious imagery. These radicals believed that following God's clear commands as revealed in Scripture required faithful believers to begin reforms immediately, not at the pace of politicians and councils.

To handle the new disruptions, the Zürich council called for a disputation to be held on October 26, 1523. Zwingli and the council ultimately agreed that the prohibition against graven images in Exodus 20:4 required the removal of images from churches. However, they insisted that the government, not public outcry, would set the pace for reforms, which would proceed at an orderly pace. The council's decisions revealed a tension between the urban and rural agitators' desire for an immediate reform of the church along biblical lines and those who wanted an orderly reformation that took political realities into consideration.

On the second day of the disputation, Conrad Grebel called for the outright abolition of the mass. Zwingli dismissed him, saying, "Milords [the council members] will discern how the mass should henceforth be properly observed." Simon Stumpf countered, "Master Ulrich! You have no authority to place the decision in Milords' hands, for the decision is already made: the Spirit of God decides. If therefore Milords were to discern or decide anything that is contrary to God's decision, I will ask Christ for his Spirit and will teach and act against it."[7] Stumpf and his companions refused to let the political machinations of the city council override the clear commands of Scripture. God would not wait for councils to do what was clearly commanded.

Zwingli's willingness to slow the pace of reform outraged and alienated some of his followers. In a letter to his brother-in-law, Grebel scorned Zwingli's decision to postpone the reformation of the mass, writing, "Whoever thinks, believes, or says that Zwingli is acting as a true pastor, thinks, believes and says impieties."[8] Instead of following the clear commands of Scripture and the guidance of the Holy Spirit, Zwingli had acquiesced to allowing the city council to set the reforming agenda. Like Luther before him, Zwingli found that appealing to the authority of Scripture could be a double-edged sword. Even though Zwingli and the council abolished the mass eighteen months later, his followers no longer trusted him to thoroughly and biblically reform Zürich's churches.

While the pace of reform in Zürich slowed, the expectation for reform grew steadily outside of the city and among the Zürich sodality and the Castelberger group. The rural communities increasingly attempted to take complete control of their parishes. In the summer of 1524, the question of infant baptism arose as an additional practice ripe for reform. Wilhelm Reublin encouraged parents in Witikon and Zollikon not to baptize their children. However, when the Zürich council learned that newborns had not been baptized, they ordered parents to bring their children for baptism or face a fine of one silver mark.

In Zürich, Grebel, Manz, and others began to identify more with the rural protests than with the official reforms in the city. Skeptical of Zwingli's commitment to reform, they wrote letters to leading German reformers, including Martin Luther, Andreas von Karlstadt, and Thomas Müntzer, for guidance on how to proceed. In the fall of 1524, they wrote three letters to Karlstadt, who had demonstrated a similar refusal to slow reforms to spare the weak in Wittenberg in 1522. Inspired by Karlstadt's call to reform, Castelberger and Manz had five thousand pamphlets printed for distribution throughout the reforming networks.

Though Müntzer was less influential on the proto-Anabaptist movement than Karlstadt, the Grebel-Manz group's letters to Müntzer provide an invaluable window into the critical ideas that motivated the emerging Anabaptist movement. Their letter to Müntzer dated September 5, 1524, reflects a growing sense of alienation from Zwingli and a set of convictions that had the potential to grow in several directions. The authors criticized the Zürich reformers for their "false forbearance"—for suppressing God's clear Word by seeking to wait until everyone accepted the reforms.

The radicals' guiding principle was to implement only those things that the Scriptures had commanded while removing practices and traditions that were not biblically mandated. They agreed with Müntzer's call to preach only the pure gospel but criticized him for continuing to chant during worship and for defending his reforms by force, since "true believing Christians are sheep among wolves, sheep for the slaughter." The authors declared that the Lord's Supper would be the joyful eating of "an ordinary [loaf of] bread" without veneration or belief in the Catholic doctrine of transubstantiation. They called on

Müntzer to create a church based on the rule of discipline established in Matthew 18, seeking God's will through prayer and fasting. Because "faith is required of all who are saved," children would not be baptized, because they had no knowledge of good and evil. They found no support for infant baptism in the Scriptures and believed that Müntzer shared their view that it was an "abomination."[9]

By that point, the radicals wished to thoroughly revise or reject nearly all of the late medieval church's sacramental system, fundamentally reshaping the relationship between the clergy and the faithful. They would continue to baptize and take communion with one another, but the experience and meaning of these rites would no longer hold sacramental power. However, it is not clear to historians whether the radicals intended at this point to reform the entire city of Zürich or to create a new separate church of only the committed believers. In autumn of 1524, Anabaptist visions for a properly reformed church seem to have wavered between a church for "upright, Christian people" who had decided to join and a church for everyone, regardless of their commitment.[10]

By December 1524, the radicals had solidified their position around baptism. According to their understanding of Scripture, baptism was a visible sign of an individual's faith and commitment to a new life in Christian community. Only adults could understand and make this type of commitment; therefore, the rite was reserved for them. Zwingli replied that the Scriptures neither forbade nor commanded infant baptism. He argued that even though infant baptism was neither commanded nor forbidden, it was similar to circumcision in that it initiated infants into the faith and the community.

On January 17, 1525, Zwingli and the radicals met in front of the magistrates to dispute the issue of baptism. Most likely, the magistrates never seriously considered Manz, Grebel, and Reublin's arguments against infant baptism. Ultimately, the council sided with Zwingli and commanded the radicals to "forsake their opinion and be peaceful."[11] The next day, the council issued a mandate, declaring that "all those who have hitherto left their children unbaptized shall have them baptized within the next eight days. And anyone who refuses to do this shall, with wife and child and possessions, leave our lords' city, jurisdiction, and domain, and never return."[12] On January 21, a new mandate ordered the closing of the radical Bible schools and gave three of Zwingli's radical opponents, Hans Brötli, Ludwig Haetzer, and Andreas Castelberger, eight days to leave Zürich's territories.

Later that same day, several of the leaders gathered in the home of Felix Manz's mother Anna to consider their response to the mandate. After prayer, George Blaurock, a former priest, asked Grebel to baptize him. Blaurock knelt and Grebel baptized him, then Blaurock baptized the others as well. At this point, the small group could properly be called "Anabaptists," or rebaptizers. Their opponents used the term to mock those who practiced adult baptism, because Anabaptism was punishable by death in the Holy Roman Empire. However, the movement's members did not believe that they were *re*-baptizing anyone. In the coming years, they referred to themselves as Brethren (*Brüder*) or baptism-minded (*Taufgesinnten*).

Spreading the baptism message

Despite the council's mandates, the new movement's members were undeterred, and they began spreading their message throughout the surrounding countryside. They found a more receptive audience there than in Zürich. The day after the baptismal service, Hans Brötli traveled to Zollikon, where he baptized Fridli Schumacher by a well. On the same day, Grebel celebrated communion in Jacob Hottinger's house. Grebel cut a simple loaf of bread and distributed it to those gathered there "to symbolize that they would henceforth live a Christian life."[13] In defiance of Zürich's mandate, Manz, Grebel, and Blaurock spent the week going house to house to lead Bible studies, baptize believers, and solidify the movement in Zollikon.

The eight days of baptisms in Zollikon quickly expanded beyond a commitment to lead new and sinless lives into an attempt to apply biblical models to all areas of life. One account reported that villagers attempted to emulate the early Christian church's community of earthly goods described in Acts. The Anabaptists in Zollikon "broke the locks off their doors, chests, and cellars, and ate food and drink in good fellowship without discrimination."[14] The entire village appeared overcome with the power of the Anabaptists' renewal message, with at least one report of a person weeping and crying over sin before being baptized. Stimulated by spiritual revival, the early Anabaptist movement now sought to renew church, economics, and society.

52 *Radicals & Reformers*

Fig. 2.1 In this sixteenth-century illustration of the Zürich disputation on January 17, 1525, Conrad Grebel, Felix Manz, and Wilhelm Reublin (*bottom*) debate the secular lords (*left*) and theologians (*right*). Manuscript page adapted from Heinrich Bullinger and [by the hand of] Heinrich Toman, [Kopienband zur zürcherischen Kirchen- und Reformationsgeschichte], ([Zürich], 1605–6). Zentralbibliothek, Zürich, Ms. B 316, f. 182v.

As the Anabaptists continued to spread to more villages, they began to intersect with other protest movements that were also reaching their boiling points. The Anabaptists sought to connect their calls for reform with the local grievances of peasants, whose agitation had grown. In areas throughout southern and central Germany and Austria, these common men and women in the countryside, towns, and mining regions rose in protest against the authorities in 1525 in what was derided as a "Peasants' War" by aristocratic opponents.[15] Anabaptist missionaries traveled through these areas, where peasant demands—reforming the tithe and gaining local control of the church—overlapped with Anabaptist reforms. They found it easier to preach in areas where peasants had already undermined the control of the magistrates, which helped Anabaptism develop into a mass movement. On Palm Sunday, 1525, Conrad Grebel baptized between three hundred and eight hundred people in the city of St. Gallen, and in many villages the Anabaptists officiated at mass baptisms and mass celebrations of the Lord's Supper.

Since the Anabaptists and peasant armies both called for biblical economic practices, the lines between peasant unrest and Anabaptist reforms were not always clear. Wilhelm Reublin and Balthasar Hubmaier were Anabaptist leaders who also worked among the peasant revolutionaries. After the peasants were crushed by the authorities, a few veterans, like Hans Hut and Melchior Rinck, joined the Anabaptist movement, becoming central leaders and missionaries. The historian James Stayer has shown that the Anabaptist emphasis on community of goods was an outgrowth of peasant demands for economic reform.[16] Despite significant intersection and overlapping with armed peasant insurrections, the Anabaptist movement remained primarily a religious renewal movement rather than a political uprising.

Anabaptism's appeals to the power of the Holy Spirit for renewal provided women freedom that they did not normally enjoy in the church. By claiming authority directly from God, women in the movement could prophesy, missionize, and lead. Authorities arrested the lay leader Margret Hottinger for the crime of Anabaptism in 1525. According to the court records, Hottinger testified "that she holds infant baptism to be incorrect and rebaptism to be right. Likewise she asked milords that they prove infant baptism to her; if they can prove to her that infant baptism is correct, then she will desist."[17] A year later it was reported that Hottinger continued to inspire Anabaptists through her spiritual discipline, prophetic authority, and personal charisma.

Like Hottinger, Agnes Linck was a self-appointed lay leader. She claimed that the Lord had baptized her directly, "in spirit and truth." In 1528, authorities in the Swiss city of Solothurn arrested her for heresy. Under examination, she admitted to rejecting both the traditional Catholic and the new Reformed understandings of the Lord's Supper. She also mocked the saints and wanted to buy a Bible without any images in it. It became clear that she had been instructing others in iconoclastic and anticlerical ideas. The authority of the Holy Spirit and Scriptures provided women like Margret Hottinger and Agnes Linck the room to express their religious convictions in nontraditional ways. But eventually, as Anabaptists grew compelled to define more precisely the boundaries and core convictions of the movement, more traditional gender roles were reestablished. In the transition from a radical renewal movement to institutional stability, the Holy Spirit was deemphasized in favor of traditional understandings of biblical and cultural gender norms.

Still, the authority to read and interpret Scripture, guided by the Holy Spirit, gave common men and women the ability to seize control of their religious destiny. They no longer needed to wait for bishops, theologians, or politicians to decide to reform the church; they could establish a scripturally faithful church on their own. Guided by the Bible and the Spirit, they gained the spiritual confidence that they were faithfully following Christ as disciples. Sustained by prayer and inspired by the Scriptures, they were willing to follow their convictions even when doing so might lead to exile, imprisonment, or death. They knew that their faithfulness would be rewarded after death.

The quest for unity

However, in a context of rapid growth and sociopolitical unrest, it soon became clear that Anabaptists did not share a common vision for how the church that baptized adults should relate to the world around it. Some Anabaptists rejected the swearing of oaths and declared that Christians could not serve as magistrates. Felix Manz rejected the use of violence in self-defense, whereas Johannes Brötli accepted armed protection when traveling. Heinrich Alberli recruited soldiers to protect the nascent church at Waldshut, where Balthasar Hubmaier, who became an Anabaptist after Grebel and Reublin visited Waldshut and soon became one of the most articulate Anabaptist theologians, had baptized nearly the entire town in April 1525. That year, Hubmaier published the first systematic defense of adult baptism, *On the Christian Baptism of Believers*. Like Grebel, he called for the reform of baptism and the Lord's Supper along biblical lines and the practice of discipline following the guidelines of Matthew 18. However, he never demanded that an adult-baptizing church separate from the world. In fact, he never even argued that believers reject the sword and become nonresistant. Hubmaier and the Anabaptists in Waldshut attempted to establish an official civic church, albeit one that practiced adult baptism. Still, Waldshut was the most important Anabaptist community for nearly eight months, until Austrian forces regained control of the city in December 1525.

By 1526, the armies of the Swabian League had crushed the massive peasant uprising and revolt in southern Germany and the Tyrol. The peasants' demand for divine justice and a fairer economic system came to a bloody end after professional armies killed around a third of the peasant forces. The sheer scale of the insurrection shocked princes and magistrates into demanding stricter control of the reforming process and favoring order over change.

Partially because Anabaptist preachers and adherents could be found among the peasant forces, authorities gradually viewed Anabaptists' religious reforms as a seditious threat to political order for undermining traditional civic order and stability. By March 1526, Zürich had threatened to drown all rebaptizers. As it increasingly became clear that no town or city would implement citywide Anabaptist reforms, the movement affirmed a vision for a church as a voluntary gathering of baptized believers outside of the traditional, territorial church model.

In 1527, a group of Anabaptists met in the small town of Schleitheim to craft a set of shared convictions. Michael Sattler, a former Benedictine prior, is thought to have been the author of the seven articles known as the *Schleitheim Brotherly Union*, or Schleitheim Confession. The articles attempted to provide unity to the movement in face of "false brethren" who threatened internal unity and external persecution by both Protestant and Catholic authorities. Although some Anabaptists, like Balthasar Hubmaier, rejected the authority of the Schleitheim Confession, the document crystallized the convictions of the movement at a moment when its future seemed to hang in the balance.

The seven articles affirmed Anabaptist unity around the core principles of separation, obedience, and discipline. Baptism was the sign that one was voluntarily following God and walking in obedience. Believers would separate themselves from the sinful world and submit themselves to congregational discipline. Because it was merely a commemorative meal for members, the Lord's Supper symbolized the unity of the church and its separation from the world. The new community would choose or dismiss their own leaders from within, thereby affirming a primary goal of the Zollikon protests and the Twelve Articles of Memmingen, a key document of the so-called Peasants' War that swept through much of German-speaking Europe in 1525. Although God established rulers and government to keep order and protect the innocent, Schleitheim stated, followers of Christ would abstain from bearing the sword to defend themselves and their church. Finally, the sword and the oath belonged in the kingdom of the world, and members of the kingdom of Christ therefore had to reject them. Amid disagreements among the Radicals about the extent to which they planned to reform all of society, about the use of violence, or about how they would worship, the Schleitheim principles were intended to unify the group around a commitment to separate, nonresistant communities.

After Schleitheim

The Schleitheim principles played a significant role in providing Swiss Anabaptist congregations a shared vision for renewal. This unity was founded on a dualistic worldview that reflected the Anabaptists' experience of being persecuted and viewed as a threat by the rest of the world. Persecution forced the Anabaptists to go underground and become a separatist movement. The Schleitheim unity provided the theological justification for the separation. From this point on, to become an Anabaptist in Switzerland meant accepting the likelihood that one would suffer for one's faith.

On January 5, 1527, Zürich authorities sentenced Felix Manz to death for Anabaptism, since "such doctrine is harmful to the unified usage of all Christendom, and leads to offense, insurrection, and sedition against the government, to the shattering of the common peace, brotherly love, and civil cooperation and to all evil."[18] In a cruel parody of Manz's adult baptism, the authorities rowed Manz out in a boat on the Limmat River to drown him. Despite the horrific circumstances of his death, Manz remained steadfast in his faith. With his mother and friends encouraging him from the banks, he sang, in Latin, "Into your hands, Lord, I commend my spirit," as he was thrown into the river.

Authorities arrested Michael Sattler, author of the Schleitheim Articles, and his wife Maguerita soon after the Schleitheim meeting. They charged Michael with nine offenses, which included not believing in the sacraments of communion, baptism, or anointing; not believing in the virgin Mary; and the refusal to swear oaths. He had also left the Benedictine order and married Maguerita. Finally, the authorities charged that "he has said, 'Should the Turk invade this land, one should not resist him. And, if it were right to wage war, then he would rather march against the Christians than against the Turks,' which is certainly a great offense, to march against us with the greatest enemy of our holy faith."[19]

Michael Sattler responded to the charges and concluded by calling on the authorities to summon their best scholars and the Bible for a public debate. Echoing Luther, he declared, "If they show us with Holy Scripture that we are in error and wrong, we will gladly retract and recant, and will gladly suffer condemnation and the punishment for our offence." The judges replied, "O yes, you disreputable, desperate, and mischievous monk, you think we should debate with you? Sure enough, the hangman will debate with you, you can believe me."[20] The judge ordered Michael to be torn with red-hot tongs and burned at the stake. According to one account, Marguerita Sattler "could not be turned away from her faith by any human grace or words. In great joy and strong faith she accepted and suffered death. God be praised! Thus she was drowned."[21]

From 1526 to 1530, the Swiss Anabaptists followed the separatist principles proposed in the Schleitheim Articles. Inspired by the early church, they pooled their resources to provide for their members' basic needs. A congregational order printed with the Schleitheim Confession stated, "Of all the brothers and sisters of this congregation none shall have anything of his own, but rather, as the Christians in the time of the apostles held all in common, and especially stored up a common fund, from which aid can be given to the poor, according as each will have need, and as in the apostles' time permit no brother to be in need." While it was not quite the true community of goods eventually practiced by the Hutterites, a concern for mutual support and charity became a common trait of all Anabaptist groups in the sixteenth century.[22]

As noted earlier, as the Anabaptist movement became more formally structured and less focused on spiritual renewal, women were increasingly excluded from leadership roles. Gender roles within the movement began to align with the patriarchal norms of sixteenth-century society. Nevertheless, women continued to play a crucial role in spreading the movement through their personal networks and everyday activities. Women disseminated Anabaptist teachings in secret in their kitchens, during sewing circles, and while selling goods in markets. Some Swiss Brethren women managed to exert informal influence in

Fig. 2.2 Authorities take Felix Manz to a fishing platform in the Limmat River, where they drowned him. Manuscript page adapted from Heinrich Bullinger and [by the hand of] Heinrich Toman, [Kopienband zur zürcherischen Kirchen- und Reformationsgeschichte], ([Zürich], 1605–6). Zentralbibliothek, Zürich, Ms. B 316, f. 284v.

the seventeenth century—in the village of Beutelsbach, near Stuttgart, Lutheran authorities attempted to prevent Margaret Hellwart from spreading Anabaptist teachings in the region by chaining her to the floor of her home at least twenty-one times between 1610 and 1621.[23]

Despite constant persecution from authorities, the Swiss Anabaptist movement developed from a diverse association of scholars and peasant agitators to a separatist community that aimed to achieve spiritual renewal through a literal interpretation of the Bible. While they initially sought to reshape society and the church, their focus shifted toward forming congregations separated from the sinful world, awaiting Christ's return. The sixteenth-century theologian Johannes Kessler wrote that the Anabaptists "shun costly clothing, and despise expensive food and drink, clothe themselves with coarse cloth, [and] cover their heads with broad felt hats. Their entire manner of life is completely humble. They bear no weapon, neither sword nor dagger, but only a short breadknife."[24] But the desire to separate from an unredeemable world did not prevent Swiss Anabaptists from spreading their vision of renewal and reform. As they fanned out through the German-speaking lands, those who referred to themselves as Swiss Brethren soon met others who shared a similar vision for a church of adult believers.

Looking ahead: Rightly remembering Anabaptist history

If you were to take a stroll along the west bank of the Limmat River in Zürich, you would find a plaque that reads, "Here in the middle of the Limmat River, Felix Manz and five other Anabaptists were drowned from a fishing platform during the Reformation between 1527 and 1532. The last Anabaptist executed in Zürich was Hans Landis in 1614." Unveiled in 2004, the plaque was created after a series of events and meetings between Reformed leaders and Anabaptist delegates, which culminated with an official apology by the Reformed church for the persecution of Anabaptists during the tumult of the Swiss Reformation. In 2020, the Lutheran World Federation, the Vatican, and representatives of Mennonite World Conference published a joint document studying their distinctive teachings of baptism and church membership.[25]

In recent decades, the global Anabaptist community has carefully discerned how to commemorate the five hundred years since George Blaurock's baptism of Conrad Grebel. They have committed to "rightly remember" their history as a result of the dialogues of reconciliation

Fig. 2.3 Troops raid a Swiss Anabaptist gathering in May 1527, capturing fifteen of them, including Jacob Falck and Heini Reimann. Manuscript page adapted from Heinrich Bullinger and [by the hand of] Heinrich Toman, [Kopienband zur zürcherischen Kirchen- und Reformationsgeschichte], ([Zürich], 1605–6). Zentralbibliothek, Zürich, Ms. B 316, f. 245v.

between Anabaptists and other Christians. When studying their history together, they commit to accuracy, reading each other's stories empathetically, and the shared goal of remembering rightly in order to draw all Christians closer to Christ. Recognizing that the story of Anabaptists in Switzerland did not end with the execution of "heroes" in the 1520s but rather has continued to the present allows contemporary Anabaptists to focus on one another's gifts rather than narratives of heroic superiority. The commemorations also seek to acknowledge that Anabaptism has expanded beyond the descendants of the Swiss Brethren to become a global renewal movement, as we shall see in the chapters ahead.

— THREE —

South German Anabaptists

Mysticism and Community of Goods

In 1529, the traveling needle merchant Hans Nadler appeared before the authorities in Erlangen, Bavaria, to be cross-examined about his missionary activities. "Wherever I travelled in the land," Nadler testified, "if I met or found a good-hearted person in inns or on the street, I gave him instruction from the Word of God."[1] He would inquire, "My brother or sister, a Christian must suffer much. Are you prepared, for the sake of truth, to suffer persecution, contempt, scorn, the forsaking of house, yard, wife and child, all for the sake of the Lord?" If the person answered yes, Nadler continued to instruct them that "you must receive the Word of God like a child and must be born anew." A follower of Christ, Nadler taught, must submit completely to the will of God. "If you submit yourself to God in this way and divest yourself of the world, it will hate, will be opposed to you and will say all kinds of evil of you."[2]

Hans Nadler, an illiterate merchant, taught new converts by linking the teachings of the rebaptizing movement to parts of the Lord's Prayer to help common people understand the fundamentals of the faith.[3] Nadler's court testimony provides a valuable window for studying Anabaptism as it developed in South Germany, Austria, and Moravia, where, as Swiss refugees mixed with apocalyptic-minded peasants, a stream of Anabaptism developed that emphasized the importance of spiritual suffering and submission.

Multiple Anabaptist origins?

When earlier historians identified the spiritual essence of Anabaptism, they pointed to what they claimed was the "genuine" Anabaptism as originated in Zürich with the Grebel/Manz circle before spreading to other parts of Europe. In his influential 1944 essay "The Anabaptist Vision," American historian Harold S. Bender proposed a version of authentic Anabaptism that, much like the Swiss group, emphasized three points: the essence of Christianity as discipleship, the church as a brotherhood, and an ethic of love and nonresistance.[4] The Anabaptists, Bender suggested, were the true culmination of Luther's Reformation.

In the 1970s, scholars challenged Bender's tidy and idealized picture of Anabaptist origins. Instead, they argued that baptizing movements arose from three separate regions: Switzerland, South Germany/Austria/Moravia, and the Low Countries (Belgium and the Netherlands). While each movement shared the practice of adult baptism, they had distinct theological emphases. For example, members of the Swiss movement read Scripture with Luther's sense of *sola scriptura*, instituting only what was explicitly called for in the Bible, especially the New Testament. The South German/Austrian/Moravian stream integrated elements of German mysticism into their beliefs. In the Low Countries in the north, the preaching of adult baptism was combined with an apocalyptic expectation and the unique teachings of Melchior Hoffman. Today, scholars no longer argue for such sharp boundaries between the groups, especially between the Swiss and southern German streams, which began influencing each other and developing networks soon after their first encounter. It is important to remember that there was never a "pure Anabaptism" that spread to other regions; each movement had different emphases influenced by the theological sources they drew from and the social-political contexts where they emerged.

Theological and practical experimentation flourished in the relatively tolerant land of Moravia among the South German and Austrian Anabaptists who lived there. Moravian communities surpassed the Swiss cities as the most important centers of Anabaptist thought and practice. The South German/Austrian Anabaptists, who emerged after the failed commoners' revolution of 1525 and were disappointed by Luther's social conservatism, combined his concept of salvation of faith with medieval mysticism, a focus on economic sharing, and eventually, elements of Swiss separatism. Their sermons exhorted believers to yield their will to God's (akin to the *Gelassenheit* of pre-Reformation mystics). In the painful process of spiritual self-denial, true faith would be forged within the soul of the believer. This process of spiritual rebirth and yielding would produce a new life that produced "good fruit" in the faithful (Matthew 7:17). Baptism, they preached, was the outward sign of this inner regeneration and marked membership into the community of the faithful.

Hans Denck and the renewal of inner life

When the tremors of the reforming movements began to shake up the church, the mystic baptizer Hans Denck was working in Nürnberg as the principal of the St. Sebald School. The city was caught up in the fervor of reform that was sweeping other urban areas. During this time, Radical Reformers Thomas Müntzer and Andreas von Karlstadt each passed through the city and printed pamphlets there. To rein in the radical movements, the city's Lutheran pastor had three artists arrested for suspicion of denying the real presence of Christ's body and blood during communion. Denck, who had by this time embraced at least some of this radical theology, eventually appeared before the city council to be examined for his ideas regarding the Lord's Supper. On January 21, 1525, on the same day that the Grebel/Manz circle performed the first adult baptisms in Zürich, Nürnberg banished Denck. City authorities threatened him with death if he should return within fifteen kilometers of the city and confiscated his property to provide for his wife and children, who were permitted to remain in Nürnberg.

It is difficult to retrace Denck's exact itinerary after Nürnberg before his arrival in St. Gallen, Switzerland, at some point in 1525, where he encountered a group of Anabaptists. When he arrived, the local baptizing movement was still caught up in the revolutionary fervor of the peasant unrest; they were willing to defend their preacher, Hans Krüsi, with force. It is unclear whether Denck had already arrived at his own nonresistant position at that time. When the authorities expelled him from St. Gallen several months later, it was not for advocating adult baptism or nonresistance, but for preaching universal salvation.

In September 1525, Denck arrived in Augsburg, where his Anabaptist sympathies eventually came to light. He met Balthasar Hubmaier and, in early 1526, baptized one of Müntzer's close associates, Hans Hut. When word of Denck's unorthodox teachings reached Augsburg's magistrates, local Lutheran leaders challenged him to a public disputation, but Denck fled the city before the debate could be held and traveled to Strasbourg, a city with a tolerant reputation. His radical reputation had preceded him, and local Anabaptists, including Michael Sattler, kept him at arm's distance. After he debated Martin Bucer, the city's leading reformer, the city expelled Denck for providing evasive answers to their questions about his orthodoxy. He continued to move from city to city, translating the Old Testament and disputing baptism with others. Denck managed to keep moving one step ahead of the repression of radical reform until he eventually succumbed to the plague in Basel in 1527.

Denck emphasized the importance of the unwritten, inner Word of the Spirit over the written outer Word of Scripture, thereby adding a new flavor of Anabaptism to the biblicism and humanism of the Zürich circles. The reform of the church depended on believers' yielding themselves completely to God's Spirit and living a holy life. According to Denck, truly sanctified believers could understand God's unmediated revelation and did not need the outer ceremonies of the church for their salvation. Baptism and communion would be celebrated as testimony to God's faithfulness to humanity, not because they were obligatory or because they dispensed grace. As Christians yielded to the work of the Holy Spirit in their lives, they would be regenerated. Subsequently, they would be able to imitate Christ in all things.

Fig. 3.1 The charismatic preacher Thomas Müntzer was one of the most influential of the Radical Reformers of the sixteenth century. Engraving from *Apocalypsis, or The revelation of certain notorious advancers of heresie* (London, 1655). Scan courtesy of Mennonite Archives of Ontario, Conrad Grebel University College, Waterloo.

Denck was one of the least polemical Radical Reformers; his desire to avoid the destructive discourse of theological debates guided much of his thought. He believed that the Holy Spirit was accessible to everyone, and that disagreements about theology or the meaning of

Scripture would dissipate once individuals opened themselves to the universal revelation of God's Spirit. He also believed that those who truly followed Christ could not use violence or coercion, and therefore they could not serve as magistrates or judges. His beliefs demonstrate a path to the rebaptizing principles of adult baptism and defenselessness through spiritual practices, in contrast to the emphasis on scriptural authority that the Zürich radicals used to arrive at similar positions.

Hans Hut: Suffering prophet

Denck's baptism of the bookseller Hans Hut on Pentecost of 1526 is perhaps his most significant contribution to the larger baptizing movement. Hut had earlier joined Thomas Müntzer's movement in the heady days of the peasant uprising. When Müntzer fled Mühlhausen in 1524, he asked Hut to print the pamphlet *Vindication and Refutation* in Nürnberg. Inspired by Müntzer's criticisms of infant baptism, Hut chose exile from the town of Bibra rather than have his child baptized. During the Peasants' War of 1525, he was present with Müntzer at the crushing defeat of the commoners at Frankenhausen, where thousands of peasant soldiers were killed. After the peasants' movement came to its bloody end, Hut's burning desire for radical renewal of church and society was rekindled in the baptizing movement.

After his baptism by Denck, Hut began an extraordinary career as a minister and prophet. In a remarkable eighteen-month period, he traveled across the German-speaking territories, preaching his message of the world's imminent end. He founded congregations in towns and villages across southern Germany and into Austria with the aim to identify and "seal" 144,000 believers before the world ended in 1528, as Hut believed was prophesied in Revelation 7:3–4. When he baptized new converts, he did so by marking their foreheads with a *T*, representing the Greek letter *tau*, which sealed them as one of those chosen to join the army that would enact God's vengeance on the ungodly at Christ's return. At his trial, Hut distinguished his vision from the goals of the 1525 Peasants' War:

> The peasants were not right about their uprising, for they had sought their own and not God's honour. . . . A Christian may well have a sword but . . . it must remain in the scabbard until God tells him to take it out. Before then they would all be scattered and tried.

Finally the Lord would gather them all together and himself return. Then the saints would punish the others, namely the sinners who had not repented.⁵

Hut converted the revolutionary hopes of the peasants into an apocalyptic baptizing movement. His "provisional pacifism," which set him apart from other baptizers, claimed that the world would be renewed at the second coming of Christ, and it resonated with many. His success, however, was short-lived. In 1527, he was arrested and subjected to brutal torture. Hut died of asphyxiation caused by a fire in his prison cell. Not to be denied their vengeance, the authorities burned his corpse at the stake.

Hut's vision for renewal combined themes of Swiss Brethren thought with emphases of other Radical Reformers. Like the Swiss, he emphasized following Christ. However, he infused his theology with the marks of medieval mysticism: yieldedness (*Gelassenheit*), suffering, and regeneration. To spread his message among common men and women, Hut used images taken from everyday life. According to his "gospel of all creatures," creation reveals the gospel truth that lower orders of creatures must suffer at the hands of higher-order creatures. Plants and farm animals, for example, suffer so that humans can thrive. In the same way, believers should submit themselves to spiritual suffering in order that God's divine purpose could be fulfilled. After Hut's death, Leonhard Schiemer and Hans Schlaffer continued to spread the "gospel of all creatures" across southern Germany and Austria. Over time, the apocalyptic expectation in their message withered away, and the mystic suffering of the soul developed into the physical suffering of martyrdom.

Augsburg: Crossroads of Anabaptism

Swiss refugees and Hans Hut's missionaries connected with each other in various cities, such as Augsburg, Strasbourg, Esslingen, and Nikolsburg. Despite their distinct geographic origins, these different baptizing groups shared leadership and provided material support to each other as they worked through their theological differences. The surviving inquisitorial sources in these cities offer invaluable insights into how the underground movement functioned and how the groups collaborated despite theological differences.

Fig. 3.2 Hans Hut, apocalyptic Anabaptist missionary. Engraving by Christoffel van Sichem (I), *Portrait of Johannes Hus*, 1677. Rijksmuseum, Amsterdam, RP-P-1908-3927.

Between 1527 and 1528, the Anabaptist community in Augsburg rapidly increased in numbers, surpassing that of any other city. Hans Hut's followers merged with Swiss Anabaptist refugees, and the new group shared resources, despite significant differences in their views. While the Swiss Anabaptists hoped that the Schleitheim Articles would bring unity, disagreements persisted. In an August 1527 interrogation, Hut distanced himself from Schleitheim's position on the sword. He affirmed, "Some imagined that Christians should not bear weapons; indeed they made a regulation of the subject in Switzerland. [I] put a stop to that and showed that this was not ungodly and forbidden."⁶ When interrogated, members of Hut's movement either denounced Schleitheim's principle of separation or lacked any familiarity with it. At the same time, Hut's apocalyptic predictions lacked authority among many of the other members of the Augsburg congregation.

In Augsburg, women played a key role in sustaining and spreading the Anabaptist message. Some women actively spread the movement by word of mouth among friends and family. For example, the records report one woman attending an Anabaptist gathering at the invitation of a maid. Other women opened their homes for meetings, delivered messages between members, and distributed alms to the poorer members. Women's sewing circles became places where members could gather to sing hymns and share testimonies with each other. After becoming an Anabaptist in November 1527, Susanna Doucher used her house as a meeting place and donated food and money to those who gathered there. For these activities, the city branded her on each cheek and exiled her from the city.

When the underground congregation gathered, preachers often exhorted members to provide alms for less fortunate members. Although her first name is unknown to us, Laux Kreler's wife distributed money to the poor and sick and gave housing to refugees and women whose husbands were thrown into prison. In 1528, the Krelers' charitable activities drew the attention of the authorities, who exiled them from the city.⁷

According to historian John Oyer, the Anabaptists practiced the following techniques to run their underground church:

> 1. Do not ask or learn the name of your baptizer or of any travelling minister. Do not learn the name of the man or woman who provides free housing and food if you are a refugee. Then you will be unable to disclose their names if you are caught and taken into court and tortured.
>
> 2. Hide the leaders at different places; disguise them; have them remain anonymous or use pseudonyms. Move them out of town or village on their itinerant ways when it becomes dangerous to keep them longer.

3. Meet secretly: in a forest a gravel pit, some isolated building at the edge of a village where the group can sing hymns without being heard, within the city in the more isolated homes that have been hung with blankets, etc., on the inside to block spying eyes, or in very small groups in normal city houses where people gather anyway for routine social purposes.

4. Greet each other simply so as to allay suspicion, but in some environments with an exchange that indicates to each party the Anabaptist inclination of the other. One says, "God greet thee, sister in the Lord." The other answers, "God thank thee, sister in the Lord."[8]

By 1528 the pressure from Augsburg's inquisitor was too much; the congregation broke up and dispersed to Esslingen and Strasbourg. In Esslingen, Müntzer's followers, Swiss Brethren, and Hut's converts cooperated in forming an Anabaptist congregation. Esslingen had only recently become a Protestant city, and it repressed, rather than exterminated, nonconformist gatherings. To avoid the harsher penalties imposed on leaders, the congregation spread leadership responsibilities throughout the congregation. Some members who recanted (denounced their Anabaptist convictions) attended sermons in the state churches while continuing to attend Anabaptist meetings. They might also carry a weapon on civic guard duty and swear oaths when called to do so. Instead of banning these "weaker" members, the Anabaptists appear to have understood that these compromises allowed the congregation enough flexibility to continue to gather without drawing too much attention to themselves.

Strasbourg, Augsburg, and Pilgram Marpeck

As it discerned the best way to reform its churches, the relatively tolerant city of Strasbourg attracted religious refugees and reformers from across Europe. In 1537, the city on the Rhine River did not repress dissenters; it outlawed only those who rejected Christian government and fomented disunity. Until 1533, it was a bastion of toleration and religious discussion. Anabaptist leaders like Wilhelm Reublin, Hans Denck, Jakob Gross, Michael Sattler, and Melchior Hoffman all passed through the city.

Pilgram Marpeck's arrival in Strasbourg in 1528 marked an important shift in the city's Anabaptist movement. Though it is not certain when Marpeck first became sympathetic to Anabaptist beliefs, he had already left his position as a mining official in the Tyrol region and had been baptized and ordained by the Austerlitz Brethren in Bohemia and Moravia. When he arrived in Strasbourg, Marpeck began to lead one of the Anabaptist groups in the city and worked with other leaders to develop a confession that called for adult baptism. Marpeck believed that the state church was not fully reformed, because it did not produce the fruit of a regenerated life. Despite his criticisms, Marpeck was not arrested, and he was hired by the city as a forestry supervisor. He left Strasbourg after a dispute with reformer Martin Bucer about infant baptism and traveled to Switzerland, Tyrol, Moravia, South Germany, and Alsace.

Marpeck eventually settled in Augsburg, where he worked as an engineer for the city from 1544 until his death in 1556 while leading an underground Anabaptist congregation. Like Hut, Marpeck did not share Schleitheim's rejection of the state. He proposed that rulers and magistrates should not intervene in church affairs; however, he thought that it was possible for Christians to work for the state so long as they did not have to use coercive force as part of their work. Marpeck wrote, "But when people in political authority are Christians or become Christians (as I heartily wish and pray) they may not use their previous physical force, power and rule in the kingdom of Christ."[9]

Tyrolean and Moravian Anabaptism

In the following years, several separate groups grew out of the mystical and apocalyptic seeds planted by Hans Denck and Hans Hut. A few continued to promote Hut's apocalyptic vision for renewal after his predictions failed to come true. After Hut's death, Augustin Bader took up the apocalyptic banner and prophesied that the forces of the Ottoman Empire would invade Europe, overthrowing the Habsburg Empire. Once all evil had been destroyed, Christ's kingdom would be established, and Bader's own son would rule as the Messiah. Bader's brand of apocalypticism never found many adherents and died out after his execution in 1530.

Hans Denck's mystical and Spiritualist emphases lived on in the writings of Hans Bünderlin, Christian Entfelder, and Jakob Kautz. These writers maintained that individual regeneration by the power

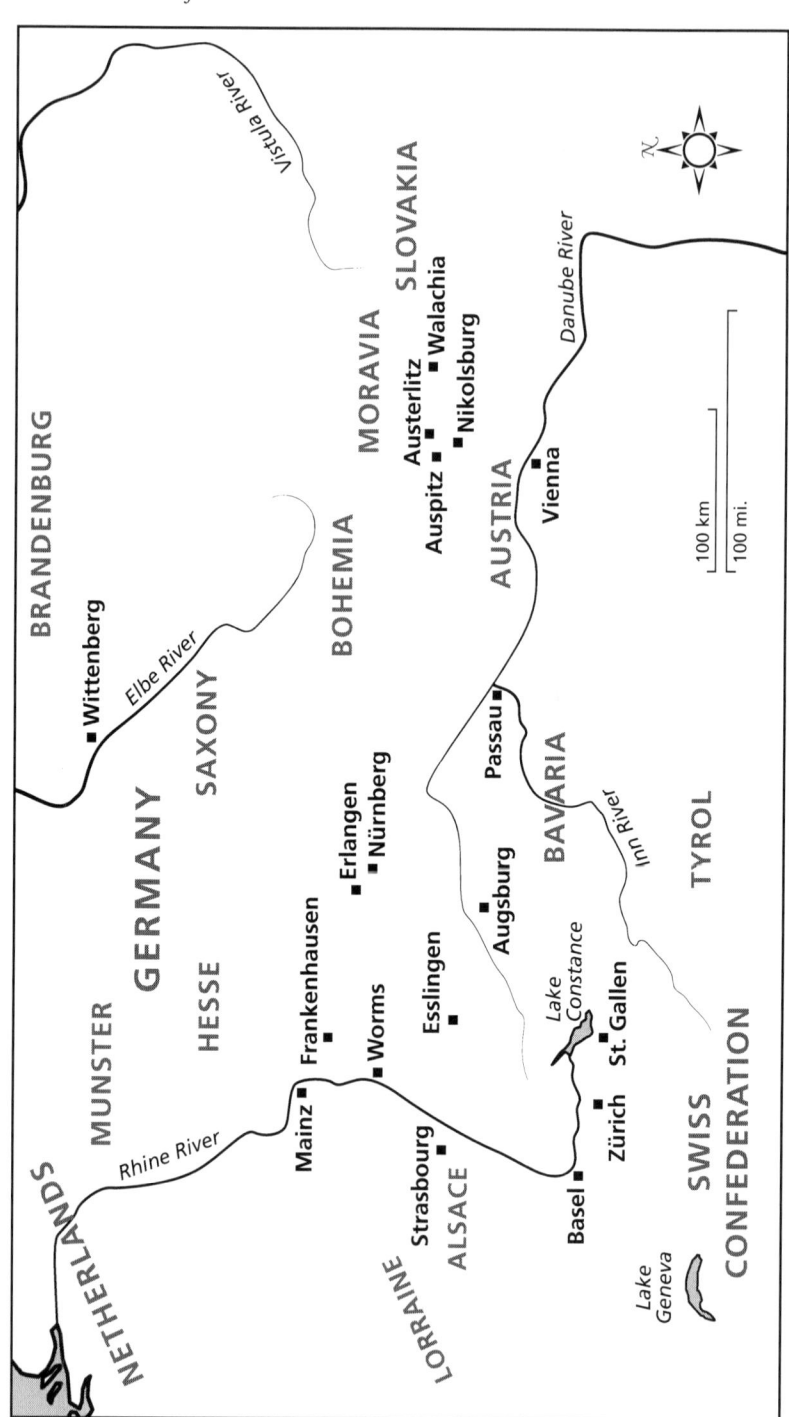

of the Holy Spirit was all that was necessary for salvation and renewal of the church. Their argument, that the sacraments were only signs of inner changes, opened baptizers to the tendency to downplay the importance of external practices. Some Spiritualists, like the missionary Bünderlin, assumed that only the inner life of the regenerated believer mattered, which led Bünderlin to reject all church ordinances or "ceremonies" as unnecessary or even harmful.

Pilgram Marpeck, on the other hand, saw in this position a dangerous tendency. Marpeck emphasized the incarnation and humanity of Christ as a counterpoint to the Spiritualists and their focus on the inner spirit over the external letter of Scripture and the individual's inner life over the church as the body of Christ. While scholars disagree about the long-term legacy of Marpeck and his followers, his advocacy for a church that was both fully visible and spiritually regenerated was an important contribution and possible solution to the tension between Anabaptists who advocated for an internally spiritualized faith and those who practiced a legalistic biblicism.[10]

Tyrolean Anabaptism, which emerged at the same time, combined mysticism, apocalypticism, and a form of Swiss-style separatism. The door for Anabaptism in the Tyrol was opened by the peasant uprising led by Michael Gasmair. When his revolutionary movement to form a democratic, egalitarian, Christian society failed, peasants in the valleys and mountains of Tyrol were primed to join the baptizing movement, as many disgruntled peasants had before them. When revolutionary movements failed, some peasants grew open to radical religious solutions to their spiritual and economic discontent.

George Blaurock was the first missionary in the region, and Leonard Schiemer and Hans Schlaffer followed, spreading Hut's ideas in the mountains and valleys around the Inn River. For many of the peasants in Tyrol, the rebaptizing reformation was their first taste of the Reformation. Converts to this early form of Tyrolean Anabaptism included the remarkable noblewoman Helena von Freyburg, who remained true to her new convictions despite pressure from government officials. She used her considerable financial resources to lodge Anabaptist leaders, including Pilgram Marpeck. For her faith, Helena von Freyburg endured imprisonment, exile, and the loss of much of her lands and property.

The importance of God's direct call in an individual's life may have helped legitimize women's roles within the movement. Historian Linda Huebert Hecht conducted a thorough study of court records and found a high number of women members among the South German/Austrian Anabaptist groups.[11] Although there are no records of women performing baptisms, women played an active role in spreading the faith, particularly through their family networks. Austrian authorities arrested many women for Anabaptism—nearly half of those arrested. Many were tortured and executed alongside their husbands. The authorities considered married women like Anna Gasser just as responsible as their husbands for providing aid and shelter to Anabaptist refugees. After her husband Hans was executed in 1529, Anna fled to Moravia, leaving behind her home and children.[12]

Nikolsburg's Anabaptist reforms

The most numerically significant South German/Austrian movement was the communitarian Hutterite community that emerged among the refugees in Moravia. Authorities in Germany and Switzerland increasingly considered Anabaptists to be a disease that needed to be eradicated in order to save the body politic. Those who escaped interrogation and execution fled to Moravia in search of toleration—including Balthasar Hubmaier, Margret Hottinger, and Pilgram Marpeck.

In 1526, Hubmaier and his wife Elsbeth Hügeline had arrived in Nikolsburg, Moravia (now Mikulov in the Czech Republic), after fleeing Waldshut in 1525 and traveling through Zürich and Augsburg. In Nikolsburg, a city of roughly three thousand inhabitants, Hubmaier found rulers—members of the noble Liechtenstein family—who were receptive to his ideas for church renewal through a program of believers baptism, memorial supper, the ban, and iconoclasm. By the "restitution of the Christian Church according to the word of God,"[13] Hubmaier hoped that Nikolsburg would replace Luther's Wittenberg as the beacon of church renewal and reform. Within a few weeks, Hubmaier convinced Leonhart von Liechtenstein and the city clergy to implement his reforms. Although the changes initiated from the clergy, not the laity "from below," they appear to have enjoyed immense success. In May 1527, an eyewitness recalled seeing seventy-two people baptized per day in the state-sanctioned church.

Word of the new "Emmaus" in Moravia attracted more people from Switzerland to the Tyrol as they sought a refuge from persecution. As Swiss Brethren arrived, they grew uneasy with the Nikolsburg reforms. Even though adherents of different streams lived side by side for over a year, some Swiss objected to Hubmaier's acceptance of brethren serving as magistrates and bearing the sword. Influenced by the Schleitheim Articles, other Swiss maintained that congregations, not city officials, should choose their clergy. At the same time, Hans Hut's followers continued to expect the imminent return of Christ, whereas Hubmaier did not believe that signs could precisely predict the onset of the end times.

In the spring of 1527, Hans Hut arrived in Nikolsburg and the tensions between the different Anabaptist groups came to a head. Hut disagreed with the mass baptisms, the lack of communal sharing, and Hubmaier's close relationship with city officials. The lord of Liechtenstein called for a debate between the leaders, but the disputation focused on Hut's end-times predictions rather than on questions of church order. Eventually, Hut and his followers left Nikolsburg with the help of Hubmaier's opponents. Hubmaier stated that "the gulf between the baptism he taught and that of Hut was as great as the difference between heaven and hell."[14]

Hut's message found a warmer reception among the Swiss and Tyrolean refugees than among the Nikolsburg residents who were accustomed to Hubmaier's state-directed reforms. The early Anabaptists had understood the sharing of goods in Acts 2 and 4 to be not just a model for them to follow, but the mark of the true church. In addition to biblical faithfulness, the sharing of goods grew out of the South German ideal of yieldedness. The refugees from the Tyrol and Switzerland complained that the resident Anabaptists in Nikolsburg should have been more generous with their houses and possessions in a spirit of Christian charity. They labeled Hubmaier and Leonhard von Liechtenstein as "sword-bearers" (*Schwertler*) for violating the Schleitheim Articles' prohibition against bearing the sword. Those who refused to bear the sword or pay war taxes were called staff-bearers (*Stäbler*). The irreconcilable differences between the *Schwertler* and the *Stäbler* about the role of government and violence eventually splintered the Moravian baptizing movement.

The Austerlitz Brethren

In March 1528, the Habsburg authorities in Vienna executed Hubmaier for charges of rebellion and heresy. Three days later, they drowned his wife Elsbeth Hügeline. In that same month, Leonhard von Liechtenstein banished the *Stäbler* from Nikolsburg. In search of safety yet again, the group of two hundred refugees resettled in the nearby community of Austerlitz (now called Slavkov u Brna). They quickly established the doctrine of the "community of goods" as a mark of the true church. To put it into practice, they appointed two "servants of temporal needs" who "spread out a cloak in front of the people, and each one laid his possessions on it with a willing heart—without being forced—so that the needy might be supported in accordance with the teaching of the prophet and apostles," as laid out in Isaiah 23 and Acts 2, 4, and 5.[15]

Led by Jakob Wiedemann, the communities at Austerlitz rapidly grew as word spread of the "promised land" in Moravia. Anabaptist leaders brought their flocks to Austerlitz to join the attempt to live fully in accord with the model of the early church as recorded in Acts 2. The weaver Philip Plener brought the Philipites from the Rhineland, the Palatinate, and Württemberg to settle in nearby Auspitz. Later that year, Gabriel Ascherham led his followers (the Gabrielites) from Silesia to Austerlitz and found a settlement of twelve hundred followers practicing community of goods. Jacob Hutter had led another flock of refugees from Tyrol to Moravia to seek safety and to begin practicing community of goods in the early 1530s. And yet it did not take long for persecution to follow them there, too. Many of the members were imprisoned in the city of Passau. During their imprisonment in the dungeons of the castle, they wrote the hymns that make up the nucleus of the *Ausbund*, the hymnal still used by the Amish of North America today. In the face of this increased persecution, the group would eventually leave Moravia in 1535.

The concept of the community of goods was highly appealing to seekers from various regions. During the early years of the German Reformation, commoners held on to the hope that the biblical ideals of justice and equality would become a reality, thereby overturning the existing political and church orders. All Anabaptist groups shared the belief that the gospel had economic implications, even more so than nonresistance. The Swiss Brethren, for instance, held that believers in Christ, while still living in traditional family households, should share their possessions with each other. And it was in pursuit of the ideal of a complete sharing of possessions that those who, after the defeat of the peasants' movement in 1525, continued to hope for a more just society flocked to Moravia.

The biblical ideals and hope for socioeconomic revolution similarly attracted many seekers to Austerlitz, but these noble aspirations sparked contentious disputes and growing acrimony among the Anabaptist groups that converged there. During the summer, the congregations heard sermons together in the open air. However, during the winter months, they needed to meet in three separate buildings, which generated disunity in teaching and practice. Rival congregations accused each other of being "false Ananiases" (Acts 5), and each claimed to uphold the true apostolic model. The bitterness often grew out of a sense of actual or alleged inequality between the leaders and their followers, as well as between women and men.

Wilhelm Reublin, an early leader of the Zürich movement, arrived in Austerlitz in December 1530. Reublin expected to find a radical community of social equality upon his arrival, but he instead discovered authoritarian leaders who forced their followers to enter unwanted marriages. Instead of building up spiritual equality, Reublin wrote, these leaders reserved the best food and rooms for themselves. Frustrated at the lukewarm reception in Austerlitz, Reublin launched a separate Bible study and became a leader for the dissenting voices.

In January 1531, Jakob Wiedemann asked the Austerlitz Brethren to choose between his leadership and Reublin's leadership. Reublin defended himself by accusing the Austerlitz elders of not bearing Christian fruit, allowing wealthy members to have better living conditions, permitting the wives of prominent leaders to eat separately from the common table, believing that baptism is the saving work of justification, preventing him from preaching, and failing to provide equal care for all children. Despite Reublin's personal connections with several influential Anabaptist leaders, including Conrad Grebel, Felix Manz, and Michael Sattler, among others, the Austerlitz Brethren banned him, accusing him of being "one who incites and makes unhappy."[16]

Shortly thereafter, Reublin led a group of three hundred men and women on a difficult winter journey to the nearby farming community of Auspitz (now called Hustopeče in the Czech Republic). However, the early days of the Auspitz community were not easy, as few members had experience in agriculture or vineyards. Disunity and hostility also followed them to Auspitz. When Reublin fell ill and was bedridden, it was discovered that he had hidden a large sum of money, despite the congregation's dire financial situation. Reublin was expelled as a "lying, unfaithful, treacherous Ananias,"[17] and he left Auspitz and eventually renounced Anabaptism altogether.

In 1535, the Holy Roman Emperor Ferdinand I intensified efforts to cleanse his realm of Anabaptist refugees and their heresy. News of the bloody siege in the northwest-German city of Münster might have convinced the nobles of the dangers of Anabaptism. Ferdinand I compelled his Moravian nobles to comply with his edicts and expel any Anabaptist groups that they still harbored. In the "great persecution" of 1535, the Austerlitz Brethren lost their martyred leader Jakob Wiedemann and dispersed to other cities—the Gabrielites returned to Silesia and the Philipites fled to Austria and South Germany. Despondent, many of the Austerlitz groups reexamined scriptures and concluded that the community of goods was intended to be the model only for the early church. Only the Auspitz congregation continued to practice the community of goods.

Jacob Hutter and the Hutterites

Initially, the group that gathered in Auspitz in 1531 preserved good relations with the other refugee immigrants, including the Philipite and Gabrielite congregations. But soon after the congregation's founding, the Auspitz Brethren found themselves without a leader after removing several founders for moral lapses or other reasons. In 1533, Jakob Hutter, a charismatic leader from the Tyrol, filled the leadership vacuum; however, during the leadership struggle, he soured Auspitz's good relations with the leaders of other immigrant congregations.

With little theological training, Hutter had previously become leader of an Anabaptist group in South Tyrol in 1529. He led his flock first to Austerlitz, then after the 1531 schism, to Auspitz. His followers eventually began referring to themselves as the Hutterische Brüder, or

Hutterites. Hutter's firm leadership alienated other Anabaptists in the region, but it attracted refugees from Tyrol, who arrived in a mass migration, fleeing persecution. Hutter led the Hutterites for only two years before he fled back to the Tyrol, where he was captured in 1535 and executed in 1536. Hutter's leadership, however, was firmly imprinted on the spirit of his congregation, which combined the *Gelassenheit* of South German Anabaptist mysticism with the separatism and pacifism of the Swiss Brethren. Thanks to successive years of strong leadership, the Hutterite movement survived years of persecution, migration, and economic struggle.

The Hutterites became passionate missionaries, sending out pairs of evangelists across Germany to invite others to join them in Moravia. Between 1529 and 1621, the Hutterites founded around one hundred communities, or *Bruderhöfe*, in Moravia and neighboring Slovakia, with a total of twenty to thirty thousand members. Their communal way of life led to extraordinary economic growth, especially during the "golden period" of their history during the second half of the sixteenth century. They became known as skilled clockmakers, bakers, masons, weavers, coppersmiths, and millers. The Hutterite history records indicate a strict gendered division of labor. One sixteenth-century observer noted,

> Nowhere do I see men and women together but everywhere each sex was performing its own work apart from the others. I found rooms in which there were only nursing mothers, who [were] without the supervision of men. . . . The duty of caring for the nursing mothers and children was committed to the nursing mothers alone. Elsewhere I saw over a hundred women with distaffs. One was a washerwoman, another a bed-maker, a third a stable-maid, a fourth a dish-washer, a fifth a linen maid, and so all the others had a particular work to do. And just as the duties were systematically assigned to the women, so each one of the men.[18]

The devastating violence of the Thirty Years' War (1618–48) proved too much for many Hutterites. They abandoned their Moravian *Bruderhöfe*, and some of the Slovakian survivors found it too difficult to maintain communitarian economic practices and the principle of nonresistance. Andreas Ehrenpreis tried to invigorate the surviving groups with a renewed spiritual fervor and revival of the old discipline. After Ehrenpreis's death, the Hutterites economic misery continued. The increasingly absolutist Austrian Habsburg rulers tolerated many religions in the seventeenth century, but they increased the repression of the Hutterites by removing children from their parents and confiscating printed materials. In 1665, the Hutterites reached out to the Mennonites in the Dutch Republic for financial aid. Eventually, most Hutterites in Habsburg lands converted to Catholicism, but their communities continued to retain a memory of their communal past.

After moving to Transylvania (Romania), the Hutterites dwindled to thirty or forty members before a group of Lutheran migrants joined the colony and rejuvenated the community. In 1767, in the face of persecutions and repression, the Hutterites crossed unmarked mountain passes to enter Walachia (Romania) in search of favorable conditions. Three years later, they took up their trek again after a new war between Turkish and Russian forces brought renewed suffering. Finally, in 1770, Count Rumyantsev, a Russian general, offered to host them on his Ukrainian estate. In 1859, the Hutterites reestablished Hutter's vision of communal economic life and began to thrive economically, until the Russians implemented universal military conscription in 1870. All the Russian Hutterites immigrated to the United States in 1874, where they settled and grew again.

The continuing Hutterite story demonstrates Anabaptism's ability to adapt and thrive in new contexts. As Swiss, Tyrolean, and South German refugees gathered in Moravia, they forged one of the most powerful articulations of radical reform. Moravian Anabaptism's dynamic combination of mysticism, yieldedness, and community of goods thrived in the "golden years" of toleration in Moravia. The conflict-ridden early years also show how disputatious economic idealism can become when it is combined with biblicism and charismatic leadership.

Looking forward: The Holy Spirit and mutual aid

In addition to the continuing Hutterite tradition, the development of the South German movement highlights two emphases threaded throughout the history of the Anabaptists: the presence of the Holy Spirit and mutual aid. Despite a reputation as somber biblicists, Anabaptists have from the beginning emphasized the importance of the work of the Holy Spirit in following Christ and understanding Scripture. Many of the urban and educated Dutch Mennonites of the seventeenth century, for example, continued to emphasize the role of the Spirit in the interpretation of Scripture through the seventeenth century, even to the point of downplaying external ordinances of the church.[19] The revival movements of the nineteenth and twentieth centuries ignited a missionary impulse to engage the world at home and abroad (see ch. 7). The Indonesian Anabaptist conference now known as the Jemaat Kristen Indonesia (JKI) began as a charismatic revival movement that met in house churches (see ch. 12). As the movement grew, its mission included social services to their members and the surrounding community. Now, JKI has some of the largest Christian congregations in Indonesia.

Mutual aid, or community of goods, was often a response to economic need and an attempt to model the new Anabaptist congregations on the first congregations as recorded in Acts 2 and 4. While most Mennonite groups eventually abandoned full community of goods, they continued practicing mutual aid and charity for their members and for co-religionists abroad. In addition to the charity programs for their own members, the prosperous Dutch churches formed committees to help persecuted Swiss Anabaptists emigrate to safe lands in the seventeenth and eighteenth centuries. More recently, Dutch and North American Mennonites provided aid for Russian Mennonites suffering during the revolution of 1917 and the subsequent anarchy and civil war.[20] Since the Second World War, Anabaptists have expanded their charitable circles to include relief and charitable work for those without direct connections to the Anabaptist tradition, such as schools for children in the West Bank and disaster relief after devastating storms in Nova Scotia, Florida, and Louisiana.

— FOUR —

Apocalypticism in the North

Melchior, Münster, and the Mennonites

In the early hours of February 11, 1535, the residents of Amsterdam were awoken by a procession of naked men and women winding their way through the city's narrow streets, crying, "Woe, woe, woe! Heavenly Father. Wrath, wrath, wrath!" During a late-night prayer session, their leader had thrown his clothes into a fire and ordered everyone else in the room to do the same. When the naked Anabaptists were arrested, they claimed not to be ashamed of their nakedness and refused to cover themselves on that frosty winter morning.

Amsterdam's magistrates were already on edge after a similar event the year before, when several Anabaptists marched through the city waving swords and shouting, "God's blessing is over the right side, and God's blessing is over the left side of this city." These Dutch Anabaptists were eagerly anticipating the signs and omens that would herald the formation of a New Jerusalem, where the members of God's elect would be marked by adult baptism.

Fig. 4.1 Four Anabaptists walk with drawn swords through the streets of Amsterdam, March 22, 1534. Etching by anonymous, *Zwaardlopers te Amsterdam* (Sword Runners in Amsterdam), 1534. Rijksmuseum, Amsterdam, RP-P-OB-78.498.

The fervent apocalyptic expectations culminated in the "Anabaptist kingdom" in the nearby city of Münster, where prophets summoned Anabaptists from across northern Europe to await Christ's return. After a lengthy siege and battle, Catholic troops ended the Anabaptist kingdom in Münster in 1535, sealing Anabaptists' reputation as dangerous fanatics and alarming magistrates across the Holy Roman Empire.

The stream of Anabaptism that eventually spread from the Low Countries (what is today modern Belgium, Luxembourg, and the Netherlands) to northern Germany, Poland, and Ukraine had its origins in the violent apocalyptic tumult of the 1530s. The prophetic vision of a New Jerusalem from where God's army and the elect would conquer and purify the world was over time replaced with the goal, inspired by Ephesians 5:26–27, of creating "spotless" congregations of reborn believers. Anabaptist history includes the occasional return of periods of prophetic and spiritual seeking, but never with the force and chaos of the 1530s. For several generations after Münster, Anabaptists across Europe had to refute any association with the revolutionary legacy of their origins.

Melchior Hoffman: Founder of Dutch Anabaptism

At first glance, Swiss and Dutch Anabaptism seem to have arisen from similar origins. Both grew out of late medieval criticisms of the sacraments. In both regions, reformers called for believers baptism to renew the church and society through personal transformation of believers' lives. However, unlike in the south, the northern stream of Anabaptism was shaped by the theology of the extraordinary reformer and self-fashioned prophet Melchior Hoffman.

Hoffman, a former fur trader turned zealous lay preacher, emphasized the imminent return of Christ and the power of the Holy Spirit. After preaching in Sweden and northern Germany, Hoffman arrived in Strasbourg in 1529, where he became an influential figure among Anabaptists.

In Strasbourg, Hoffman mixed his earlier apocalyptic expectations with the other reforming ideas swirling around the city. He began to preach the doctrine of the celestial flesh, claiming that salvation could come only through a purely divine Christ untouched by human nature. Therefore, the infant Christ was manifested by the Holy Spirit within Mary and was born of her without taking anything from her nature or substance. Christ's human nature, he taught, did not come from Mary but was created by God. Hoffman believed that believers could conquer their flesh by regeneration through the Spirit, just as Christ conquered earthly flesh through his purely divine flesh. These regenerated believers would yield to God's will until "godly authorities" could bring about God's justice, thereby justifying their suffering.

Fig. 4.2 Melchior Hoffman, Radical Reformer and originator of Anabaptism in northwest Europe. Engraving by Christoffel van Sichem (I), *Portrait of Melchior Hoffman*, in or before 1677. Rijksmuseum, Amsterdam, RP-P-1937-1344.

Before coming to Strasbourg, Hoffman had already taught that spiritually gifted individuals could know God's plans for the end times. In Strasbourg, he met the prophets Barbara Rebstock and the married couple Lienhard and Ursula Jost; through them he grew convinced that he was Elijah returned to inaugurate the last days. The spiritual authority of the Holy Spirit bestowed women like Ursula Jost and Barbara Rebstock with remarkable authority in reforming circles in Strasbourg, where there were up to seventeen Anabaptist male and female prophets. Ursula and Lienhard Jost's visions warned of the coming judgment of the rich and powerful and a cataclysmic battle between good and evil, for which the righteous would seal their loyalty and God's covenant with adult baptism.[1] Those marked by adult baptism would not join the fight, Hoffman wrote, but they would aid the God-ordained defenders of the gospel through nonviolent means.

It is unclear whether Hoffman formally joined any of the baptizing groups in Strasbourg, but when his advocacy on their behalf and his prophetic proclamations angered the authorities, he quickly fled the city. Hoffman then took his message of the coming end times north to the region of East Friesland (in northwest Germany), where he baptized three hundred people in a church in Emden. Many of these individuals were from the Low Countries, and when they returned to their homes, they spread Hoffman's apocalyptic message. Hoffman later returned to Strasbourg in 1533 and allowed himself to be arrested, as one of his followers had prophesied that Christ would come to free him from jail. Hoffman continued to prophesy in jail for several more years until his death in 1543 after a long and miserable imprisonment.

Melchiorites and the Anabaptist "kingdom" of Münster

Hoffman's message found fertile ground in the Low Countries, where a small group of clergy and educated artisans had been reading the works of Luther and Erasmus and critiquing indulgences, fasting, relics, saints, purgatory, church hierarchy, and monasticism. A group known as the Sacramentarians rejected the Catholic teachings on the sacraments, especially the idea that the elements of the communion meal became the actual blood and body of Christ. Although most Sacramentarians did not join baptizing reform movements, Hoffman's apocalyptic messengers found people ready for radical changes. However, when one of his missionaries was executed by authorities, Hoffman suspended his baptizing activities for two years.

Despite Hoffman's moratorium on baptisms, his message continued to spread, especially among skilled artisans. The barber-surgeon Obbe Philips, for example, preached the message of "the imminent destruction of all tyrants" and established Amsterdam as a center for the Melchiorite movement. Obbe's leadership was eventually eclipsed by

Fig. 4.3 Gathering of Anabaptists performing adult baptisms in a house.
Etching by anonymous, *Doop der wederdopers* (Baptism of Anabaptists), 1535. Rijksmuseum, Amsterdam, RP-P-OB-78.485.

the zealous Anabaptist Jan Matthijs, a baker from Haarlem. Through his fiery preaching and charismatic personality, Jan Matthijs took up the prophetic leadership of Melchiorites. At one meeting, he "carried on with much emotion and terrifying alarm, and with great and desperate curses cast all into hell and to the devils to eternity who would not hear his voice and who would not recognize and accept him as the true Enoch."[2] Awed by Jan Matthijs's fiery passion, the Melchiorites acknowledged him as Enoch, a biblical prophet of the end times, and God's envoy. Jan Matthijs reversed Hoffman's baptismal ban and sent out pairs of apostles to spread the Melchioritic message and baptize believers with the sign of the Tau, which was believed to designate the 144,000 elect servants of God.

As mentioned earlier, Melchiorite ideas also took root in the city of Münster in Westphalia, where the political situation allowed Anabaptists to attempt to establish a godly city, which would come to a bloody end in 1535. In late 1533, the reforming preacher Bernhard Rothmann had set the wheels in motion when he split Münster's city council by calling for a civic reformation whereby the magistrates would reform the city and promote true religion, echoing Zwingli's council-driven reform of Zürich's churches. Rothmann began as a moderate reformer, but he gradually advocated Melchiorite teachings, including adult baptism.

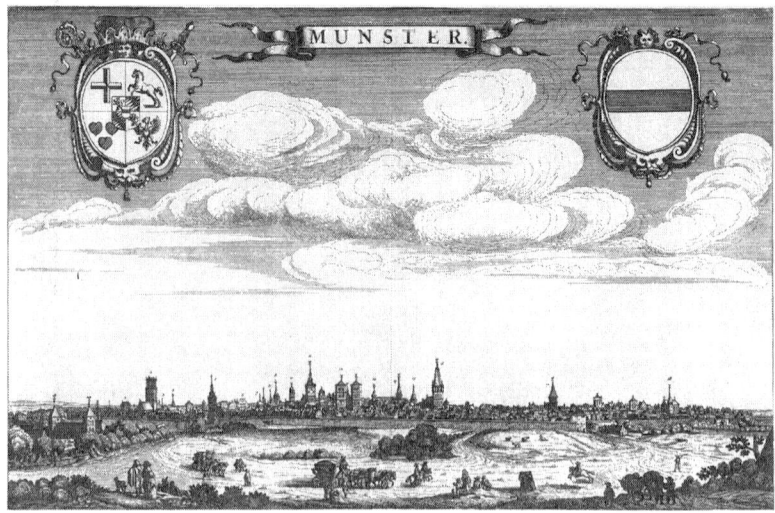

Fig. 4.4 A 1648 view of travelers approaching Münster. Etching by anonymous, *Gezicht op Münster* (A View of Münster), 1648. Rijksmuseum, Amsterdam, RP-P-OB-77.017.

In January 1534, several of Jan Matthijs's apostles arrived in Münster. The Melchiorite emissaries baptized Rothmann, who began baptizing other people; in January alone, fourteen hundred people—a quarter of the city's population—were baptized. In that same month, the apostle Jan van Leiden arrived. Sensing the opportunities in joining with Rothmann's radicalizing civic reforms, Jan van Leiden sent for Jan Matthijs and other Dutch Melchiorites to join him in Münster.

Melchiorites from across northwest Europe flocked to Münster, which had replaced Strasbourg as the city where they joyfully anticipated the imminent coming of the New Jerusalem. News of Rothmann and others baptizing believers in Münster spread rapidly, and there was excitement and anticipation that the end times had begun. The city would become a haven for those who had received baptism marked with the sign of the Tau. Non-Anabaptist residents of Münster, aware of the emperor's 1529 decree condemning Anabaptists to death by fire, sword, or other means, began to flee the city in late January. Their departure, coupled with the influx of Melchiorites, paved the way for Rothmann's allies to win the council elections on February 23, 1534. After the elections, non-baptized people left the city if they could, leaving behind a population of women and children that far outnumbered the men, mostly from the property-less class. As a result, the Anabaptists were free to establish a Christian government with the aim of renewing both the church and society.

When the prince-bishop of Münster, Franz von Waldeck, besieged the city, the Anabaptists inside compelled everyone remaining—many of them married women whose husbands had fled—to receive baptism as a way to root out persons of questionable loyalty. The newly baptized were given a token inscribed with DWWF, which stood for "The Word has become flesh" (*Dat Word Wird Fleis*).[3] Messengers were sent out from the city to call for believers to join the New Jerusalem. Despite the besieging army, men and women continued to come to the city with the hope of witnessing the signs and wonders that heralded the coming of Christ.

The increasingly unstable Jan Matthijs arrived on the day of the February election. However, he would not spend long in the New Jerusalem. Around Easter, Matthijs and some of his companions charged the troops outside of the city in hopes of initiating the end

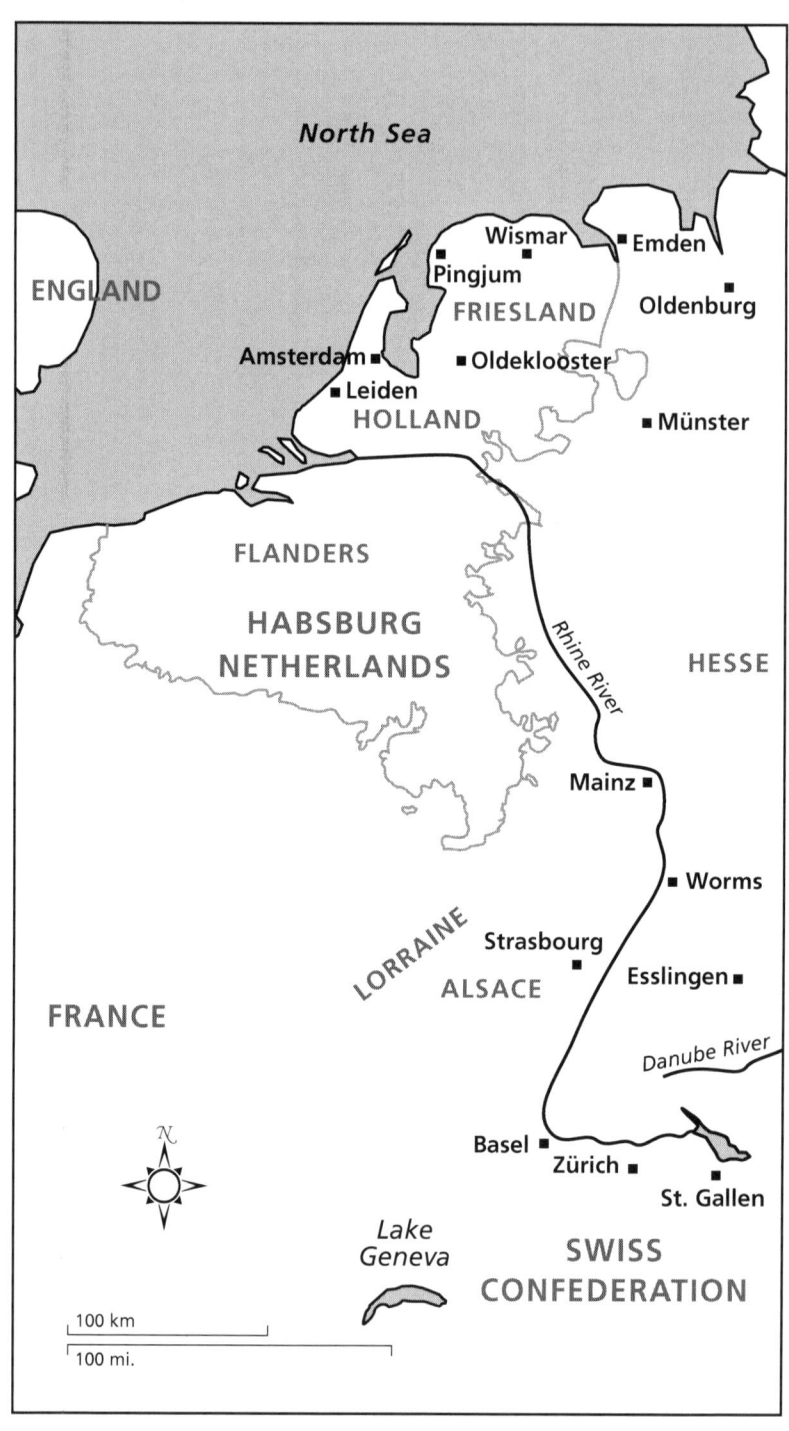

times, but the besieging soldiers quickly cut Matthijs to pieces. In the resulting apocalyptic crisis, Jan van Leiden assumed leadership of the city, replacing the city council with a band of twelve elders and proclaiming himself king. After the failure of Christ's appearance that Easter morning, 1534, Münster's message changed. No longer a New Jerusalem where believers could find refuge, the city was now the new Israel that would dispense God's vengeance on the wicked.

In February and March of 1534, missives from Münster had arrived in the Low Countries, appealing for "the Children of God" to travel to Münster to save themselves from God's imminent wrath. The faithful were instructed to bring only money, linen, and weapons, since the city would be able to provide the rest for them. Several thousand Dutch men and women set out for Münster. Most never made it; five ships of the faithful were stopped in Amsterdam's harbor on March 21, 1534, and others were detained on the way between March 21 and 24. Most of the pilgrims were simply disarmed and given amnesty. In Amsterdam, several Melchiorite men ran through the streets with swords, crying out, "The day of the Lord is coming, the day of the Lord is coming," to warn of God's wrath on the unrepentant.[4] Despite the failure of the trekkers and the execution of the sword-bearers, the faithful continued to expect God to deliver them during the coming apocalypse.

In the summer of 1534, self-appointed king Jan van Leiden introduced polygamy in Münster. A lack of trustworthy firsthand sources obscures why he introduced the practice. Women outnumbered men in the New Jerusalem; women had stayed behind to look after family affairs, and former nuns had been some of the strongest advocates for adult baptism. In addition, among the Melchiorite immigrants, there were twice as many women as men, perhaps owing to the appeal that prophetic practices provided for female participation in the movement.

Perhaps to address this gender imbalance, Jan van Leiden instituted polygamy and eventually married sixteen women, many of whom connected him to prominent families. The justification for polygamy was drawn from Old Testament examples. In practice, the introduction of polygamy allowed patriarchal leaders to assert male authority over women and facilitated the distribution of food rations to households. To accommodate the arrival of the pilgrims, the city implemented a system of communal living and housed newcomers in the homes of those who had left.

In the end, the fate of Münster was inevitable. By the late spring of 1535, the city was defended by only a small number of men against the prince-bishop's forces. On June 25, 1535, the besiegers breached one of the gates and took over the city. Some locals were granted safe passage, but most men were executed in the following days. Many women were spared after they renounced their faith. Jan van Leiden and two other leaders were put on display in cages until their brutal execution in January 1536. The fate of Bernhard Rothmann, the original Münsterite reformer, remains uncertain.

Fig. 4.5 Portrait of Jan van Leiden as king of the Anabaptist kingdom at Münster. Engraving by Jan Muller, *Portrait of Jan van Leiden, a Dutchman and Leader of the Münster Anabaptists*, ca. 1615. Metropolitan Museum of Art, New York, Harris Brisbane Dick Fund, 1917, 17.3.910.

The movement reforms after Münster

The fall of Münster in 1535 marked the end of any hope that Anabaptists could collaborate with city authorities to establish a New Jerusalem. The events there solidified the perception of Anabaptists as dangerous extremists, prompting rulers throughout the Holy Roman Empire to take action to eliminate them. The term *Anabaptist* became a pejorative label for all who supported adult baptism, and they became subject to the imperial decree that ordered their execution. Like the Swiss Anabaptists who unified their movement at Schleitheim in response to persecution and internal differences, those in the north who advocated for adult baptism had to decide the future of their movement.

Post-Münster Anabaptist Options

Initially, the Melchiorite survivors went underground and developed into four streams:

Münsterites continued to advocate the establishment of a New Jerusalem following the model of Münster. A few even proposed retaking Münster itself. However, this group soon withered and died.

Batenburgers went further than even those at Münster in justifying the use of the sword. Under the leadership of Jan van Batenburg they used terrorist tactics—killing livestock and burning crops—to strike fear in those who did not accept their doctrine and those who persecuted Anabaptists. Like the Münsterites, they practiced polygamy and community of goods. The Batenburgers were most active during the 1530s, but there are a few records of activity after 1544.

Melchiorites rejected violence, but they maintained the prophetic and visionary practices of the early Melchiorite movement. This remnant group mostly existed in the Rhineland area of northwest Germany.

Obbenites were named for Obbe Philips, the leader who had commissioned Jan Matthijs but eventually rejected the Anabaptist movement around 1539. Despite the loss of one of their strongest leaders, the movement worked to form peaceful, separate congregations of righteous believers. After Münster's finale and Obbe's departure, Dirk Philips and David Joris became leaders of the peaceful Melchiorite remnant.[5]

94   *Radicals & Reformers*

Initially, the most important leader after the fiasco in Münster was the glassmaker David Joris. His followers, sometimes called the Davidjorists, were primarily of a Spiritualist movement. Like most Spiritualists, they believed that sacraments were mere externalities, which allowed them to tolerate a certain degree of Nicodemism—outwardly conforming to the Catholic Church while inwardly dissenting. Through his personal charisma and visions, David Joris quickly rose to prominence in the Melchiorite movement. He facilitated an agreement among Melchiorite delegates at an August 1536 conference at Bocholt. In the same year, he had a series of visions that laid claim to his spiritual authority and his identity as the "third David," succeeding King David of Israel and Christ.

An Influential Voice

Some of the most important Anabaptist leaders were initially followers of David Joris. At the age of twenty-four, Anna Jans and her husband Arent Jansz van der Lint joined the Melchiorites in the heady days when thousands flocked to Münster to take part in the New

Fig. 4.6 As she walked to her execution, Anna Jans handed her infant son to a spectator, beseeching him to care for her child. Etching by Jan Luyken, *Anneken Jans Gives Her Child to a Baker...*, 1685. Rijksmuseum, Amsterdam, RP-P-OB-78.426.

Jerusalem. She authored a song which declares, "I can hear the trumpet sounding." The lyrics ring with eschatological excitement and fervent anticipation of the vengeance of the unrighteous by the "great vine press of the wrath of God."[6] "The Trumpet Song" became a popular anthem of the Melchiorite movement. It rejoices in the coming punishment of the godless, and it encourages the faithful—those sealed with the baptismal sign of the Tau—to take up their harps and sing in anticipation of their inheritance. David Joris published "The Trumpet Song" in a collection of spiritual songs and composed his own song echoing its sentiments.

Through her song and relationship with David Joris, Anna Jans was a prominent Anabaptist leader. In 1538, while she was returning from England, Anna Jans and a female traveling companion were arrested in Rotterdam after a witness recognized a song they were singing. Authorities drowned Anna Jans on January 20, 1539.

David Joris led a Melchiorite movement that stretched from England to Oldenburg, in northern Germany. After 1536, he tried to win over the Melchiorites in Strasbourg, whom everyone considered to be "the Elders of Israel" because of their early relationship with Melchior Hoffman. In June 1538, he traveled to Strasbourg to seek their approval of his leadership. Wary of Joris's reliance on personal, subjective revelation, the Strasbourg Melchiorites were unwilling to anoint David Joris as Hoffman's successor. Lienhard Jost's and Melchior Hoffman's prophecies, they contended, were based on Scripture and reason. When the prophet Barbara Rebstock asked to speak to Joris under the inspiration of the Holy Spirit, Joris refused to listen to her. The Strasbourg group defended her right to speak, because "she has been of the fear of the Lord for many years."[7] Ultimately, David Joris failed to win the Strasbourg Melchiorites' approval of his leadership. Although he failed to attract many followers in Strasbourg, Joris became the most important leader in the movement from 1536 to 1539. His distinctive beliefs included his claim to be the "third David" who possessed authoritative access to truth. Joris did not try to build new congregations but emphasized the spiritual perfections of individuals.

In the aftermath of the persecution of hundreds of Joris's followers in 1539 by Catholic Habsburg authorities, including Anna Jans (see sidebar, pp. 94–95) and his mother, Joris himself became a target and fled for his life. He found refuge in Antwerp in the same year and then moved to Basel in 1544, where he lived under the alias Jan van Brugge until his death in 1556. This meant that Joris could no longer lead the Dutch Melchiorite movement through his charismatic personality. As a result, Menno Simons, Dirk Philips, and other Obbenites were more easily able to take over the leadership of the movement, and Joris abandoned Anabaptism for Spiritualism.[8]

Menno Simons's new direction

A farmer's son, Menno Simons started his religious career at the age of twenty-eight as a Catholic vicar in the Frisian village of Pingjum in 1524. Shortly thereafter, Menno began reading Luther and questioning the doctrine of transubstantiation. When he turned to Scripture seeking answers to his doubts, he concluded that the church had deceived him. Menno continued searching the Bible for answers after he was transferred to the church at Witmarsum in 1532, where he continued to dispense the sacraments that he no longer believed in.

Eventually, Menno learned about adult baptism and Hoffman's teachings, but he remained ambivalent about joining the movement, even though he believed that infant baptism was unscriptural. It is not clear what led Menno to finally receive adult baptism. But the brutal repression of the Münsterite attack at the nearby monastery of Oldeklooster and the final defeat of the Münsterite defenders challenged Menno to act. He could no longer hide in the comfort of his pulpit while others were willing to die for their faith. In the summer of 1535, he received baptism and began to rebuild the Melchiorites into a peaceful movement through his tireless preaching and writing.

By 1540, Menno's talents had become well-known, and several representatives asked him to become an elder and care for "the great sufferings and need of the poor oppressed souls."[9] After Hoffman's prophecies failed to materialize, dejected apocalyptic Münsterites found a spiritual home in the peaceful, separatist congregations led by Menno and Dirk Philips. Menno's tireless journeys and writings prevented the northern Anabaptist movement from imploding. Menno's most important work, *Dat Fundament des christelyken leers* (*The Foundation of Christian*

Fig. 4.7 Menno Simons. Print by Christoffel van Sichem (I), *Portrait of Menno Simons*, 1677. Rijksmuseum, Amsterdam, RP-P-1911-547.

Doctrine), first published in 1539, served as the theological bedrock for his followers.

Menno adopted and developed Hoffman's teaching on the celestial flesh of Christ, but at the heart of his theology lay the doctrine of regeneration—the lengthy process of a believer's repentance and conversion, often marked by spiritual anguish. The Holy Spirit's transformation of the believer was sealed with baptism and demonstrated through good works. Whereas David Joris's Spiritualist followers could discard externalities, Menno insisted on a visible gathering of the regenerated. The disciplined church was to be the pure bride of Christ, without spot or wrinkle. Unlike Swiss Anabaptists, Menno wrote more approvingly of government, which he believed God had ordained to punish the wicked and protect the innocent. Despite Menno's more supportive stance, the authorities persecuted the faithful, fulfilling Menno's expectation that true believers would suffer for their faith.

Menno traveled extensively to maintain the scattered church and defend it from attacks from Catholic and Protestant opponents. Although Menno admitted that his opponents outmatched him in debates, his arguments and theological defenses provided the intellectual framework to support his flock into the seventeenth century. Menno also wrote against Anabaptist and Spiritualist opponents— "corrupt sects" that threatened the unity of the movement from within. Most of the disputations centered on either the use of violence or the relation between the spirit and the letter of biblical interpretation. In *The Foundation-Book*, Menno condemned violence, polygamy, and rebellion. And soon after becoming an elder, he confronted the gifted preacher Adam Pastor for his belief that Jesus was purely human.

Menno's most tireless campaign was against the Davidjorists' Spiritualism. In addition to his rebuke of David Joris's messianic pretensions, Menno insisted on the need for the faithful to avoid attending state church services, baptisms, and marriages. The Davidjorists, on the other hand, allowed their followers to attend them, since "to the pure, all things are pure."[10]

Growth and dissent

In 1541, the Court of Friesland claimed victory over the Anabaptist heresy, but the reality was quite different. Menno's pastoral and intellectual leadership breathed new life into the movement, which had grown out of the ashes of Hoffman's apocalyptic prophecies. With Menno at the helm, the Anabaptists embraced a nonviolent and separatist approach to their faith, which allowed them to flourish in the second half of the sixteenth century. Elder Lenaert Bouwens was a prolific baptizer, welcoming over ten thousand people into the Anabaptist fold between 1551 and 1582. By 1600, one-quarter of the province of

Friesland had embraced Anabaptism, a testament to the movement's strength and resilience.

As the Anabaptist movement grew, it became increasingly important for congregations to maintain purity and clear boundaries with the wider society. To achieve this, they utilized church discipline to address sin, discord, and schismatic beliefs among members. Those who persisted in such behaviors could be barred from communion and even from the congregation itself.

However, differences arose among congregations about how to implement church discipline and how severe it should be. To address these issues, Menno Simons, Dirk Philips, Lenaert Bouwens, Gillis van Aken, and other leaders gathered in Wismar in 1554 to determine shared practices. The resulting articles of the Wismar church order focused on church discipline, including guidance on whether believers could do business with banned members or their spouses.

In addition to discipline, the Wismar Articles also addressed issues such as marriages with non-Anabaptists, divorce, bearing weapons, and doing business with nonmembers. This emphasis on congregational purity and discipline became a defining feature of the Anabaptist movement, allowing it to thrive under persecution.

As Menno grew older and physically weaker, a new generation of elders pressured him to strengthen church discipline. A group led by Dirk Philips and Lenaert Bouwens thought that congregations had grown too lax in their discipline. In 1557, the aging Menno traveled to Harlingen to discuss the case of Swaen Rutgers, a believer from Emden who refused to shun—that is, socially avoid—her banned husband. Under pressure from Dirk Philips and Lenaert Bouwens, Menno sided with the stricter group.

Delegates from the Waterland region refused to accept the Harlingen decision. Dirk Philips and Lenaert Bouwens banned the Waterlanders, calling them *trekwagens*, or "dung carts," since they accepted muck into their congregations. The moderate Waterlanders called themselves the baptism-minded, or *Doopsgezinden*. When Anabaptists in Germany questioned Menno's strict practice of shunning and counseled a more moderate practice, he banned them. By the time of Menno's death in 1561, the tireless pastor had been eclipsed by the hardliners in the movement that bore his name.

In 1566, a revolt against Hapsburg rule broke out in the Low Countries. Many Mennonites fled from the south to the north, where seven provinces had established a new country, the Dutch Republic. In the second half of the sixteenth century, the Dutch Mennonites split several more times, usually over issues of discipline and the proper relationship between congregations and the surrounding society. The quest for the pure congregation "without spot or wrinkle" (Ephesians 5:27) resulted in fierce disagreements about who could discipline members and the process of pronouncing the ban or shunning. In 1567, a Flemish/Frisian split occurred; although the issues were about discipline, personality clashes often exacerbated the animosity and made it difficult for the groups to reconcile. The "Old" and "Mild" Flemish split in 1586 and the "Old" and "Young" Frisians formed in 1589, but the schisms continued over the decades, with more conservative branches insisting on greater separation from the world in which many members flourished economically. The groups who continued to hold to Menno's teachings on the celestial flesh called themselves Mennonites, whereas most others called themselves Doopsgezinden. The splits were so profound that Frisian and Flemish Mennonites maintained separate congregations in Russia centuries later.

Sword and prison: The age of persecution

The Doopsgezinden and Mennonites enjoyed greater freedom and toleration than Anabaptists in Switzerland, Moravia, or Germany. However, before the formation of the Dutch Republic in the 1570s, they too suffered for their faith. After the apocalyptic visions of Hans Hut and Melchior Hoffman had evaporated and the utopian zeal of the 1520s and 1530s waned, Anabaptists adapted to the reality that they had to go underground and would never become mass movements. A martyr-minded mentality became common to all sixteenth-century Anabaptists.

The persecution of the Anabaptists started in Switzerland when Felix Manz was drowned in Zürich in 1527. This was followed by the 1529 edict issued by the Holy Roman Emperor Charles V, which ordered that "every rebaptizer and rebaptized person of reasoning age, male or female, be executed and taken from life to death by fire, the sword or the like."[11]

In addition to an assumed connection between Anabaptists and the Peasants' War of 1525, the reports of Jan van Leiden's kingdom fanned the flames of fear of Anabaptists throughout Europe. Anxious rulers viewed Münster as conclusive proof of the perils of allowing Anabaptists to spread their message unchecked, and they acted decisively to eliminate them.

Before the Reformations, late medieval religious and civic leaders worked together to combat heresy within their territory. Although rulers' commitment to eradicate dissent through trials, torture, and execution seems repugnant by modern standards, authorities felt a religious and moral responsibility to cleanse their territory of heretics. If they allowed false teachings to spread in their city, thereby contaminating others with the disease of heresy, God would hold them accountable. In addition, it was widely assumed that religious diversity endangered the political stability of a city, state, or territory. Both Protestant and Catholic leaders believed that tolerating dissenting beliefs was detestable. As historian Brad S. Gregory notes, "It was tantamount to letting dangerous people seduce others to damnation, sully God's honor, and subvert the social fabric."[12]

Rulers fined, imprisoned, exiled, tortured, and executed Anabaptists. Anabaptists who participated in the apocalyptic or revolutionary unrest at Münster or the Peasants' War only reinforced their reputation as fanatics. In addition, the Anabaptist rejection of infant baptism in favor of adult baptism undercut the universal foundations of Christendom.

For centuries, infant baptism marked Europeans' entry into the religious and secular order at an age before they could give their consent; Anabaptists' rejection of infant baptism rejected the fundamental religious and political assumptions that knit together the social order.[13] By also refusing to swear oaths, serve in the government, or bear the sword, Anabaptists seemed to reject any participation in the social order. This only strengthened the belief among their opponents that Anabaptists were heretical seditionists, further fueling the persecution against them.[14] During the sixteenth and seventeenth centuries, around twenty-five hundred Anabaptists were executed for heresy, with the majority being men but roughly a third of them women.

The experience of persecution deeply shaped Anabaptist spirituality. They began to understand that baptism by Spirit, water, and

Fig. 4.8 In the face of persecution, Anabaptists gathered in secluded forests and caves. In this illustration from the sixteenth century, the authorities raid a nighttime meeting in the Swiss forests.
Manuscript page from Johann Jakob Wick, [Sammlung von Nachrichten zur Zeitgeschichte aus den Jahren 1560–87 (mit älteren Stücken)], ([Zürich], [1574]). Zentralbibliothek, Zürich, Ms. F 23, S. 393–94.

blood, as described in 1 John 5:6–8, was something that all believers would likely participate in. When they were baptized as adults into the church, they accepted the likelihood of suffering and even martyrdom for their faith.

Rather than fear death, some Anabaptist martyrs saw their public execution as an opportunity to share their faith. One of their opponents despaired that the Anabaptists "dance and jump in the fire, view the glistening sword with fearless hearts, speak and preach to the people with smiles on their faces; they sing psalms and other songs until their souls have departed, they die with joy, as if they were in happy company, they remain strong, assured, and steadfast to the point of death."[15] Over time, continual repression and persecution intensified the sense of separation from a world that had turned away from the narrow path of the Bible's gospel message. A worldview suffused with a sense of persecution and separation became central to Anabaptists' identity and faith.[16]

Many of the hymns and pamphlets that emerged during the sixteenth century nurtured a piety of steadfastness and suffering for the faith. In 1535, Moravian Anabaptists composed numerous hymns on death and suffering while they languished in a prison in Passau. The hymns emphasize loneliness, patient suffering, and hope that God will not forsake those who suffer for their faith. Around 1583, a publisher combined these hymns with eighty other songs, many of which were penned by martyrs, including George Blaurock, Felix Manz, and Hans Hut.[17] (Some Old Order Amish groups continue to use this combined volume, known as the *Ausbund*, today.) Originally, Anabaptists composed the songs included in the *Ausbund* and hundreds of other vernacular songs to internalize and support the biblical and contemporary command to remain steadfast in the face of suffering. At 1531 song attributed to Michael Sattler states:

> When Christ with his true teaching
> gathered together a little band,
> he said that everyone with patience
> must follow him daily, carrying the cross.[18]

The underground congregations circulated accounts of trials and letters from prisoners to their spouses. Published anonymously in 1562, *The Sacrifice of the Lord* (*Het offer des Heeren*) became a popular and important early martyrology for Dutch believers. The small, easily concealed book contained stories and songs of martyrs predominately from the Low Countries, in addition to texts about Christ, Stephen, and Michael Sattler. Set to well-known tunes, the songs provided examples of believers who remained true to their convictions during their imprisonment, trial, and execution.[19] They simultaneously cultivated the values of steadfast suffering and instructed believers in the basic beliefs, providing them with answers in case they eventually became imprisoned. A song based on the 1549 interrogation of an Anabaptist named Elisabeth before the council instructs the singer on Anabaptist thought while extolling the deacon as a model of faithfulness:

> *The Council:* "But what is it that you believe about the mass and the most worthy sacrament?"
>
> *Elisabeth:* "Of those things I've never read anything certain, but I have about the Lord's Supper, so dear.". . .
>
> *The Council:* "Tell us, did infant baptism have no benefit since you had yourself baptized again?"
>
> *Elisabeth:* "No, I did not do it 'again,' for it happened only once upon my confession."[20]

Not all the Anabaptists who faced a trial were executed. In the Habsburg Low Countries, some local magistrates refused to enact policies from distant authorities. Accused Anabaptists were not simply heretics; when judges knew them as "family members, colleagues, neighbors, fellow citizens, and sometimes even as 'good Christians,'"[21] they ruled with greater leniency. Authorities also tried to differentiate between leaders and followers, usually punishing the former with capital punishment. Women were less likely to receive the death penalty, partly because they were seldom leaders and partly because of the prejudice at the time that women were incapable of making independent decisions.[22]

Anabaptists employed several strategies to avoid punishment. Some accused Anabaptists threw themselves at the mercy of the court, acknowledging their error and recanting Anabaptist beliefs. In such cases, the courts often fined or exiled them instead of executing them. Other Anabaptists practiced a type of Nicodemism, promising to recant Anabaptism and attend state churches but then retracting their recantation and meeting secretly with Anabaptists. For example, Blasius Greiner, a glassmaker from Württemberg, was arrested and recanted at least three times between 1562 and 1571.[23] Many Anabaptists avoided persecution by moving to regions governed by more tolerant authorities. Even though the revolutionary spirit of the peasants' movements of the 1520s and the Münsterites' apocalyptic expectations in the 1530s had dried up, the charges of fanaticism and heresy doggedly followed Anabaptist groups for several centuries.

New songs, new voices, new lands: From Anabaptist to Mennonite

Mennonite theologians and historians have attempted to pinpoint the moment when the Anabaptist movement transitioned from its "radical" phase to a more settled state. This historical project aimed to determine when the Anabaptists lost the fervor of their early missionaries and martyrs. These scholars crafted an idealized image of a "golden age" of Anabaptism for contemporary Mennonites to emulate. In reality, the end of the radical moment occurred at different times for various adherents, and some lamented the loss of the utopian apocalyptic vision, whereas others saw the retreat into separatism as a lack of conviction. Women, in particular, may have regretted the restoration of patriarchal structures and the decline of female prophecy.

There is a danger that by focusing on the genesis of the movement, we gloss over the numerous ways that individuals and groups must reinterpret their ideals across new contexts in place and time. For example, as the second and third generations of Anabaptists began to raise children within the faith, they had to rethink the original emphasis on adult baptism and discipleship. Attitudes toward the authorities also changed when officials protected Anabaptists in their territory and even lobbied on behalf of persecuted Anabaptists in other lands. Just as the earliest Anabaptists drew inspiration from medieval spirituality, the writings of Erasmus, or Luther's emphasis on Scripture alone, Anabaptists would continue to be influenced and nourished by religious and cultural forces around them. To tell the stories of Anabaptists, we must balance the highest original ideals with an appreciation for how time changes all things.

Looking forward: Martyrdom and costly discipleship

According to a recent essay collection, "right remembering" of contemporary and sixteenth-century stories of those who suffer for their faith means "a conscious effort to acknowledge the complexity of every story" and telling the story "with an empathetic spirit" of the other.[24] North American Amish and Mennonites have continued to tell the martyr stories because they caution against the dangers of acculturation and testify to the possibility of loving one's enemies, even in extremely difficulty contexts; however, these North American retellers also generally enjoy religious freedom and economic comfort. While the stories serve as a reminder to pursue radical discipleship even in a time of comfort, they also reflect the reality for many Christians in the global Anabaptist community.

In the global church, persecution and suffering for one's faith is a lived experience. A 2012 report by the Center for the Study of Global Christianity estimates that hundreds of thousands of Christians have been killed for their faith since 2000. According to a 2023 BBC news item, for example, the body of a founder of the Meserete Kristos Church in Eritrea, who spent over a decade in prison for his faith, was denied burial for two weeks after his death in April 2023 because his religion was not recognized by the state.[25] In African and Asian contexts, becoming an Anabaptist often means joining a minority religion, not simply switching Christian affiliations. In these contexts, Anabaptists continue to discern how to be faithful in trying times.

— FIVE —

The Earth Is the Lord's

Seeking the Peace of the City

When twenty-five-year-old Maria Bögli arrived in Amsterdam in early August 1711, she had been traveling for over a month with over three hundred other Swiss Anabaptist refugees, sailing down the Rhine River on four boats. Dutch Mennonites had been lobbying authorities on behalf of persecuted Anabaptists for decades, to help them escape tightening restrictions on their lives. Bögli had taken advantage of the Bernese authorities' agreement to let Swiss Anabaptists sell their belongings and leave Bern. Upon their arrival in the Dutch Republic, she and the other refugees found shelter in Amsterdam warehouses while Swiss and Dutch leaders searched for a suitable place for them to settle.

Bögli, who came from Herzogenbuchsee, a village of a few hundred residents, left no record of her first impressions of Amsterdam, a financial and trading metropolis of over two hundred thousand residents. Nor do we know what she thought of the wealthy Dutch Mennonites who had made it possible for her to be there. But we do have a poem, published in 1713 by Dutch poet Pieter Langendijk, written from the imagined perspective of a recent Swiss refugee girl named Simplicity.

Langendijk imagines the refugee's tearful lament upon seeing the wealthy Amsterdammers for the first time:

> Is this the same land for which I longed
> When I lay bound in shackles and fetters?
> Do my eyes deceive me?
> Are these the same brethren, my helpers in need?
> Who, with God, were my people's protectors?[1]

Simplicity acknowledges Dutch generosity as the only "ray of virtue" that shone through the cloud of inter-confessional disputes, unbridled consumption, lewd behavior, indecent dress, and stuck-up airs of the Dutch. And she admonishes the Dutch:

> Consider a time one hundred and fifty years ago,
> Examine yourself and think about how your forebears lived.
> They labored for a treasure, an eternal reward;
> They valued splendor less than the heavenly martyr's crown.
> Generosity, it is true, is easily found in you,
> But one virtue does not wash out all other sins.[2]

Langendijk intended his poem to satirize Dutch Mennonites' wealth and social pretensions. Through the character of Simplicity, Langendijk contrasts Dutch Mennonites' luxurious lifestyles with the simple manners of the Swiss Brethren. Langendijk's poetic critique of wealth and assimilation reinforces a long-standing caricature of the Dutch Anabaptists—still common among some North American authors—that is often used as a warning about the dangers of acculturation.

Langendijk was leveling a polemical attack, and we should be careful not to assume that his poem reflects the reality of all the Dutch or the Swiss. Many of the refugees brought significant amounts of money with them. Maria Bögli, for example, was able to purchase a house and a plot of land for herself soon after the refugees settled in the Dutch village of Kalkwijk.[3] The Swiss newcomers eventually joined conservative Dutch Mennonite congregations in the area who were theologically similar in belief and practice.

The satirical bite in Langendijk's poem relies on the notion that a trans-European Mennonite identity united the Swiss and Dutch.

The poem assumes that the groups *were* related despite the different geographic origins, languages, levels of urbanization, and practices of church discipline. By the beginning of the eighteenth century, many of the Anabaptist groups across Europe understood themselves to belong to the same movement. In response to appeals for help during waves of repression, the Dutch Mennonites provided financial assistance and petitioned local and national authorities to intervene on behalf of the Swiss Brethren and other persecuted Anabaptists across Europe.

At the heart of their interventions and appeals for toleration was an assumed common identity among all "Mennonites" as both respectful dissenters from the official church and as obedient subjects of the state. To defend the Swiss against charges of sedition and heresy, the Dutch grafted them into their Mennonite identity. This common, transnational identity became an important strand of a much larger network that kept Mennonites across the continent in contact with others who held to adult baptism, separation from the world, non-swearing of oaths, and defenselessness.

Some historians describe the period of 1600–1700 as a time when Anabaptists transitioned from Anabaptist to Mennonite. This process could describe several traits of Anabaptist history during this time. To shake the rebellious and heretical stain of rebellion and the Peasants' War, Anabaptists frequently called themselves Mennonite instead of Anabaptist. They thereby constructed a new historical identity that united all Mennonites with the patient suffering of the martyrs of the sixteenth century and the obedient subjects of the seventeenth.

As the Anabaptist movement evolved into distinct Mennonite traditions, regional differences intensified, resulting in a diversity of understandings of what it meant to be Mennonite. This diversity increased as Mennonites migrated to different parts of the world seeking toleration and economic opportunities, leading to new Mennonite identities at local and transnational levels. As these traditions took shape, clashes often occurred between and within Anabaptist groups over how to faithfully express the Anabaptist convictions, especially with those nearest to them. Over time, some groups chose to separate themselves from the surrounding society by moving to new lands or by maintaining distinctive dress and language as a way to mark community boundaries. Other groups integrated, choosing to open themselves to the surrounding culture as they looked for new ideas or ways to live out their faith.

Fig. 5.1 Portrait of Swiss man and woman who migrated to the Dutch Republic wearing traditional clothing. Etching by Karel Christiaan Fuchs, in E. Maaskamp, *De kleedingen, zeden & gewoonten in de Nederlanden in den aanvang der 19e eeuw* (Amsterdam, 1829). Rijksmuseum, Amsterdam, RP-P-1896-A-19274.

The promises and perils of new contexts
In the seventeenth and eighteenth centuries, Anabaptists had to adapt to three historical phenomena that were part of the transition from the late-medieval society into modernity: religious toleration, state-building, and the Enlightenment. Some Anabaptist groups resisted these broader social changes in order to remain true to their understanding of their tradition. Others saw opportunities to practice their faith in safety and new resources for intellectual growth.

Religious toleration
During the second half of the 1500s, Anabaptists and the religious and political authorities gradually tolerated each other. After the turmoil of the 1530s, Anabaptist missionaries continued to convert new members, but they went underground, reestablished traditional gender roles, and no longer expected the second coming of Christ. From the Low Countries to German lands, Anabaptists worked to convince rulers that they had nothing to fear from them. In some territories, tolerant rulers who did not believe that Anabaptists were seditious heretics protected them. The German Lutheran lord Bartholomäus von Ahlefeldt, for example, permitted Menno Simons to live out his final years in the village of Wüstenfelde despite pressure from the king to remove him.[4] Dutch authorities stopped executing Anabaptists in 1571, and the Swiss followed in 1614.

Whether they lived in the tolerant Low Countries or under the repression of the Swiss lands, all Anabaptists had to discern what it would mean to be faithful Christians as they passed the faith on to their children, built institutions, and earned their living. In tolerant contexts, calls for separation from the surrounding world made less sense. In the seventeenth century, Anabaptists increasingly called themselves Mennonites or the baptism-minded (*Doopsgezinden* in Dutch, *Taufgesinnten* in German) to distance themselves from the violent legacies of the Peasants' War and Münster. As Mennonites cultivated a reputation as hardworking, loyal dissenters, authorities recruited them to migrate in exchange for exemptions from military service and the freedom to practice their faith as they wished. Dutch Doopsgezinden, grateful for the toleration they had been granted and aware of the persecution of the Swiss Brethren, included a prayer of gratitude for their authorities in the *Martyrs Mirror*, a collection of martyrs stories from 1660 that Anabaptists continue to read today.

Martyrs Mirror Prayer for Secular Authorities

"On the other hand, the authorities whom thou hast set in our fatherland, the blessed Netherlands, that are at present free from the constraint of conscience, free from domineering over the most holy faith, and above all, free from the blood of Thy servants and saints, be pleased to bless them, out of Thy heavenly habitation, with the abundance of Thy wisdom and grace, a foretaste of which Thou hast permitted them to have already, many years ago."[5]

State-building

The lack of strong, centralized states meant that Anabaptists could negotiate with local officials for toleration. Rulers granted Mennonites special privileges (*privilegia*), or private laws, that applied only to them. Privileges authorized Mennonite practices of marriage, worship, burial, and the right to operate private schools. Granted special exemptions from the civic obligations of other subjects, like exemption from military service or war taxes or the freedom to establish parochial schools, Mennonites thrived. When rulers saw political or economic benefits to Mennonite settlements, they were willing to grant a series of special liberties and obligations that afforded Mennonites inequality before the law while protecting their religious freedoms.

Governments would eventually extend similar privileges to future settlements in Poland, Russia, Canada, and Paraguay, protecting Mennonites whose religion would otherwise have conflicted with the law of the land. However, when Mennonites lacked a powerful political backer, they could suffer at the hands of disgruntled citizens or officials. From the seventeenth century through the twentieth, Mennonites were offered privileges to settle in marginal lands. But as states centralized their powers, new governments revoked old privileges, and many Mennonites migrated to other countries where they could negotiate better terms for themselves.

The Enlightenment

During the eighteenth century, the intellectual movement known as the Enlightenment electrified the public sphere. Its proponents argued that reason, not tradition or religion, should govern human life. They envisioned an "enlightened" society that guaranteed the natural freedom and liberty shared by all people (usually assumed to be all white men). The American and French revolutionaries in 1776 and 1789 justified their revolts using the ideas that "all men are created equal" and are "born and remain free and equal in rights." In the nineteenth century, newly drafted constitutions eliminated many of the legal inequalities that had secured Mennonite privileges. Influenced by Enlightenment ideas, reforming legislatures and rulers argued that all citizens of a state enjoyed equal rights before the law. As a corollary, all citizens were also beholden to the same responsibilities, including universal conscription, or the obligation to serve in the military when summoned.

Mennonites were among the groups that embraced the new theories of equality and human rights, which gave them theoretical equality before the law. For example, Dutch Mennonites had previously been excluded from holding office and certain professions, but new constitutions made members of all faiths equal before the law, allowing them to participate in all areas of society, including the government. Similarly, when Napoleon's empire expanded across Europe, German Mennonites were granted full rights of citizenship under the Napoleonic law code, but they lost their military exemptions.

Other, mostly rural, Mennonites continued to set themselves apart from the surrounding society. They viewed themselves as a light on a hill, and they worried that the new constitutions would erode or replace the earlier privileges they had secured from previous rulers. They believed that equality with other faiths would erode their exemption from military service, which was easier to secure in the unequal societies of premodern Europe. As they encountered new centralizing states and powerful Enlightenment ideas, some Anabaptist groups in the seventeenth and eighteenth centuries chose to embrace them, others to resist them, and still others to migrate to new lands where they could live under premodern understandings of privileges.

Settlements in Hamburg and Altona

While the exact timeline of Mennonite migration to northern Germany remains unclear, it is known that Mennonites began settling in the region toward the end of the sixteenth century. Many governments in the area proactively invited Mennonites to settle, recognizing the benefits that their skills, tools, and reputation for hard work could bring to the region, having seen the positive impact of Mennonites in the Low Countries.

Since only Lutherans could publicly worship in the cultural and economically powerful city of Hamburg, Mennonites established a congregation in nearby Altona in 1601. The first Mennonites who settled in Altona had to pay an annual protection tax to the Count of Schauenburg. In return, they could bury their dead, practice trades, and hold (quiet) services. Mennonites were forbidden from converting Lutherans, joining most guilds, and building churches. With the death of each Schauenburg count, the growing congregation had to renegotiate the conditions of their freedom.

Altona's Mennonites were forced to be a distinct economic and religious community, and their economic success in shipping, textiles, and whaling eased their assimilation. As they developed businesses and integrated into the surrounding society, Mennonites had to carefully reflect on how to live out their commitments in a society that tolerated rather than persecuted them. The prevalence of the North Sea trade meant that Mennonite merchants had to choose whether to arm their ships. In 1694, the congregational leader Gerrit Roosen cautioned merchants against arming their ships, lest their desire for wealth overcome their faithfulness to God. Despite warnings that members who armed their ships would face discipline, some Mennonite merchants armed their ships, nonetheless.[6] Roosen himself was involved in the manufacture of gunpowder, illustrating how questions of nonresistance grew more complicated as Mennonites discerned how to be faithful in a tolerant context. Like the Dutch Mennonites, Altona's merchants felt that you could be nonresistant and still trade in gunpowder if you did not use it yourself.[7]

As Mennonites integrated into North German society, they started to speak German, rather than Dutch. With growing tolerance toward them, their identity became more fluid, and they started to choose marriage partners from outside their religious group. Mennonite merchants became affluent by dominating herring fisheries and whaling, and sometimes sought partners from other communities with a similar social standing. However, conservative members of the congregation were concerned that mixed marriages could weaken faith commitment and religious identity, leading to occasional conflicts within the church.

Mennonites in the Vistula Delta and Poland

In sixteenth-century Poland, the first Anabaptists, who were refugees from Holland, settled near the cities of Elbing and Danzig (Elbląg and Gdansk in Polish). Menno Simons and Dirk Philips each visited the refugee communities and their young congregations, some of which lasted through the twentieth century. Although Anabaptists could not initially live in the city of Danzig itself, nearby lords invited them in to drain the surrounding swampland and improve canals in the Vistula Delta. Mennonites who lived in the urban centers of Danzig and Elbing faced the most restrictive policies. Because their beliefs, dress, and use of Dutch language marked them as a distinct group, Mennonites often became the target of disgruntled citizens and magistrates. As a result, the Mennonites paid extra taxes to calm their critics.[8] Despite their secondary political status, Mennonites prospered by investing in textile mills and distilleries and using their agricultural skills.

The era of privileges and special status began to end for Mennonites in the Vistula Delta when the region came under the rule of the Prussian king Friedrich II in 1772. Mennonites requested that the new king grant them the same privileges that the Polish rulers had given them,

Fig. 5.2 A 1625 Danzig street scene. Etching by Aegidius Dickmann, *View of the Golden Gate at the End of the Langstraat in Danzig* in Views in and around the City Danzig series, 1625. Rijksmuseum, Amsterdam, RP-P-1901-A-22338.

in particular the freedoms in worship, education, and business, and exemptions from the military. To make a good impression, they donated "two fatted steers, 400 pounds of butter, 20 cheeses, 50 pairs of chickens and 50 pairs of ducks" to a banquet in honor of the new king.[9]

Hoping to maintain good relations with authorities, Mennonites tried to remain within the conditions of their privileges. Nevertheless, tensions flared occasionally, endangering the precarious status quo. The Prussian state had forbidden Mennonites from baptizing new converts, since doing so would reduce the potential number of men who could serve in the military. In 1780, Heinrich Donner ignited controversy when he baptized his Lutheran maid into his Orlofferfelde congregation. Conservative Mennonites who desired a stricter ban of mixed marriages complained to the Prussian administration that Donner was undermining the Charter of Privileges. Although Friedrich II dismissed the complaints, most Mennonites subsequently banned mixed marriages, fearing that the government might punish the Mennonites for violating the terms of their privilege. Previously moderate congregations changed their practice and slowed Mennonites' engagement with the surrounding society.[10]

Mennonite exemption remained a sticking point, however, because Prussian military recruitment was linked to land ownership. Therefore, Mennonite farms reduced the potential number of men the government could enlist. In 1789, Friedrich II's successor, Friedrich Wilhelm II, issued a "Mennonite Edict," which officially forbade Mennonites from purchasing land, banned mixed marriages, and levied new taxes for military exemption on top of those that already existed. Prussia, a particularly militaristic state, exerted tremendous pressure on the Mennonites to serve in the military by making it nearly impossible for young Mennonite men to buy property. In response, Mennonite congregations adopted more conservative positions toward marriage with non-Mennonites. There was concern that mixed marriages would antagonize the authorities, who saw such marriages as covert proselytization. Over the coming decades, Mennonites in Prussia would continue to petition the king for military exemption, but they increasingly found it too difficult to make a living, and many families emigrated to Russia, where they would not have to serve in the military. By 1850, three times as many Mennonites lived in the Russian Empire as in the Vistula Delta.

Mennonite beginnings in the Russian Empire

In 1788, four hundred Prussian Mennonite families, who were mostly landless, left their homes for the Russian Empire. They hoped to settle along the Dnieper River, a major trade artery in what is now Ukraine. However, upon arrival, the settlers were disappointed to learn that they would be building their settlements along the smaller Chortitza River, which had rocky and less fertile soil. In the early years, the Chortitza settlers struggled with disease and hunger, which was worsened by the Russian government's slow delivery of promised supplies. The colonists also had to navigate policies of self-governance, a lack of ministers who could baptize and marry members, and tense relations with the local nomadic people.

Despite these challenges, the Chortitza colony thrived, and in 1803, they were joined by an additional wave of Mennonite immigrants from Prussia who settled a hundred miles away along the Molochna River. With significantly more fertile soil than the "Old Colony" at Chortitza, the Molotschna colony grew three times as big as the first settlement, which tended to be more socially and theologically conservative. According to the historian Leonard G. Friesen, "Both were deemed the Mother Colonies, and although both functioned cooperatively

Fig. 5.3 A postcard showing Chortitza, 1908. "Chortitza." Reproduced by permission of Mennonite Heritage Archives, Winnipeg, 132-17.0.

in times of crisis, it can also be said that their relationship was often highly competitive and occasionally fractious."[11] In 1853, Mennonite immigrants from Prussia established the Am Trakt colony along the Volga, and a subsequent wave from Prussia formed the Alt-Samara, or Alexandertal, colony.

Mennonite identity, Friesen argues, solidified around three traits. First, the religious identity of the settlers was congregationally centered. Sitting in a U-shape during worship reinforced the importance of congregational life by forcing members to look each other in the eyes. Second, the ban on proselytization prevented new members from joining and reified distinct cultural practices and the development of an ethno-religious tradition distinct from neighboring German settlements. The Russian government considered all those living in a Mennonite settlement to be Mennonite, even when they did not

Fig. 5.4 Portrait of Govert Bidloo, one of the most famous physicians of the seventeenth century and personal physician of William III, Stadhouder of Holland and king of England. Engraving by Abraham Bloteling, after a painting by Gerard de Lairesse, c. 1680–c. 1690. Rijksmuseum, Amsterdam, RP-P-1905-4423.

Fig. 5.5 Portrait of Anna Stinstra-Braam, deaconess of the United Mennonite Congregation in Harlingen and one of the richest women in Harlingen. Oil on canvas by Tibout Regters, *Anna Stinstra-Braam (1738–1777)*, 1763. Amsterdam Museum, donation of P. de Clercq and P. van Eeghen.

Fig. 5.6 Rembrandt's *Syndics of the Drapers' Guild* illustrates Mennonites' economic success in the tolerant Dutch Republic. The Mennonite merchant Volkert Jansz is shown standing to the left; the group also includes Catholic, Remonstrant, and Reformed members. Oil on canvas by Rembrandt van Rijn, *De waardijns van het Amsterdamse lakenbereidersgilde, bekend als "De Staalmeesters,"* 1662. Rijksmuseum, Amsterdam, loan of the municipality of Amsterdam, SK-C-6.

adhere to the religious tradition. Third, the self-governing colonies developed administrative structures that eventually wielded tremendous authority over their members' lives.

Eventually, there were over fifty Mennonite colonies in the Russian Empire, spreading out from Ukraine to Crimea, the Caucasus, and Siberia. Over the next two centuries, the descendants of Mennonites from the Russian Empire would re-create the colony model as they migrated to countries like Canada, Mexico, Paraguay, and Bolivia. As described in subsequent chapters, the colony model's strength was that it allowed Mennonites to control the borders of their churches and communities. The potential danger lay in the indistinct lines between membership in the church and community.

Mennonites in the Dutch Republic

The Dutch Republic had tolerated Anabaptists since 1572, but the government barred them from serving in government and certain professions. Nevertheless, Mennonites were thankful for the toleration they were given, and in gratitude, they offered their money and prayers to the authorities. When France and its allies invaded the Republic in 1672, Mennonites donated shoes for the soldiers and served as firefighters, and congregations in Friesland donated four hundred thousand guilders (over $2 million USD in today's dollars) toward the war effort. Mennonites' assistance in the war effort improved the public perception of the dissenters and helped erase the blemish of Münster.

As the attitude of the surrounding society toward Mennonites changed, they increasingly participated in cultural and economic life. Agatha Deken coauthored the first Dutch novel. The poet and playwright Govert Bidloo taught anatomy at Leiden University and became personal physician to William III, the Dutch head of state and king of England. One of the richest women in the province of Friesland, Anna Stinstra-Braam, collected over two hundred works of art. It is no wonder that the differences between the wealthy Dutch congregations and the Swiss refugees struck the poet Pieter Langendijk so profoundly in 1711.

Toward the end of the eighteenth century, Mennonites found themselves in a difficult position. Despite their rising economic and cultural status in Dutch society, they were still treated as second-class citizens. Some Mennonites began to question their traditional stance against bearing weapons and joining the growing Patriot movement, which attempted a democratic revolution in 1787. François Adriaan van der Kemp, a Mennonite preacher, became a captain in a militia group and published pro-Patriot pamphlets, inspired by the American Revolution. Mennonites played a prominent role in the 1795 Batavian Revolution that overthrew the Dutch Republic and put an end to the traditional exemptions from military service that Mennonites had enjoyed since 1576.[12] While not all Mennonites were in favor of the new government, many seized the opportunities provided by the revolutionary regime.

During the eighteenth century, the number of Doopsgezinden declined sharply, from around 160,000 to 30,000, and many congregations disappeared entirely. Conservative Mennonites attributed this decline to unrestrained toleration and overly intellectual rationalism, which they believed weakened their identity. On the other hand, progressives who embraced new scientific discoveries and broader intellectual horizons accused the orthodox inflexibility of traditionalists for the stagnation and decline. While the reasons for the decline are not entirely clear, it is likely that there were multiple influences, including economic stagnation and a shortage of pastors for rural areas. Additionally, some members had married spouses in the Reformed church, which shared a rationalistic and undogmatic outlook with the Doopsgezinden but did not have the second-class stigma that prevented Mennonites from reaching public office.[13]

Fig. 5.7 Cartoon parody of Dutch pastor François Adriaan van der Kemp as half-preacher and half-soldier. Van der Kemp was an active participant in the Patriot Revolution of 1787 and later moved the United States, where he became friends with Thomas Jefferson and John Adams.
Etching by anonymous, "Spotprent op de Leidse predikant F.A. van der Kemp, 1786," 1786. Rijksmuseum, Amsterdam, RP-P-OB-85.549.

Modern North American Mennonites have held up the decline of the Dutch Doopsgezinden as a warning that the lure of wealth and social prestige will inevitably lead to the loss of the radical Anabaptist spirit.[14] However, this may be an ungenerous and simplistic interpretation. The Dutch Mennonites used their considerable wealth and education to benefit Anabaptists across Europe. To heal old divisions, Dutch Mennonites wrote multiple confessions of faith. Over time, Dutch Mennonites grew less enthusiastic about confessions, worrying that they would supplant the authority of the Bible. Other Mennonites continued to value written confessions as defenses against worldly pressure and proof of their orthodoxy to authorities who might wish to rescind their toleration.[15] In 1664, the discord grew into vitriolic sermons and arguments that spilled out of the church onto the street in a conflict that outsiders ridiculed as the "War of the Lamb." Although many Dutch Mennonites rejected the need for written statements of faith, other Anabaptist groups adopted Dutch confessions as their own. Many Plain Anabaptists, for example, continue to hold the 1632 Dordrecht Confession of Faith as their own today.

The Dutch also donated a significant amount of time and money to secure the toleration or migration of persecuted Anabaptists across the continent. Although there were tentative connections between various Anabaptist groups, the development of a trans-European Anabaptist/Mennonite identity truly began with Hans de Ries's publication of an expanded martyrology in 1615. The book, *History of the Martyrs, or Genuine Witnesses of Jesus Christ*, expanded older Dutch martyr stories by adding accounts of Anabaptists from Switzerland, Germany, and Moravia, thereby arguing that they had all suffered for the same convictions. When Dutch editors expanded the martyrologies, into what came to be called the *Martyrs Mirror*, they added contemporary accounts of repression in Swiss and German lands. The literary work paralleled relief efforts by the Dutch on behalf of the Swiss Brethren, Palatinate Anabaptists, Hutterites in Slovakia, and Mennonite settlements in West Prussia. Dutch Mennonites lobbied rulers for relaxation of repression, and when that failed, they paid for their resettlement in the Dutch Republic or North America.

By writing martyrologies and aiding in the migration of other Anabaptists, the Dutch created a broader Anabaptist unity. One sign

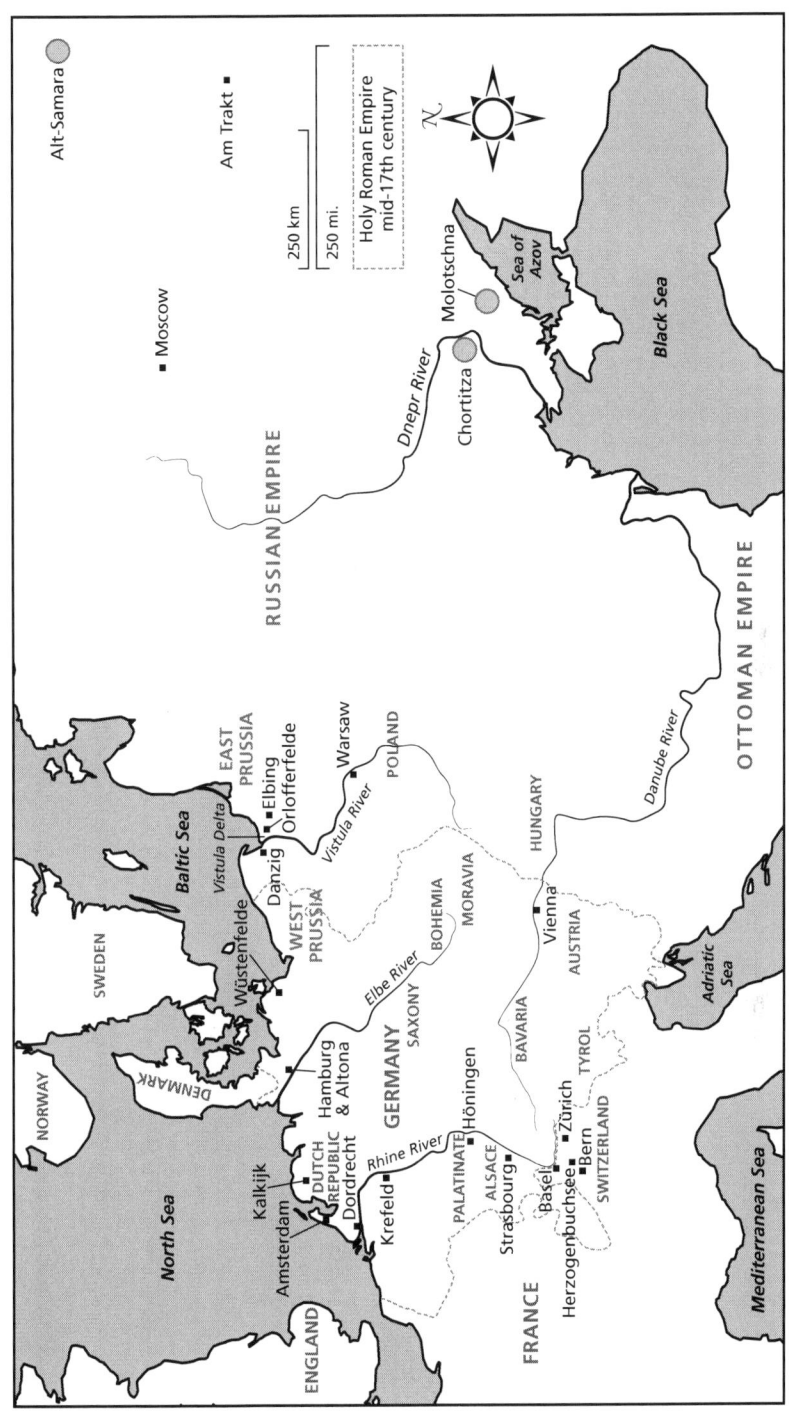

of this transnational network is the number of Anabaptist groups who began to call themselves "Mennonite," even though they had no direct connection with Menno Simons and even though the Dutch preferred to label themselves as Doopsgezinden, or baptism-minded. By using a Dutch name, other groups could graft themselves into the Doopsgezind reputation as obedient dissenters in the Dutch Republic and shed the Anabaptists' sixteenth-century reputation as traitorous heretics.

Suppression and migration in Germany and Switzerland

Swiss authorities viewed Anabaptists as seditious heretics who threatened the stability of the country, and they continued and intensified their suppression of Mennonites through the eighteenth century. They complained that the Mennonites "are not embarrassed to scream out at the ministers and supporters of our churches, calling them a brood of adders, scorpions, tearing wolves and grasshoppers from hell."[16] After being freed from prison upon a promise to cease preaching, some Swiss Mennonites returned to their old lives. They defiantly refused the oath, and they refused to carry arms in defense of the homeland. In a 1645 letter, one Swiss official complained that they even had to arrest Anabaptist women who had begun to foment unrest and speak disrespectfully of the authorities after the arrests of their menfolk. Barbara Bruppacher, for example, exclaimed that she wanted to vomit every time she walked by a Reformed church.[17] It was clear to the Swiss government that authorities needed to combat such a seditious movement.

Swiss Mennonites found creative ways to avoid persecution, some of which likely confirmed the authorities' negative opinions. To evade official scrutiny, Mennonites moved to sparsely populated valleys, and worshiped in caves or secret rooms in barns. They also were willing to compromise in nonessential matters. For example, they mumbled forced oaths, hid their children when authorities came around, or even allowed their children to be baptized, since coerced infant baptisms were worthless in their opinion. Similarly, if forced to swear an oath of recantation, some Mennonites did so with the belief that a coerced oath was invalid.[18]

In the eyes of their neighbors, Mennonites' simple, honest lifestyle was a powerful critique of the official Reformed church. Although the authorities successfully eradicated Anabaptism from Zürich and Basel, the number of Bernese Mennonites continued to grow, which led the authorities to increase their repression.

When they learned of the edicts against the Swiss Brethren, Dutch Mennonites used their wealth and political connections to lobby on behalf of the Swiss. When Zürich authorities executed the elderly preacher Hans Landis in 1614 for repeatedly returning from exile, Dutch Mennonite leaders petitioned their own rulers to write letters of protest to their Swiss counterparts. Later in the century, Swiss letters to the Dutch recounted the stories of members languishing in prison. Although the death penalty was no longer used, many Swiss Brethren died imprisoned or sentenced to service on galleys. Elisabeth Hützny, for example, was taken to a Zürich prison in 1639 "under rigorous duress" and died after suffering "many unhealthy days."[19] The Relief Fund for Foreign Needs organized and financed Dutch activities and helped refugees settle into the Palatinate and Alsace. In 1711, harassment of the Mennonites intensified, and the Dutch Mennonites hired diplomats to negotiate the conditions by which many Swiss refugees would migrate down the Rhine River to more tolerant locations in the Dutch Republic, southern Germany, or North America.

North America

The first Mennonites to settle in North America were wealthy Dutch-speaking Mennonites from the Krefeld region of northwest Germany. Prosperous merchants like William Rittenhouse paid special taxes to William Penn to purchase privileges and land in Germantown, Pennsylvania. In 1690, Rittenhouse, the owner of a successful paper mill, became the first Mennonite minister in North America. The urban Mennonites in Germantown differed from the rural, "plain" Mennonites who migrated to Pennsylvania in the eighteenth century from southern German and Swiss lands, but both groups crossed the Atlantic seeking economic opportunities and religious toleration.

In 1785, the descendants of the early Mennonite settlers in America claimed that their "predecessors came from a far country to America to seek religious liberty,"[20] but the motivations for leaving Europe were likely a combination of religious and economic drivers. For many eighteenth-century German emigrants, North America was an unattractive location; the travel costs and physical risks were high, and the weak colonial governments were not strong enough to guarantee the protection of settlers. However, weaker governments might have been attractive to Anabaptists who had faced decades of legal difficulties in Europe. Overall, Mennonite migration patterns to North America closely match those of the other Germans who moved away from the lands along the Rhine to improve their prospects in the Americas. At a time when many German speakers migrated to escape the economic struggles gripping the Palatinate, Alsace, and Switzerland, the possibility of religious toleration was an additional incentive for Anabaptists.[21]

One advantage that the Mennonites and Amish who set foot in Philadelphia had over other immigrants was the organizational and financial aid provided by the Dutch. Dutch ministers initially tried to dissuade Mennonites from leaving the Palatinate by warning them of the shipwrecks, pirates, and the dangers of sea voyages. Nevertheless, when German Mennonites or Amish needed funds to make the trip, the Relief Fund for Foreign Needs provided loans or grants for the migrants. For example, when the Martin, Gerber, and Horsch families ran out of funds near the Dutch border, the committee gave them enough to complete their transatlantic voyage.[22] The Dutch committee members had not exaggerated the potential dangers to the prospective emigrants. In his diary, Hans Jacob Kauffman recorded the deaths of twenty-two children and two adults among the Amish passengers crossing the Atlantic on the *Charming Nancy* in 1738.[23]

Upon their arrival, Amish and Mennonites tended to settle near co-religionists who had made the transatlantic trip earlier. Unlike the Prussian Mennonites who would migrate to Russia in the nineteenth century, North American Anabaptist immigrants did not settle in self-contained colonies. Their proximity to other German-speaking immigrants smoothed the transition to the colonies, but it also opened their members to outside influences and religious movements.

In 1745, to firm up Anabaptist commitments, especially commitments to nonresistance, several Pennsylvania leaders asked the Dutch to help finance the publication of a thousand copies of a German translation of the *Martyrs Mirror*. They worried that they had traveled "to so distant a land without sufficient assurance concerning freedom of conscience." As "the flames of war seem to be mounting higher and higher," the authors hoped to "make every preparation for the steadfast constancy in our faith."[24] At that point, the project was too expensive to proceed, but the letter-writers were correct in their sense that their relationship with the colonial society would be tested.

Soon after its outbreak in 1776, the American Revolution forced Amish and Mennonites to reassess their relationship with the surrounding society. Before the revolution, Mennonites in Pennsylvania, Maryland, and Virginia had voted and held local office while maintaining their nonresistant beliefs. The Patriots forced colonists to choose sides, passing "Test Acts" that required oaths of allegiance to the revolutionary government and calling on all adult males to bear arms to secure their liberties. The Patriots pressured Mennonites to take part in the new revolutionary nation, one that was built on an armed citizenry. They thereby alienated many Anabaptists from the new nation they were forging. Few Mennonites joined either party. When he refused to manufacture muskets for George Washington's army, John Newcomer—a renowned gunsmith from Lancaster Country, Pennsylvania—was fined and lost the right to make weapons. In 1778, ten Mennonites were exiled from Pennsylvania and all their property was sold, including food for their children and the women's spinning wheels.[25] Mennonites and Amish who refused to renounce the British monarch lost the right to vote until 1789. Many Mennonites considered themselves loyal to the British Crown and supported the British military. They felt more confident that their religious freedoms would be better protected by the British government and believed that, because a ruler's power came from God, Christians should not rebel against a divinely ordained government.

After the war, the Mennonites faced the challenge of deciding what it meant to become subjects of the new American government. They had to grapple with complex questions such as whether they could become American citizens and bear the shared rights and responsibilities of all Americans or remain as subjects who benefited from the protection of the British monarchy.

In 1789, thirty Mennonite families who felt they could not stay in the new country migrated from Pennsylvania to the Niagara Peninsula in present-day Ontario. The *Pennsylvania Gazette* claimed that the Mennonites were leaving because they had been denied the right to vote during the American Revolution because of the Test Acts. However, it is also likely that the Mennonites were motivated by the search for affordable farmland to pass on to their children. The revolution heightened the sense of separateness that many Mennonite and Amish members already felt from the world around them and reaffirmed the importance of maintaining a distinct religious and cultural identity from the larger society.

The American Revolution of 1776 and the French Revolution of 1789 developed new republican understandings that all people (at least the free, predominantly white, male ones) were the sovereigns of the nation. The Declaration of Independence of the American colonies, for example, declared that "all men are created equal." Napoleon Bonaparte expanded the French Revolution's concept that all citizens were equal before the law across much of Europe. Some Mennonites, like the Dutch, welcomed the ideas of people's rights and equality before the law as a way to remove centuries-old barriers to opportunities. Other Mennonites struggled against the emerging consensus that equal rights for all entailed the equal duty to bear arms to defend those rights. In the wake of these movements, the age of privileges and loopholes ended, and many Mennonites found themselves arguing *against* the equality offered to them.

Transnational connections

> "My Beloved Brother! In body we are far from each other, but through the blood of Jesus we are always close in spirit even if we cannot see our faces here in the transitoriness, nevertheless love will urge us to pray to God, the father of all for each other."
> —1820 letter from Isebrand Wiebe, Herrenhagen, West Prussia (Pielica, Poland) to Benjamin Eby, Bishop in Berlin (Kitchener, Ontario)[26]

By the nineteenth century, the Anabaptist movement had solidified into several traditions that reflected differing theological convictions and relations with their surrounding contexts. In the towns and cities of the Netherlands, most Mennonites and Doopsgezinden lived and worked seamlessly alongside their Reformed, Catholic, and Jewish neighbors. In Switzerland, many Swiss Brethren were active participants in the social dynamics of rural life, until centralized repression pushed them into a more separatist existence. As we shall see in the next chapter, the relations with their neighbors were positive enough that many of the "true-hearted ones" acted as a bridge between the Swiss Anabaptists and the world. In Prussia and the Russian Empire, Mennonites moved to new territory, where they were relatively free to govern themselves until the second half of the nineteenth century.

Despite distinct characteristics and separate traditions, the groups increasingly considered themselves part of a larger, shared tradition. United by a common martyrology, seventeenth-century Doopsgezinden from the Netherlands worked across divisions to relieve the suffering of persecuted members in Switzerland and the Palatinate, who began calling themselves Mennonites in order to be grafted into the reputation of their northern brethren. Hutterite elders traveled to the Dutch Republic to request "a good contribution" during a time of suffering.

One indication of the remarkable transnational sense of connectedness can be seen in a small booklet published in 1840 that collected letters written between Mennonites in Ontario, Pennsylvania, Bavaria, Prussia, and Hamburg. Although the letters present only one side of a conversation, they provide glimpses into the common issues with which Mennonites would grapple in the coming century. For example, the Brenkenhofswalde congregation in Prussia struggled with the loss of members who moved to Russia. A correspondent from Bavaria reported growth in their congregation, adding that "we are subjected to military service, which strikes us very severely, and most unfortunately, we must accept because we are forced to do so by our esteemed government. Therefore, you yourself can likely imagine, dear brother, how the old people must feel when their sons are taken."[27] Writing from Friedrichstadt on the Eider, in northern Germany, minister Carl Justus van der Smissen wondered whether Ontario Mennonites also struggled with spiritual lethargy in their members. "Or has among you too, as in so many places among our brethren in the faith, coldness and indifference entered in, so that indeed the outer respectable conduct is there, but an active consciousness of sinfulness is lacking?"[28] As they faced these outer and inner threats in the coming years, Mennonites would find spiritual resources from both outside sources and their own tradition.

Since the eighteenth century, Anabaptism has grown to become a global church through migration and mission. Despite distance and differences in language and culture, various expressions of the movement continue to have an understanding that there is a shared Anabaptist-Mennonite identity. Mennonite World Conference (MWC) has more than a hundred member churches in over fifty countries and is the largest international body of Anabaptist-related churches. When a church is in crisis, MWC calls on its members to support one another through aid and prayer, just as the Swiss Brethren appealed to the Dutch. In 2022, MWC circulated the appeal by the leader of Associated Mennonite Brethren Churches in Ukraine for spiritual and financial support after Russia invaded Ukraine, as well as Rev. Alphonse Kisubi Kassa's "cry of alarm to the different faithful members of the Mennonite church around the world" on behalf of the members of Communauté des Églises des Frères Mennonites au Congo (CEFMC—the Mennonite Brethren church in DR Congo), who had been displaced by war. While a common identity and shared history is a type of fiction, it is a powerful fiction that can call others to act.

— SIX —

Renewal and Revitalization

Seventeenth- and Eighteenth-Century Anabaptists

In 1758, five German Mennonite elders gathered to investigate the young minister Peter Weber, who was chosen by lot the previous year to lead the congregation at Höningen. According to the investigating elders, Weber had held private meetings "in any place he desired." Because they were outside of the officially sanctioned gathering places, these meetings put other Mennonites at risk. In addition, Weber had taken communion with people from outside of Mennonite circles and complained to the Dutch Mennonite pastor Johannes Deknatel about the spiritual impoverishment of the Palatinate Mennonites. Finally, by pursuing his own ecumenical interests instead of the greater good of the church, the investigating report concluded, Weber demonstrated "spiritual pride." In the interest of preserving traditional practices, the elders removed Weber from his post, but he continued to influence Mennonites across southern Germany.

Weber had been looking for ways to reenergize Mennonites' spiritual life. In a 1761 letter, he complained that "many preachers are as suitable to preach as oxen are suited to play the organ" and worried that Mennonites were more concerned with shallow spiritualties and external appearances than they were with their inward lives.[1] Like many Mennonites in the seventeenth and eighteenth centuries, he drew from outside traditions to revitalize a faith that he felt was no longer relevant in a context of toleration and relative isolation. Other leaders had also grown disturbed by Mennonites marrying non-Mennonites, dancing, drinking, playing cards, and even bearing arms. Baptism into an inherited tradition no longer seemed to carry the same commitment to radical discipleship.

Weber's solution was to borrow language from the Pietist movement to foster the inner life of Mennonites and preach "redemption through faith in Christ and His sacrifice" instead of good works. Although the concepts of grace and faith that Weber used were innovations, he never saw them as opposed to the traditional Mennonite values of costly discipleship and the need to combat rising individualism with church discipline.[2] Weber reshaped and reinterpreted the values of other traditions to serve Anabaptist goals.

Over the course of the seventeenth and eighteenth centuries, Mennonites had proved to be loyal subjects, and rulers were more willing to tolerate them. One official in the Palatinate, the area where Peter Weber lived, remarked, "No better, more industrious, and competent subjects are to be found, who, with the exception of their religion their faith and their error, should serve the members of other faiths as an example in morals as well as in working night and day."[3] But economic success and religious toleration proved to be a mixed blessing for the Mennonites. Many leaders worried that their younger members had forgotten the faithful sacrifices of the early Anabaptists.

Thieleman J. van Braght had printed the *Martyrs Mirror* in part to admonish readers to reflect on the stories of faithful martyrs in order that they could withstand the spiritual dangers of "numerous large, expensive and ornamented houses, countryseats of splendid architecture and provided with towers, parks magnificent as a paradise, and other embellished pleasure-grounds" and "the wearing of clothes from foreign countries, whether of foreign materials, uncommon colors or

Fig. 6.1 With the *Martyrs Mirror*, the preacher and poet Thieleman van Braght made an important contribution to the formation of a transnational Mennonite identity. Engraving by Abraham Bloteling, *Portrait of Tieleman van Braght*, in or after 1664. Rijksmuseum, Amsterdam, RP-P-1904-1048.

of strange fashions."⁴ Van Braght hoped that the martyrs' stories would reenergize Mennonites' commitment to defenseless discipleship and simplicity.

This chapter tells the story of how Anabaptists attempted to create strong, long-lasting congregations. In the centuries after the early Anabaptists, their descendants interacted with their neighbors, often discovering helpful spiritual and intellectual resources. As tolerated Mennonites developed social, business, and intellectual networks with their neighbors, they borrowed ideas that still shape Mennonite life centuries later. Other Anabaptists moved in the opposite direction and drew sharper lines between their congregations and the surrounding society and culture. Both responses created new understandings of how to be faithful disciples that diverged from early Anabaptism, but which were helpful in new, tolerant contexts.

Anabaptist worship

The sixteenth-century Anabaptists rejected many medieval worship practices. They criticized the Catholic churches for their baptismal fonts, stained glass windows, reliquaries, and shrines as biblically unsound and a waste of a parish's resources. When Conrad Grebel, Felix Manz, and George Blaurock baptized Zollikon villagers and took communion with them in January 1525, they broke with centuries of Christian liturgical tradition and undermined the role of the priestly class. While they opened participation in worship to all who were gathered, not just the priests, they also limited membership to those who chose to follow Christ.[5] Baptism was the profession of faith by which one joined the church, and the Lord's Supper united the believers with God and each other.

In the early days of Anabaptism, worship was influenced by traditional Catholic practices, the biblical model of the New Testament church, and the ever-present threat of persecution. Because early Anabaptist worship was clandestine, historians have limited records from which to draw their conclusions. However, a 1572 eyewitness account by the Lutheran priest Elias Schad describes his visit to a secret, nighttime meeting of two hundred Anabaptists in a forest outside of Strasbourg. He recounts a candlelit service during which five leaders "read a passage from the New Testament and then preached for about 15 minutes. Prayer then followed these five sermons, lasting for about 30 minutes. Then there was a call for those who did not understand to be instructed by the elders. Or if God's Spirit led, one could address the whole group." After the sermons and greetings, the members knelt to pray, "murmuring as if a nest of hornets were swarming."[6] Legal records from trials show that Anabaptists also met informally. For example, women in Augsburg met over sewing circles to read Scripture or hear a brief message.

Formal patterns of worship developed as Anabaptists built churches, founded institutions, and trained leaders in the following centuries.

Initially, preaching was done by trained theologians or ministers; however, after the death of the first generation, preaching responsibilities fell to craftspeople and farmers in the south and doctors and teachers in the north. Dutch Doopsgezinden sponsored the first seminary in Amsterdam in 1735 to meet the needs of increasingly educated and culturally sophisticated members. Elders, ministers, teachers, and deacons led congregations and weekly worship. In addition to paying for trained pastors, Anabaptists integrated worship practices from other traditions. This process of integrating new practices continues into the present day, as Mennonites across the globe continue to draw spiritual sustenance from charismatic, Catholic, or local traditions.

Meetinghouses

To escape persecution and public attention, early Anabaptists met in homes, in caves, at work, or on boats. While persecution drove the Anabaptists underground, their emphasis on the belief that the church was the gathered believers, not a building, made the location for their meetings less important than the message they shared. Magistrates in

Fig. 6.2 Pieter Pietersz Bekjen preaches in a rowboat on the Amstel River, 1568. Etching by Jan Luyken, in Caspar Commelin, *Beschryvinge van Amsterdam . . .* , 1693. Rijksmuseum Amsterdam, RP-P-OB-44.426.

the north were the first to allow congregations to build church structures, but the buildings had to remain hidden from public view. The churches were not truly clandestine (everyone knew that Mennonites gathered there), but they allowed authorities to preserve the public pretense of religious unity.[7] Throughout Europe, the first meetinghouses remained plain with little decoration that could identify them as church buildings to passersby.

Music
Communal singing was at the heart of Anabaptist worship. An early exception to this was in Zürich, where Conrad Grebel prohibited singing, perhaps in reaction to the excessive ornamentation in the city's traditional masses. Other Anabaptist leaders did not share Grebel's aversion. Dutch and German hymnbooks were published in the 1560s. The Psalms were favorites among the Dutch, but new tunes and lyrics from other traditions expanded the musical repertoire over time. Among the Swiss Brethren, the hymns of the *Ausbund* were central to their spiritual identity and kept the memories of suffering martyrs alive for many generations.

Communion
The earliest records suggest that Anabaptist gatherings regularly included a celebration of the Lord's Supper. The whole assembly participated in the service, using everyday cups or ladles. The simplicity of Anabaptist communion likely arose in the context of persecution and missionary activities that required a combination of secrecy and accessibility.[8] Over time, regional differences with common patterns developed. Instead of breaking bread at every meeting, congregations took communion once or twice a year, usually after a weeklong period of confession when members tried to reconcile with God and each other. Whether it was in the urban congregations of Amsterdam or a rural church in Alsace, taking communion was a way to publicly proclaim one's membership and good standing in the congregation.

Baptism
Among the first generation of Anabaptists, adult baptism—and with it the decision to leave the old church—was for those who had repented

and desired to walk in the resurrection. Adult baptism was not a decision to be taken lightly; it opened up the real possibility of suffering for faith. For children raised in established Mennonite congregations, however, the decision to be baptized and join did not carry the same weighty consequences.

Before baptism, candidates participated in a period of instruction in church teachings, usually with the help of a confession of faith. At the baptism service itself, believers might have given a personal testimony and promised to give and receive counsel with other members. The act of baptism usually followed the traditional practice of pouring or sprinkling water on the head of the baptismal candidate, but controversies about proper form arose in the seventeenth century in Germany and in nineteenth-century Russia, when the Mennonite Brethren argued that baptismal candidates needed to be fully immersed in water during baptism.

Fig. 6.3 A baptismal service in the church "Bij 't Lam" in Amsterdam, 1780–90. Etching by Cornelis Brouwer, *Doop-Plechtigheid bij de Mennoniten*, 1780–90. Rijksmuseum, Amsterdam, gift of Mrs. Brandt, Amsterdam, and Mrs. Brandt, Amsterdam, RP-P-1905-385.

Spirituality

Swiss Brethren spirituality was grounded in a deep knowledge of the Scriptures. Their *Concordance* (*Concondanzt vnd zyger*) provided a convenient way to study the Scriptures and place their story in the larger biblical narrative. The *Concordance* organized verses under topical themes for which biblical references might help them in their spiritual life, as well as help them defend themselves if they ever had to enter a debate. Swiss Brethren devotional life and identity was also strengthened by a collection of beloved writings by various Anabaptist authors called *Golden Apples in Silver Bowls* (*Güldene Aepffel in Silbern Schalen*). Together with the *Ausbund*, these three books were foundational to Swiss Brethren identity and devotional life.[9]

Among the Dutch, praying aloud replaced the earlier practice of silent prayer. Some of the earliest published songs were the martyrs' songs that were included in martyrologies. The Waterlander Doopsgezinden were the first to sing the Psalms following the fashion of the Reformed church, and other congregations soon adopted the practice. Historian Piet Visser has suggested that one positive outcome of the various splits among the Dutch Mennonites was a tremendous flowering of hymnals. Each congregation and division published their own hymnal to unite the group among a common corpus of songs. By 1800, Dutch Anabaptists had published over 150 hymnals with fifteen thousand different songs.[10] Many congregations had also installed organs to accompany their songs.

Pietism as renewal

In the seventeenth and eighteenth centuries, some Mennonites felt that the traditional worship and devotional practices no longer met their spiritual needs. With the easing of persecution, Mennonites interacted more freely with their neighbors, and the ponderous songs of the martyrs and sermons delivered by uneducated farmers no longer nourished the spiritual life of younger, often educated members. Other Mennonites complained that tolerated Mennonites had grown lax and lost the passionate commitment of their persecuted forebears.

In mixing with their neighbors, these younger Mennonites encountered Pietism and found a spiritual resource of great depth. Pietism was a complex historical phenomenon that emphasized personal conversion, social activism, biblical study, and godliness. It arose in the 1670s in Reformed and Lutheran churches as a reaction against an increasingly sterile religiosity. Hungry for church renewal and a warm, personal spiritual life, Mennonites formed small groups for Bible study and prayer and formed connections with Dutch and German Pietists. The Pietists inspired Mennonites who were dissatisfied with traditional spiritual practices that seemed to focus more on the traditions of the religion rather than the inner life of the believers. There were many similarities between the Anabaptists and the Pietists; the Pietists saw Anabaptists as models of Christians who died for their faith, and the Anabaptists hoped that Pietism could help revitalize their churches.[11]

Anabaptists who were interested in renewing their churches formed a network that included churches in the Dutch Republic, Krefeld, Hamburg, Altona, and the Palatinate. In a 1757 letter to Peter Weber, Amsterdam Mennonites lamented that "no one feels the need for a gracious savior, because everyone lives virtuously; confident that their salvation is certain, the whole congregation is on the verge of tumbling to their death."[12] Johannes Deknatel was a minister in one of the largest Amsterdam Mennonite congregations as well as a Pietist author. South German Mennonites took his writings to Pennsylvania in the eighteenth century and then on into Canada in the nineteenth. Deknatel translated Pietist hymns into Dutch and financially supported German Pietist leaders. In 1804, Christian Burkholder published a book in America titled *Useful and Edifying Address to the Youth*, which included the typical Pietist and Anabaptist themes of personal repentance, new birth, and discipleship. For Burkholder, discipleship rested on conversion, repentance, and humility.[13]

Anabaptist communities influenced by Pietism cultivated an awareness of the importance of the inner spiritual life of the believer and a greater attention to prayer. Other congregations saw Pietism's influence as a danger to traditional Anabaptist emphases and disciplined members who embraced it. However, many Mennonites believed that Pietism supported the fundamental Anabaptist commitment to Christian discipleship. Peter Weber, for example, believed that a personal relationship with God should lead believers "to do good deeds, to suffer on behalf of the faith and to build up the welfare of the congregation."[14]

The close connection between Anabaptists and Pietists continued in North America. Under the leadership of Alexander Mack, a group of German Pietists known as the Schwarzenau Brethren resolved to live by New Testament principles and the model of the early church. When they moved to North America, they settled in the same areas as Mennonites in Pennsylvania and Virginia. Eventually, Mack's followers developed into the Church of the Brethren and attracted many Mennonites as members. Today, the Church of the Brethren have strengthened their identity as part of the Anabaptist movement and, along with Mennonites and the Quakers, are identified as one of the "historic peace churches."

Fig. 6.4 Portrait of Dutch Mennonite preacher Johannes Deknatel, whose Pietist devotional writings were treasured by Mennonites throughout Europe and North America. Etching by Cornelis van Noorde, *Portrait of Johannes Deknatel*, 1759–61. Rijksmuseum, Amsterdam, gift of Mrs. Brandt, Amsterdam, and Mrs. Brandt, Amsterdam, RP-P-1903-A-23356.

Rationalism as renewal

Spurred by phenomenal wealth, the Dutch Republic grew into an important intellectual and cultural center in Europe during the seventeenth century. In painting, science, and philosophy, the young country saw its cultural life flourish, and Mennonites participated in many of the important trends of the time. The Enlightenment, as noted earlier, refers to a broad range of seventeenth- and eighteenth-century ideas, practices, and movements that questioned traditional knowledge to improve individuals, institutions, and society. Although contemporary scientific arguments that the universe worked without the active intervention of God opposed traditional Christian worldviews, many Mennonites adopted rationalistic Enlightenment ideals to revitalize their faith and reform broader Dutch society. Mennonites became doctors, mathematicians, and publishers. The merchant Martinus Houttuyn, for example, was an amateur mathematician who promoted Isaac Newton's ideas and published a thirty-seven-volume work of "animal, plant, and mineral diversity."[15] Other Mennonites furthered the Enlightenment through their work as booksellers, publishers, engravers, or translators. The influence of the Enlightenment spirit is best seen in the training courses of the Amsterdam seminary, where candidates for the ministry used "a collection of air pumps, magnets, electrical generators, Leiden jars, telescopes, microscopes, and optical instruments" to study natural sciences alongside theology. The instruments enabled the study of natural laws to learn more about God and how to use those principles to improve society.[16]

Several wealthy Mennonites established organizations to make the world a better place. Some of the groups were small and had closed memberships, like the group Tot Leerzaam Vermaak (For Instructive Pleasure) formed by six Mennonites for the sake of sharing essays and ideas. Other Mennonites participated in larger groups that were open to everyone. In 1778, Pieter Teyler van der Hulst, a merchant and Mennonite deacon, left an estate that endowed the Teylers Foundation. The foundation opened a museum in Haarlem to share Enlightenment ideas through its exhibits of the natural sciences and sponsored essay contests to address contemporary philosophical questions.[17] In 1777, the clockmaker Willem Writs was a cofounder of Felix Meritis, a society where people interested in literary and scientific pursuits could meet at the Temple of Reason, built in 1784.[18] In the same year, the Maatschappij tot Nut van 't Algemeen (Society for Public Welfare) was formed in the home of the preacher Jan Nieuwuenhuyzen. "The Nut," as the society was eventually known, was influenced by the Enlightenment conviction that the middle class had the duty to improve the lives of their social inferiors through education and philanthropy.[19]

Separation as renewal

By the end of the seventeenth century, many Anabaptists lived in territories where they enjoyed relative toleration. Freedom from persecution meant the freedom to plant roots, raise their children, and build lasting institutions. Most felt gratitude for sympathetic authorities who protected them and intervened on behalf of persecuted Anabaptists in other lands.

Some Swiss and South German Anabaptists had grown concerned at the degree to which some of their co-religionists had made peace with the surrounding world. They criticized increasingly comfortable

Fig. 6.5 The 1791 meeting of the Society for the Public Welfare, founded by Dutch Mennonite minister Jan Nieuwenhuyzn. Etching by Cornelis Bouwer, *Hoofdvergadering van de Maatschappij tot Nut van 't Algemeen*, 1791, after drawings by Daniël Kerkhoff. Rijksmuseum, Amsterdam, RP-P-OB-86.204.

Fig. 6.6 Demonstration of the electrifier in the Hall of Physics in the building of the Felix Meritis society in Amsterdam, inaugurated in 1789. Several of the founders were members of Mennonite congregations.
Etching by Reinier Vinkeles (I), *Zaal der Natuurkunde in Felix Meritis*, 1789, after drawings by Jacques Kuyper and Pieter Pietersz. Barbiers, 1801. Rijksmuseum, Amsterdam, RP-P-OB-70.321.

relations with non-Anabaptist neighbors as a betrayal of the faith for which their ancestors had died. Although their tradition had taught them to separate from the world, the world had grown friendly toward them. In Switzerland, a growing number of people viewed the Anabaptists as model Christians when compared to the stale religiosity of the official Reformed church. When authorities investigated the increasing allure of the Anabaptists, one woman denied being an Anabaptist, claiming, "No, to tell the truth I am not worthy to be an Anabaptist . . . they are such a holy people."[20]

After two centuries of persecution, Swiss Brethren depended on the support of sympathetic neighbors who interceded for them or even hid them. These half-Anabaptists (*halbtäufer*), or true-hearted (*treuherzige*) people, admired the Anabaptists but could not take the step of accepting believers baptism. The Swiss Brethren struggled with how to consider their true-hearted friends who were not baptized. Some were thankful for the support and declared that it was up to God to pass judgment on who was truly saved. Others maintained that the truehearted were not saved, and the Anabaptists needed to separate from them and rely only on God to protect them.

One of the strongest advocates for greater separation was Jacob Amman, who had converted to Anabaptism in 1680. In the 1690s, when Amman moved his family to the more tolerant region of Alsace, he was upset to find that Alsatian Anabaptists had lost a sense of their separation from the world. Amman advocated for clearer boundaries between believers and the corruption of the surrounding society to recapture the uncompromising separation of the 1527 Schleitheim Confession. Further supporting Amman's separatist position was the 1632 Dordrecht Confession of Faith, which many Alsatian ministers had signed on to in 1660. Penned by the Dutch, Dordrecht called for congregations to shun, or socially avoid, those who had fallen into sin. With a more robust church discipline, Amman longed to renew the church by clarifying and sharpening borders with a corrupting world. With the zeal of a convert and influenced by Pietist spirituality, Amman called for a more active faith than he found among the Swiss Anabaptists. The Swiss group, led by Hans Reist, preferred a more settled, inward religious expression, perhaps to ensure that they could continue to live at peace with their neighbors.

Separation and Shunning

As found in the Schleitheim and Dordrecht Confessions, both the Swiss/South German and Dutch Anabaptist traditions called on their members to separate both from the fallen "world" and from members who had fallen into sin. In times of cultural change or persecution, the principle of separation helped the Anabaptists maintain a strong religious identity, but sometimes at the expense of breaking relationships with their worldly neighbors or "fallen" church members. The Dordrecht Confession continues to be the official confession of faith for the Old Order Amish communities.

Schleitheim Confession (1527), Article IV

We have been united concerning the separation that shall take place from the evil and the wickedness which the devil has planted in the world, simply in this; that we have no fellowship with them, and do not run with them in the confusion of their abominations. So it is; since all who have not entered into the obedience of faith and have not united themselves with God so that they will to do His will, are a great abomination before God, therefore nothing else can or really will grow or spring forth from them than abominable things. Now there is nothing else in the world and all creation than good or evil, believing and unbelieving, darkness and light, the world and those who are [come] out of the world, God's temple and idols. Christ and Belial, and none will have part with the other. To us, then, the commandment of the Lord is also obvious, whereby He orders us to be and to become separated from the evil one, and thus He will be our God and we shall be His sons and daughters. . . .

From all this we should learn that everything which has not been united with our God in Christ is nothing but an abomination which we should shun. By this are meant all popish and repopish works and idolatry, gatherings, church attendance, winehouses, guarantees and commitments of unbelief, and other things of the kind, which the world regards highly, and yet which are carnal or flatly counter to the command of God, after the pattern of all the iniquity which is in the world. From all this we shall be separated and have no part with such, for they are nothing but abominations, which cause us to be hated before our Christ Jesus, who has freed us from the servitude of the flesh and fitted us for the service of God and the Spirit whom He has given us.[21]

Dordrecht Confession of Faith (1632), Article XVII. Of Shunning the Separated

Concerning the withdrawing from, or shunning the separated, we believe and confess, that if any one, either through his wicked life or perverted doctrine, has so far fallen that he is separated from God, and, consequently, also separated and punished by the church, the same must, according to the doctrine of Christ and His apostles, be shunned, without distinction, by all the fellow members of the church, especially those to whom it is known, in eating, drinking, and other similar intercourse, and no company be had with him that they may not become contaminated by intercourse with him, nor made partakers of his sins; but that the sinner may be made ashamed, pricked in his heart, and convicted in his conscience, unto his reformation. 1 Corinthians 5:9–11; 2 Thessalonians 3:14

Yet, in shunning as well as in reproving, such moderation and Christian discretion must be used, that it may conduce, not to the destruction, but to the reformation of the sinner. For, if he is needy, hungry, thirsty, naked, sick, or in any other distress, we are in duty bound, necessity requiring it, according to love and the doctrine of Christ and His apostles, to render him aid and assistance; otherwise, shunning would in this case tend more to destruction than to reformation.

Therefore, we must not count them as enemies, but admonish them as brethren, that thereby they may be brought to a knowledge of and to repentance and sorrow for their sins, so that they may become reconciled to God, and consequently be received again into the church, and that love may continue with them, according as is proper. 2 Thessalonians 3:15.[22]

Hoping to clarify the church's position on separation and sin, Amman and three other elders traveled to Switzerland in 1693 with several proposals. It was the practice for Anabaptists to prepare for communion by reflecting on their relationships with God and others. If relationships were broken, members were to refrain from taking communion until they had reconciled with God and each other. Those who refused to mend their ways were banned from the Lord's Supper. Amman called for more frequent communion, which would have resulted in greater attention to discipline. His group wanted to give ministers and elders the authority to make the final decision about discipline, whereas the Swiss had traditionally required the entire congregation to approve an excommunication. Amman also introduced footwashing to the Swiss congregations. The practice was called for in the Dordrecht Confession but had not previously been practiced by the Swiss. Dordrecht's influence can also be seen in Amman's belief that a "corrupt" member had to be "shunned by all members . . . , whether in eating or drinking and other similar fellowship without any partiality."[23] Amman also argued that believers should not attend state churches and that true-hearted sympathizers could not be saved unless they publicly confessed with their mouths what they believed in their hearts.

Inspired by Schleitheim's separatist tradition and the precepts of Dordrecht, Amman hoped to renew the church by clarifying its separation from the world. In Alsace, where local authorities welcomed Anabaptist groups, the Swiss Brethren transplants were dismayed at how easily the boundaries between the church and the world could be blurred when there was not persecution. Amman's proposals refocused attention on drawing lines between the two. In the canton of Bern, authorities had been intensifying their pressure on Anabaptists to conform, so the Swiss were painfully aware of their conflict with the world. In addition, they had never signed on to the Dordrecht Confession. Led by the elder Hans Reist, many Bernese "Reistians" rejected Amman's proposals as divisive innovations, not traditions that needed rekindling. They relied on true-hearted neighbors and family for their survival; if Christ had eaten with sinners and tax collectors, surely the Bernese Anabaptists could socialize with people performing charitable deeds.

Despite the groups' attempts to come together as one, the differences between the Reistians and the Amish—as followers of Jacob Amman came to be known—grew increasingly heated and acrimonious. Swiss refugees in Alsace saw Amman as a faithful reformer who restored traditional Anabaptist teachings on separation and discipline. However, the Reistians saw him as a hot-headed schismatic. Efforts by Palatinate Mennonites to resolve the split failed. Despite Reist's willingness to admit that he had been lax in administering discipline, Amman banned and shunned him and many of the Palatinate Mennonites who had hammered out the compromise. Several years later, Amish leaders acknowledged that they had been too quick to ban and shun others, and they symbolically excommunicated themselves as an act of penitence. Reist's groups rebuffed the overture and remained cool toward subsequent attempts at reconciliation.

From 1711 on, Swiss Anabaptism was split into two groups: the Amish and the Reistians, who eventually called themselves Mennonites. In addition to the disagreements about how far to separate from the world, economic differences may have also divided the groups. In 1711, a Dutch diplomat speculated that the Mennonites, who were less willing to immigrate, had more land and money than the Amish, who were quicker to take advantage of an opportunity to leave for the Dutch Republic.[24] The bitterness continued on both sides for years to come. Mennonites nearly refused to share the same barge out of Switzerland with Amish refugees.

Despite the animosity, Mennonites and Amish often settled near each other in southern Germany and in North America. Still, the Amish practiced a more rigorous church discipline, incorporated footwashing, and adopted a humbler style of dress with untrimmed beards. In 1702, a Catholic priest remarked that Amish men "have a long beard and the men and women wear clothing made only of linen cloth, summer and winter." Mennonites who followed Reist appeared in their dress "about like the Catholics" and "have shorter beards." While the Mennonites built churches, the Amish continued to meet in their homes.[25]

Even though the issues change over time, questions about discipline and relationship to the surrounding world have continued to drive wedges in the Anabaptist movement. As early as the sixteenth century, the splits between the Frisian, Flemish, and Waterlander Mennonites arose over a disagreement about how faithful disciples should relate to the surrounding world and how discipline could be used to clarify that relationship. In the nineteenth century, the issues might have been Sunday schools, and in the twentieth century, splits occurred over owning cars and telephones or holding English-language church services. To renew the faithful discipleship, Anabaptists repeatedly ended fellowship with other Anabaptists to create congregations "without spot or wrinkle." For some, faithful discipleship has meant that purity is more important than unity.

Looking forward: New sources for renewal

In 1697, Gerrit Roosen, the venerable preacher and elder of the Hamburg-Altona congregation, wrote a letter expressing his dismay at the Amish split. In northern Germany, congregations like Gerhard's seldom shunned offenders, nor did they spend much time worrying about how members dressed. Although members should avoid luxury, Gerhard wrote, "I think it appropriate to follow the customs of the land and that of the people one is with and of one's surroundings."[26] Gerhard's concern for inner piety over outward appearance reflected the attitude of most Dutch and North German Mennonites. Only a few of the most conservative churches in the north practiced shunning or dressed differently from their neighbors. In the south, greater separation and clearer external markers were seen as the keys to spiritual renewal.

It is difficult to discern what role the new ideas played in the numerical decline or growth of Mennonite communities. The historian Michael Driedger has argued that it would be wrong to believe that

Pietism and rationalism were forces that happened *to* Mennonites. Johannes Deknatel's pietistic writings and Martinus Houttuyn's promotion of the sciences are examples of how Mennonites participated in and contributed to new intellectual and spiritual ideas with the hope of reforming and revitalizing the Anabaptist traditions.[27]

Since the sixteenth century, Mennonites and other Anabaptists have been drawing water from new spiritual wells. Some Mennonites continue to call for greater use of the intellectual tools of science and higher education. Other groups reject contemporary trends and strive to remain separate from the surrounding culture. In India, some Mennonites have found helpful theological resources in other theologies—such as Dalit theology, which draws from liberation theology and Black theology—that emphasize God's preference for the poor and outcast. Because many converts in India are part of the Dalit, or lowest level of Indian society, stressing God's presence among the poor has helped the development of an indigenous and non-Western theology in India.

At several times throughout the history of the movement, integrating other approaches has proven invaluable to the long-term survival and even growth of the Anabaptist garden. Anabaptist churches constantly change and adapt in response to or in cooperation with the surrounding society and culture. Sometimes they wither, and sometimes they blossom.

— SEVEN —

Movement and Modernity

The Nineteenth Century

In the nineteenth century, Mennonites across Europe and North America were swept up into the modern age—with all its benefits and drawbacks. Innovations in science and technology, combined with consumer demand, led to the industrialization of the economy and society. Industrial economies produced affordable mass-produced goods but destroyed traditional economies and continue to threaten the environment. Nineteenth-century social reformers sought solutions to the poverty and displacement that arose from rapid urbanization; they pushed governments to develop social safety nets. The nineteenth-century intellectual battles between modern reason and mass culture on one side and the vision of a traditional faith on the other continue to divide churches and society today. By the end of the nineteenth century, Europe and North America had begun the process of religious pluralization that picked up speed and intensified in the twentieth century.

In many Western societies, religion was displaced from the center of cultural life—but not completely sidelined. Modern scholars began to study religious traditions as products of their historical context rather than divine revelation. In response to the inroads of this theological and cultural shift, some conservatives insisted on clearer separation from the surrounding culture while others developed their own intellectual rebuttal to the challenges to traditional social and religious authorities. The modern age also witnessed the growth of new religious movements in the West, such as the remarkable rise of the evangelical and charismatic churches. The religious plurality that emerged during the Reformation took root in the modern age, when the Anabaptist free church model grew more common.

As Mennonite and Amish communities engaged more with the outside world and took part in the rapid changes shaping Europe and North America, they faced the challenge of defining their relationships with broader culture and with each other. They found it increasingly important to clarify their values and practices to assess the degree they should embrace or reject modernity. As society grew more comfortable with religious plurality, many Anabaptists found it easier to assimilate into the culture, even if they were not aware that they were doing so. To take advantage of the opportunities of the modern world, some Mennonites dismissed traditional practices as moldy relics of a bygone age. Others would draw more clearly defined lines between the church and the surrounding culture. The resulting cultural clash divided churches, but it also sparked new partnerships and galvanized Mennonites to seek greater interaction with the broader world.

European Mennonites and the promises of modernity

During the nineteenth century, Dutch Doopsgezinden experienced what some historians call their golden age. In 1815, the Kingdom of the Netherlands granted Mennonites the same social and legal rights as other religious groups, leading to an increase in membership and the church's overall growth. As a result, wealthy merchants and factory owners served as deacons in their congregations and members of the mission board. With the removal of social barriers, Doopsgezinden increasingly adopted the nationalist mood of the country and even held political positions. Samuel van Houten, a Doopsgezind cabinet minister, proposed social welfare laws, including a ban on child labor for those under twelve.

One of the leading figures was Samuel Muller, who attempted to chart a course for the church through the theological currents of the age. Muller, who was raised in a Mennonite orphanage, received a scholarship to study in the Mennonite seminary in Amsterdam. Thereafter, he became pastor of the important congregation in Zaandam. He was one of the founders of the General Mennonite Conference (Algemene Doopsgezinde Sociëteit, or ADS), which almost all the Dutch congregations had joined, ending nearly all the schisms from the previous centuries. In addition to teaching at the seminary, Muller went on to serve on the Mennonite Mission board and the Dutch Bible society. He used his position and influence to renew Mennonite life by training pastors who were skilled preachers, familiar with Mennonite history, and able to teach the youth. He revised the seminary curriculum to focus on biblical study rather than physics and mathematics, which had previously been taught. Despite Muller's attempts to maintain a distinct Mennonite theology that combined biblical values with the best of liberal theology, by the end of the century, Mennonites had fully assimilated into Dutch society, contributing to science, literature, and politics, but had shed traditional teachings and practices of separation and nonresistance. They continued to practice adult baptism and were known for placing a high value on individual choice.

Fig. 7.1 Samuel Muller, nineteenth-century Dutch Mennonite scholar and leader.
Engraving by Dirk Jurriaan Sluyter, *Portrait of the Professor Samuel Muller*, after a painting by Jacobus Schoemaker Doyer, before 1845. Rijksmuseum, Amsterdam, RP-P-1907-3399.

The Russian Mennonite commonwealth

In the nineteenth century, the largest population of Anabaptists lived in the Russian Empire, mostly in Ukraine. The Mennonite colonies there grew into self-governing communities, which historians have described as the "Mennonite commonwealth." Like other settler communities in Ukraine, Mennonites were responsible for town planning, education, insurance, and public order. They valued the ability to form their own communities and live out their faith without government interference. The terms of their *privilegium* granted autonomy for the villages, travel grants, religious freedom, and exemption from military service. It also restricted the Mennonites from selling land to new families without permission from officials. The experience and pattern of living out Anabaptist values that developed in Russia later became the model for Mennonite practice in Mexico, Belize, Bolivia, Argentina, and Paraguay. For these Anabaptists, separation did not mean avoiding certain "worldly" activities; rather, it meant the establishment of isolated colonies.

Despite these restrictions, Russian Mennonites prospered economically. They established schools, charities for widows and orphans, and ran successful businesses and institutions. One of the most remarkable leaders was the farmer Johann Cornies. Cornies's successful experimentation with new sheep breeding techniques caught the attention of national authorities, who appointed him lifelong chair of the Agricultural Union in 1836, giving him control of many areas of farming in Molotschna. In addition to reforming village education, Cornies promoted agricultural innovation throughout the colony and started the transition from a purely agricultural economy toward some of the earliest industrialization in the Russian Empire.

While Cornies's leadership laid the foundation for economic success, his top-down methods sometimes met resistance among those who resented his power, which came from the government—not the community or church. In response to the Agricultural Union's directives to plant trees, one mayor planted all the trees upside down. In response, Cornies charged the mayor with disrespecting the tsar and compelled him to appear before the church, which excommunicated and shunned him. Cornies's legacy among Mennonites is mixed. The Mennonites who first migrated to North America viewed him as a dictator who pushed innovation even when it was not wanted. Other

Fig. 7.2 The powerful leader Johann Cornies reformed the Mennonite communities of south Russia.
Johann Cornies, [before 1846]. Image reproduced by permission of Mennonite Heritage Archives, Winnipeg, 062-2.0.

Fig. 7.3 Johann Cornies's nearly ten-thousand-acre estate Taschenak, in southern Russia, which remained in his family until the Soviet Revolution.
Taschtschenak, Johann Cornies estate, 1895–1914?. Photo reprinted by permission of Mennonite Heritage Archives, Winnipeg, PP-4-044-232.0.

Mennonites who enjoyed the economic benefits of his reforms consider Cornies an enlightened reformer who set the colonies on a safe course for the future.

The story of the disobedient mayor highlights a recurring tension of the Mennonite commonwealth model: the relation between church and village governance was often unclear. Since the Mennonites ran their own villages, they had to decide how to collect taxes and police themselves. When members sinned, it was not always clear whether the congregation or village should discipline the offender. To be married or hold office in the village, residents had to join the church. Because land ownership was linked to church membership, some villagers may have joined the church out of practical necessity or because of ethnic identity rather than theological commitment.

During the second half of the nineteenth century, the Mennonites were drawn further into society. After Russia's humiliating defeat in the Crimean War (1853–56), the Russian government sought to modernize the country as quickly as possible. To achieve this, they ended serfdom in 1861, centralized education, made Russian language mandatory, and tried to instill a new sense of Russian nationalism and loyalty to the tsar. In 1871, Alexander brought the Mennonite colonists into legal equality with the recently freed serfs and state peasants, thereby ending Mennonite legal autonomy. With the introduction of universal military conscription in 1874, it seemed to many Mennonites that they were being asked to compromise too far.[1]

In response, eighteen thousand people, a third of all Mennonites in the empire, left Russia for Canada and the United States. The Canadian government had promised Mennonites freedom of religion, military

Fig. 7.4 A view of the oldest Mennonite church in Chortitza, 1900. The girls are wearing white aprons over their school uniforms. Photo courtesy of Gerhard Peter Rempel/Mennonite Archives of Ontario, Conrad Grebel University College, Waterloo, 1405.

exemption, and control over education. The American promises were similar, but without the guarantee of military exemption. In Canada, the government offered large "reserves" of land in Manitoba for Mennonites to settle. Railroad agents and boosters helped Mennonites settle in the United States along the railways that crisscrossed the prairies. Most of those who chose the potential of North American promises over the unknown direction of Russia were religiously more conservative, including many Mennonite Brethren and all the Kleine Gemeinde (German for "little church") and Hutterites living in Russia. For those who remained, the period between 1874 and 1917 became a "golden age" of economic success and spiritual revival.

Those who left believed that God had presented them an opportunity to renew the church by making it central to their lives again. Old Colony elder Johan Wiebe addressed a gathering on the Red River in Manitoba in 1875, declaring that Canada presented them with "an entirely different order from the one . . . accustomed to in Russia—to deal with everything according to the gospel, . . . the teaching of Christ which the apostles had received from the Lord more than 1800 years ago."[2] In Canada, they established their villages along the models they knew from Ukraine and quickly established new institutions for education and insurance.

The settlements in Kansas, Nebraska, Minnesota, and Manitoba were facilitated with the support of the Mennonites already living in North America, even though they had different historical origins. In 1870, the *Herald of Truth*, a paper found in many homes of the Mennonites and Amish of the United States, began reporting on the struggles and migration of Russian Mennonites to North America, expressing "our sympathy for our brethren on the other side of the ocean" and offering to "extend the welcoming hand, and if need be also material aid."[3] Just as the Dutch Mennonites had supported the migration of Swiss Anabaptists to America in the 1700s, their descendants mobilized aid on behalf of an Anabaptist group with a similar theology and different cultural background. Despite the early inter-Mennonite cooperation, the Low German–speaking Russian Mennonites scattered on the plains between Manitoba and Kansas had more in common with each other than with the Pennsylvania German–speaking Amish and Mennonite communities to the east.

New revivalisms

In the nineteenth century, Mennonites in Europe and North America drew from both Anabaptist and Pietist spiritual traditions. North American Amish and Mennonites continued to embrace their Anabaptist roots by reading the *Martyrs Mirror* and singing hymns from the *Ausbund*, but they also incorporated new Pietist songs. Russian Mennonites read Menno Simons's writings and also adopted literature and songs from German Lutheran Pietists. Rather than abandoning their Anabaptist beliefs, Mennonites and Amish borrowed aspects of Pietism that aligned with their convictions, such as believers baptism, yieldedness, and a suspicion of worldliness. According to historian Theron Schlabach, "By 1800 Mennonite and Amish had accepted so much from Pietism that ever since, many perceptions of what it is to be 'Mennonite' are probably at least as Pietistic as Anabaptist."[4]

In the middle of the nineteenth century, a revival spread through the German-speaking villages in Ukraine. Among the Mennonites, the German preacher Eduard Wüst found an audience thirsty for spiritual revival. Many Mennonites were dissatisfied with the spiritual state of their churches. Instead of "a faith learned by rote,"[5] they wanted evidence of genuine conversion and repentance of sin in believers. Wüst's preaching satisfied a deeper spiritual longing among Mennonites who no longer found the traditional sermons read from the pulpits satisfying. His "mission festivals" stressed personal salvation and the urgent need for missionary work. In 1860, eighteen Mennonites came to a new understanding of faith and celebrated communion without the permission or presence of traditional church leadership. This new group led to the formation of a movement known as the Mennonite Brethren Church.

The Mennonite Brethren required baptism by immersion instead of the traditional pouring and sprinkling and encouraged a renewed interest in the sixteenth-century Anabaptist writings, especially Menno Simons. Their lively worship stressed the presence of the Holy Spirit and even led to spiritual excesses, including book burnings and abuses of authority by several leaders who called themselves *Die Sterke* (the Strong). After struggling to contain the spiritual excesses, Mennonite Brethren leaders passed the "June Protocol" in 1865, which established the principle that no one leader should have authority over all the church and also challenged the divisive introduction of animated worship practices of music, dance, and shouting. After Mennonite Brethren moved spiritual authority from charismatic individuals to the congregation, they were able to reestablish order. Eventually, the mission work of the Mennonite Brethren in the Russian Empire died down—although they would go on to plant many churches in North America and across the world.[6]

New revival movements disrupted and rejuvenated Anabaptist churches. Members who desired a revitalized spiritual life often found resources such as Sunday schools, new music, or revivalism in contemporary movements outside of Mennonite churches. When they brought the new resources back into the church, conflict broke out between the revived members and those who wanted to preserve traditional practices. Exuberant spirituality could lead to division or abuse of power at times. However, many of the new spiritual practices would provide welcome water for the roots of the Anabaptist tradition.

Old Order movements reject modernism

While some Anabaptist groups discovered new spiritual resources outside the church and brought them in, others reinforced the separation from surrounding culture to preserve their sense of traditional Anabaptist identity. In Canada and the United States, modernizing movements forced Anabaptists to assess how much they would enter a surrounding culture that stressed progress, individualism, technology, and formal ways of organizing institutions. Some Amish and Mennonites saw modern innovations as an opportunity to make the church relevant to others outside of traditional Anabaptist communities. Others worried that the emphasis on individualism, materialism, and technological progress would undermine the community and traditional values of humility, modesty, and separation. They asked whether the church should be a "city on a hill" separate from the world or "salt of the earth" mixed in with the rest of society. As a result of these nineteenth-century discussions, some groups drew closer together in new ways while others chose to split, leaving fault lines that still divide Anabaptists in streams visible today.

Among the Amish, the debates settled on the status of their Ordnung, the unwritten traditions that guided every part of daily life.

According to David Beiler, a Lancaster County bishop, truly reborn believers would be instructed and guided in the Ordnung in "meekness, humility, patience in adversity."[7] In doing so, they would align themselves with the order that God desired for the world. In the face of changing contexts, some Amish asked whether the Ordnung needed to adapt to be relevant, or whether it had to stand firm as a bulwark against the surrounding world. The tensions bubbled over in different places at different times. Two bishops in northern Indiana—Isaac Schmucker and Jonas D. Troyer—had begun to wear more stylish clothing, send their children to public schools, and serve in local political offices. These changes struck other Amish as prideful efforts to fit into the surrounding culture. Minister John E. Bontreger declared that the innovators had "started a new church according to their own opinions."[8] In Pennsylvania, a division among the Mifflin County Amish began in the 1860s between those who understood baptism in streams to be the biblical mode—instead of the usual practice of pouring water—and those who wanted to avoid innovations and the disruptions they caused. Perhaps Old Order Amish bishop David Beiler's memoirs summarize the conservative sense that Amish were too accommodating to the changing social order when he lamented that Amish had earlier gone to church barefooted instead of in "fine shoes and boots," and that children were going "to school every winter for months at a time" and spent their time "telling jokes and in unprofitable conversation."[9] While some of Beiler's concerns about dress, using machines to cut sausage meat, or singing schools seem superficial, they reflect a deep concern for members to take their faith commitment seriously instead of carelessly accommodating themselves to the winds of the world's popular sentiments blowing around them.

To settle these disputes, several conservative leaders proposed holding a nationwide *Diener-Versammlung*, or ministers' meeting, to "put together and achieve an agreement suitable to the peace and forbearance of the Gospel."[10] The first of these meetings was held in 1862, not long after the American Civil War broke out. Over fifteen hundred people attended the first *Diener-Versammlung*, including many laypeople attracted by the preaching. Despite agreeing on positions against using lightning rods, posing for photographs, and joining militias, it became clear that most delegates tended to be open to innovations.

Conservatives, however, felt that the meetings failed to tackle the fundamental nature of the disagreements.

The conflict reached its peak in 1865, when traditionalists presented a new order to the other delegates. Church unity, they suggested, could be kept so long as everyone adhered to the rules they were proposing, which stood against acculturations like "brightly colored, striped, or flowered clothing," new hymns, and fancy furniture. The majority appear simply to have ignored the conservative Ordnung. Thereafter, those who wanted clearer lines to be drawn stopped attending the *Diener-Versammlungen*, which continued nearly annually until 1878. Known as the "Old Order," these traditional Amish would become one of the most visually distinct Anabaptist groups, maintaining the clearest separation from the surrounding culture. The Old Orders maintained a distinct dress, worshiped in homes, and shunned entertainment that was too worldly.

A similar desire to strengthen the walls of separation happened among Mennonite groups in opposition to Sunday schools, evangelistic meetings, and other innovations that were finding their way into the church. In response, Old Order Mennonite groups formed in Indiana (1872), Ontario (1889), Pennsylvania (1893), and Virginia (1901). Like the Old Order Amish, the Mennonite groups avoided some of the technological innovations of the modern age. However, the Old Order Mennonites worshiped in meetinghouses rather than homes, and the clothing styles differed between the groups. Old Order groups had earlier split from the Brethren in Christ, in 1843, because of that group's strong opposition to worshiping in meetinghouses. Similar divisions also splintered the Church of the Brethren between 1881 and 1883, when a small group felt that the church was accepting too many of the innovations of the modern consumerist age. While the various Old Order Anabaptist groups have different origins, they reflect a collective dissatisfaction with how North American culture threatened their separate identity and eroded their traditional values of simplicity, modesty, and humility.

Two splits among the progressive Amish Mennonites illustrate the complex strategies of negotiating change being used during that time. Henry Egly, a young bishop in Adams County, Indiana, had a spiritual awakening in response to a serious illness and began to preach that only those who had an identifiable conversion experience could join the church. The group that followed Egly combined some traditional Amish dress practices with religious expression borrowed from the outside world, such as the use of Sunday school materials and the prohibition of alcohol.[11] The Egly Amish—following the pattern of more modern groups—sponsored Mathilde Kohm as a missionary to the Congo in 1896 and funded a Bible institute in Bluffton, Ohio. A second split happened when the progressive bishop Joseph Stuckey refused to ban a member who taught that God would ultimately save everyone. Although Stuckey had resisted innovations like Sunday school and portrait photography, his members sent their children to public schools, dressed more fashionably, and used modern hymnals. By the twentieth century, Amish groups ranged from the progressive Stuckey Amish to the most conservative Old Order congregations.

Initially, the differences between the Old Order Amish and the progressive majority would not have been readily apparent to outsiders. While they were open to changing the Ordnung and accommodating new scriptural understandings, the progressive majority did not completely embrace broader society. Most continued to prohibit musical instruments, "unnecessary, grand household furnishings," and "pompous carriages" while continuing to practice rigorous church discipline.[12] As their relationship with their Mennonite neighbors warmed, most of the accommodating Amish referred to themselves as "Amish Mennonites." Younger members frequently spoke English and became more comfortable interacting with the broader culture. Mahala Yoder, a young Amish Mennonite woman, wrote a letter to her sister that described a trip to the city to shop for spring hats, playing card games, and partaking in popular pastimes, including the orchestra and circus.[13] Like other denominations—including Mennonites—Amish Mennonites built institutions, created conferences, and published their own periodicals.

A third way of living out the Amish tradition began in 1910, when several leaders in Michigan founded the Conservative Amish Mennonite Church to distinguish themselves from both the Old Order Amish and Amish Mennonite branches. In addition to reaffirming the 1632 Dordrecht Confession, the Conservative Amish Mennonite Conference called for greater separation from the world's taste in fashionable clothing, secret societies, life insurance, and government offices. In addition to their focus on evangelism and personal holiness, the

Fig. 7.5 Cars parked for the first Sunday school conference held by the Amish Mennonites in Ontario at the Wilmot meetinghouse (now Steinmann Mennonite Church). Old Order Amish groups had rejected church buildings, cars, and Sunday school. Photo courtesy of Steinmann Mennonite Church/Mennonite Archives of Ontario, Conrad Grebel University College, Waterloo, 160.

conference differentiated themselves from the Old Orders by adopting progressive positions against the use of tobacco and alcohol.

In the early 1900s, the progressive Amish Mennonites formalized their close relationship with the "Old" Mennonite Church by merging their conferences.[14] The desire to create formal institutional structures demonstrates the degree to which the Amish Mennonites had replaced the traditional local, congregational polity of the Amish with the formal institutional structures popular among other mainstream North American denominations. The merging of the groups was not a "hostile takeover"—within days of voting to join with the Mennonites, one of the trustees of the Clinton Frame Amish Mennonite Church in Goshen removed the word "Amish" from the congregation's sign. The merger strengthened both groups, allowing them to better face the challenges of the twentieth century by pooling their energies and ideas. It was so complete, according to the historian Paton Yoder, that many Amish Mennonite congregations soon lost their collective memory of their origins in the Amish Anabaptist tradition.[15]

The decision to separate from other Anabaptists also affected the Dutch-Russian stream of Anabaptism. In 1812, Klaas Reimer and a small group of followers broke from other Mennonites in the Molotschna colony in order to enforce stricter discipline. Dismayed at what he perceived to be Mennonites' low morals and willingness to contribute to the Russian military's campaign against Napoleon's advancing army, Reimer gathered a small group around him to worship in homes. His group was dismissively referred to as the "Little Church," or Kleine Gemeinde, but they embraced the term as a sign of their faithfulness. Like the conservative Amish and Mennonites, the Kleine Gemeinde remained separate from the world and other Mennonites. During the nineteenth century, they condemned many activities as worldly, including card-playing, smoking, drinking, higher education, musical instruments, and mission work. Now known as the Evangelical Mennonite Conference, the Kleine Gemeinde has remained one of the most conservative Russian Mennonite groups in North America.

War and the nation

As revolution changed the political landscape in Europe and North America, Mennonites entered into a period of renegotiating their role in the world around them. The French Revolution temporarily upset the balance of power in Europe, and its armies spread revolutionary ideas of equality and liberty across the continent. After Napoleon's defeat at Waterloo (1815), the political status quo was restored, but the legacy of the French Revolution would continue to reverberate into the twentieth century. The ideas of the revolution contained the seeds for liberal democracy, totalitarianism, and political violence. Even those states that rejected French revolutionary ideals saw nationalism's potential, especially in stoking the support of citizenry for service in the military. A new aggressive form of nationalism germinated throughout absolutist regimes like Prussia and Russia as well as more democratic countries like the Netherlands, the United States, and Canada. Mennonites' reactions to these larger political forces reflected whether they hoped to play a larger role in the world around them.

In the Netherlands, Dutch Mennonites had already shed the last vestiges of their peace position by the 1780s. Many Mennonites supported the French Revolution and were willing to fight to support it when French forces arrived in Holland. When war broke out against

Belgium in 1831, many Dutch students joined the army, including several Mennonite seminarians.

As Mennonites grew less willing to emigrate and more open to theological currents in the surrounding culture, the pull of German society and the restrictions in marriage and property rights led Prussian Mennonites toward greater identification with a German national identity. Those who had the strongest reservations against serving in the military had emigrated by 1880, and progressive, urban Mennonites urged their members to give up nonresistance as a relic from the past. Once they allowed the decision to serve in the military to rest on the conscience of the individual, Mennonites eased the path toward serving with a free conscience. Thereafter, Mennonite identity was associated with their status as a "free church" rather than with the practice of nonresistance.

In the United States, tensions over whether slavery would be allowed in the western territories exploded into a bloody civil war that cost over 620,000 lives. Although American Mennonites and Amish had traditionally forbidden slaveholding, they had not been active abolitionists, and a few Mennonites even owned enslaved people. Mennonites believed that it was up to God, not politics, to change the world.[16]

While they did not work to end slavery, Mennonites in the east petitioned their representatives to protect their conscientious objector status to avoid military conscription as the issue pushed the nation toward war. Lancaster Mennonites were protected by the fiery warmonger Representative Thaddeus Stevens, who created and protected alternative possibilities for Mennonites and Amish, large voting blocs in his district. However, midwestern Mennonites, like Ohio bishop John M. Brenneman, refused to rely on the goodwill of officials, which was according to him to "lean on a broken reed."[17]

Conscripted Mennonites in the North could pay exemption fees or buy substitutes to take their place to serve in the front. Mennonites saw hiring someone else to serve as an acceptable alternative to joining the military. Some Mennonites struggled with this decision. Charles Krehbiel had emigrated from Europe to Illinois to avoid serving in the Bavarian army, but when war broke out in the U.S., he hired a substitute to take his place in the Union army. According to some accounts, when his substitute returned from the war "looking like a skeleton,"

Krehbiel financially supported him for the rest of his life.[18] In the Confederate states, Mennonites who were forced to serve fired their guns into the air, refusing to shoot at their enemies. The Confederate army eventually assigned them to noncombatant duty.

The few men who did fight in the war were likely already marginal members of the church before the war began. When three brothers from Ohio joined the war, their father Jon Herr mourned, "I little thought that wee was raising children to goo to war . . . but it really now is so and I am often overcome that I can't keep back the tears when I think of the thousands which have already gone to an untimely grave." Their mother Barbara "wept bitterly day and night."[19] When veterans returned home after the war, they were usually disciplined by their home congregations. When Abraham Schneck returned to Bluffton, Ohio, his community called him "Krieg Schneck" (War Schneck) and ostracized him.

The Mennonites who remained in Russia after 1871 spent years negotiating a new agreement with officials for an alternative form of service. Securing exemptions stalled when disappointed officials discovered that Mennonites could not speak Russian. One official exclaimed, "You have been in Russia for seventy years and still cannot speak Russian? That is a sin!"[20] In the end, the government agreed that

Fig. 7.6 A group of men posing in the uniform of the Russian forestry service [ca. 1905–14]. Photo reprinted by permission of Mennonite Heritage Archives, Winnipeg, 686-15.0.

Mennonites could fulfill noncombatant service in the medical corps or the forestry service.

The eighteen thousand Mennonites who moved to the North American prairies to escape Russian conscription in the 1870s did not share their new neighbors' scarred memories of the war and were as suspicious of the American state as the Amish and Mennonites who were already there.[21] The Civil War ended slavery in the United States, but questions about war, political engagement, and racism continued to challenge Mennonite identity in the coming years.

The "quickening" at the end of the century

In the nineteenth century, Mennonites in Europe and North America entered a period of rapid acculturation and engagement with the surrounding culture. European Mennonites were already culturally enmeshed with the surrounding society, and they had been building institutions and denominations since the eighteenth century. These efforts included newspapers to unite the varieties of German Mennonites, urban church plants, and international missions. North American Mennonites, who had kept their distance from the rest of Canadian and American society, perceived a need to establish new rationalized and formalized institutions of church life during the latter part of the century. Some historians have referred to this new period as the "awakening" of Mennonites in North America. The historian Theron Schlabach has suggested "quickening" as a more appropriate term, since the Mennonites were not spiritually asleep, but the pace of their activities picked up dramatically.[22]

Before the US Civil War and the arrival of Mennonites from Russia, the largest branch of Anabaptists in North America was the (Old) Mennonites. A smaller, progressive group of Swiss Mennonites known as the General Conference comprised recent immigrants from Europe whose culture was already different from those who had been in North America for several generations. All North American Anabaptists shared a piety that called on believers to humble themselves before God and others. Mennonite positions of separation and nonresistance arose from the need to follow the "meek and humble" Jesus. Practically, the believer's humility expressed itself in daily life in myriad practical ways, including plainness in clothing and furniture.

In the second half of the century, progressive Mennonites embraced new professions, higher education, and new evangelical emphases. Many Mennonites called for more preaching in English and a revitalized church life. Realizing that their members were already studying materials from outside groups, progressive leaders set up printing shops and began establishing their own schools to discern and modify the adoption of these new ideas. Instead of embracing the new initiatives uncritically, they wanted to guide their dissemination among Mennonite groups. One proponent of embracing innovative approaches argued, "If we let *not* our light shine before men that they may see our good works, by neglecting to maintain and build up such institutions . . . then we are doomed to sink into the valley of oblivion, a well-deserved obscurity."[23]

One of the most important leaders in these new endeavors was John F. Funk, who had left his lumber business in Chicago to begin a publishing house in Elkhart, Indiana. Funk published over 120 titles, half of which were in English and the other in German. Funk launched the newspapers *Herald of Truth* and *Herold der Wahrheit* to bind

Fig. 7.7 John F. Funk's publications were an important force in unifying the church in the late nineteenth century.
John F. Funk, in Meditation, 1913. Photo reprinted by permission of Mennonite Church USA Archives, Elkhart, Indiana, John F. Funk Photographs, HM4-154, box 1, folder 1.

scattered Mennonite congregations together. He published materials to support the progressive innovation of Sunday schools, and he led evangelical meetings. Funk's publications advertised his new German edition of the *Martyrs Mirror* and the newly translated English edition that continues to be read in the twenty-first century.

Funk and other activists started a new age of progressive optimism among (Old) Mennonites. Immigrants from Russia and Prussia had traditionally been less suspicious of the surrounding culture and had experience creating institutions. A few years after their arrival, Russian immigrants began planning for a school "in which capable young men . . . could acquire the necessary training for teachers."[24] In 1887, the need for education evolved into the founding of Bethel College, in North Newton, Kansas, one of the earliest Mennonite institutions of higher education in North America.

These progressive activities brought the Mennonite churches into greater involvement with the surrounding culture. The ideas driving evangelical Protestantism also provided Mennonites with the theology, devotional material, and music to accompany them into the world. The new ideas paved the way for their assimilation into American and Canadian culture. Instead of the traditional language of humility, the activists preached on the "manliness of God" and used military language to inspire their hearers to go forth into the world like soldiers marching into war. When they borrowed from modern spirituality, Mennonite preachers often unhooked the question of personal salvation from the Mennonite distinctives of discipleship, simple dress, and peace.

Sensing this, an 1871 statement by tradition-minded Virginia leaders warned that the desire for Sunday schools was the desire to follow the fashion "amongst the highest, the proudest, and the dressiest classes of our country." They warned that when Sunday schools encouraged children to learn through competition, they promoted "a spirit of pride and exaltedness."[25] There was a danger, they cautioned, in borrowing too freely from groups who were not opposed to warfare.

By the end of the nineteenth century, Anabaptists in Europe and North America had been forced to decide how much they could accommodate with the surrounding culture. The groups who decided to emphasize sharper separation from the surrounding world grew further apart from those who chose to accommodate and integrate aspects of modernity. United by newspapers and new institutions, activist Mennonites drew from Protestant circles to create a new institutional identity that brought them into greater involvement with the surrounding culture. While it may have altered their worldview in ways that they were not aware of, it also encouraged them to move beyond traditional cultural connections and take the gospel to domestic and international mission fields. The new activist and optimistic identity continued into the twentieth century, when it crashed against the horrors of global warfare.

Indigenous relations

As Mennonites spread across Europe and North America, they did not move into empty spaces. They built their homes, farms, and businesses on land where governments had recently conquered or displaced Indigenous or other peoples. Settlements were a way for national governments to claim territory. The Mennonites in Russia benefited from the imperial government's desire to settle Ukraine. In the Americas, European rulers had long used the "Doctrine of Discovery," a series of papal decrees issued in the fifteenth century, to justify the displacement of Indigenous groups. According to the doctrine, the first Christian nation to "discover" a land automatically controlled it and could seize it from non-Christian natives. Governments tried to solidify their claim over lands they had acquired through policies like the 1862 US Homestead Act and the Dominion Lands Act of 1872 in Canada, which promised farms to settler families to encourage expansion. In 1870s Manitoba, the government offered Mennonites the "East Reserve" and "West Reserve," land that a recent treaty had marked for settlement, often to the detriment of the Métis people who had been living there.[26] Rail companies in both countries sent emissaries to Europe to promote settler expansion on Indigenous lands.

It is unclear whether the Amish and Mennonites who settled in northern Indiana knew the history of the Potawatomi land that they purchased in 1841. The Potawatomi had been coerced to sign a series of treaties ceding their lands to the federal government, and by 1838 most of the Potawatomi had migrated to new territory in Kansas. However, Chief Menominee, who never signed a treaty, refused to leave and he and others were forcibly marched on the "Trail of Death" by an armed militia, who burned the Potawatomi crops and destroyed their village. During the westward march, forty-two people—mostly children—died of heat and disease. While the Mennonites did not actively promote Chief Menominee's expulsion, they benefited from his people's removal.

Even where there were good relations between settlers and locals, Mennonite settlement facilitated government control over its territory. For example, Mennonites in the Paraguayan Chaco peacefully cohabitated with the Indigenous Guaraní in the 1920s, but the settlement of the Mennonites was part of the Paraguayan government's dispute with Bolivia over who controlled the land. As recently as 2016, Low German Mennonites from Mexico looking for fertile land bought twenty thousand hectares in Colombia that may not have clear legal title and where there has been considerable displacement of the people who lived and owned land there. While it seems clear those swept up in "Colombia fever" did not have political motives, the disputed land may not stand up to legal challenge.[27]

In the late twentieth century, North American Mennonites began to acknowledge their complicity in the displacement of Indigenous peoples from their lands. In response, Mennonites have sought ways to address historical wrongs and build better relationships with Indigenous groups. The Return to the Earth project, initiated by principal peace chief of the Cheyenne and Mennonite minister Lawrence Hart, "supports Native Americans in burying unidentifiable ancestral remains now scattered across the United States and enables a process of education and reconciliation between Native and Non-Native peoples."[28] On the eve of the five hundredth anniversary of Christopher Columbus's first contact with the Americas, the Mennonite Church called on its members to

1. Refrain from a triumphalist spirit in celebrating this event in favor of humble gratitude for the benefits experienced in these new lands.

2. Recognize the greed and devastation that characterized the coming of the Europeans, and repent of our participation in the unjust exploitation of native peoples.

3. Seek to understand more accurately the rich history of native peoples, hear their stories, feel their pain and learn from their values and patterns of life.

4. Rejoice that even through suffering many Native Americans received the Gospel message and share in the body of Christ.

5. Recognize the leadership of the United Native Ministries Council (UNMC) and learn to know and support in love and prayer the member congregations and congregations eligible for membership in the Council.

6. Advocate for appropriate redressing of injustices done to native people in the past, and for just and constructive programs of human betterment for native peoples now and in the future.

7. Renew a commitment to the mission of Christ in North America that is sensitively inclusive of peoples of all nations, tribes, peoples and tongues.

8. Reaffirm the global nature of the church and its mission and resist the provincial attitude characteristic of nationalistic celebrations.[29]

Into the twenty-first century, North American Mennonite churches continue to work at dismantling the Doctrine of Discovery and building relationships with their Indigenous neighbors.

Home and rural missions

Among North American Anabaptists, missions did not mean traveling to new countries. In the early days of missions, the first North American Mennonites who reached out to new immigrants in cities or rural communities would have seen themselves as crossing into "heathen" territory; New York or Arizona would have been as foreign to them as Java or Hyderabad. For the Mennonite Brethren, Mennonite, and Brethren in Christ missionaries who left their relatively homogeneous German-speaking communities, working in isolated mountain towns or moving to the cities would have felt like foreign missions. The middle of the nineteenth century saw a burst of missionary activity as Sunday schools and mission society journals stoked enthusiasm among

Anabaptists, who increasingly copied models for missionary work from other Protestant groups. In the United States, another influence of Anabaptist missionary interest was the broader culture of American expansionism surrounding the Spanish-American War. A feeling of Anglo-Saxon superiority buttressed a growing sense that missionaries helped spread Western civilization and push back against Catholicism in colonies abroad and among urban immigrants at home. Instead of avoiding the world, many Anabaptists now saw it as a field for missions.

The first missionaries were not part of official denominational initiatives, but bold individuals or families who struck out on their own to share the gospel. Perhaps half the American Mennonites who went on overseas missions left under the auspices of non-Mennonite agencies. By joining nondenominational organizations like the Christian and Missionary Alliance, they could distance themselves from the ethnic and denominational elements of their faith.

Eventually, initiatives became part of denominational mission boards. In 1893, several young adults led by Menno S. Steiner established the Chicago Home Mission. Under the motto "Where the sick are healed, the needy clothed, the hungry fed, and to the poor the Gospel is preached," the mission began as a series of Sunday school conferences, but it expanded into mothers' groups, sewing classes, a medical clinic, and a daycare for newly arrived immigrants. Denominations were usually cautious in their support of mission projects, but many of the projects needed the financial and administrative support that denominations could provide. In 1896, the project came under the direction of the newly formed Mennonite Evangelizing Board of America. In 1929, Ignacia and Manuel León began teaching Sunday school in Spanish, and David Castillo became the first Hispanic Mennonite pastor. Although small in number, the Spanish-speaking congregation in Chicago would become the launching pad for many Latino Mennonite leaders.

In addition to urban missions, Anabaptists planted churches in rural communities. The (Old) Mennonite Church started 430 rural congregations, which were often supported by members of parent congregations. Clara Brubaker, who served the rural communities in the Ozark Mountains of Missouri, was typical of those who left their home communities to build new churches. Like Brubaker, many of the church planters were bivocational, working outside of the congregation to support their ministry. In 1897, Brubaker donated land for a school near Birch Tree, Missouri. In addition to teaching in the school for many years, she taught Sunday school and visited the elderly and sick in the rural community. A prolific writer, Brubaker wrote seventy-eight articles to encourage others to contribute to the missionary cause.[30]

Despite the sacrifice of those who led them, few of the rural or urban church plants grew exceptionally large. But the mission enthusiasm also transformed and renewed the individuals and congregations who supported them. And significantly, missionary activities broke down traditional barriers between the church and the world, and as we shall see in later chapters, foreign and domestic missionaries' encounters with new cultures challenged their understanding of race and religion. As a result, in the twenty-first century, the typical Anabaptist is no longer a rural, white European.

Looking forward: Cultural discernment

Christianity is always embodied in culture. Attempts to separate or identify the "pure gospel" from the way it is expressed underestimate how worship, music, clothing, parenting styles, and technology are difficult to separate from how faith is expressed, passed on, and lived out. Anabaptists, like all Christians, continue to actively or passively engage in culture. The Old Order Anabaptists' Ordnung is an attempt to clarify which technologies and culture bind a community together and which lead to greater individualism and division. Hutterite colonies have maintained their traditional dress and language while adopting modern technologies. Even more "mainstream" Anabaptists continued to hold some separation from the surrounding culture into the middle of the twentieth century. To a certain degree, the polarization among North American Mennonites can be traced to people's decisions about what theological or cultural streams to adopt.

Since the 1960s, when Anabaptist churches in Asia and Africa gained control of their congregations, they have discerned what parts of the tradition taught by foreign Anabaptist missionaries have been culturally determined and whether there are parts of their own culture they could incorporate. In subsequent chapters, we will see how the use of drumming and movement or dance in worship were banned by early twentieth-century missionaries, who did not always require converts to adopt the conservative dress worn by North American Mennonites or Brethren in Christ members but did force assimilation in other ways. Increasingly, African churches today are using traditional music in their worship.

In more recent Amish Mennonite church plants, however, new believers in Africa or Latin America have often adopted the clothing and head coverings of the sending denominations. Like the nineteenth-century Mennonites and Amish, Anabaptists around the world continue to resist or adapt to cultural innovations, though they may not always be aware that they are following a longer tradition of doing so.

— EIGHT —

To the Ends of the Earth

Anabaptist Missions

At his 1921 baptism at the Nyanga mission, Daniel Kitamba became one of the earliest converts to join a Mennonite church in the Congo. His marriage to Ruth Isaka in 1926 was the first Christian celebration of marriage in the same mission. Kitamba went on to become a teacher in the schools that Mennonites opened in the Kasai region and a tireless missionary of the gospel message. While on a mission in 1936, Kitamba was killed by a bolt of lightning. Still today, Congolese Mennonites consider Kitamba's sudden death to have occurred "in the line of duty" while practicing and spreading his faith. The seeds that Kitamba and other converts planted in the Congo grew during the country's colonial history, transformed after the foreign missionaries had to leave the Congo, and continue to bloom. Today, there are about 225,000 Anabaptist believers divided among three branches of the Congolese Mennonite denominations.

After four centuries as a faith content to remain within its own communities, Anabaptism expanded beyond its ethnic borders in the nineteenth and twentieth centuries. Parts of Kitamba's story are emblematic for how this fundamental transformation of Anabaptism began. At the end of the nineteenth century, Mennonite and Brethren in Christ missionaries from North America and Europe began to evangelize outside their traditional communities by moving to cities and other countries. The remarkable success of the missionaries' work, which usually included the foundation of schools and medical clinics, depended on the sacrifices of local preachers like Kitamba. In addition to developing new members, the missionary movement in turn changed Anabaptists by exposing them to new theological and social influences.

Modern Anabaptist missions

Although the sixteenth-century Anabaptists spread their message across northern Europe, persecution eventually forced the churches to retreat underground. The conditions of their toleration often prohibited Anabaptists from proselytizing—recruiting others to join their faith. Apart from the urban and socially engaged Dutch, Mennonites in Europe and North America were content to keep to themselves and cultivated a reputation as "the quiet in the land:" humble and peaceable people who refrain from active participation in public life.[1] In many Hutterite, Amish, and Mennonite communities, cultural and religious identities grew intertwined. Folkways, languages, and foods knit communities together, creating a powerful sense of belonging and mutual support. Although these traditions helped communities and congregations form tight bonds and allowed them to survive transcontinental displacement, they blurred the lines between faith and culture. The resulting boundaries made it difficult for outsiders to join and made Mennonites less likely to reach out to others.

Traditionally, Anabaptist missionary outreach was simply sponsoring traveling ministers to serve their own members in isolated settlements. If new members joined from outside of the community, it was through marriage. As traditional authorities and practices were challenged in the nineteenth century, the denominations changed. Many saw these changes as progress, and as linked with economic success and stability. Progressively minded Anabaptists desired to share their tradition with others. Inspired by evangelicals from other traditions, nineteenth-century Mennonites were convinced that they needed to reach beyond their own members to save the souls of the lost, and they were also convinced that there would be positive benefits for their home congregations. At first, they traveled to isolated rural communities, and

Fig. 8.1 Congo Inland Mission school, Nyanga Station. Photo reprinted by permission of Mennonite Heritage Archives, Winnipeg, PP-Photo coll. 166-156.0.

then they started sending missionaries to other countries and planting mission posts in cities. After years of moving to areas where they could live out their faith in relative isolation, Anabaptists moving to new cities and countries had to discern what it meant to be a disciple in new cultures and contexts.

Indonesian beginnings

The stories of those who joined Anabaptist churches are as diverse as their countries of origin. Some joined the churches founded by missionaries, whereas others identified as Anabaptist or Mennonite only after discovering similar convictions on their own. Some groups blended their own traditions with Anabaptist ideas, and others found freedom by rejecting much of their previous religious practices. The story of the diverse origins of the Mennonite churches in Indonesia reflects patterns that would continue as the tradition grew in new lands.

In 1847, Mennonites in the Netherlands founded a mission society, and the first Anabaptist missions in the modern era began. They sent Pieter Jansz to the Dutch East Indies (now Indonesia), a country under Dutch colonial rule. Jansz was later joined by Hillebrandus Klinkert, and the two worked to translate the Bible into the Javanese and Malay languages. As German and Russian Mennonites grew interested in missions as well, they donated money toward the Dutch efforts in Indonesia. Missionary work provided one of the first opportunities for transnational Mennonite cooperation, especially among those from areas where revival movements had stimulated an interest in reaching out to others. Russian Mennonites Heinrich Dirks and Agnetha Schröder worked in South Tapanuli on the island of Sumatra from 1870 to 1881. When they returned to Europe, Dirks traveled extensively to promote mission work among Russian, Dutch, and North American Mennonites.

Jansz chose to open a school and carry on his mission work in the area around Mount Muria on the northernmost part of the island of Java. By 1856, he had baptized fourteen people, but he found it difficult to carry out evangelistic work in a predominantly Muslim region at a time of increasing conflict between the Dutch Indies government and the Javanese. Because Christianity was regarded as the religion of the oppressor, Jansz realized that evangelism had to be carried out by Javanese leaders who would spread Christianity and build community among the converts.[2]

The anti-colonial mystic Ibrahim Tunggul Wulung shaped the young Javanese church more profoundly than any European missionary. The early years of Tunggul Wulung's life are unclear. After a struggle against the colonial regime, he had a life-changing, mystical experience. He found a scrap of cloth with the Ten Commandments written on it, and he tried to learn more about the faith that taught those precepts. Once he discovered Christianity, Tunggul Wulung saw in it a new, powerful wisdom that recognized Christ as a messianic king who served humanity. In 1852, he converted to Christianity, and at his baptism in 1854, he took the name Ibrahim.

Tunggul Wulung's initial efforts to form a partnership with Pieter Jansz floundered. The Dutch missionary criticized Tunggul Wulung's teachings for integrating Christianity with a syncretic mix of Islam, Buddhism, and Javanese mysticism. Tunggul Wulung viewed Jansz as a typical controlling foreign missionary who was twenty years his junior. Inspired by an idea from Tunggul Wulung, Pieter Jansz established Dutch-run agricultural colonies where Javanese Christians could avoid social ostracism and create a social foundation for their religious life. Uninterested in deferring to missionaries who dominated these new

180 *Radicals & Reformers*

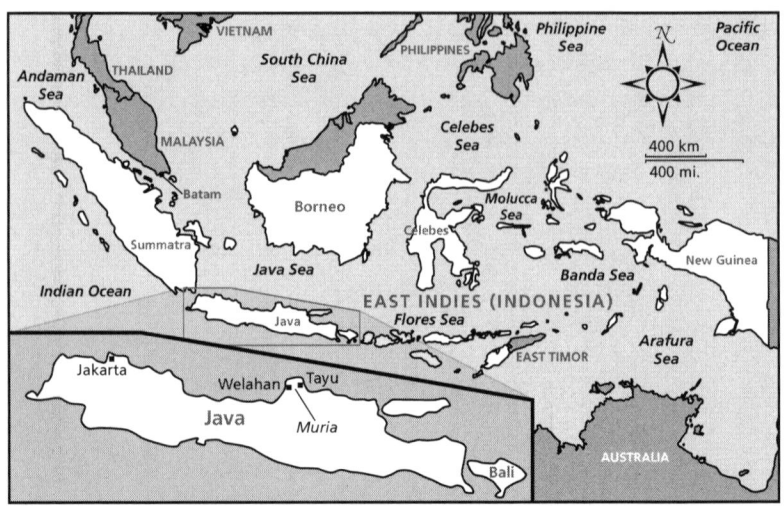

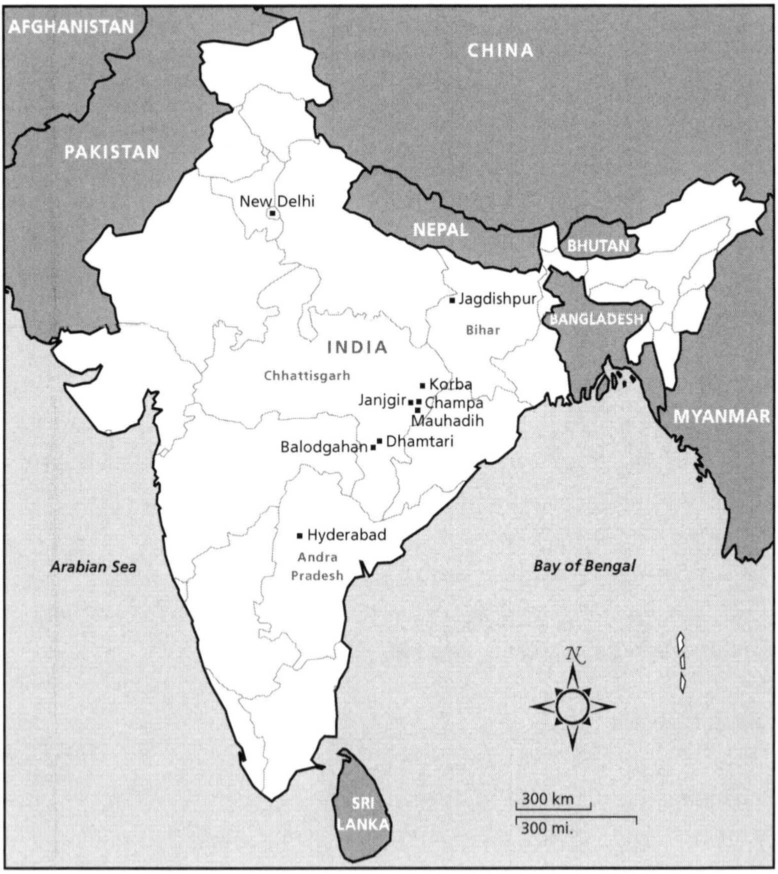

villages like village chiefs, Tunggul Wulung set out to create his own movement.

Along with his wife and fellow mystic Endang Sampurnowati, Tunggul Wulung preached a Javanese gospel and established his own independent Christian communities near Mount Muria. By establishing new Christian villages like Bondo, he hoped to evade the Dutch government's labor obligation and ease the separation of converts from their traditionally Muslim families and communities. For thirty years, Tunggul Wulung traveled across Java, preaching a Christian message that met the needs of the Javanese people. The power of Jesus' name freed Javanese people from malevolent spiritual forces and worked miraculous healings. The promise of a coming "Just King" provided hope for those who desired freedom from Dutch rule. Upon his death in 1885, Tunggul Wulung left over one thousand followers in four congregations under the leadership of his grandson Rustiman. In the hope of establishing a more modern organization, Rustiman contacted Pieter Jansz's son Pieter Anthonie, who commissioned him to baptize Tunggul Wulung's followers. Members of the Muria Javanese Church, known today as the Gereja Injili di Tanah Jawa (Evangelical Church of Java), or GITJ, continued to acknowledge the spiritual legacy of Tunggul Wulung as late as the 1980s.[3] The church that the Janszes and Tunggul Wulung started remains rural and strongly Javanese in its theology today.

Muria Christian Church of Indonesia

While the Dutch focused their missionary work on the Javanese population of northern Java, a separate Mennonite movement developed among the Malay-speaking Chinese community in the 1920s. As with the Javanese, religion was intricately linked with Chinese social identity and community. The Chinese churches—which tended to be wealthier and better educated than the Javanese ones—also started in the Mount Muria region of northern Java. Both groups were examples of Anabaptist communities whose growth was driven by local leaders who provided converts with an alternative way of life that allowed them to break ties with their traditional communities.

The leaders of the new movement, married couple Sie Djoen Nio and Tee Siem Tat, had followed Confucianism before becoming

Christians. Sie Djoen Nio began reading the Bible, and the couple's children were then baptized as Catholics. In 1917, Tee suffered a prolonged spiritual malaise and a bodily illness that neither traditional nor Western medicine could cure. After Sie Djoen Nio told her husband about the healing miracles of Jesus she had read about in the Bible, Tee attended several Christian gatherings. As he learned more about Jesus, he was gradually healed in his body and spirit, leaving him miraculously at peace and freed from his spiritual burdens. To commemorate his recovery, Tee purchased fifteen birds from a passing bird merchant and released them. After his conversion, Tee radically reordered his life, handed his business over to his children, and became a powerful evangelist.

Tee shared his faith with his friends and neighbors. When they sought to affiliate with other churches, Tee's growing congregation in Kudus first contacted the Salvation Army and the Seventh-day Adventists, but they ultimately associated with the Dutch Mennonite Mission board, which was willing to work with the Chinese Indonesians. Tee was attracted to the traditional Mennonite emphases on the Bible, believers baptism, discipleship, and the rejection of violence.[4]

Fig. 8.2 Sie Djoen Nio and Tee Siem Tat established the Muria Christian Church of Indonesia. Mr. & Mrs. Tee Siem Tat, Chinese Mennonites in Indonesia. Photo reprinted by permission of Mennonite Heritage Archives, Winnipeg, 280-50.0-009.

As the group grew, a strong communal identity knitted the young church together, because when new members converted, they had to break ties with their communities. They were not allowed to send their children to traditional Chinese-language schools and were excluded from traditional wedding and burial practices. Eventually, the young congregation bought their first church building with their own funds, after a falling out with the Dutch missionaries over funding for the building.

Under Tee's leadership, the Kudus group spread their message into the surrounding communities. Often, while Tee preached, Sie Djoen Nio met with the women. Converts like Sie Giok Gian became evangelists and traveled from house to house spreading the message of Jesus, healing the sick, and casting out evil spirits. The miracles, according to Sie Giok Gian, were testimonies for Jesus. As the churches grew, the traditional Chinese leaders grew angry with people who no longer turned to them for burial, wedding, or other services. When Tee Siem Tat began to preach in the village of Welahan, local Confucian temple workers threw stones at his car. When the temple workers threw stones the next time they returned to the area, Tee and his colleagues threw bread. Surprised, the Confucians asked why they threw bread rather than go to the police. Tee replied, "The Mennonite teaching tells us that we have to repay violence by doing well."[5]

Upon Tee's death in 1940, the leadership of the eight congregations was left to his children and their spouses. Originally called the Chinese Mennonite Christian Church, the group changed its name to Muria Christian Church of Indonesia (Gereja Kristen Muria Indonesia, or GKMI) to reflect their desire to reach beyond the Chinese communities at a time when rising Indonesian nationalism contained anti-Chinese sentiments. They looked for ways to reach beyond the Chinese community, and many started using Indonesian family names instead of Chinese ones.

Missions and growth in India

While the Chinese and Javanese churches in Indonesia developed from the seeds Tee and Tunggul Wulung planted, the Indian Anabaptist churches were founded by European and North American mission and service projects. Most Indian Anabaptists are members of the low-caste

Dalits, or poor farm laborers, or from tribal backgrounds. These were groups that fell out of the *varna*, or caste, system that divides Hindu society into socially unequal groups. The caste that one is born into determines one's identity, occupation, and social status. Christianity, including Anabaptism, was a way for members of the lowest echelons of Indian society to improve their social standing. By converting, they could find higher self-respect in their new faith than in the Hindu social structures that kept them locked into humiliatingly low social statuses.

The first Anabaptists who traveled to India were the Russian Mennonite Brethren missionaries Abraham J. and Maria Martens Friesen. By building on the success of earlier American Baptist missionaries, their work among Telugu speakers in southern India enjoyed remarkable success. Soon, the Russian Mennonite Brethren sent six more couples. Inspired by the Friesens' success, American Mennonite Brethren established a mission station near Hyderabad in 1899. Having grown to over two hundred thousand members, the Conference of the Mennonite Brethren Church is now one of the largest Anabaptist conferences in the world.

The success of these early missions depended on local evangelists and pastors. In their letters home, the missionaries noted that the "natives" did most of the evangelical work. The local evangelists, who were Dalits with no formal education, typically preached a message of Christian equality, which sometimes contrasted with the relatively lavish lifestyle and large homes of the Westerners. As the missionary compounds grew to include schools, hospitals, and clinics, the missionaries had to spend more of their time on administrative duties, which forced them to rely on the local preachers to go out and evangelize. Fortunately, the local preachers easily connected with their listeners, who shared their Dalit background and became interested in their message.

Many of the Western workers first felt a call to go to India in response to a severe famine in the 1880s and 1890s; the priority for the early years was to feed starving people. Several years after Mennonite Brethren from the Russian Empire started their mission among Telugu-speaking people of Andhra Pradesh, the (Old) Mennonite and General Conference Churches in North America each sent workers to the state of Madhya Pradesh as a response to the devastating famines. The (Old)

Mennonite Church built a mission in Dhamtari, which became the foundation for the Mennonite Church in India (MCI). The General Conference Mennonite Church, now known as the Bharatiya General Conference Mennonite Kalisiya (BGCMC), eventually established separate missions in Champa, Korba, Janjgir, Mauhadih, and Jagdishpur. Over time, they also built orphanages, an elementary school, a theological school, a hospital, and a church. In 1906, the Mennonite Church mission board bought the entire village of Balodgahan and became the landlord for the village.

While the initial focus of the missions was caring for the physical needs of Indians, many of those who received aid later joined and became important leaders in Indian churches. In 1900, MCI worker Jacob Andrew Ressler reported that the missionaries fed fourteen

Fig. 8.3 In 1908, the Mennonite Church purchased the "outlaw" village of Balodgahan, Chhattisgarh State, to provide self-sufficient farms for Christians and orphans. The church established there celebrated its hundredth anniversary in 2006. Photo reprinted by permission of Mennonite Church USA Archives, Elkhart, Indiana, Mennonite Board of Missions Photograph Collection, India National Leaders, 1948–1964, IV-10-7.2, box 5, folder 3, photo #31.

thousand people twice daily.⁶ Many of the converts to the church included people who worked at the mission stations, patients suffering from Hansen's disease (leprosy), and orphans who grew up in the care of the stations.

MCI missionaries' care for their members even included matchmaking. They arranged the marriage of Stephen Solomon and Phoebe Sheela, who had been orphaned and lived at the station as children. After studying at the University of Calcutta, Solomon became a prolific writer who translated tracts and books into Hindi, taught at the Mennonite Higher Secondary School, and was ordained as a minister after his retirement in 1970. Sheela, the first woman university graduate in the Mennonite Church in India, taught in mission schools and municipal high schools. By 1916, there were around 9,500 members in roughly two dozen BGCMC churches, and there were 488 members in MCI churches in 1912. The mission of the Mennonites in India had a social dimension in addition to the gospel message. Aaron Massy, a seventy-seven-year-old Mennonite from Dhamtari, reflected, "I was a beggar in the past. Today my son is a doctor. This is the blessing of the

Fig. 8.4 Phoebe (Sheela) and Stephen Solomon, teachers and deacons in the Dhamtari church. Photo reprinted by permission of Mennonite Church USA Archives, Elkhart, Indiana, Mennonite Board of Missions Photograph Collection. India National Leaders, 1948–1964, IV-10-7.2, box 5, folder 3, photo #08.

Mennonite mission in this area."[7] When India gained independence, much of the educational, relief, and missionary work would be taken over by local Indian leaders.

Missions and growth in China

The first Mennonite church in China was started in 1905 by Henry C. and Nellie Schmidt Bartel. With fifty dollars and a few coworkers, the Bartels set out to establish an independent, locally controlled Mennonite church. Known as the Christian Church Gospel Association (Ji Du Jiao Fu Yin Hui), the young church relied on local leaders from the beginning, because of limited financial support from abroad. The Christian Church Gospel Association held short-term Bible schools for their Chinese coworkers, who would travel out into the countryside to evangelize. On "Full Sunday," the first Sunday of each month, all members of the church gathered to worship at the church in Tsao Hsien, which could hold over one thousand worshipers. Because local missionaries, like Wang Hsuen Ch'en, lived among the people in the countryside, the church continued to grow under the repressive Communist regime that took over the country in the 1940s. After the foreign missionaries were deported, the church suffered, and its membership dropped from twenty thousand in 1949 to one hundred in 1958. In 1978, the government again allowed Christians to gather; the Tsao Hsien church has since grown to thirty thousand members who meet in forty-six locations throughout the region. Though the Bartels were initially missionary entrepreneurs who set off on their own, they eventually received support from Krimmer Mennonite Brethren, Mennonite Brethren, Evangelical Mennonite Brethren, and the Missionary Church Association. While the church no longer has Anabaptist connections, the congregation recognizes the contributions of the Mennonites to the community's founding.

In 1911, General Conference missionaries Henry J. and Maria Miller Brown founded a small church in Kai Chow (now Puyang of Henan Province). Mennonite Brethren missionaries started a church among the Hakka community in Fujian Province in 1912. This church was reorganized as the Hakka Mennonite Brethren Conference in 1920 and managed by an executive committee of twenty-one Chinese members. The Methodist mission board invited the Mennonite Church mission board to take over a Methodist congregation in Hechuan and set up a clinic in 1947. After the Communist Party's restrictions on foreigners in 1950, the foreign missionaries had to leave China and lost all contact with the congregation back in Hechuan.

The General Conference and Mennonite Church missions to China, like those to India, sought to provide a holistic mission by combining the gospel message with social relief, schools, and clinics. Some converts saw Christianity as the source of Western technological dominance and converted for social advancement. Women who converted were able to break away from some of the patriarchal structures of Chinese society. In the General Conference churches, women took leadership roles, and in the 1930s and 1940s, Qing-Feng Lee served as moderator. The gospel of Christian equality also rejected the traditional practice of binding young girls' feet to restrict their growth, which was considered a sign of status and feminine beauty.

In China, Mennonites from North America struggled to overcome the perception that Christianity was an insidious arm of Western cultural imperialism. Evangelical slogans that called on the church to "conquer China for Christ" and talked about waging "spiritual battles" fanned the suspicion that missionaries were the vanguard for the front lines of a looming political and cultural war.

Missionaries had indeed adapted the language of American nationalism and anti-Catholicism campaigns among immigrants in cities and overseas territories. The American missionary M. S. Steiner saw great opportunity in his country's victory during the Spanish-American War of 1898 to convert the new American colonies. He wrote, "The 8,000,000 benighted, priest-ridden, oppressed souls of the Philippine Islands are tired of Spain's misrule. . . . They will listen to messengers from our land. The same is true of Cuba at our door."[8] Whether or not they were aware of it, Mennonite missionaries became part of the efforts to westernize the world and Americanize immigrants.

Mistrust of missionaries in China was fueled by the evangelists' rejection of Chinese cultural practices among those who converted. For example, the missionaries' critique of ancestor veneration undercut the importance of children's duty to respect their elders, making it difficult for some converts to be both Christian and Chinese. When the missionary Henry J. Brown threw down the memorial tablet of a Chinese deacon, the deacon grew offended at the idea that he would have to stop respecting his ancestors and no longer perform acts expected of sons toward their parents. In Fujian Province, locals protested that the construction of a Mennonite church disturbed the feng shui of ancestral graves. When missionaries introduced Western medicine, local villages perceived it as magic and accused missionaries of stealing children to use in their magical preparations.

Although Anabaptist missionaries saw some success in their efforts in China, the eventual development of a truly indigenous Chinese Christianity allowed the churches to survive under repressive regimes. Chinese leaders had insisted on more autonomy in church functions like weddings and funerals and in the management of church funds; despite missionaries' resistance to turning over control to local leaders, the push toward indigenization strengthened the Chinese churches. Chinese Mennonite churches had suffered during the multiple wars, conflicts, and political upheaval in the first half of the twentieth century, including the Japanese occupation during World War II and the establishment of the People's Republic of China in 1949. Under the Communist regime, the Chinese churches cast off the Western cultural practices after the sponsoring denominations had to leave the country. This led to the growth of an assimilated, Chinese Christianity that shed the baggage of its association with Western cultural imperialism.

Mission among Indigenous North Americans

In 1880, the General Conference church sent Samuel Schmidt Haury and Susanna Hirschler Haury to the Arapahoes in what is now Oklahoma. They were joined by Heinrich R. Voth, who traveled among many different Native American groups. During his travels, Voth met with the Hunkpapa Lakota leader Sitting Bull (Tȟatȟáŋka Íyotake). Sitting Bull was then leading the Ghost Dance revival to inaugurate a new age where the white settlers would disappear, the dead would rise, and the bison would return. At a time when Native American rights and ways of life were under assault by the American government and settlers, the Ghost Dance promised an apocalyptic vision of a world turned upside down. Because the ceremony of the Ghost Dance had no drums and used Christian-style singing, Voth proposed closer cooperation with Sitting Bull's movement. Sitting Bull declared that his movement had much in common with the Mennonites and called on his

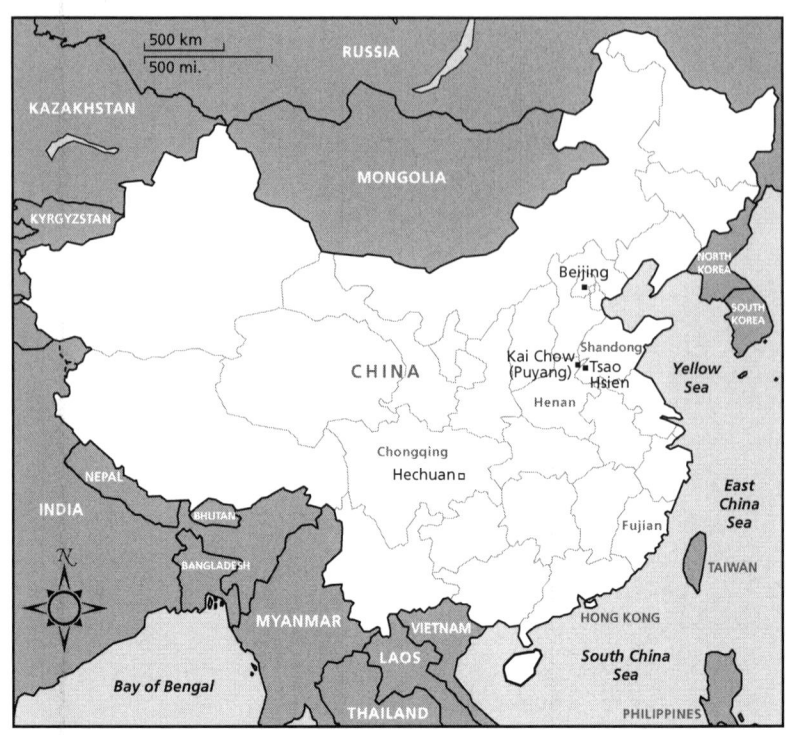

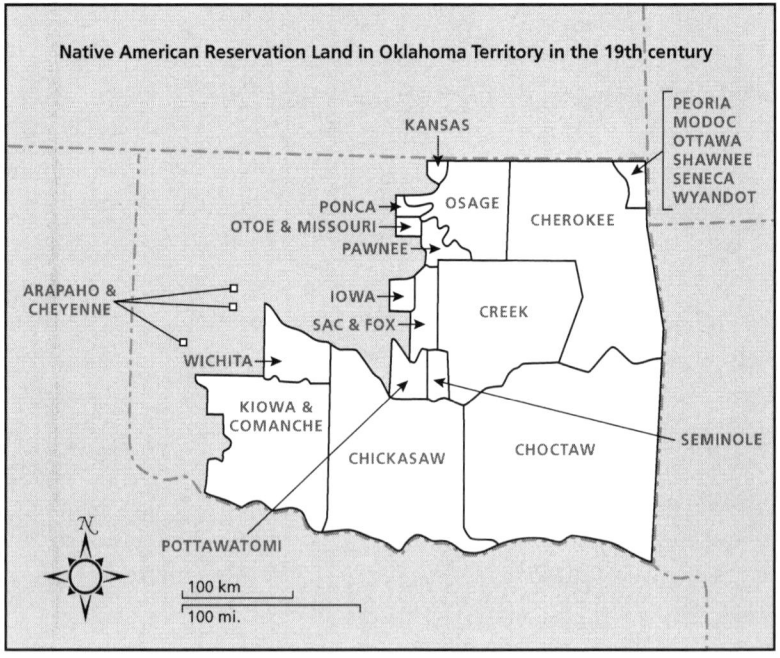

people to attend Sunday school, but when the Ghost Dance messiah failed to appear, the interest in the Christian message evaporated. It was clear that the movement was an effort to preserve Indigenous cultural identity at a moment of crisis and not an offshoot of Christianity.

Although Voth looked for ways to accommodate Native American spiritualities, most Anabaptist missionaries worked with secular authorities to use schools and missions to assimilate Native Americans into the broader American society. Even Voth argued for the need to "undermine the heathenish customs and the superstitions of this people and open their eyes."[9] North American Anabaptist groups from the Beachy Amish to the Brethren in Christ tried to establish churches among Indigenous peoples, including the Sioux and Cree in Manitoba, Ojibwe in Ontario, Creek and Choctaw in Alabama, and Hopi and Navajo in the American Southwest. Indigenous people were slow to join Mennonite churches, which were reluctant to accommodate Indigenous spiritualities and practices. Mennonites often shared the same colonialist assumptions of the surrounding culture.

Despite significant mistrust, there were times when Mennonite and Indigenous traditions merged successfully. The Cheyenne of Oklahoma, many of whom had survived the Washita massacre of 1868, have had a tradition of a peace chief, who works to secure peace between tribes and with the authorities. Some Cheyenne who joined the church became leaders in both the Cheyenne and Mennonite communities. John Peak Hart was a Christian and a peace chief, and his son Homer Hart joined the Mennonite church. Homer's son Lawrence Hart became a Mennonite minister and Cheyenne peace chief, combining the traditions of his father and grandfather.[10] Julia Yellow Horse Shoulderblade was a Northern Cheyenne member who also bridged the two traditions. She and her husband James were among the first Cheyenne Mennonites in Montana to sing Cheyenne spirituals, which combine Cheyenne tunes with lyrics written by Cheyenne Christians. In 1982, these songs were published in the hymnbook *Tsese-Ma'heone-Nemeotȯtse (Cheyenne Spiritual Songs)*.[11] Shoulderblade and the Harts demonstrated ways for the Anabaptist message to be sung in new tongues. However, just as in China, India, or Indonesia, when Anabaptists spread the gospel, they had to discern how much of their message was cultural and how much it could be acculturated into a new context.

Fig. 8.5 Eugene Standing Elk (*left*) and Thomas Horseroads, Northern Cheyenne delegates to the General Conference Mennonite Church session in Freeman, South Dakota. 1923 General Conference Mennonite Church meeting. Photo courtesy of Mennonite Library and Archives, Bethel College, North Newton, Kansas, 2014-0617m.

Fig. 8.6 Lawrence Hart, He'amavehonesvestse (Sky Chief), Cheyenne peace chief and Mennonite pastor. Pastor Lawrence Hart, 19--. Photo reprinted by permission of Mennonite Heritage Archives, Winnipeg, 492-222.0.

Shifting Mennonite identity

The interest in spreading the gospel outside traditional Anabaptist communities exposed fissures within the churches and created new areas of disagreement. Conservative groups worried about potential changes that the missions might introduce to the church. Most Old Order groups remained skeptical of the need for missions, preferring to witness by remaining separate from the world. However, mission efforts also energized the spiritual lives of many members and prepared them to meet the challenges of greater engagement with the surrounding world during the twentieth century.

While missionaries were taking the gospel message to new contexts, the American leader Daniel Kauffman spearheaded one effort to halt the creeping influence of modern theology and culture in the church by drawing up a list of clearly defined teachings and practices to reassert a clearer separation between the church and surrounding culture. Beginning with his book *Manual of Bible Doctrines* (1898), Kauffman edited and wrote several texts that listed doctrinal fundamentals that shared much of the theological outlook of the time, as well as several ordinances particular to the Anabaptist-Mennonite faith, including nonconformity in dress, nonresistance, prayer coverings for women, and footwashing. He also rejected the oath, birthday celebrations, modern fashion, and membership in secret societies. Kauffman's arguments, while popular among many in the (Old) Mennonite Church, made it difficult for missionaries to adapt the gospel when traveling in a new land.

Missionaries tried to acclimate Christianity to new cultures without moving too far from the traditions of the organizations that sponsored them. For example, Kauffman and many others considered women's prayer covering to be an ordinance, which put it in the same fundamental category as baptism and communion. In India, one proposal was to allow women who converted to wear local coverings rather than traditional Mennonite devotional coverings. Footwashing also easily translated in the Indian context because Indians also understood the theology behind humbling oneself to wash another's feet.

Many missionaries were theologically progressive and already critical of the cultural elements of Mennonite practice, which they readily discarded in the host countries. Some adaptations appeared to

Fig. 8.7 Daniel Kauffman at his typewriter, ca. 1913. Photo reprinted by permission of Mennonite Church USA Archives, Elkhart, Indiana, Charles L. Shank Family Papers, HM1-638.

move too far. In China, General Conference missionary Edmund G. Kaufman performed marriages that integrated traditional Chinese elements, and when other missionaries criticized him, he handed control of the church to local leaders. When missionaries returned home, they began to question what was essential and what was "cultural baggage" in traditional Anabaptist practices. This led to conflict with traditional Mennonites who saw the practices as clear markers over and against the surrounding culture.

When Mennonites went overseas or moved to urban neighborhoods, their holistic message usually combined care of physical needs with the gospel message. Sometimes they downplayed traditional teachings, like the peace position, along with Mennonite dress distinctives such as plain coats and prayer coverings. In the mission field, there was also an effort to downplay the differences between Christian denominations and to emphasize Christian unity. As a result, while North American Mennonites emphasized modest clothing and prayer coverings as markers of faithfulness at home, the central message from Mennonites overseas was often no different from that of other Protestant missionaries.

At the same time, there were other areas where North American or European Mennonite missionaries linked the gospel message closely

Fig. 8.8 Early relief workers Vesta Zook (*left*; later Slagel) and Vinora Weaver (later Saltzman) traveled to Constantinople to work for MCC in providing relief to southern Russia refugees.
Photo reprinted by permission of Mennonite Church USA Archives, Elkhart, Indiana, Vesta Zook Slagel Papers, 1921–1982, Photographs, 1921–1922, HM1-403, box 2, folder 5.

with Western culture. Early Mennonite and Brethren in Christ missionaries in Africa prohibited local converts from dancing, singing traditional songs, and playing African instruments like drums. Instead, they taught hymns translated from English and German, creating the impression that correct worship had to be done in the European or North American fashion. These cultural assumptions were laced with racial prejudices of white Euro-American cultural superiority.

While overseas or in cities, missionaries were exposed to ideas and organizations that led to changes back home. For example, missionary women often had more freedom abroad than in their home congregations. In 1921, while sailing to join relief workers in Turkey, Vinora Weaver and Vesta Zook tossed their bonnets into the Atlantic Ocean once they were sure that they would no longer have to report to conservative superiors in North America. The act was representative of the increased opportunities for women like Zook, who went to college and then served in mission or relief efforts at home or abroad.

Looking forward: Missions in a new lens

Over the course of the twentieth century, Anabaptist churches fundamentally transformed; the typical Anabaptist is now no longer a rural and white European. The missionaries' work in the cities and internationally reflects a pattern that would be typical in many different contexts. In the Congo, just as in Indonesia, China, and India, the success of church plants relied on local Congolese spreading the good news to their own people. By the twenty-first century, the Mennonite missionaries' work transformed Anabaptism by opening its cultural and theological boundaries to new influences and expanding it into a global movement. The pace of the transformative process that began in the late nineteenth century would significantly quicken after World War II, when Anabaptists across the globe had to adapt to a dramatically altered world.

As contemporary Anabaptists celebrate their movement's growth into new countries and communities, some North American and European Mennonites have also reexamined the assumptions or preconditions that once inspired them to engage the world as a mission field or potential new settlement. They recognize that when they first came to North and South America, Mennonites were often parts of government efforts to subdue Indigenous groups via white Euro-American immigrants. In seeking to avoid inflicting violence on others in Europe, Mennonite migrants to the Americas benefited from the violent subjugation of Indigenous peoples. Beyond North America, missionaries were often invited to set up churches by colonial governments who desired to control local populations. Especially in Canada, contemporary Mennonites have focused on building mutual relationships with Indigenous neighbors. This has ranged from territorial acknowledgments at public events, reshaping the narrative of their settlement's impact on Indigenous peoples, and reassessing their participation in the residential school system that took children from their communities and caused long-term harm.[12] The challenge in the twenty-first century is for Anabaptists to build relationships with one another across the globe while simultaneously remembering the history of migration and mission with eyes open to the power behind the theology and politics that facilitated it.

— NINE —

Age of Cataclysm

1914–45

"What monstrous events have occurred between the time I last wrote and now. The Czar has been dethroned! Russia has become a Republic! We here in the South have only heard the echo of the storm. In the North, however, it has raged like a hurricane. How it shall end God only knows."[1] Written in the middle of the First World War on the eve of the Russian Revolution, this entry from the diary of Mennonite villager Anna Baerg, dated March 11, 1917, notes the young woman's feelings as her country stood balanced on the precipice of change. It is unlikely that the twenty-year-old daughter of a farmhand, let alone many others, could have guessed that within several years, the area where Mennonites had established their colonies in Ukraine would be engulfed in the chaos and catastrophe of civil war and anarchy. Anna Baerg and her family would flee Russia for Canada, leaving behind the shattered ideals and bittersweet memories of a Mennonite commonwealth.

The wars and revolutions of the early twentieth century fundamentally transformed Anna Baerg's world, as they did for thousands of other Mennonites. The era between the outbreak of the First World War in 1914 and the end of the Second World War in 1945 was a transformative period for many Anabaptists as they faced intense challenges to their theological convictions and relationship to their nations and communities. The wars introduced destructive military innovations, totalitarian forms of government, and some of the largest movements of peoples in history. Some Mennonites would be uprooted, others would support repressive regimes, and others would become victims of totalitarian forces. By the end of this era, Anabaptist churches in Asia and Africa had begun to work toward separating from the churches that had planted them. Even Anabaptist communities that did not directly experience the brutality of modern warfare reevaluated their relationship with the surrounding society and governments that increasingly expected everyone to contribute to and support their nations' wars.

World War I

In early August 1914, patriotic festivities for the declarations of war broke out on the streets of Europe. Enlisted men celebrated their mobilization for battle, and nearly everyone expected a short conflict lasting only a few months; governments confidently predicted a decisive victory for their country's military. However, instead of a short war, the conflict dragged on for four years, and the devastation of modern warfare produced death and destruction unlike anything that Europeans had experienced for several generations. The First World War witnessed the advent of modern weapons, mass conscription, and governments' increased control and surveillance of their subjects' lives. By its end, the conflict had destroyed an entire generation of men, toppled empires, and shook many people's confidence in the benevolent hand of science and reason. This war was the first of several cataclysmic events that reshaped Mennonite life in the twentieth century.

Mennonites in wartime Germany

Western European Mennonites shared a common wartime experience with their neighbors. As they integrated into modern, industrialized, democratic society, German, Dutch, and French Mennonites no longer held the doctrine of nonresistance on the eve of hostilities. Churches had occasionally reminded their members of traditional Anabaptist teachings on nonresistance, but the decision whether to serve in the military became a matter of individual choice. German Mennonites maintained the distinctive practices of adult baptism, separation between church and state, and refusal of the oath, but they embraced many other aspects of German identity.

In the German Empire, legal provisions allowed for Mennonites to serve a noncombatant role, such as medic. But of the two thousand German Mennonites who served in the military during the First World War, over two-thirds chose to serve as part of the regular military. As with other German churches, Mennonite periodicals carried obituaries of men who died. By the end of the war, four hundred Mennonite soldiers, or four percent of all German Mennonite men, had died. When the provisions of the Treaty of Versailles (1919) redrew the borders of the new German state, congregations in Alsace, Danzig, and parts of West Prussia found themselves living in new countries. Like many other Germans, Mennonites resented Germany's defeat and the terms of the peace conditions, but they did not reevaluate their participation in the war or its legitimacy.

Fig. 9.1 Published by South German Mennonites, *Christlicher Gemeinde-Kalendar* listed the death notices of German Mennonite soldiers. Scan courtesy of Milton Good Library, Conrad Grebel University College, Waterloo.

Russian Mennonites amid war and revolution

Before the First World War, Russian Mennonites had worked out an agreement with the tsar's government to allow their young men to perform an alternative service in lieu of the military obligations. After the government initiated universal conscription in the 1870s, the migration to North America had convinced the Russian authorities to find a way to accommodate the Mennonites, whose cultural and social contributions were vital to the agricultural life of Ukraine. The government had initially proposed that conscripted men serve in the army medical corps, but the Mennonites felt that this would contribute to the military efforts. Instead, they devised a plan by which Mennonite men could serve in the forestry corps, which were funded and run by the Mennonite communities.

When the war broke out, Mennonites in the Russian Empire quickly declared their allegiance to the tsar and the fatherland by opening their hospitals to the wounded soldiers and sending money, food, and clothing to aid those in their care. To create an additional alternative to the traditional forestry service work, Mennonite leaders reached an agreement with the government for Mennonite men to serve in the medical service. Publisher David H. Epp, in an editorial in the *Botschafter*

Fig. 9.2 A group of Alternative Service men in Russia. Photo courtesy of Elvera (Bergen) Goetz/Mennonite Archives of Ontario, Conrad Grebel University College, Waterloo, MAO M2004Goe 2 – Group of Alternative Service men, 1916.

newspaper, wrote, "Our confession forbids us as Mennonites to spill blood, but binding [up] wounds we hold to our sacred duty." He concluded his editorial by asking God "to intercede for our beloved monarch, for the greatness of his realm, and the strength of his armies."[2] Between 1914 and 1917, around seventy-five hundred Russian Mennonites served in the forestry service and around six thousand served in the medical services.

Despite demonstrations of their loyalty, Russian Mennonites soon encountered problems. Worried that their German origins suggested divided loyalties, Russian military leaders were reluctant to send Mennonites to the front lines. Increasing anti-German animosity led the government to ban German-language periodicals, forbid the public speaking of German, and demand that farms registered to Germans near the front be registered and prepared for liquidation. As the war dragged on, Mennonite communities struggled to pay the cost of maintaining the thousands of young men in the forestry or medical services and suffered under the economic constraints of a wartime economy.

When the tsar abdicated in 1917, many Mennonites, like many others in the country, welcomed the fall of the old regime as an opportunity to create a fundamentally new Russian society. No one would have had a sense of the brutal events that would devastate Ukraine and Russia over the following years as armies vied to seize control of the state or plunder the countryside. In March 1918, Mennonites, terrified by the breakdown of law and order, welcomed occupying German forces as liberators, greeting them with *Zwieback* and *Schinckenfleish*, traditional Mennonite foods. Under the Germans, churches were reopened, and community life briefly resumed in the Mennonite commonwealth, but the conditions of the treaties that ended war required German forces to retreat, leaving Mennonites vulnerable to neighbors who now viewed them as traitors.

Before they withdrew, German forces trained Mennonite self-defense units, known as the *Selbstschutz*. While most Mennonites maintained the ideal of nonresistance, they did not condemn those who took up arms to defend their families and communities. During the chaos of 1919, the *Selbstschutz* at the large Molotschna settlement fought against the troops of Nestor Makhno's feared anarchist forces. Makhno, who may have previously worked on a Mennonite farm, led a hundred thousand men under the banner of the black flag of anarchism. His forces plundered Mennonite homes and brutally murdered hundreds of men, women, and children. Malnourished and weakened by disease, Mennonites did not even have the strength to bury their dead. In the face of Makhno's anarchic terror, Mennonite men trained in the *Selbstschutz* defended their villages from marauders committing murder and rape.

After several successful *Selbstschutz* actions, the young Mennonite diarist Anna Baerg wondered about the mixed blessing of Mennonites defending themselves when centralized authority collapsed. She wrote,

> The skill and effectiveness of the *Selbstschutz* should not go to people's heads, however. We should thank God for our safety. I spoke of the great "evil;" and are not the war and conscription an evil? A necessary one, perhaps for the sake of survival, but an evil nonetheless, for it has brought with it so much sorrow already. That our pacifism has gone to shambles is only one of the consequences—and now there is no turning back.[3]

As they skirmished and plundered across southern Ukraine, the armies also spread typhus where they went, and many communities languished under the disease, which killed over 10 percent of the adult population. The *Selbstschutz* had also fought the Bolshevik Red Army, which further branded Mennonites as traitors in the eyes of the future Soviet state and alienated them from their neighbors. A Red Army general complained that the Mennonites refused to defend the country, but when it came time to defend their farms and families, they were ready to fight. By 1922, the Bolshevik army had gained control of Ukraine and Russia, and it became clear that the Mennonite commonwealth lay in ruins.

At the outbreak of World War I in 1914, thousands of Mennonite conscientious objectors had declared their commitment to both Russia and their nonresistant ideals by serving in the forestry and medical services. After eight years of war, revolution, disease, and anarchy, thousands of Mennonites looked to emigrate, whereas others began rebuilding their lives in the new Soviet state. The nineteenth-century model of self-governing Mennonite settlements became impossible in Soviet Ukraine and Russia, but it remained the faithful pattern by which to organize church and society for later Mennonite colonies in Latin America.

Age of Cataclysm 203

Fig. 9.3 A crowd at the departure of emigrants leaving Russia in 1923. When this wave arrived in Canada, they were known as *Russländer* (Russians) to differentiate them from the *Kanadier* (Canadians) who had arrived in the 1870s. Photo reprinted by permission of Mennonite Heritage Archives, Winnipeg, 665-116.0.

Fig. 9.4 The Johann Jakob Dyck family inside a freight car, 1923. The train car has been adapted for the long journey from Russia. Interior of immigration train, 1923. Photo reprinted by permission of Mennonite Heritage Archives, Winnipeg, 665-113.0.

Amidst Chaos and Suffering, the Search for Meaning

In his journal, teacher Dietrich Neufeld vividly described the suffering and chaos that Nestor Makhno's forces left in their wake: "We scarcely have strength enough to rejoice over the Anarchists' departure. Family heads are worried about the immediate future. It's time for the fall seeding, but the horse stalls are empty. Corpses are lying about on the streets and roads where the marauding bands of Makhno made their mad dashes. Why did it happen? What now? Those are the vexing questions to which there seem to be no valid answers."[4]

Responses to war in Canada and the United States

As nonresistant German-speaking pacifists, Anabaptists in North America were also under suspicion of treasonous loyalties. Although the war was fought in Europe, Canada declared war in 1914 and the United States, previously neutral, entered the war in 1917. The conflict had quickly grown into a "total war" in which all citizens, not just soldiers, were expected to contribute to the war effort. Governments used propaganda to stoke the fires of patriotic frenzy and encouraged their populations to financially support the war by purchasing war bonds or paying special taxes. Both the Canadian and US governments passed military service laws in 1917, and Mennonites and Amish now had to define their place in countries at war.

Churches taught the peace position as a matter of tradition, but some congregations emphasized it more than others did. After the First World War, C. L. Graber recalled, "I was taught nonresistance at home, in Sunday school, in church all my life and it never entered my mind to do anything else except to refuse military service." However, Wilmer Shelly, from eastern Pennsylvania, remembered, "When World War I came, up until that time in my home church I had never heard anything about conscientious objectors [or] of the Mennonite position on war. I had never received any instruction or mention of a conscientious objector."[5] Overall, Mennonites and Amish in North America had continued to teach the peace position, even if their commitment to the principle in a time of war had not been tested for several generations.

When the war broke out, Mennonite and Amish responses varied according to their particular stream and when they had immigrated to North America. Mennonites whose families had emigrated from Russia in the 1870s still had close familial and linguistic ties with Germany. They were concerned about the war's impact on European Christians and were more likely to express pro-German sentiments. The editor of the General Conference *Christlicher Bundesbote*, Carl H. A. van der Smissen, wrote that the war was "a punishment of God for the godlessness of man in so-called Christendom," but he also argued that Russia and France had forced Germany into the war.[6] Abraham Schellenberg, editor of *Vorwärts* out of Hillsboro, Kansas, lamented anti-German bias in most media and supported German war aims, including raising money for the German Red Cross, and this resulted in an official investigation of his paper.

Swiss-American Mennonites who had lived in North America for several generations, like Daniel Kauffman, editor of the (Old) Mennonite *Gospel Herald*, denounced the conflict more strongly. Kauffman wondered whether "in the midst of trial, persecution, insults, etc., we would manifest a meek, submissive spirit, suffering rather than to inflict suffering upon others, dying rather than to kill?"[7]

Mennonites and Amish in the United States had not had to struggle with the question of conscription since the Civil War, when they had avoided military obligations by paying fines or hiring substitutes to take their place. Canadian Mennonites had worked to secure exemptions from the government when they emigrated from Europe and the United States in the nineteenth century. Whereas Mennonites had previously been able to separate themselves from wartime spirit and activity, this new kind of total warfare compelled nonresistant churches to ask new questions. Some asked whether they could buy war bonds or work in a munitions factory. Could their conscripted men fill noncombatant roles in the military? If they served as noncombatants, would they wear military uniforms? Would they drill? Could they help build latrines or serve in the mess?

Canada enacted conscription in August 1917, followed soon thereafter by the Wartime Elections Act, which disenfranchised all conscientious objectors. To clarify the implications of these acts, Ontario Mennonites sent a delegation to Ottawa, and the Non-Resistant Relief Organization (NRRO) raised money to ease the war's suffering. An extraordinary collaboration between Old Order, General Conference, (Old) Mennonite, Amish Mennonite, and Brethren in Christ Churches, the NRRO intervened when tribunals refused to grant Mennonite men exemption from conscription. Ontario Mennonite women sewing circles also cooperated in the formation of the "Ontario District" to gather clothing and money for those suffering domestically and abroad. Although confusion about the implementation of Canada's conscription laws resulted in the imprisonment of some religious conscientious objectors, Canadian officials routinely granted indefinite leaves of absence for religious conscientious objectors.

As the United States moved from a neutral policy to a declaration of war, peace churches rushed to negotiate exemptions from conscription. Anabaptist groups drew different lines of noncooperation and sent separate delegations to Washington, making it difficult to speak to the government with a united voice. Ethnic and theological diversity also complicated the lobbying efforts. The General Conference Mennonites, Mennonite Brethren, and Krimmer Mennonite Brethren (who had withdrawn from the Kleine Gemeinde in 1869) told government representatives that they would be willing to work in agricultural service, the Red Cross, or even in noncombatant military service. (Old) Mennonite Church representatives rejected participation in any service under the authority of the government, whether combatant or noncombatant. Their leaders also threatened to excommunicate members who purchased war bonds or worked in munitions factories.

The original conscription legislation made no provisions for conscientious objectors, or COs. To make it difficult for COs, the War Department deliberately delayed a final decision on alternative service options and ordered conscripted men to report to camps, wear a uniform, and train like other recruits. Leaders like Secretary of War Newton D. Baker hoped that conscientious objectors would abandon their convictions after arriving in the camps. Without an alternative for conscientious objectors, it is likely that many men signed up in response to the patriotic fever gripping the country, or that they found it easier to join than endure the intense pressure to follow orders.

Once COs arrived at their camps, they tried to remain true to their nonresistant convictions. If they wore the uniform, drilled with other recruits, and obeyed orders, noncombatants were generally treated well. However, if they refused to cooperate by refusing to follow orders or wear the uniform, they suffered for their convictions. Other recruits "baptized" Mennonites with buckets of manure or dunked them in latrines. Some COs dug their own graves and were told that they were going to be buried alive. Jesse Hartzler, a Mennonite from Missouri, was kept on a bread and water diet, lashed with straps, and kept in solitary confinement.[8]

Perhaps the most harrowing story is that of the Hutterites David, Joseph, and Michael Hofer with their brother-in-law Jacob Wipf, all conscientious objectors. Officials at Alcatraz penitentiary and Fort Leavenworth beat the men with sticks, hanged them by their hands from the ceiling, forced them to stand all day, and kept them on a starvation diet. After continual deprivation, malnutrition, and abuse, Joseph and Michael Hofer died. When their bodies were returned home, their families discovered that they had been dressed in the uniforms that the men had refused to wear.[9] The hostility toward conscientious objectors in the United States was so alienating that nearly all the Hutterite colonies moved to Canada soon after the war.

The realities of the country's crusading spirit and the hostility that Anabaptists faced from other Americans caught Anabaptists unprepared. The Espionage Act of 1917 and Sedition Act of 1918 reduced the freedom of expression of all Americans, so when the Amish Mennonite newspaper *The Budget* printed a letter in 1918 that discouraged readers from buying Liberty bonds, a grand jury charged the editor, Samuel H. Miller, with attempting "to cause or incite insubordination, disloyalty, mutiny and refusal of duty in the military and naval forces of the United States."[10]

Eager to wage war at home and abroad, vigilantes tried to force Anabaptists to buy war bonds or fly the flag as a demonstration of their loyalty. Mennonite Churches in Inola, Oklahoma, and Fairview, Michigan, were burned to the ground; other buildings were painted yellow, a color associated with cowardice. A mob in Kokomo, Indiana, painted the minister yellow and shaved his head.

Mennonites came under intense pressure to contribute to the Red Cross to demonstrate their loyalty. Some conservative groups felt that the Red Cross was too tightly integrated into the war effort. When Jacob Stehman, a Mennonite from Missouri, refused to give to the Red Cross, a mob of fifty men tarred and feathered him. Other Mennonites donated or worked with the Red Cross, as did those in Russia. Silas Grubb, editor of *The Mennonite*, argued that contributing to the Red Cross was a way to combat evil by supporting the good. He wrote, "We only show ourselves loyal citizens if in this time of suffering we are ready to contribute something that will bear favorable comparison to the sufferings and sacrifices made by those who serve under the colors."[11] Many Anabaptists, like Stehman, sought to justify their citizenship while also maintaining a distinct identity.

Consequences of war

After the war, North American Mennonites grew less confident in the benefits of greater assimilation into the surrounding culture even as they engaged with it more vigorously. The backlash during the war confirmed the separatist convictions of conservative groups, like the Old Order Amish and the Old Order Mennonites, and reaffirmed their desire to clarify the lines with the world. Despite the realization that maintaining their traditional convictions could entail greater sacrifice in the future, Anabaptists grew resolute in their strengthening of Mennonite identity. W. S. Gottshall, the pastor of a General Conference congregation in Bluffton, Ohio, wrote, "There must be a more distinct separation of our people from the world and politics if we want to be recognized as different from others and stand familiar on our peculiar Mennonite Principles."[12]

At the same time, the war had lowered many barriers between North American Mennonites and the wider world. To demonstrate their place in America, Mennonites in Kansas, Nebraska, and South Dakota stopped using German, previously a key part of their Mennonite identity. When they returned from the military camps, conscripted men brought back new ideas and goals that they had picked up while they were away from traditional church authorities. While working to secure exemptions from conscription, Mennonite leaders had learned how to navigate the corridors of governmental power. They also learned the benefits of cooperating with other like-minded peace churches, such as the Quakers, as well as other Anabaptist groups when lobbying for conscientious objector provisions.

Efforts toward inter-Mennonite cooperation continued to develop with the Mennonite response to a severe famine that struck Ukraine. In 1921–23, the policies of the Soviet government exacerbated severe drought conditions. The Molotschna colony sent three leaders to Europe and North America to request assistance and secure help with immigration. When the Soviet Mennonites grew frustrated dealing with multiple Mennonite organizations, a special meeting of existing Mennonite charitable and relief organizations gathered in Elkhart, Indiana, to centralize their efforts to send aid to Ukraine. The newly formed Mennonite Central Committee sent aid workers Arthur Slagel, Clayton Kratz, and Orie Miller to Europe in 1921, but the relief did not arrive there until 1922. MCC, along with Dutch Mennonite relief organizations, sent aid and workers to Mennonites in Ukraine and Russia to alleviate their suffering. In the Soviet Union, Mennonites also formed committees to negotiate with authorities in Moscow to secure emigration rights for Mennonites in Ukraine and across the Soviet Union. Between 1923 and 1929, 22,000 Mennonites immigrated to Canada. In 1929, another 1,000 were allowed to immigrate to Brazil, and 2,000 left for Paraguay.

The Canadian government stopped all Mennonite immigration after World War I, partially in response to the Mennonites' refusal to participate in the war effort. In 1922, after several years of negotiation, the government finally allowed Mennonites to immigrate again. Over the next eight years, approximately 21,000 Mennonites migrated from Russia to Canada. Known as the *Russländer*, this group tended to be more educated and urbanized than the earlier Russian Mennonite settlers, the *Kanadier*, though they settled in farms in Ontario, Manitoba, and British Columbia. The Russländer would become one of the largest Anabaptist groups in Canada, establishing numerous schools, colleges, and newspapers.

As the Russländer were arriving in Canada, 7,000 Russian Mennonites from the 1870s immigration were preparing to leave Canada for either Mexico or Paraguay. During the war, the governments of Manitoba and Saskatchewan had implemented standardized schooling that required English language curriculum and raising the

Fig. 9.5 The Red Gate at the border between Finland and the Soviet Union. Anna Baerg and her family left the Soviet Union on June 29, 1924. In her diary, she recorded, "Ahead we can already see the red and white Latvian flag waving. And admittedly, as we leave our old homeland, a feeling of relief goes through my whole being as if a heavy load is lifted from me." (*Diary of Anna Baerg*, 1916–1924, 137). Photo reprinted with permission from Mennonite Heritage Archives, Winnipeg, CA MHC PP-8 – Photo Col. 500-516.0.

national flag; they also trained teachers in order to improve schools and instill greater national identity. Believing that this violated the terms of the religious autonomy they had received when they first immigrated to Canada, half of the Old Colony Mennonites—named for their origins in the colony of Chortitza in Russia—accepted the Mexican president's invitation to settle in the states of Durango and Chihuahua. The Mexican *privilegium* granted them "complete freedom to practice your religious principles and to live according to the rules of your church without being molested or in any way restricted," including freedom from military service, swearing oaths, and interference in their schooling.[13] For the Old Colony Mennonites, Mexico was an opportunity to stop the march toward assimilation and live out their religious convictions free from outside interference.

In the Soviet Union, officials had begun forcing Ukrainian agriculturalists onto collectivized farms. They identified landowners, including many Mennonites, as *kulaks*, or wealthy peasants who resisted reform. In 1929, a campaign forced dekulakization of villages, in which enemies of the new Soviet order were deported or executed. To avoid dekulakization, Mennonites and other farmers voluntarily gave up their land and livestock. Others burned their crops and killed their cattle as an act of resistance. Mennonite communities also lost their spiritual leadership in the arrests and deportations. Of the seventy-two clergy members in the Molotschna colony, for example, only ten preachers remained in 1932; the rest had been exiled or killed. To feed the Red Army and the urban populations, Soviet authorities increasingly demanded greater yields and confiscated crops from farmers, leading to the famine of 1932–33, which caused the deaths of six to seven million people. It is not known how many Mennonites were affected by dekulakization and the famine, but scholars have concluded that Mennonites suffered both because of their religion and because of their wealth.

In addition to collectivization, dekulakization, and famine, Mennonite communities in the Soviet Union suffered during the period known as the Great Terror, when Stalin ordered the purges of "undesirable populations." The plight of Soviet German communities during the famine sparked sympathetic interest in Germany, where campaigns raised money for German communities in the Union of Soviet Socialist Republics, or USSR. Stalin and other Soviet leaders became suspicious that the charity was evidence that German populations had divided loyalties. Like other Soviet Germans, Mennonite men were taken away, often in the middle of the night, to be interrogated, tortured, exiled, or executed. Stalin's purges of millions of suspected enemies left the agricultural population with a gender imbalance, with women outnumbering men two to one. There is some evidence that half of all Mennonite families were without male heads of households by 1938. To overcome this hardship, women collaborated and supported each other—for example, by combining households in the winter to preserve heat. To make sense of such sufferings, the communities held on to the conviction that they were living in the end times, and that God would overcome the authority of the Soviet state.

Postwar Cooperation and Conflict

Determined that another war would not take them unaware again, North American leaders took steps to set up a future alternative service program and buttress the nonresistant position among their members. In the United States, Mennonite church leaders worked with the Church of the Brethren and Quaker churches, now collectively known as "peace churches," to lobby for an official alternative service. They pushed for a more flexible program to allow conscientious objectors to perform work of national importance under direction of civilians instead of being inducted into the military, as had been the case in World War I. Eventually, these efforts bore fruit with the passage of the Selective Service and Training Act of 1940. The end proposal bore many similarities to the forestry and medical alternatives available to Russian Mennonites during World War I.

As leaders endeavored to strengthen the teaching of the nonresistance position in congregations and colleges, it grew increasingly clear that Anabaptists held a spectrum of positions on the teaching and its implications. The American Henry J. Krehbiel, chair of the General Conference board of publication, called for the abolition of all war, whereas other Anabaptists held that wars would continue until the end of time. Remembering how quickly other pacifists had compromised their convictions in the Great War, Mennonites were wary of working too closely with outside peace movements. The Lancaster Mennonite bishop John H. Mosemann Sr. believed that the peace movement was a "satanic delusion" that would only smooth the slippery slope to modernism and liberalism. George R. Brunk, an influential conservative leader from Virginia, warned against popular social movements that attempted to change the world without Christian conversion. Despite some different emphases, most Anabaptists affirmed a nonresistant stance while rejecting pacifism, which they considered coercive and unbiblical.[14]

Anabaptist cooperation also bent under the pressure of the rancorous debate between liberals and modernists roiling the broader Protestant world. While the Mennonite groups were also raising questions about the resurrection, virgin birth, and biblical inerrancy, Mennonite conservatives added into the conversation the traditional Mennonite positions on nonconformity, which they also held to be fundamentals required

Fig. 9.6 Seen as the source of modernist influence, Goshen College closed between 1923 and 1924 for reorganization, and many of its faculty left for Bluffton College. This cartoon from the *Sword and Trumpet* portrays Mennonite educational institutions as the mill that turns out debauched alumni, and into which parents blindly throw their money and children. Ink drawing, "The Patrons, Proprietors, and Products of the Mill," *Sword and Trumpet*, April 1930, 19.

for salvation. Mennonite fundamentalists charged Bluffton College and Goshen College with promoting modernist ideas among their students. While there were very few true modernists among Mennonites, some supported the Social Gospel movement and critical approaches to the Bible. Conservatives like Daniel Kauffman, editor of the (Old) Mennonite Church periodical *Gospel Herald*, hammered against colleges and suspected modernists in editorials. A group of Virginia (Old) Mennonites founded the *Sword and Trumpet* in January 1929 to resist modernism. Its masthead claimed that it was "Devoted to the Defense of a Full Gospel, With Especial Emphasis upon Neglected Truths, and to an Active Opposition of the Various Forms of Error that Contribute to the Religious Drift of the Times." Mennonites drew deeply from fundamentalist polemics to preserve traditional Mennonite teachings. The vitriolic disputes totally bypassed the Old Order Anabaptist groups, who continued to maintain their traditions.

Renewal through history

To bypass the bitter doctrinal debates between fundamentalists and liberals, North American scholars looked for alternate ways to define Mennonite identity. Historians, trained in the leading European and American universities, turned to the Anabaptist story instead of Scripture or doctrine to find the essence of the church. As early as 1885, Cornelius H. Wedel described a pattern of *Gemeindechristentum* (congregation Christendom) marking Anabaptist and Mennonite traditions. Wedel's emphasis of congregational autotomy and doctrinal freedom reflected the General Conference tradition in Kansas at that time. The Mennonite history of another theologically progressive historian, C. Henry Smith, emphasized individual autonomy, education, and progress in a way that intertwined Anabaptist history with the mythology of the United States. Smith's and Wedel's versions of Mennonite history and essentials were especially popular among General Conference Mennonites.

In 1943, Harold S. Bender delivered a talk titled "The Anabaptist Vision" as his presidential address to a gathering of the American Society of Church History. Bender defined the essence of Anabaptism as a commitment to discipleship, a voluntary church separated from the world, and the application of love and nonresistance to all human relationships.[15] The Anabaptists, he argued, carried the arguments of Luther and Zwingli to their conclusion and were the culmination of the Reformation. Bender's vision of Anabaptist essentials, which he later published, inspired a generation of Mennonite church leaders and teachers. The emphasis on lay leadership, mutual aid, nonresistance, discipleship, and biblical study set out by "The Anabaptist Vision" informed a new generation as they increasingly rubbed shoulders with the rest of the world, going forth convinced that their tradition represented Christianity at its purest. Despite eventual scholarly criticisms of Bender's history for rejecting Anabaptists he found objectionable, like the Münsterites, his synthesis of Anabaptist ideas continues to inspire many readers from within and outside of the Anabaptist tradition.[16]

Growing global bonds

A growing interest in Anabaptist history deepened the sense of a shared identity among Mennonites across Europe and North America. This common Mennonite or Anabaptist identity could be found in the *Martyrs Mirror*, which included stories from across Europe and had encouraged the Dutch Doopsgezinden to advocate for Anabaptists across Europe. In the 1870s, Swiss Mennonites in North America had helped with the immigration of Russian Mennonites to the prairies of Canada and North America. Then, in the 1920s postwar period, Christian Neff, pastor of the Mennonite congregation in Weierhof, Germany, called for a new, international gathering of Mennonites. Held in 1925, the conference marked the four hundredth anniversary of the first Anabaptists in Switzerland in 1525. In 1930, a second conference in Danzig, Germany, focused on the need to coordinate the relief efforts on behalf of Soviet Mennonites. The 1936 gathering in the Netherlands commemorated the four hundredth anniversary of Menno Simons's conversion from Catholicism in 1536. The themes for the three conferences helped in the promotion of a Mennonite World Conference at a time when many North American Mennonites remained hesitant or indifferent about its value. Over the decades, MWC would expand to include the Brethren in Christ and Anabaptist groups from across the globe. While the Old Orders and some conservative groups have never joined MWC, today it represents churches from across the globe who trace their theological roots in the sixteenth-century radical reformation groups.

World War II

German Mennonites and the Third Reich

After World War I, Mennonites in Germany, like many other Germans, felt humiliated by the country's defeat, and they distrusted the new democratic government to fix the economic collapse (1929–32) and stand up to a threat from the Soviet Union. The terms of the peace treaties directly affected areas where Mennonites lived: Prussia was cut off from the rest of Germany, and France gained control of the Alsace. Mennonites, like many Germans, welcomed Hitler's rise to power in 1933 and his promises to restore order and resist Communism.

Over the next twelve years, Mennonites seldom expressed opposition to National Socialist ideology. Although some German Mennonite leaders had reemphasized Mennonite history and the peace tradition after World War I, most understood their political leaders to be acting as God's instrument on earth. As Emil Händiges, the editor of the journal *Mennonitische Blätter*, wrote, "Honouring the temporal authorities and the social order in accordance with the apostolic witness, we hold it to be the duty of Christians to serve our nation and state conscientiously."[17] There appears to have been more support for secular authorities among Prussian Mennonites then among southern German Mennonites. In general, Mennonite congregations and individuals supported Nazi (National Socialist) Party goals to return the country to stability, rebuild the economy, separate church and state, and restore national honor. The racial and nationalist policies also appealed to Mennonites in Germany, Paraguay, and Canada who saw themselves as part of a global Germanic people. For example, the Canadian Mennonite newspaper *Der Bote*'s coverage of ethnic nationalistic concepts of Germanism was overwhelmingly favorable between 1930 and 1939.[18] For many, Hitler's promise to fight Communism also resounded deeply with Mennonites who had been following the stories of Mennonites suffering in the Soviet Union. When the Nazi Party reintroduced military conscription in 1935, Mennonites did not object. After war broke out in 1939, some Mennonite men joined the medical corps instead of the military, but they generally obeyed their conscription orders.

After the war, German Mennonites reassessed their wartime experiences. At the 1948 Mennonite World Conference in Goshen, Indiana,

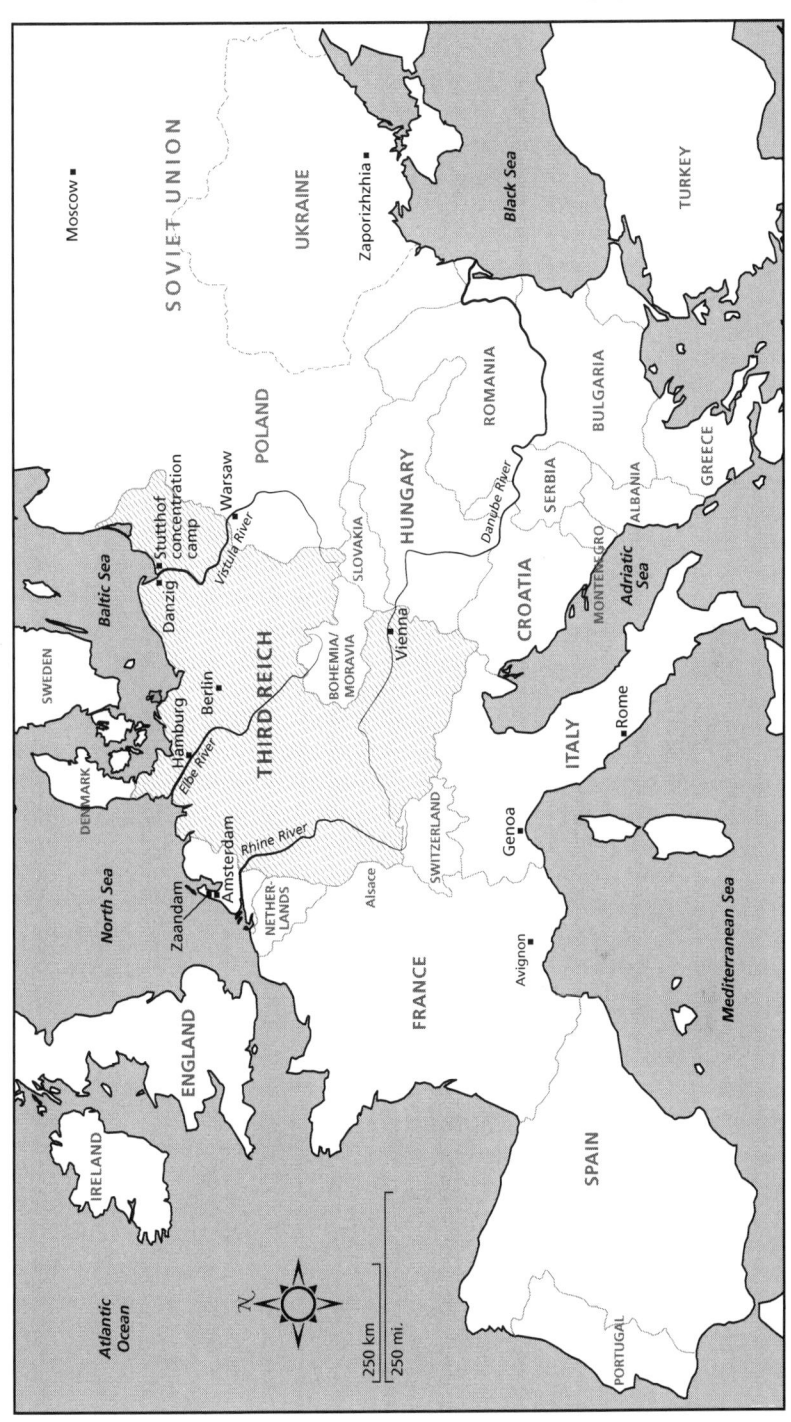

German pastor Dirk Cattepoel asked for forgiveness, especially from the Dutch and French members. "As a Christian from Germany," he said, "I would confess with all my heart how deeply it burdens us that so much distress, so much cruelty, and so much destruction has come over others through men of our nation."[19] When marking fifty years since the end of the war, one German conference confessed for when they had "valued their commitment to the state higher than their duties to Mennonite brothers and sisters in the Netherlands and France. . . . Nearly all Mennonites remained silent in the face of Nazi crimes against Jews and others. . . . We can only plead for forgiveness with the words of the Lord's Prayer."[20] More recently, historians and German Mennonites have acknowledged that German Mennonites benefited from Nazi racial policies and that some actively participated in carrying out the regime's atrocities.

The Stutthof concentration camp—located near Danzig, an area which had the highest density of Mennonites in the world—inflicted starvation, mistreatment, and random violence against its prisoners. Although it is difficult for historians to judge whether guards with common Mennonite last names were Mennonite by ethnic association or by religious upbringing, Mennonite factories and farms in the area used concentration camp prisoners—Soviet prisoners of war, political prisoners, and nearly fifty thousand Jews—as essentially slave labor. For example, in his machine factory, Gerhard Epp relied on the forced labor of five hundred Stutthof prisoners from 1942 until the end of the war. There is also considerable evidence that soldiers with Mennonite backgrounds were involved in the killing of Jews, including serving in the notorious *Einsatzgruppen* and working as camp guards in extermination camps.

Mennonites under occupation

There was no singular, shared Anabaptist experience of World War II. National loyalties or ethnic identity shaped Anabaptists' wartime experiences more than religious convictions. While German Mennonites considered the National Socialist government to be God's ordained authority to whom they pledged their loyalty, Mennonites in the Netherlands resisted German occupiers out of their sense of loyalty to their country and compassion for Jewish neighbors. Anabaptists in China, the Netherlands, France, Indonesia, and the Soviet Union experienced World War II under occupation by Japanese or German forces. The turmoil of the war and upheaval of the postwar settlements strengthened the independence of some churches and led to the dissolution of others.

Mennonites in the Netherlands

Before the outbreak of war in Europe, some Dutch leaders, like pastor Frits Kuiper, had warned about the dangers of National Socialism. Others, like Cornelis Bonnes Hylkema, strongly supported the domestic Dutch Fascist party, the Nationaal-Socialistische Beweging (NSB). Initially, many Dutch looked to Hitler as Europe's best defense against the Soviet Union. However, when German troops occupied the Netherlands in 1940, attitudes toward Germany quickly changed as the Dutch adapted to life under occupation. German or Allied bombing destroyed Doopsgezind church buildings in Rotterdam, Vlissingen, and Nijmegen and damaged many others. Pastors, whose training left them unprepared for wartime ministry, worried about spies or collaborators in their congregations who might report them for delivering critical sermons.

Many Dutch Mennonites resisted German efforts toward the Nazification of their country and the implementation of anti-Jewish laws. Mennonite leaders protested so-called occupation measures such as the dismissal of Jewish civil servants from their jobs. Some members actively undermined German efforts to transport Dutch Jews out of the country. For example, Geertje Pel-de Groot of Zaandam hid a Jewish baby, Marion Swaab; after a neighbor betrayed her, Pel-de Groot was killed in Ravensbrück in February 1945. Minette "Mies" Boissevain-van Lennep, a member of the Amsterdam congregation, was also arrested for saving many Jewish children. She survived the war, but her husband died in a concentration camp, and her two sons were executed in 1943.

The experience of occupation threw Dutch Mennonites into new moral quandaries. Pastors took care to temper their criticisms of the Germans for fear of informers sitting in the pews. Before the war, most Dutch Mennonites had not been opposed to serving in the military. Even some of those who had argued for nonresistance before the war felt that the occupation warranted the use of force. Mennonites helped members of the Dutch resistance free prisoners, print illegal newspapers, forge documents, commit sabotage, and rescue downed Allied pilots. Believing that they were living in an exceptional moment in history, the Dutch Mennonite peace group did not speak up or protest against the resistance.

Overall, Dutch Mennonites' experience of the war mirrored that of their non-Mennonite neighbors. The historian Gerlof Homan has suggested that Mennonites resisted the occupation and anti-Jewish policies to the same degree that their neighbors did. When they later reflected on why they hid Jewish families, Mennonites recalled that they did so out of a common sense of human decency, not out of religious or uniquely Mennonite convictions.

Anabaptists in Indonesia

The crisis of World War II in Europe provided the impetus for the autonomy of the Javanese churches in the Dutch East Indies. When Germany invaded the Netherlands, it severed communication between the Dutch mission board and their missionaries. Japan, allied with the Germans, became a potential enemy of the Dutch East Indies. Japan also desired Indonesia's rubber and oil resources. Under pressure from local congregations, European missionaries handed over leadership of the Javanese congregation to local leaders in 1941. In December of that year, Japanese forces began their invasion, and the collapse of the Dutch colonial government created a power vacuum.

As the Dutch authorities withdrew, gangs of Muslim youth began a campaign to force Christians to return to Islam. Many Indonesians considered Christians disloyal because of the churches' connection to European churches. Gangs attacked the homes and shops owned by Christians, especially Chinese descendants, who were targeted because of their ethnic difference and supposed wealth. Javanese Christians protected Chinese brothers and sisters, but the gangs eventually targeted Javanese groups. Youths captured and tortured leaders of congregations in Tayu, Samyandi, Oesada, Yosep, Soeyono, and Menadij. There were accounts of miraculous signs or interventions that protected believers. S. Djojodihardjo later recalled that when his father, a preacher in the town of Pati, was confronted by an angry crowd, "the people in the church saw a vision of a white-robed man with his arms stretched heavenward. They gained strength from the vision, and the angry crowd did not harm."²¹ After Japanese troops conquered the affected areas and restored order, the violence subsided. However, the flight of Chinese Christians from the Muria region was so significant that some congregations never recovered.

Mennonites in China
The war period had profound effects on the church in China. Some historians trace the outbreak of World War II to July 7, 1937, when Japan launched a total war against China. In 1931, Japan had seized China's northeastern province of Manchuria, renaming it Manchukuo. From its puppet state, Japan launched its full-scale invasion of China six years later. During the occupation of eastern China, it was difficult for foreign missionaries to continue their work. The Japanese authorities forced all Protestant Christians to unite under one umbrella organization and restricted missionaries' activities. After the defeat of Japan and a civil war, the Chinese Communist Party established the People's Republic of China in 1950. With the advent of the Cultural Revolution in 1965, all remnants of the churches were erased from the country. Some clandestine Christians remained Mennonite in their beliefs and practices, but Western mission boards lost all contact with Chinese Christians until 1978, after the Cultural Revolution had ended.

Mennonites in the Soviet Union
When Germans invaded the Soviet Union on June 22, 1941, Soviet officials—fearing that ethnic Germans would be sympathetic to the rapidly advancing German forces—issued an order to forcibly relocate them far from the front. Mennonite villagers, apart from women with children, were relocated to the north and Siberia, where they worked in mines and forests in harsh conditions. Rapidly advancing German forces overran the Crimea, Ukraine, and the Caucasus region before the Soviets had removed all the ethnic Germans in those regions.

The remaining villagers, whom the military administration classified as *Volksdeutsche*, or ethnic Germans, welcomed the invading military as liberators from the Soviets. Life for the *Volksdeutsche* improved significantly under the German occupation. Many Mennonites were especially grateful for the opportunity to hold religious services, revivals, and choir practices, and they hoped that their lives might return to normal. The military administration fostered German identity through schools and centers that promoted the idea that the Ukrainian *Volksdeutsche* maintained some of the purest forms of German culture. Many young Mennonite men served in the German army, and Mennonite women found work as interpreters for the German military and administration.

Mennonites, along with other Soviet Germans and Ukrainians, also participated directly in the Holocaust, including in "actions" in which Jewish men, women, and children were murdered. These murders happened outside of Mennonite villages, including a massacre in 1942 outside of Zaporizhzhia. Over the course of three days, German military forces, along with local police forces, murdered over thirty-seven hundred Jews and buried their bodies in a shallow grave. According to eyewitnesses, two Mennonite brothers, Ivan and Jacob Fast, worked as part of the police forces. There are also accounts of several Mennonite

Fig. 9.7 German soldiers raise the flag over the village of Halbstadt, Molotschna Mennonite settlement, as SS Reichsführer Heinrich Himmler observes [1942]. Flag raising ceremony in Halbstadt. Photo reprinted with permission of Mennonite Heritage Archives, Winnipeg, 351-15.0.

women working as translators for Einsatzgruppe murder squads and informing on potentially subversive forced laborers.[22]

The story of Soviet Germans under German occupation is complex. Some Mennonites supported the occupying forces because of their German identity, anti-Semitism, or hatred of the Soviet system. Others were shocked when they learned of the German treatment of their Jewish friends and neighbors whom they had lived alongside and suffered with during the years of Soviet dekulakization. Many Mennonites were also indifferent to what was going on around them as they focused on day-to-day survival. Many had already begun to identify more as Soviets than as Germans. Today, as new archival sources are opened in the former Soviet Union, historians are beginning the painstaking process of piecing together the story of Soviet Mennonites as perpetrators, benefactors, and victims of Nazi policies in Ukraine.

Amish and Mennonites in the United States and Canada

In the evening of January 4, 1943, several Mennonite families gathered at the train station in Galt, Ontario, to say goodbye to their sons. Noah Bearinger later recalled, "It was a cold winter evening and many parents had gathered to see their boys leave. They sang farewell songs as we were loaded and started moving into the dark."[23] Bearinger and the other young men were setting off for Montreal River Camp in Ontario, one of several camps where Canadian Mennonite men performed alternative service during World War II.

When the Second World War broke out, North American Mennonites wanted to do more than simply avoid military service, as they had tried to do during World War I. Mennonites hoped to negotiate a workable compromise with their governments that would allow them to maintain their nonresistant identity while contributing to society. Rather than withdrawing from the world, Mennonites increasingly understood nonresistance to mean that they carried a social responsibility to bear a positive witness of reconciliation to the world.

Canadian Mennonites who immigrated in the 1920s remembered the Russian forestry and medical corps that they had served in during World War I and indicated their willingness to work within similar Canadian programs. Mennonites from the earlier migration maintained that the conditions of their immigration in the 1870s excluded them entirely from the requirements of conscription acts. The government and representatives of peace churches eventually agreed on an alternative service program like the Russian model. In the Alternative Service Work (ASW) program, conscripted men could contribute to Canadian society by working in forestry camps provided by the state and funded by churches. Eventually, ASW expanded its options, allowing some of the 7,543 conscripted Mennonite men in the program to work in schools, hospitals, farms, and factories. Many other Mennonites and Amish had farm deferments and never had to decide what they would do if they were conscripted.

In the United States, most Amish and Mennonite men eligible for the draft received a deferment, usually for agricultural labor. Of the remaining conscripted Mennonites, 4,536 men (46 percent) served in the Civilian Public Service (CPS), a program for conscientious objectors like ASW in Canada. In the camps and units, the men performed a variety of public services, including logging, fighting fires in remote forests, and providing mental health care. These programs took the men away from their communities to new environments where they worked, ate, and slept among conscientious objectors from a variety of faith backgrounds.

While the men were away, women supported them with care packages and letters. Hundreds of wives and girlfriends moved near camps

Fig. 9.8 A busload of Alternative Service workers register at Green Timbers Forestry Station, Surrey, British Columbia. Photo courtesy of J. B. Martin/Mennonite Archives of Ontario, Conrad Grebel University College, Waterloo, 3.1.

to be near their partners, and many other married women managed farms and businesses and raised children without their husbands. With many men in CPS and ASW camps, student bodies at Mennonite colleges grew disproportionately female. A few women volunteered to serve as nurses in Europe, including areas under threat of German bombing or occupation.

Despite the possibility of alternative service, 4,500 Canadian and 5,200 US men with traditionally Mennonite names served in the military, either in the regular service or in noncombatant roles.[24] Because the numbers of enlistees are based on the last names of men who joined and not their religious affiliation, it is difficult to discern the prewar religious commitment of the enlistees. The numbers serving in the military were higher among more acculturated groups like the General Conference Mennonites or Brethren in Christ than among the more traditional, rural groups, like the Old Orders.

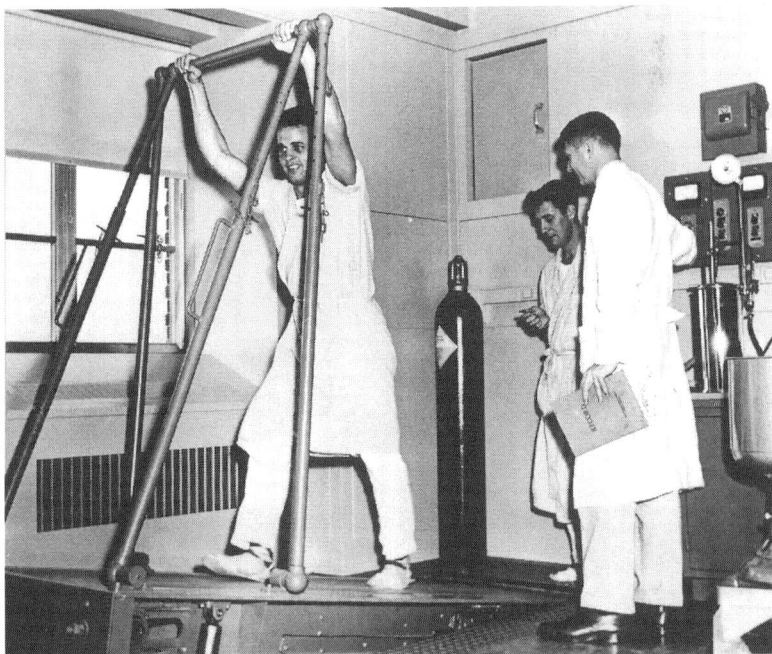

Fig. 9.9 Some conscientious objectors performed their alternative service as patients in experiments, like this man at the National Institutes of Health at Bethesda, Maryland, in 1958. Photo courtesy of *Canadian Mennonite/* Mennonite Archives of Ontario, Conrad Grebel University College, Waterloo, 2337.

In general, men who served did not join early or during the periods of greatest "war hysteria" in 1940 and 1941, which may indicate a reluctance to join the military. Sheldon Martin, for example, initially joined the ASW, but when his wife needed expensive medical treatment, Martin enlisted. Others joined because they believed in the cause or making a greater contribution to the national effort. Ontarian Gerhard "Gerry" Thiessen found the work at ASW camps to be menial and believed that too many Mennonites were interested in avoiding danger rather than being committed to nonresistance. In 1943, he joined the Canadian Air Force, where he served until the end of the war. It is unclear how many Anabaptists who served were active members of congregations before the war or whether their home churches excommunicated them upon their return.

A complex story

An honest account of Anabaptists' experiences in the first half of the twentieth century is difficult to encapsulate into a tidy narrative. During times of war and political upheaval, individuals and communities must make multiple ethical choices—both little and big—about how to make their way in a time when normal mores no longer seem to apply. While stories of faithful resistance to nationalist militarism continue to inspire Anabaptists a century later, it is tempting to pluck out and remove the threads that do not live up to current ideals. Between 1914 and 1945, many Anabaptists resisted nationalism, but others served in the military. A small number took part in the Holocaust, but a few hid Jewish children. In the twenty-first century, historians and church members continue to recover evidence and tell new narratives that both hold up steadfast faithfulness and confess grievous sins. Including the full range of Anabaptist responses to war tells a more truthful story that provides an opportunity to grapple with both human frailty and steadfastness.

There are also stories of meaningless suffering from this period, from which it is difficult to tell tales of either heroism or failure. Like many Christian groups, Anabaptists have treasured accounts of devout martyrs who remained true to their principles, even when it led to their imprisonment, exile, or death. However, it is more difficult to find meaning in the stories of the countless victims who were not

Fig. 9.10 A photograph of the Mennonite Eby family taken in September 1942. In April 1943, the oldest son, Gordon, joined the Canadian Air Force. Photo courtesy of Gordon C. Eby/Mennonite Archives of Ontario, Conrad Grebel University College, Waterloo, 137.

targeted for their faith but were nonetheless swept up in the horrors of war. Across the globe, Anabaptists continue to fall victim to the political and ethnic violence around them. In 2017, the indiscriminate killing in the Kasai region in the Democratic Republic of the Congo recalled the bloody chaos and violence faced by Russian Mennonites after the Russian Revolution. In the Kasai region—the birthplace of the Congolese Mennonite church—thousands of Mennonites were among the 1.5 million people displaced by the violence between government soldiers and militias in a conflict fueled by economic disparity and ethnic tension. In addition to struggling to feed their families, the displaced Congolese Mennonites lost loved ones in the violence. Adolphine Tshiama, the president of the women's group that is part of the Mennonite Church of the Congo, lost her brother and several of his family members. Even though it may be harder to make theological sense of such senseless violence, these accounts can be as important to tell as the stories of the sixteenth-century martyrs or those who were imprisoned or killed for refusing to serve in the military. As Anabaptists wrestle with these stories, they develop a broader understanding of suffering to give it purpose other than something to revere.

Many historians who write for the church try to paint a realistic portrait of the Anabaptist and Mennonite past that looks at more than the heroic age of the sixteenth century. But Anabaptists, inevitably shaped by the broader cultural forces, have not always lived up to the church's ideals. Stories of faithfulness and failure lead individuals and groups to reflect on their own fallibility and how nationalism, populism, and ethnic violence continue to be powerful temptations in the twenty-first century.

— TEN —

A Transformational Era

1945–present

In 2022, Mennonite World Conference and Mennonite Church Eastern Canada (MCEC) gathered for business and worship in Indonesia and Ontario, respectively. Gatherings such as these regularly bring Anabaptists together to network, vote, and worship, and they have become important moments for the Anabaptist institutions created during the twentieth century. These recent events—centered on community building and worship—illustrate some of the remarkable changes that have radically reshaped the Anabaptist movement's identity and expression after the end of the Second World War.

On April 29 and 30, moderators Arli Klassen and Diane Lichti led Mennonite Church Eastern Canada delegates in a hybrid annual gathering, where participants adopted a new identity statement and welcomed to full membership Meheret Evangelical Church, an Amharic ministry in Kitchener, Ontario, for people from Ethiopia and Eritrea. Gathered online and in person, delegates also welcomed six other congregations as provisional members: Centre Béthésda Mennonite de Québec, Burning Bush Forest Church, Église de Dieu Réparateur des Brèches, Église Mennonite Agape, Goshen Mennonite Church, and The Meeting Place. Worship was led by musicians from the Lao

Mennonite Fellowship of Canada, Grace Lao Mennonite Church, the Chin Christian Church choir, and the Markham Christian Worship Centre youth choir. In her address, MCEC executive minister Leah Reesor-Keller used the parable of the mustard seed to reflect on the gathering as a metaphor for the church: "This tiny seed is laden with unthinkable and unimaginable potential when the Spirit of God is at work unleashing the seed's power. The kingdom of God is always changing and growing in unexpected ways. We as the people of MCEC need to also be changing and growing, seeking God's surprising kingdom revealed to us in new ways as the world around us is constantly in flux."[1]

Later that year, Mennonite World Conference held its assembly in the city of Salatiga on the Indonesian island of Java. Anabaptists from forty-four countries gathered for several days in early July, and hundreds of others joined virtually at home or together in watch parties. The assembly concluded with a Sunday morning worship at Semarang in the twelve-thousand-person capacity Holy Stadium, the home of the Anabaptist congregation JKI Injil Kerajaan—one of the largest Christian congregations in Indonesia. The worship team from the eighteen-thousand-member JKI Jakarta Praise Community Church started the gathering with high-energy rock music, and worship services throughout the week reflected various music styles from around the world.

At the four well-attended sessions, speakers reflected on Anabaptist efforts to build peace and ease suffering in Europe, Asia, Latin America, and Africa. Hong Kong pastor Jeremiah Choi spoke on how the Chinese government's repression of demonstrations led to a 10 percent loss of members in his congregation, Agape Mennonite Church. In her talk, Ethiopian leader Tigist Tesfaye Gelagle encouraged those gathered to view one another as "significant" so that Anabaptists from around the world might worship together amid suffering and oppression. "Unless we are significant to each other, there is no celebration of togetherness," she said. "Seeing significance in others crosses barriers. I can forget my pain if I am significant to you."[2] Reflecting on European Mennonites' response to Russia's invasion of Ukraine in February 2022, Salomé Haldemann of France wondered whether Mennonites from areas that had seen war and suffering could help strengthen the peace position among European Mennonites. The next assembly was planned for 2028, to be hosted by the Meserete Kristos Church in Ethiopia—the largest Anabaptist denomination in the world, with 370,000 members.[3]

These two gatherings highlight the remarkable developments in the Anabaptist movement after World War II. Social, technological, and political transformations of the modern world have expanded the movement beyond the Swiss/German and Dutch/Russian ethnoreligious traditions that sustained and nourished Anabaptist identity and practice over the previous four centuries. In North America and Europe, Anabaptists now worship in dozens of languages. Most significant for its future direction, Anabaptism has transformed into a truly global movement of 2.13 million baptized believers in eighty-six countries. In 2022, Mennonite World Conference estimated that two-thirds of baptized Anabaptists were African, Asian, or Latin American.[4]

Women, whose activity and roles in the church had been significantly constrained in earlier centuries, now lead classes, congregations, and conferences in churches across the world. All three of the Mennonite communities in Congo, for example, ordain women. In 2013, Communauté Mennonite au Congo (Mennonite Church of Congo, or CMCo) approved the ordination of women, following the practice of the other two Congolese Mennonite communities. In 2000, Communauté des Églises de Frères Mennonites au Congo (Mennonite Brethren Church of Congo) approved women's ordinations, followed by Communauté Évangélique Mennonite (Evangelical Mennonite Church of Congo, or CEM) twelve years later. According to Charlotte Djimbo Ndjoko, a Mennonite Brethren woman living in Kinshasa, women "have struggled along with men for years and years for this ordination. Men have resented them. Thanks be to God that these men have now recognized that women have a place in the church in pastoral ministry and evangelization. We are very happy. We will support them as Mennonite sisters. And we invite other women and girls to join them."[5]

These trends were not unique to Anabaptists. In the second half of the twentieth century, technological innovation, ideas of economic and gender equality, and the end of empires fundamentally transformed society and Christianity across the world. The trend for greater diversity grew out of seeds planted in the nineteenth century, and as those seeds continue to bloom, it remains unclear what shape Anabaptist thought and practice will take in the coming decades. The growth of global Christianity and modernity's societal and cultural shifts have led to a flowering of Anabaptist practices and idioms, thereby redefining what it means to be a "typical" Anabaptist in the global, modern age. Statistically, a typical Anabaptist today is a Congolese Mennonite, and a typical North American Anabaptist is an Amish farmer.

While many Anabaptist groups have been inspired by feminist, postcolonial, or liberation theology to open leadership roles to women and LGBTQ+[6] members, others work to maintain more traditional patterns of leadership and membership, often drawing from North American evangelical theological resources. As has been true since the second generation of Anabaptists in the sixteenth century, all Anabaptists must discern what parts of their traditions are essential to their core identity and convictions, which cultural practices can be given up, and whether they can cooperate or take inspiration from ideas and traditions around them.

As the plurality of Anabaptist voices and experiences increases, the task of writing a unified and comprehensive history of the past century becomes difficult. At times, it can be unclear how a Hutterite from Manitoba is related to a member of a Spanish-speaking Mennonite church in a South Texas city or a member of a Mennonite colony in Paraguay, yet all of them would still identify with the Anabaptist tradition (or at least parts of it). The following chapters highlight examples from the twentieth and twenty-first centuries. Unfortunately, this means that there are many Anabaptist stories from around the world that go untold in these pages. While the history is not exhaustive and its conclusions must be provisional, the following chapters are intended to provide an overview of the rich tapestry of Anabaptist practices and worship.

A worldwide pattern

Since the 1970s, Christianity's center has shifted from Global North to South, thereby truly becoming a world religion. Scholars such as Lamin Sanneh and Philip Jenkins have documented this transformative process, increasingly leading to an understanding of the history of Christianity as a global phenomenon that has grown beyond its traditional borders.[7] Long intertwined with Western culture and society, Christianity has been in a period of numerical decline in Europe and North America. Simultaneously, it has rapidly grown as the main religion for many people in postcolonial countries, especially in sub-Saharan Africa and the Asia-Pacific region.[8] In 1910, two-thirds of the world's Christians lived in Europe; in 2010, roughly one-quarter did. That relative decline relates to both fewer European Christians as well as the remarkable growth of world Christianity. In 2010, 26 percent of Christians lived in sub-Saharan Africa, 37 percent in the Americas, and 13 percent in the Asia-Pacific region.[9]

The growth and global identity of Mennonite and Anabaptist churches have mirrored these global trends, forcing scholars to rethink how they write the history of a movement that has been fundamentally transformed. Since the 1990s, the scholarship on worldwide Anabaptism has grown, documenting histories that had been previously unwritten. At its 1997 assembly, Mennonite World Conference commissioned five volumes of the Global Mennonite History Series to write the history of the world movement, using local authors when possible.[10] These volumes and other histories that have followed continue to enrich our understanding and appreciation of the great diversity in Anabaptism.

Historian Jaime Prieto has argued that mission and migration were the two forces that drove the remarkable growth and spread of Anabaptism in Latin America.[11] John D. Roth and other scholars have added a third force—contextualization—to help explain what has happened.[12] According to missiologists—scholars of the methods and purposes of missions—a key driver of the explosive growth of world Christianity since the 1960s has been an idea that Protestants call "contextualization" and Catholic missiologists refer to as "inculturation," or the careful work by local leaders and laity of translating the gospel into their own contexts, making it authentically theirs and allowing it to meet their local needs.[13] Instead of having to give up one's culture and become German, Canadian, or American in order to become a Christian, one can be an Ecuadorian, Congolese, or Korean Christian because the good news rings deeply and authentically true in any culture and context.

Within each country, conference, and congregation, Anabaptists have their own background and dynamics, and groups would tell their history and express their Anabaptist identity differently. Yet the common forces of mission, migration, and contextualization help us understand a common process that continues to unfold.

In the nineteenth century, some Mennonites in Europe and North America appeared to have recaptured the missionary zeal that marked the sixteenth-century Anabaptists' urgent call for repentance and regeneration (see chs. 3 and 8). The spark for missions and active engagement of the world was rekindled and strengthened by the experiences of young men and women in alternative service to conscription during the First and Second World Wars. North American young people spread out across their own countries and the world to serve in the name of Christ in service programs such as Mennonite Central Committee, Mennonite Disaster Service, Mennonite Voluntary Service, and the Pax program. These programs emphasized meeting practical needs rather than spreading the gospel message. However, by embodying a Christianity that emphasized daily discipleship, reconciliation, service, and community, these young people were practicing

Fig. 10.1 Mennonite Disaster Service volunteers assist after a tornado in Udall, Kansas, on July 28, 1964. Photo courtesy of Mennonite Library and Archives, Bethel College, North Newton, Kansas, 2005-0107m.

a type of mission outreach, even if they did not explicitly seek converts. Other Mennonites drew from Western Protestant models of missions and created programs designed specifically to spread the gospel.[14] Like nineteenth-century missions to India and China, some of these evangelizing initiatives worked to meet both spiritual and physical needs. After serving in cities or internationally, North American Mennonites returned to their home congregations with their worldview significantly expanded, leading to a growing sense of connectedness with Mennonites and Christians around the world and beyond the Anabaptist tradition.

Unfortunately, in many countries, memories of the encounters with Western missionaries during the colonial era include both pain and joy. For example, in his autobiography, the first African bishop of the Tanzanian Mennonite Church, Zedekiah Marwa Kisare, recounts the "colonial mentality" of missionaries who refused to teach him English or assumed that Africans had to become Western to become Christian. He recalls, "Up to this time [1963] the missionary approach to our African heritage was to say that it was all savagedom, *ushenzi*. There was no effort to connect the gospel message to our traditional faith."[15] From Indonesia to Congo, mission societies were often reluctant to ordain or equip converts to take leadership in their own denominations or congregations. The legacy of the power imbalances during the early mission years has taken decades to heal.

Anabaptism also spread thanks to the migration of German-speaking Mennonites fleeing war or seeking greater religious freedom. In 1927, 266 conservative Canadian Mennonite families unwilling to adapt to educational reforms moved to the harsh and inhospitable "green hell" of the Paraguayan Chaco to establish the Menno Colony. Mennonites fleeing Stalin's Soviet Union in the 1930s and the devastation of World War II in the 1940s joined them in Paraguay, establishing new colonies in the Chaco and eastern Paraguay as well as eventually in Bolivia, Uruguay, and Brazil. Along with Mennonites from the 1920s migration to Mexico, they became part of the approximately quarter million Low German–speaking Mennonites who continue to seek farmable land across South and Central America.

To a lesser extent, domestic migration in the United States and Canada also spread Anabaptism into new, usually urban, contexts,

Fig. 10.2 Mennonite colonists travel by oxen cart to the Paraguayan Chaco, where they settled, forming Menno Colony in 1928. Photo reprinted with permission of Mennonite Heritage Centre, Winnipeg, 518-28.0.

where people learned to live out their faith in new ways. Already by 1972, two-thirds of North American Mennonites no longer lived on farms, and they were increasingly educated and professional. While they often looked back on a rural past with nostalgia, Mennonites had to learn how to be faithful in towns and cities.[16] Urban church plants for Mennonite transplants eventually attracted new members who did not share the same ethno-religious past. In addition, missions for new immigrants developed into congregations, and others, like some of the francophone congregations who joined MCEC in 2022 as described in the beginning of this chapter, started autonomously but found a home in the Anabaptist movement.

This translation of the Anabaptist tradition to new urban contexts occurs throughout the world. To support church planters in urban areas where their youth were moving, leaders of the Muria Christian Church of Indonesia (Gereja Kristen Muria Indonesia, or GKMI) established the Foundation for Missions and Charities (PIPKA) in 1965. With careful reflection on how to reach out to groups beyond the traditional ethnic Chinese communities, the GKMI established new congregations in cities across Java and across the Indonesian islands of Celebes, Batam, and Bali. Just as many North American Anabaptists work at moving beyond an ethnic understanding of what it means to be a Mennonite or Brethren in Christ Anabaptist, GKMI has become one of the few ethnically diverse Christian churches in Indonesia and has collaborated with churches in Hong Kong and the Philippines in sending missionaries to Singapore and Mongolia.[17]

Sometimes the process of religious contextualization happened before new Christian groups joined the Anabaptist movement, as in the Indonesian examples of Ibrahim Tunggul Wulung, Sie Djoen Nio, and Tee Siem Tat (see ch. 8), whose conversions and theologies flowed out of and integrated their Indonesian worldviews. In Africa, the contextualization process became easier after newly decolonized governments forced foreign missionary groups out. While the newly independent churches struggled with their new autonomy after years of forced reliance on Western support, they were now freer to discern together how to express their Anabaptist identity.

The contextualization of Anabaptism is not a quest for a culturally "neutral" faith. Rather, it asks how Scripture and Anabaptist beliefs can makes sense for believers in Los Angeles, California, or Bulawayo, Zimbabwe, in the same way that older traditions speak to and express the experiences and spiritual questions of Anabaptists living in rural Lancaster County, Pennsylvania, or urban Hamburg, Germany. Despite the variety in Anabaptist practice, most believers across the world share some common beliefs (discipleship and adult baptism), and in many but not all groups, some experiences and practices are prevalent (Pentecostalism and peacemaking).

Anabaptist center: Discipleship and service

As Anabaptists have spread through cities and villages across the world, the way they practice and express their faith invariably, and perhaps necessarily, transforms whenever they encounter novel ideas, cultures, and social structures. This transformation is thoughtfully and intentionally processed in meetings and Bible studies, when a pressing question compels believers to discern together how to respond. Traditionally, Anabaptists collectively discerned what faithful discipleship in response to Christ as revealed in the Bible would look like. For example, members of Evangelical Mennonite Church of Burkina Faso (Eglise Evangélique du Burkina Faso) in Sidi, Burkina Faso, grew uneasy when the living chicken and four liters of millet beer (*dolo*) that they paid in return for access to farmland were used for sacrifices to the spirit of the land. Instead, they proposed an alternative gift of money and produce, even though it could mean that they would lose access to the land and therefore have to leave Sidi. In 2015, the believers in Sidi proposed that they would help the priest harvest his crop in lieu of the sacrifices, which helped reduce tensions and allow them to continue to worship in Sidi.[18] Anabaptists believe that faithfulness means following Christ, even if it potentially means they might suffer as a result. The questions of faithfulness change, but discipleship continues to be a hallmark of Anabaptist practice.

Anabaptist center: Peacemaking

For many believers, the call for disciples to be nonviolent peacemakers has become a hallmark of their Anabaptist identity. For centuries after the Reformation, Anabaptist commitment to nonviolence meant the refusal to serve in the military. Since World War II, the peace position has evolved into more proactive expressions, including advocating and working for social justice and reconciliation.

While many Anabaptists throughout the world share this conviction, the gospel of peace is lived out in a variety of ways. The Meserete Kristos Church (MKC) in Ethiopia provides vocational training for prisoners and prepares communities to receive the prisoners upon their release. At a 2019 gathering of Anabaptist peace workers, Ethiopian leader Tewodros Beyene linked this reconciliation work with the mission work of the church: "The church's peace work should have a vision of mission. We have a *gospel* of peace and need to be evangelists who call others to peaceful relationship with God."[19] At the same conference, Mennonite attorney Katherine Torres spoke about her work as coordinator of Puentes para la Paz (Bridges for Peace) to engage Christian denominations in the Colombian peace process. "Nonviolence is the gift of Anabaptists," Torres said. "Anabaptists work at peacemaking out of a strong sense of community."[20]

The teaching and practice of nonviolence, peacemaking, and reconciliation will look different depending on a community's contexts and influences. Most separatist and Old Order groups continue to define nonviolence as the refusal to serve in the military or defend oneself from aggression, but they are less active in political activism on behalf of others. Mennonites are divided on how to relate to the government and to congregational members who serve in the military or police forces. Describing the practice of some congregations in the Organización Cristiana Amor Viviente in Honduras, researcher Reynaldo Vallecillo writes, "In Honduras we have not had a civil war, and people don't have a bad opinion of [the] military. We associate the military with projects of peace . . . so we have people from the military in our churches, which opens the possibility for participating."[21] In Canada, Mennonites such as Jane Philpott and Ed Fast have served as members of national or provincial parliaments, and in Paraguay, Arnoldo Wiens, a Mennonite pastor, ran for presidential office in 2013.[22] Despite the lack of a consistent Anabaptist peace position, the commitment to peace and reconciliation has attracted many new members to the Anabaptist tradition.

Suffering for the faith: Persecution

In 2007, the Vietnamese government officially formalized the legal status of Hội Thánh Mennonite Việt Nam (Vietnam Mennonite Church). Representing around half the Anabaptists in Vietnam, most of these congregations grew out of the ministry planted by Eastern Mennonite Missions in 1957 and restarted in the 1980s. Beginning in 1998, a second movement of indigenous congregations supported by Vietnamese Canadian Mennonites formed into the Mennonite Church in Vietnam, or Evangelical Mennonite Church.[23] Although both groups adopted the same confession of faith, members in the Evangelical Mennonite Church endure periodic arrests, beatings, and imprisonment by government authorities.

In June 2014, Vietnamese security police raided a gathering of pastors and theological students who had been meeting in Ben Cat town, twenty kilometers north of Ho Chi Minh City. The attendees included Le Thi Phu Dung, president of the Evangelical Mennonite Church, and local pastor Tran Minh Hoa. At eleven at night, police with loudspeakers demanded for the doors to be opened, and uniformed and ununiformed men stormed the building, assaulting teachers and students before arresting seventy-six persons. The authorities encouraged bystanders to throw stones at the building, breaking windows and roof tiles. After their release from prison, the arrested members returned to the building to clean up, but local gangs continued to pelt the building with bricks, stones, and rotten eggs.

In a Global Anabaptist Profile survey of twenty-four Mennonite World Conference churches, a significant number of respondents reported experiencing some form of persecution. While the survey did not ask members to specify what type of persecution occurred or who committed it, the survey's results suggest that the experiences of the unregistered Mennonite Church in Vietnam are shared by other Anabaptists. While European or North American Mennonites rarely reported persecution, 36 percent of respondents in Africa and 17 percent in Latin America said that it was "often" the case. For example, 73 percent of the respondents in Communauté des Églises des Frères Mennonites au Congo and 41 percent of members in Communauté Mennonite au Congo reported experiencing persecution often.[24]

Anabaptists in the West may not share the same experiences of persecution, but they often attempt to intervene on behalf of those who are suffering.[25] Anabaptists from across the world wrote on behalf of SangMin Lee, a Mennonite conscientious objector from South Korea sentenced to eighteen months in prison in early 2014 for refusing to complete his mandatory military service for reasons of faith. "Right before Jesus was arrested by soldiers," Lee had explained, "Peter tried to protect Jesus and cut off a soldier's ear with a sword. Jesus told Peter he could have called the angels to protect him. However, he chose not to. As a Christian, this is the most powerful scripture for me and the reason I believe in Jesus Christ."[26] After Lee's trial, a letter-writing campaign was initiated by the Institute for the Global Study of Anabaptism in Goshen, Indiana, and Justapaz, a Colombian Mennonite peace and human rights organization. Just as the Dutch Mennonites sent fact-finding missions, raised funds, and appealed to Swiss authorities for the toleration of the Anabaptist co-religionists in the 1600s and 1700s, Anabaptists from around the world sent letters to Lee in prison, letting him and the prison authorities know that he was not forgotten.[27]

Embracing the Holy Spirit: Pentecostalism

In July 1963, the influential Javanese Mennonite leader Soehadiweko Djojodihardjo attended a Bible study in Pati to discern how the church might revitalize the spiritual life of its members. At one point, Djojodihardjo attended a prayer meeting, after which he suddenly felt that my whole body moved. Then later my tongue and my mouth moved too, slowly at first, then becoming more pronounced and faster. Finally my diaphragm moved, as though it was squeezed, so that sounds came out of my mouth. Strange words came forth forming sentences which I did not understand myself. I continued to speak in tongues for about half an hour. A feeling of tranquility and joy came over me such as I had never experienced in times past. At night when I prayed again, this experience repeated itself. My mouth and my tongue moved. Later words came out as before.[28]

As he later reflected, that spiritual awakening changed Djojodihardjo's life. His disposition improved, sermons came more easily, "as though what I say when I preach is entirely controlled by the Holy Spirit," and his prayers for the sick were answered.[29] God healed members who were suffering from illness and spiritual oppression.

Like Djojodihardjo, members of the fastest-growing Anabaptist churches practice a spiritual life that expects the Holy Spirit to produce the gifts experienced in the early church, including speaking in tongues, healing, deliverance from demons, and prophecy. Whether and how churches experience the charismatic gifts relates to their history, context, and culture. Anabaptists in African churches are more likely to report experiencing deliverance from demonic oppression, whereas Latin Americans are more likely to have experienced a miraculous healing.[30] According to a survey of North American Anabaptists, racialized, minority Mennonites were more likely than other groups to report having had a charismatic healing.[31] The charismatic movement has shaped many white Mennonites in North America since the 1970s, and new Anabaptist congregations are more likely to comprise migrants from the Global South, who bring with them their experiences of the gifts of the Spirit. At the same time, many North American and European Mennonites, shaped by a rational, scientific worldview, are skeptical of spiritual expression and miracles. As Anabaptists in Africa, Latin America, and Asia shape Anabaptism in the future, the nature of the movement will likely have more of the spiritual expression of the sixteenth-century Anabaptists who emphasized the power of the new birth brought about by the power of the Holy Spirit.

The ties that bind

As the Anabaptist movement sprouts and grows in new lands, it inevitably changes as it encounters new contexts—just as the movement adapted and changed over the previous five centuries. Church bodies celebrate the growing domestic and global diversity of the faith family, but the growth can raise questions of what ideas or practices bind members together into a global peoplehood. The authority of the pope unites the Roman Catholic Church, the Augsburg Confession provides theological authority for Lutherans, and a clear set of doctrinal positions binds the global Reformed and Baptist groups.[32] A single authority or specific articulation of theology has never united Anabaptists. Even though Anabaptists have fashioned many confessions of faith over the previous centuries, there has never been one confession with a singular authoritative power over all Anabaptists.

Anabaptist growth has happened without centralized planning and parameters, resulting in myriad expressions, all which claim to be part of the global Anabaptist community.[33] Sometimes, churches in Asia, Africa, or North America were planted by Western mission agencies with clearly identified Mennonite or Anabaptist principles, but other missionaries downplayed Anabaptist distinctives and focused on the personal salvation of new converts. Some groups discovered Anabaptism after they had already discerned the values of discipleship, community, and peace from their own reading of Scripture. Mennonite leaders who lack easy access to Anabaptist-themed seminary training attend interdenominational institutions, which can influence their theology. All these histories produce a rich variety of Anabaptist expressions.

— ELEVEN —

Continuity and Change

Anabaptists in Africa

In July 2009, the Mennonite and Brethren in Christ delegates attending the fifteenth Mennonite World Conference (MWC) assembly in Asunción, Paraguay, participated in a powerful moment of reconciliation. Mennonite World Conference president Danisa Ndlovu and Ishmael Noko, general secretary of the Lutheran World Federation (LWF), embraced in celebration and affirmation of a mutual commitment to work toward the healing of relationships between Lutherans and Anabaptists.[1] Meetings and discussions between Anabaptist and Lutheran church leaders led to a statement the following year from the LWF asking for forgiveness from Anabaptists for persecution by Lutheran authorities in the sixteenth century and beyond.[2]

After years of working toward reconciliation, the culminating ceremony in Paraguay was a significant ecumenical moment, but Ndlovu and Noko's embrace in Asunción also illustrated the shifting center of gravity of churches long associated with German and northern European ethnic groups. Both men were born in what is now Zimbabwe in southern Africa. In addition to his work as MWC president, Ndlovu served as bishop of Ibandla Labazalwane KuKristu eZimbabwe (Brethren in Christ Church in Zimbabwe) until 2014, and Ishmael Noko had been a professor and dean at the University of Botswana. While there have been African Christians since the earliest history of the church, the first Anabaptist missionary presence there began in the 1890s, and much of the African church's significant growth happened in the second half of the twentieth century. There are now more baptized Anabaptists in Africa than there are members in North American Mennonite and Brethren in Christ churches.

Pakisa K. Tshimika and Doris Dube's excellent introduction to the first volume of the Global Mennonite History Series provides an overview of the complex and diverse histories of Mennonite and Brethren in Christ churches in Africa.[3] Like the continent itself, African churches are a "mosaic of many cultures, ethnic and tribal groups as well as languages."[4] Worship is expressed in the local culture, giving each congregation a unique flavor. However, in multicultural urban contexts, especially in central Africa, congregations may worship in three or four languages. Focusing in on a particular country or region makes the complexity of the history clearer. Narratives must be nuanced accordingly, but there are common themes in the history of sub-Saharan African Anabaptists.

According to Tshimika and Dube, "Any person who takes time to listen to elders in African villages can report stories about African spirituality and the role God played in our lives before the arrival of missionaries."[5] African converts often understood the Christian God to be the same as the Higher God, creator of all life, that they had always seen revealed in creation and their communities. In many African societies, the primary spiritual interaction was through the ancestors, who had direct access to God while also understanding the lives of the living. Jesus Christ, therefore, became the new mediator for humanity, or the Supreme Ancestor. In regions of east Africa, Islam had been present for centuries, and Orthodox Christianity, first established in Ethiopia in the fourth century, had been that country's prevalent religion for centuries.

During the 1500s through 1800s, Western missionaries arrived in sub-Saharan Africa, first in coastal areas, than later traveling into the interior of the continent while the empires and transatlantic slave trade of Christian nations were also expanding. Before the imperial age of the nineteenth and twentieth centuries, African missionaries planted

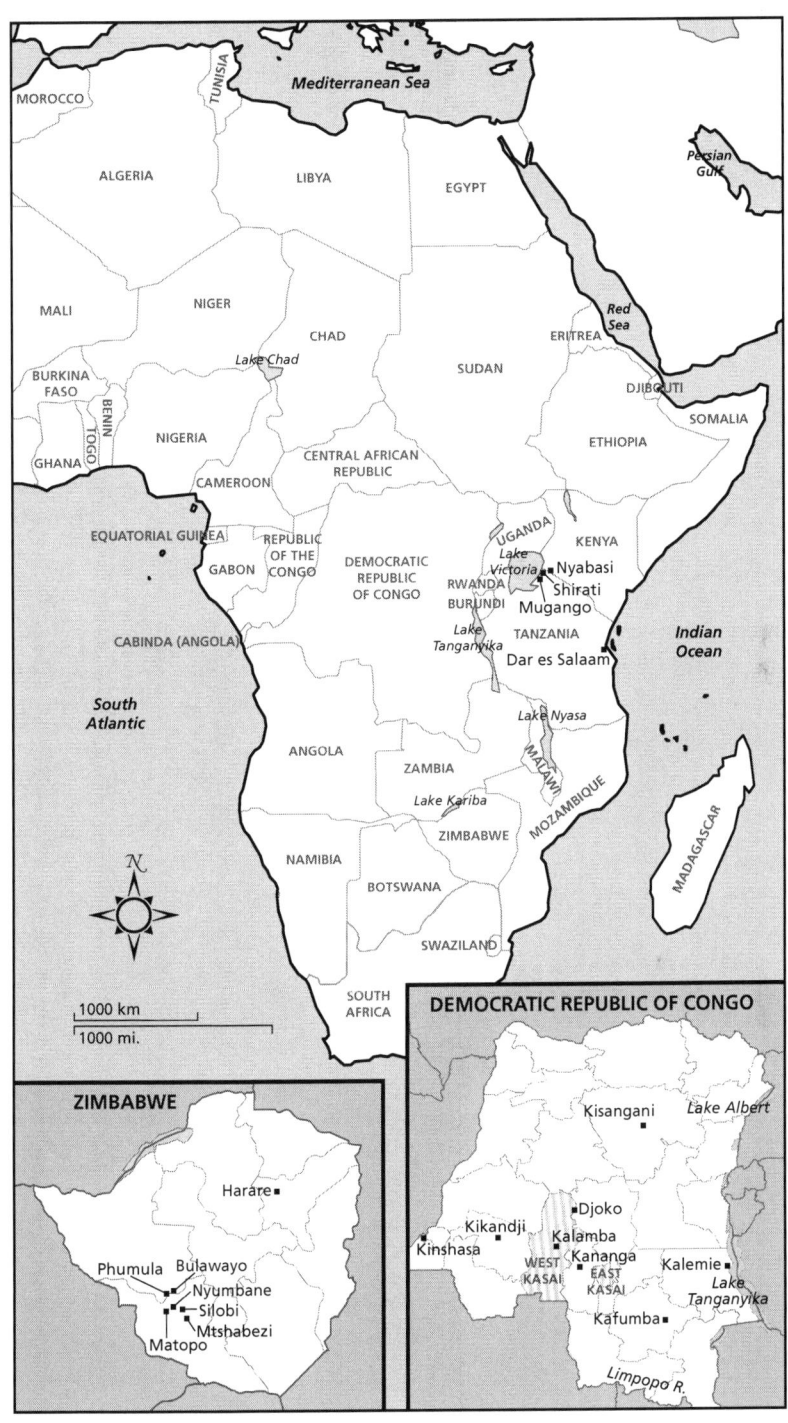

churches away from the coasts, further into regions of Africa beyond European control. For nearly fifty years, for example, the Anglican missionary and bishop Samuel Ajayi Crowther planted a series of Yoruba-led churches in Yorubaland and Niger. In the late nineteenth and early twentieth centuries, Western imperial powers expanded away from the coasts and into the interior, seeking to directly control and govern the continent. At the end of Crowther's career, European missionaries replaced African leaders, and the model of a self-governing and indigenized church was abandoned until it returned after the end of the colonial period.[6]

European colonial administrators divided countries among churches and mission agencies, linking the spread of Christianity with the spread of imperial administration and industrial and trading companies. Because African territory was parceled out to avoid conflict and competition between Protestant missionary groups, rural people became Mennonite, Lutheran, or Anglican because of where they lived, not necessarily because they had chosen a particular expression of Christianity. After political independence, many people whose Christian identity was an accident of geography rather than choice have wondered what it meant to become Anabaptist, Mennonite, or Brethren in Christ when it had been the only option available.

Cities were an exception to this pattern, because authorities allowed multiple Protestant groups to establish congregations in urban areas. When rural Anabaptists migrated to the city, they worshiped and built churches with others from their ethnic group, and transplants from their home communities subsequently joined them. Anabaptist believers in cities worked, lived, and sometimes worshiped with Christians from a variety of ethnic backgrounds, so they had to discern what practices and beliefs were essential to their faith and which traditions were particular to their home communities. Members who returned to their villages from the city took these insights with them.

In the 1960s, as African countries gained political independence from foreign powers, churches also called for their independence from Western influences. Some Western mission organizations handed responsibility over to local leaders, while some resisted giving up control. As Africans began leading their own churches, they realized how little they had been trained for succession. This led to tension between the desire for local control and a continued dependence on foreign funds, a struggle that can be seen in other parts of the global church as well.

In 1960, Zedekiah Marwa Kisare—who had been an interpreter for Elam and Elizabeth Stauffer and John and Ruth Moseman, some of the first Mennonite missionaries in Tanzania (then known as Tanganyika) in the 1930s—could see these changes coming, just a few years away from his being ordained as the first African bishop of the Tanzanian Mennonite Church. In his autobiography, Kisare recalls feeling a mixture of excitement and apprehension at the prospect, writing,

> In 1960 freedom was in the air. The United Nations was pushing England to give us our independence. People began to think in radically different ways. The church too would become independent. Africans would become responsible to administer the church's programs. There was even talk of an African bishop. These were new and exciting ideas. They were also sober ideas because the future was upon us, and no one had been getting ready for the future.[7]

Fig. 11.1 (*left to right*) Ezekiel Muganda, Simeon Hurst, and Zedekiah Kisare visiting Ontario churches in 1961. Muganda and Kisare were among the first leaders ordained in Tanzania, and Hurst was a long-time missionary. All three men are wearing plain coats, commonly worn by North American Mennonite ministers. Photo courtesy of *Canadian Mennonite/Mennonite Archives of Ontario, Conrad Grebel University College, Waterloo.*

For many African churches, the years after the transfer of power to local leaders were difficult. Nevertheless, Mennonite and Brethren in Christ churches quickly grew, especially in areas experiencing political and economic hardship. When asked about that dynamic, one pastor explained that "many people in his country used to think that when they were in trouble, help would come from the outside. Now they had been disappointed by their national as well as international governments, and they realized the only hope left was in God and God alone."[8]

Tshimika and Dube observe that the fastest growth happens in churches with ministries that serve the whole person—body and soul. People who experience worship at Anabaptist-related schools, medical facilities, and community development return to their villages and establish new churches in the same model. Schools, they note, have been underappreciated for how they bring young people to faith and help create new disciplined believers. The formation of young members has become particularly urgent in war-torn regions, where Christians have had to discern how to survive amid violence and weak governmental control. Questions about Anabaptist identity and essentials of the faith will become increasingly acute in Africa, just as they will in other parts of the world, including the West, whenever there is political turmoil and instability.

Brethren in Christ churches in southern Africa

When the first Brethren in Christ missionaries arrived in Africa, they initially did not know where they would end up. When they were at sea, Elizabeth and Jesse Engle, Hannah Frances Davidson, and Alice Heisey heard that no missionaries were active in the area north of the Limpopo River, home to the AmaNdebele people. But the British mining magnate and imperial advocate Cecil John Rhodes considered missionary work a cost-efficient approach in the colonization of the region that would eventually be known as Rhodesia (present-day Zimbabwe), and when they arrived he granted the Anabaptist missionaries three thousand acres in the Matopo Hills. As was often the case in Africa, locals viewed the missionaries with suspicion, since the North Americans seemed to share the same culture as the imperial authorities and often arrived soon after Europeans claimed dominion over African territory.[9]

The missionaries who arrived on July 7, 1898, and eventually established Matopo Mission, near Bulawayo, preached the gospel message, but they also set up schools and clinics. Davidson and Heisey traveled to nearby villages with several young men who had settled in the mission, including Mlobeki Moyo, Matshuba Ndlovu, and Siyaya (last name unknown). In 1899, ten Ndebele people were baptized in the Ginqa River. One of the first to be baptized, Mlobeki Moyo later recalled how the first missionaries spread their message: "As soon as the missionaries arrived, they started preaching to the people. We would visit the people as they were involved in communal labour (*ilima*). The missionaries would join in the work as well."[10] After finishing the work, the missionaries read from the Bible, explained the message, and prayed. The missionaries, along with other Westerners, introduced Western understanding of land ownership, agriculture, and economy, replacing traditional AmaNdebele beliefs and practices, which may have precipitated long-term environmental degradation in the twentieth and twenty-first centuries.[11]

The mission focused on evangelization and providing education to rural villages. Schools trained leaders to go out and form new mission stations in villages, including Mahlabathini, Silobi, Maphane, Gale (now Nyumbane), and Mtshabezi. By the 1930s, Matopo Mission had grown into a leading center for education in practical and religious topics and started a teacher training school to meet the growing demand for trained educators. The Mtshabezi Mission, planted in 1906, became a refuge for girls whose parents planned to marry them against their wishes. Known as the *intomb Zegedini*—the girls of the gate—many of the graduates of the Mtshabezi Girls School became leaders of the Brethren in Christ church.

In 1906, Ndabambi Moyo and Gono Sibanda, new converts of the Zimbabwean church, looked to expand missions into neighboring Zambia (then known as Northern Rhodesia). They joined American missionaries Hannah Frances Davidson and Adda Engle in traveling nearly eight hundred kilometers to establish Macha Mission Station on thirty-two hundred acres among the Batonga people, despite the protests of government authorities, who thought the endeavor too perilous for women. Once Chief Macha brought his son to be educated at the mission school, the mission station took root and began teaching and evangelizing, training young people to go out and start substations in neighboring villages. Davidson traveled extensively, speaking in the local language, comforting the sick and dying, and providing medication. Her diary remains an authoritative source on the early history of Anabaptist missions, and a valuable insight on the difficulties of mission work, especially for women.[12]

The Brethren in Christ Churches of Zimbabwe and Zambia (Ibandla Labazalwane KuKristu eZimbabwe and Mbungano Yabunyina Muli Kristo, respectively) worked together as one church body as they continued to build schools and plant mission stations. When Zambia gained independence from Britain in 1964, the North American mission board gave full authority for the church to Africans, and it continued to operate as one body until a minority white government in Rhodesia (Zimbabwe) unilaterally declared independence from Britain in 1965 and closed its borders with Zambia in the 1970s, making travel between the two countries nearly impossible. During the ensuing Rhodesian revolutionary war, some young men and women raised in the church and educated in its schools joined the rebel movements.

Fig. 11.2 Stephen Ndlovu (*second from left*) speaking at the 1981 Mennonite World Conference general meeting. Also pictured are (*left to right*) Abraham Wetseh from Ghana, Mbonza Kikunga from Zaire, and Naftali Birai from Tanzania. Photo reprinted with permission of Mennonite Church USA Archives, Elkhart, Indiana, Mennonite World Conference Records, 1923–2012, X-009, box 21, folder 1.

After the end of minority rule, Zimbabwe gained independence in 1980. Independence celebrations were short-lived for many Ndebele, who were targeted by the government-backed Gukurahundi army, which tortured and killed members of the church for their Ndebele ethnicity and church participation. When squatters invaded the Wanezji Mission in the early 1980s, bishop Stephen S. Ndlovu risked his life to dialogue with the squatters rather than use violence after he traveled to Phumula Mission to comfort members there. Even today, stories of leaders' faithful perseverance shape the peace position that remains strong among the twenty-eight thousand members of the Zimbabwean church, who continue to process the pain and suffering of those years. In a recent survey, nearly 80 percent of respondents declared that they would not participate if the government should require military service.[13]

The southern African churches continue to discern what to keep and what to discard from the Western missionaries. As has been common among many African churches, drums, which play a central role in African culture, have become more common in services, and North American teachings on head coverings and jewelry are being reevaluated and rejected for being cultural practices, not theological ones. While it is no longer required for women to cover their heads in services, many still do so during solemn occasions, such as baptisms.

Since the 1980s, the Brethren in Christ (BIC) churches have expanded into Malawi, Mozambique, and Botswana. As many members seek economic opportunities in other countries, the churches have looked for ways to support their members in South Africa and London, England. In neighboring Malawi, a group led by pastor Sani Selemani Chibwana reached out to Zimbabwean leaders in 1983 to help establish a church in Malawi. The following year, three leaders and their wives visited the small group of worshipers, which would eventually grow to five hundred members when it officially registered with the state. Ephraim Disi was the first person ordained in the BIC Mpingo Wa Abale Mwa Kristu and eventually became the denomination's first president. Now with around forty-five hundred members, the Malawian church includes ministries to respond to the suffering caused by poverty and HIV/AIDS.[14]

Anabaptists in central and western Africa

In 1911, Mennonite missionaries chose a spot west of the Kasai River to begin a mission in the Congo, becoming the first Anabaptist presence in central Africa. Members of the Defenseless Mennonite Conference (known as the Fellowship of Evangelical Churches since 2013) and the Central Illinois Mennonite Conference had jointly organized the Congo Inland Mission (known as the Africa Inter-Mennonite Mission, AIMM, since 1972) to send a married couple to the Congo. Lawrence and Rose Haigh built the first CIM/AIMM mission station at Kalamba Mukenge among the Lulua people and at Djoko Punda among a variety of peoples.

Until 1908, King Leopold II of Belgium held the Congo autocratically as a private domain. After an international campaign highlighted the humanitarian atrocities of Leopold's rule, the Belgian parliament annexed the country and began to rule it as a Belgian colony. Leopold had supported Catholic missions while restricting Protestant missionary endeavors, not granting them the same access to land or support, policies which the Belgian government continued.[15] As a result, Protestant mission groups often collaborated in response to these colonial restrictions. They recognized each other as members of a shared Protestant project and downplayed doctrinal or practical differences among Protestants. Strong inter-Protestant cooperation in the Congo continues to the present day.

Success came slowly for the CIM mission. In 1917, seventeen people were baptized at Djoko Punda, which grew into an important center for Mennonite activity in central Africa. In the 1920s, Aaron Janzen, who had worked previously for CIM, founded a specifically Mennonite Brethren school-chapel mission post in Kikandji, which later moved to Kafumba to be nearer to a more secure water supply. In 1926, Luke Sengele became the first convert at Kafumba and soon thereafter helped convert thirty-seven others. From early on, the work at Kafumba was holistic, combining mission outreach with agriculture, healthcare, and educational activities. While it attempted to be self-sustaining, Janzen's mission eventually came under the control of the American Mennonite Brethren Mission (AMBM). The move provided more stability, but the new relationship would have long-term impacts.

Early converts, like Valentin Badibanga, who desired to become a "Jesus person," a *mwena Yesu*, were critical to the success of evangelism.[16] Local leaders knew the language and culture better than missionaries did, and translation work was a way for Congolese converts to exert leadership in mission work and ensure that what was preached always confirmed the presence of God in Africa before Christians' arrival. The Congolese evangelist Mutombo (last name unknown), for example, was central in the earliest CIM conversions in the 1910s. Djimbo Kubala, Nganga Diyoyo, and Ernestina Janzen, Aaron Janzen's wife, worked together to translate the New Testament into the Kituba language. The project was completed in 1943, after Martha Hiebert joined the team following Ernestina Janzen's death in 1937. Working as Bible translators, teachers, and healthcare workers, Congolese converts helped their neighbors overcome initial suspicions and prejudices about Westerners and Christianity.

Much of the initial distrust came from the close association with white missionaries and the colonial project. Missionaries started chapel-farms, school-farms, or mission stations to begin their activity and sustain the local community. Locals suspected that the schools were a way to train children to speak the language of the colonizers, and many communities were willing to send only enslaved or captured children—not their own. Missionaries created further mistrust when they forced locals to abstain from traditional celebrations, tobacco, and alcohol.

Congolese historians have described a "psychology of dependency" that grew out of the missionary work.[17] Missionaries controlled the finances of the church and provided many free services subsidized by the colonial government, and Congolese converts came to rely on the foreign funding.

In response to increasing pressure from the Congolese, the Belgian government prepared to grant independence in 1960. A few months before the political transition, Congo Inland Mission prepared to hand over control of the church to the local community. Many Congolese realized that the previous hierarchical system had not prepared them to lead their churches. As a sense of abandonment grew, the foreign missionaries considered staying in Congo to show solidarity with the church, but they decided it would be safer for them and their families to leave. A missionary later recalled, "And when the situation in the

Congo returned to normal and we returned, our Congolese friends made the following remark to us, 'When things became difficult, you left us to our sad lot.' The remarks of our Congolese friends were justified but they affected me nonetheless."[18]

An earlier exception to the pattern of colonial dependency, the farm at Kafumba was intended by missionaries Aaron and Ernestina Janzen to be a self-sufficient mission outreach that shared the economic proceeds from palm oil, coffee, and food crops with Congolese believers. The farm grew into a refuge from the exploitative practices of the nearby palm oil industry by offering a "holistic, congregation-oriented ecclesial economy."[19] Even though the wages were less than those in the broader palm oil industry, workers at Kafumba found dignity in the work that was intertwined with being baptized members of the congregation. According to the scholar Anicka Fast, Congolese believers were active in running the farm and created a new economic unit following the Russian Mennonite pattern of congregational life that first developed in Ukraine. The local autonomy and sufficiency ended, however, when the American Mennonite Brethren Mission began to subsidize Kafumba in 1943, but from 1922 to 1943, Kafumba served as an alternate economic and missiological model.

After independence, a new Congolese conference developed. In 1962, Luba people who had been working in West Kasai fled to East Kasai to escape interethnic tensions. With Rev. Mathieu Kazadi as its first president, the Evangelical Mennonite Community (CEM) began in 1962 as a thoroughly Congolese initiative. Educated from an early age at Djoko Punda, Kazadi organized congregations among the refugees in East Kasai into a regional church.[20]

By the 1970s, African Mennonites had achieved control of Congolese churches, and in 1971, the Communauté des Églises des Frères Mennonites au Congo and Communauté Mennonite au Congo became fully autonomous, as the CEM had been since its origins. At a time when the government encouraged Congolese to take pride in their culture, Mennonites began to use African names and clothing instead of the Western ones they had previously used. While most congregations were and remain rural, Mennonites also spread into cities, where they encountered Spirit-led Pentecostal churches. Renewal movements of the 1980s—which included signs of the Spirit, prayer vigils, and praying out loud—were sometimes resisted, but now all congregations use these traditional forms of worship. Women make up most of the members of the Congolese churches, and some, like Léonie Kelendende Kadi Hayalume, have been trained in Bible and theological schools.[21]

Since the 1960s, some Congolese Mennonites have lived their faith amid persecution and violence. After Congolese independence, mission stations were often attacked by rebels who associated them with the colonial powers. Rebel soldiers suspected pastor Emmanuel Wayindama because he worked as a teacher at the mission school. The rebels beat Wayindama and threatened to kill him on the spot, but he replied, "Sure you can, but if you do, that's all you can do to me." The rebels released Wayindama, who led students and families to safety.[22]

Currently numbering over two hundred thousand members, Congolese Mennonites increasingly ask themselves what it means to be

Fig. 11.3 A choir records music at a studio in Luluabourg (now Kananga), Congo, 1965. Photo reprinted with permission of Mennonite Church USA Archives, Elkhart, Indiana, Mennonite Board of Missions Photograph Collection from Congo, IV-10-7.2, box 3, folder 22, photo #1.

both African and Mennonite. Some have begun to turn to African spiritual traditions and resources rather than Western theology and history to shape their Anabaptist identity. Kinshasa pastor François Tshidimu, for example, suggests:

> Congolese Mennonite Anabaptism must be understood according to our culture. There are many valuable aspects of Congolese culture conveyed in its music, proverbs, tales, philosophy, the place it gives to blood sacrifices, the concept of what is taboo and what is holy, the idea of humans set apart by God, its sense of hierarchy, and its innate religious sprit, as well as the value Africans give to nonviolence, unity, peace, and reconciliation. All of that can be developed to solidify Congolese Mennonites' faith in Jesus Christ.[23]

East African Anabaptists

In August 1942, a wave of revival swept over the young Tanzanian Mennonite church at Katuru Hill in Shirati. First kindled in Rwanda and Uganda in 1936, this revival fire spread across east Africa, transforming churches as it went. Lives from all levels of society changed as believers repented from open and hidden sins and an unwillingness to follow Christ completely. Now referred to as the East African Revival, the movement "emphasized that at the Cross there was not white or black, educated or illiterate, missionary or African, pastor or layman. All needed to be released from sinfulness."[24] Tanzanian bishop Zedekiah Marwa Kisare recalled, "With deep sorrow we began to ask forgiveness of each other for the terrible sins we had committed. From this point onwards, I have had good fellowship with my brothers."[25]

When the revival broke out, the Mennonite presence in Tanzania (then Tanganyika) was still establishing its roots. In 1934, four Lancaster Mennonite Conference missionaries set up their first worship building in Shirati, thirteen kilometers from the Kenyan border. As in other countries, the missionaries also set up medical facilities, schools, and other social services. The missionary Elam Stauffer hoped to establish an indigenous body that was a "self-supporting, self-propagating, and self-governing church." Kisare, who as mentioned earlier would later become the first Tanzanian bishop, started working as a translator for the outdoor worship services. Growth was slow until the 1942 revival movement swept over believers at Mugango, Nyabasi, and

Shirati, and those who repented went on to preach the gospel and call for repentance wherever they could. Twelve-year-old students Wilson Ogwada and Nikanor Dhaje left school to spread the gospel message to those who had never heard it. Traveling and preaching tirelessly along the border between Kenya and Tanzania, they became the first African Mennonite missionaries to spread the gospel beyond national borders. The lay missionary Rebeka Makura brought the message of renewal to the Mennonite mission at Mugango. Together with American missionary Phebe Yoder, Makura then brought the message of repentance to other believers in Tanganyika.

A second revival in 1946 called on Christians to remove barriers and build up the body of Christ. Instead of emphasizing the gifts of the Spirit, this movement called on believers to devote themselves to Christ through confession and submission. Looking back at the growth of the church, missionaries and local believers credited the East African Revival with shaping an African Mennonite movement that

Fig. 11.4 Four Ethiopian women (names unknown), 1963. Under Ethiopia's repressive Marxist-Leninist Derg government (1974–1991), women played a critical role in sustaining and expanding the church. Photo reprinted with permission of Mennonite Church USA Archives, Elkhart, Indiana, Mennonite Board of Missions Photo Collection from Ethiopia 1963, IV-10-7.2, box 3, folder 32, photo #1.

local believers spread, led, and sustained from early on. Now known by its Swahili name, the Kanisa la Mennonite Tanzania has educational and health ministries serving over sixty thousand members.

The African revival movement in turn influenced European and North American missionaries who took the message home with them, where it awakened Mennonite believers beyond Africa. By calling all to submit equally before the cross, the East African Revival challenged class, race, gender, and authority structures among North American Mennonites.

When they returned home from their time in east Africa, North American missionaries confronted traditions of dress and discipline that seemed to have little to do with following Jesus. The liberating power of the revival inspired women like Erma Maust to teach revival and repentance in Lancaster congregations and across North America, even in the face of criticism from church leaders.[26] African missionaries like William Nagenda brought the revival from Africa to North America, where his indefatigable spirit and message challenged his audiences to be weak so that Jesus could be Lord. The East African Revival movement offered Mennonites in North America spiritual resources for the twentieth century that were not tied to traditional separatist understandings of faithfulness.

The Mennonite church in Ethiopia also developed in a surprising way, but their remarkable story happened in a context of repression rather than revival. In 1948, Ethiopian emperor Haile Selassie invited Mennonite missionaries to run several schools. The first Mennonite church began in 1951, eventually taking the name Meserete Kristos (Christ the Foundation) Church, inspired by 1 Corinthians 3:11. MKC remained small until a 1964 Pentecostal revival produced a generation of energetic and motivated young leaders. Evangelist Daniel Mekonnen's ministry of healing gained a national reputation and attracted curiosity seekers who came to investigate stories of miraculous healings for themselves.

In 1974, the Marxist military movement known as the Derg overthrew the emperor. Early on, the regime gained popularity by redistributing land to the poor and reducing rents, but it soon turned into a military dictatorship. The government forced people to take indoctrination classes, forbade anyone under twenty-five from attending church, and harassed Christian groups, including MKC. Mennonites who refused to participate and chant pro-government slogans were imprisoned, and some leaders left the country for safety.

In 1982, Marxist authorities intensified their persecution of MKC, seizing property, freezing bank accounts, and imprisoning leaders for up to fifty months. Fearing for the future of the church, in early February 1983, pastor Kedir Delchumie reorganized the church into an underground organization. For ten years, the MKC met in secret cells of five to ten people, often by candlelight in rooms at the back of members' homes. When a cell grew to be over ten members, it was split into smaller cells to avoid outsiders' attention. Sustained by hours-long prayer sessions, members met to teach and support one another. They arrived at separate times and did not allow singing or clapping at their meetings.

Critical to the leadership of the underground movement were women like Aster Debose, who was nearly killed for her association with Westerners. Leading more cell groups than men did, women had been trained by the MKC to pray and instruct their groups. Just as sixteenth-century Anabaptist women met around the spinning wheel, Ethiopian women's traditional activities were an opportunity to meet in secret, often during traditional coffee ceremonies. "If the police come," Felekech Bekele later recalled, "[the women] will say, 'It's the coffee!' The coffee ceremony takes more than two hours. You have to clean it, roast it, you do all this process. Maybe one woman is preparing the coffee at the back, but the other women are teaching."[27]

Despite its clandestine status and the persecution of hundreds of its leaders, the Meserete Kristos Church grew during the underground years. Disenchanted with the Marxist regime, new believers found a supportive community in the MKC cell network. Once the government removed the restrictions on Christian worship, it was discovered that the MKC had grown from 5,000 to 34,000 members and from thirty-four congregations to fifty-three. Since the end of persecution, the MKC has grown to become the largest Mennonite conference in the world. One of the fruits of persecution has been the MKC's continued emphasis on training leaders, evangelism, social action, and church planting, which has led to its growth to over 350,000 baptized members in over 1,100 local churches and 1,100 church-planting centers.

Those who read the stories of MKC see parallels with the history of early Anabaptism in Europe. "MKC began as a small fellowship of believers committed to following Jesus in daily life," writes historian John D. Roth. "Like the Anabaptists, MKC faced fierce opposition. And like the Anabaptists, MKC survived persecution by developing strategies for survival and growth that depended heavily on lay ministry, friendship evangelism, a commitment to discipleship training, and, above all, a deep attentiveness to the presence of the Holy Spirit."[28]

African Anabaptism: No single story

The diversity of Anabaptist expression in Africa complicates easy conclusions. Just as there is no singular African culture, there is no one Anabaptist story on the continent. While Ethiopian choirs write their own songs, some churches in Kenya and Tanzania still sing the songs from missionary hymnals. Further complicating the narrative are smaller, often independent churches who work with Mennonites without officially joining Mennonite or Anabaptist organizations. For example, Mennonite Mission Network partners with Good News Theological Seminary in Ghana in educating workers and leaders in African Initiated Churches (AICs) in biblical studies.[29] In many countries, the indigenization of Anabaptism has been developing for decades and is essentially completed, whereas others continue to discern the essential characteristics of African Anabaptism and to separate those elements from the culture of the missionaries.

Many African Anabaptists worship in contexts of political unrest and violence. In Ethiopia, two years of warfare between the government and rebels in the Tigray region have left over four hundred thousand in the region living in famine-like conditions. Eight MKC churches in the region were burned and several members killed. As the postindependence Congolese story illustrates, where the peace position was not always seen as a core teaching, practicing Christian nonviolence in areas with unrest and warfare can be especially difficult. Nevertheless, when asked, a higher percentage of African churches stated that they would not participate in required military service than did North American respondents.

The political and financial distance between African Anabaptists and Mennonites in Europe and North America continues to remain an uncomfortable reality. The legacy of the colonial patterns of dependency still looms large for some African churches, and they have worked for decades to teach their members about the discipline of stewardship. That paternalistic legacy of mission work makes it difficult to ask Mennonites in North America and Europe to lend their relative wealth for the sake of their African co-religionists. In 2022, MKC president Desalegn Abebe appealed for North American aid in the face of a severe drought exacerbated by war, climate change, and the Russian invasion of Ukraine. However, Abebe cautioned, "Helping us doesn't make you lord. . . . It doesn't make you rich, doesn't make you blessed. . . . This is a mutual thing." He added, "We are all created in the image of God."[30]

African churches feel that the gifts that they can share with the global church are spiritual. In 2019, six leaders of LMC (formerly Lancaster Mennonite Conference) traveled to Ethiopia to learn how MKC has successfully multiplied over the previous decades. Just as African missionaries traveled to North America to bring the gifts of the East African Revival movement, some authors have wondered whether the missionary plants will increasingly travel from Africa to North America. One African scholar noted,

> The material resources of our brothers and sisters in the north are indeed substantial, but our spiritual resources in the south are equally as great. We want people in the north to connect with the spiritual depth of the churches in Africa. There is an awakening, an exciting sense of being alive. The Spirit of God is being unleashed among us. Reading and praying in isolation is not the answer. We feel there is a need for a spiritual awakening in North America and Europe. It is our firm conviction that Mennonites will pioneer in that, because they are people-oriented, and that is a great advantage.[31]

— TWELVE —

Conversion and Adaptation

Anabaptists in Asia

On January 30, 2016, around one hundred men and women gathered in Seoul, South Korea, to take part in the first Korean Anabaptist Conference, a new and dynamic expression of Anabaptism. There had been a long history of Christianity in Korea, and North American Mennonites had established a vocational school and served in social welfare agencies there since 1953, but the interest in the Anabaptist Christian tradition among Korean believers gained true momentum in the 1980s and 1990s. Disillusioned with the hierarchical rigidity and militarism of the Korean churches, students like Lee Yoon Shik traveled to North America to seek answers to the question, "What is the nature of the New Testament Church and how can we bring that church into our lives?"[1] In 1996, those who were convinced that the Anabaptist tradition most closely reflected early Christianity formed Jesus Village Church (JVC), the first Anabaptist congregation in South Korea. To support the growth and outreach of JVC, Korean Anabaptists worked with mission organizations, teachers, and theologians in Canada and

Conversion and Adaptation 263

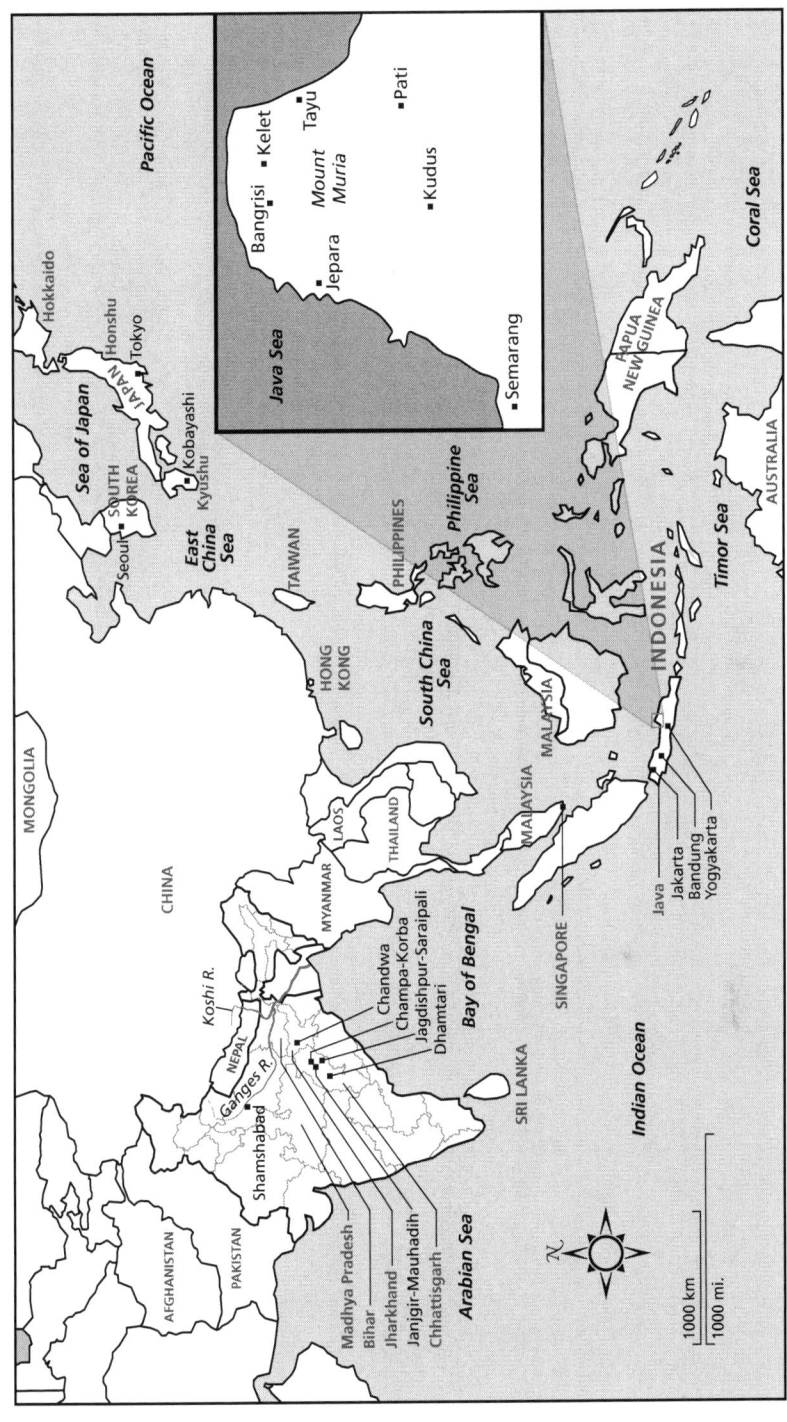

the United States to create school curriculum and a library of Anabaptist resources for the Korea Anabaptist Center, founded in Seoul in 2001. With their library and publishing efforts, Korean Anabaptists seek to change Korean Christians' negative perception of Christian pacifism, and they are finding that there is broader interest in "a healthy, biblical church, justice in the public square, and a tangible community based on the Anabaptist movement."[2]

Since World War II, Anabaptism in Asia has developed in a kaleidoscope of styles that reflect the origins, history, and culture of the local context. Some of the churches grew out of local initiatives, and others were planted by foreign mission agencies. Korean Anabaptists do not see themselves as a branch of the European or North American Mennonite tree, even though they see striking similarities between their search for a biblically authentic model of Christian community and the sixteenth-century European Anabaptists. They clarify that interest in Anabaptism arose not from missionaries, but out of the "deep desire within Korean Christians to find an alternative form of Christian expression that follows the New Testament model of Church and its head, Jesus Christ."[3]

Christianity in Asia

Comprising half the world's population, Asia is home to members of all major religions; however, most Asians identify as Muslim, Hindu, Buddhist, or nonreligious. The continent's culturally diverse people represent significant socioeconomic differences spanning the wealthy societies of South Korea and Japan to the more economically disadvantaged communities in India, the Philippines, and Indonesia. Christians in Asian contexts are often religious minorities, and the precarity of their status means that they must negotiate sensitive religious differences. Choosing to join an Anabaptist or any Christian church often leads to separation from traditional networks and social supports, not unlike the experiences of early Anabaptists.

Christianity was present in Asia long before the mission movements of the nineteenth century. According to apocryphal traditions, the apostle Thomas introduced Christianity in isolated pockets of India in the earliest days of the church. By the seventh and eighth centuries, traders had carried Nestorian Christianity to Malaysia,

China, and the Indonesian archipelago. Facing the rise of strong states such as the Muslim powers in central Asia and the Ming Dynasty in fourteenth-century China, Christian groups went underground or disappeared, whereas Korea and Japan remained relatively isolated from Christian influences. Christianity accompanied European colonization in the sixteenth century, most notably in the newly Catholic parts of the Philippines. Jesuit Catholic missionaries evangelized up to three hundred thousand Japanese believers until the ruler Tokugawa Iemitsu, suspicious of foreign influence, persecuted and eliminated Christian presence in his country. Inspired by Pietism, Moravian followers began the first modern missionary societies in Asia, and the earliest Mennonite missionaries in the nineteenth century followed the Moravian model in combining mission and relief work in India, China, and Indonesia.

The pattern of Christian privileges concluded with the end of the colonial era, and the devastating conflicts of World War II, the Korean War (1950–53), the Vietnam War (1955–75), and other Cold War proxy wars have strengthened resistance to Western ideas and influence, especially as China has developed into a new regional power. The end of the colonial period in Asia echoed the African experience, as some churches found themselves underprepared to take the reins of leadership from Western organizations, leading to struggles over leadership and control of church property. The churches in Asia have grown and now occupy leadership roles in global Mennonite organizations.

Anabaptist growth and change in Indonesia

Despite political turmoil and ethnic and religious violence, the Anabaptist-Mennonite churches that Tunggul Wulung, Tee Siem Tat, and Pieter Jansz started in Java, Indonesia (see ch. 8), continued to grow after World War II. The largely rural Gereja Injili di Tanah Jawa (Evangelical Javanese Church, or GITJ) remains concentrated in the Muria region and is mostly ethnically Javanese. In 2020, GITJ reported 117 congregations and 45,000 members. While its beginnings in the 1920s among Chinese Christians still shape its character, Gereja Kristen Muria Indonesia (Muria Christian Church of Indonesia, or GKMI) has expanded beyond its geographic and ethnic origins in its

64 congregations and nearly 16,000 members. The two older Indonesian groups have been joined in the Mennonite World Conference by the newest Anabaptist network, Jemaat Kristen Indonesia (Indonesia Christian Congregation, or JKI), which began as an intentionally indigenous prayer network. Since 1985, JKI has grown at an astounding rate into 400 congregations with 47,000 members.[4]

The stories of the three churches each reflect their unique native and missionary origins, but they share a common status as religious minorities in a predominantly Muslim country, which has shaped their history and identities.

World War II and Indonesian independence

When German forces invaded the Netherlands in 1940 (see ch. 9), they cut the nation off from the Dutch East Indies, thereby galvanizing Indonesians, led by the Muslim majority, to launch a campaign for independence. Before independence could be secured, Japan invaded the Dutch East Indies in 1942 to extend its imperial authority in Asia and secure the raw materials—especially oil—that it needed for its war in China. Initially, the Javanese greeted the Japanese army as liberators, but it soon became clear that Japan would install an authoritarian administration over the archipelago.

In the vacuum left by the retreat of Dutch colonial administrators from the Muria region, the radical Muslim organization Ansor waged a campaign of terror against Christians and ethnic Chinese, both of whom they saw as close sympathizers with Dutch authorities. Churches and hospitals were looted and damaged by mobs, and in the town of Tayu, Ansor members forced Muria Javanese leaders to disavow their faith under threat of torture and execution. The Kelet congregation organized an armed defense of their community, but opportunistic members of other congregations split church property among themselves. The loss of their leaders and destruction of their property profoundly affected Muria Javanese Christians.

Japanese authorities often encouraged Muslims to attack Javanese and Chinese Christians alike, but the mobs spared important Muria Chinese church buildings in Pati after one of the Muslim leaders reportedly said, "This is the house of the Lord Jesus."[5] Muria Chinese leaders managed to convince the Japanese authorities that they were not connected to the Dutch colonial authorities. The Japanese forbade the use of Chinese, closed Christian schools, and forced the Kudus congregation to abandon their Salvation Army hymnal and create their own songbook. Muria Chinese Christians fared relatively better than Javanese Christians, but the years of Japanese occupation, which lasted until mid-1945, were difficult for all Indonesians; famine and forced labor killed an estimated four million people.

Even before the war, both the Javanese and Chinese believers had been reevaluating their relationship to Western churches. At the first general assembly of the Javanese church, held in May 1941, Swiss missionary Daniel Amstutz proposed a statement of faith that included several Anabaptist practices, including adult baptism, rejection of the oath and military service, and nonresistance in one's personal life. Amstutz's Anabaptist items sparked strong opposition at the assembly, particularly among younger members. When it became clear that the doctrine of nonresistance would potentially alienate youth interested in joining the independence movement, it was dropped from the statement of faith. After the war, when the Dutch reclaimed control of their colony, church leaders agreed that politically active youth could join the guerrilla forces working toward Indonesian independence.

By the time Indonesia gained independence in 1949, the Muria Javanese Church had declined by half, from four thousand to two thousand members. Worried that they lacked sufficient resources to carry on their ministries, some leaders considered accepting an invitation to join the Reformed church, but the proposal was rejected in favor of continuing to maintain a Mennonite identity. The chair of the synod sent a frank letter to Daniel Amstutz, stating, "It is very clear that the churches of the Muria area no longer accept basic Mennonite teachings because we have gone to war and have taken oaths. We honestly confess that the Muria area church no longer maintains this particular identity."[6] Moved by the honest assessment, Amstutz responded that the Javanese were still welcome to consider themselves in good relationship with the Mennonite fellowship, despite all that happened during the war and the independence movement.

In contrast to the Javanese churches, the Muria Chinese congregations at Kudus, Pati, and Jepara grew during and after the war; however, it was also a time of reexamining their church structure and theology. In 1941, a new church order created the Muria Christian Church, but it was unclear how far the synod's authority would extend over individual congregations and whether the Kudus congregation and the descendants of Tee Siem Tat would continue to dominate matters. Increasingly, other members of the synod grew frustrated with the outsized role played by Tee Siem Tat's son-in-law Tan King Ien, as when he personally funded theological education in North America for his son Tan Hao An, better known as Herman Tan. In 1952, Tan King Ien funded his own travel to Basel, Switzerland, for the Mennonite World Conference, and when he returned from five months abroad, he found that the Kudus church had removed him from his roles as congregational chair and minister.

In the 1950s, the Muria Chinese Church synod attempted to clarify its theological identity, especially in relation to the Anabaptist-Mennonite tradition as taught in North America. Since its earliest days, the Muria Chinese movement had not concerned itself with theological precision, preferring to focus instead on evangelism, repentance, and baptism. Furthermore, the traditional Mennonite understanding of nonresistance had never been a central teaching point, especially during the years of the independence movement, when young Chinese Christians joined patriotic movements as expressions of national loyalty, just as young Javanese Christians had done. When Herman Tan introduced a new twenty-point confession of faith based on his studies at the Mennonite seminary in Goshen, Indiana, he met considerable resistance. Eventually, however, the synod adopted the confession, which included Anabaptist distinctives on adult baptism, discipleship, the oath, and a general peace position, and it adopted the name Muria Christian Churches of Indonesia (Persatuan Gereja-Gereja Kristen Muria Indonesia, or PGKMI), replacing the Chinese and Dutch names that they had used until then.

The Muria Javanese Church (known today as GITJ) found new growth after the waves of bloody retaliations that followed a coup attempt and the assassination of several generals on September 30, 1965 (known as G30S in Indonesia). Military reprisals targeted suspected Communists and ethnic Chinese, killing between 500,000 and 1.2 million people. The Muria Javanese Church aided victims while avoiding being swept up in mob violence, thereby standing out as an example of Christian love and charity amid horrific bloodshed. The church witnessed substantial expansion after 1965, when the government obliged all Indonesians to register membership in one of the nation's officially sanctioned religions. Former and suspected Communists preferred to join with Christian churches, since extremist Muslim organizations had perpetrated most of the bloodshed.

An era of leaders

In both Muria churches, a new generation of leaders attempted to restructure their synods in new directions and build firm foundations for long-term stability. Among the Muria Javanese (GITJ) churches, the tireless leader Soehadiweko Djojodihardjo hoped to make the Javanese churches independent from external funding. Pak Djojo (as Djojodihardjo was known) and other leaders worked closely with Mennonite Central Committee, the Dutch Mennonite Mission Council (Doopsgezinde Zendingsraad), and European Mennonite Evangelism Committee (Europäisches Mennonitisches Evangelisationskomitee, or EMEK). Djojodihardjo secured economic support for development

Fig. 12.1 Soehadiweko Djojodihardjo (*left*), an influential leader of the Javanese Mennonite Church, is interviewed at the 1967 Mennonite World Conference. Photo courtesy of *Canadian Mennonite*/Mennonite Archives of Ontario, Conrad Grebel University College, Waterloo, 4008.

projects and integrated the GITJ into international networks, including Mennonite World Conference.

Unfortunately, connection with the international networks and Djojodihardjo's leadership style contributed to ongoing patterns of dependency in the 1960s and 1970s. Djojodihardjo's significant role in multiple leadership positions drew criticism from members, especially the youth, who were looking for opportunities to serve and influence the church. When Djojodihardjo stepped down from his many positions in the mid-1980s, the church entered a period of strife around the control of church finances, resulting in similar arguments over church property and assets that also arose in African and Indian churches after the end of the missionary era. Synod meetings were sparsely attended and did not convene at all in 1990 and 1995, and a new synod was formed in 1996. Mennonite Central Committee and the Dutch mission councils mediated a reconciliation process that was completed in November 2000.

GKMI, meanwhile, was also led by a new generation, including Herman Tan, Charles Christano, Albert Widjaja, Mesach Krisetya, Andreas Setiawan, Adi Sutjipta, Chrismanto Jonathan, and Adi Sutanto. This new generation was theologically trained and desired to strengthen and centralize the synod's evangelistic activities against those of congregations, which had traditionally been the sites of earlier initiatives. Western aid agencies, accustomed to thinking of the church in institutional forms, were eager to support this effort financially. Herman Tan and others created the Foundation for Missions and Charities (also known as PIPKA) in 1965 to serve urban areas, especially those where GKMI youth were migrating for economic opportunity. Because it operated outside of the synod, PIPKA garnered significant criticism from those who pointed out that some of the money it raised might have gone to the synod instead. Eventually, PIPKA was handed over to the synod and became its main evangelical organization. In 2010, PIPKA, GKMI congregations, and Western agencies supported eighty-two mission posts. GKMI and PIPKA have deliberately expanded the church's appeal beyond ethnic Chinese Indonesians. As a result, it is now one of the few interethnic churches in Indonesia, with members from ethnic groups from across the country and mission outposts in Singapore and Mongolia.

A third network emerges

The church network now known as the Jemaat Kristen Indonesia (JKI) began as a charismatic revival movement from the island of Timor in the 1960s. At a time of anti-Chinese violence, GKMI was struggling with generational change in leadership, as young adults grew frustrated with traditional structures that made it difficult for them to use their gifts and education to serve the church. Under the leadership of twenty-year-old Agus Suwantoro, the informal fellowship group known as Keluarga Sangkakala—which had been meeting for fellowship and prayer in Semarang—organized an independent conference in Bangsri for "Workers in the Field of the Lord" (Konferensi Pelayan Ladang Tuhan, or KPLT).[7] Because the conference arose outside of church structures, some GKMI leaders were in opposition to the conference, whereas others agreed to attend and deliver addresses.

The 225 conference attendees experienced profound manifestations of the Holy Spirit during the five-day conference. Many had gifts of the Spirit, including "visions, prophecies, speaking in tongues, healing, and deliverance from evil spirits."[8] Money and food appeared when they were most needed, and some participants received the gift of locating fetishes—traditional objects of spiritual power—hidden in the homes of GKMI members. Young people spread the spiritual revival beyond Bangsri to other cities, including Yogyakarta, Bandung, Jakarta, Jepara, and Kudus. Despite the misgivings of some leaders about this new revival, GKMI worked with the young adults to start several new congregations.

Although the Sangkakala movement eventually lost momentum, some of its early leaders sought to reconstitute it in new forms. Adi Sutanto studied in the United States from 1973 to 1976 to learn how to integrate the spiritual spontaneity of the revival with an institutional framework that would allow GKMI to develop further and sustainably. When it became clear that his ideas would not be integrated by the GKMI, Adi Sutanto and his wife Sri Padmawati Adi founded a new organization called Yayasan Keluarga Sangkakala (Trumpet Family Foundation) in May 1977.

The new network began as small house fellowships, which meant that all members were asked to share their gifts with their group. Meeting weekly in the evening, the services were a time to worship, study, and eat together, thereby delivering a holistic and intimate religious experience that would not have been possible in traditional church structures. Increasingly, the vision of the movement expanded to include social ministries, including building schools, hospitals, and churches. Yayasan Keluarga Sangkakala revival meetings spread the evangelistic message to new cities, and by 1984 the prayer meetings that began in Adi Sutanto and Sri Padmawati Adi's home grew into sixteen hundred individuals meeting in forty-six groups. Adi Sutanto requested that the GKMI denomination recognize Sangkakala as a member or branch of the GKMI denomination, but the GKMI rejected the request because of the network's charismatic worship style.

In 1985, the Indonesian government enacted new regulations that required all religious communities to register with the government. This forced the Sangkakala network to organize themselves into a more formal entity known as Jemaat Kristen Indonesia, or JKI. Soon after, JKI applied for membership in the Mennonite World Conference. As JKI began to take on a more institutional structure, it faced a delicate balancing act. It sought to maintain the Spirit-filled vitality that had driven its origins while also adopting the more traditional structures of a synod or denomination. This balance was essential for JKI's growth and outreach.

Under the leadership of Adi Sutanto, JKI has nurtured an identity distinct from the two other Indonesian members of Mennonite World Conference. JKI's Indonesian theological perspective resonates deeply with the Indonesian context. With its emphasis on the gifts of the Holy Spirit, JKI is able to reach Indonesians who understand natural phenomena to manifest spiritual forces through miracles. Adi Sutanto has written, "In planting churches in Java among people that are animistic, we really need the power of the Holy Spirit, because . . . it is in particularly animistic societies that the cosmic struggle between Christ and Satan is most apparent."[9] This emphasis on indigeneity and freedom from foreign support led to an organizational structure that emphasized self-supporting congregations.

Because of JKI's loose denominational structure, each congregation is free to live out the gospel in its own context without undue interference from a denomination or synod, resulting in a wide range of church types and sizes among its four hundred congregations—including some in the United States, Australia, and the Netherlands. Given JKI's start in the Sangkakala years as small house fellowships, the rise of JKI megachurches has been a surprising development. The large congregations, which include five of Indonesia's largest churches, appeal to professional urban believers, who can still have a more intimate religious experience in smaller prayer or Bible study groups. In addition to vibrant worship services, the JKI megachurches offer holistic social services that reach thousands of people beyond the congregation, including many from the Muslim majority.

Ongoing questions

Though Indonesia is a secular state that tolerates six major world religions, Islam is the dominant religious and cultural force and enjoys significant social advantages. As minority religious groups, all three Anabaptist churches must sensitively negotiate relations with their Muslim neighbors. This is especially true for Chinese Christians, whose dual minority status can leave them especially vulnerable. As historian John D. Roth notes, "Each synod would describe itself as fully committed to evangelism, with GKMI and JKI quite vigorous in promoting their missional identity. Yet all the synods are extremely sensitive in their approach to evangelism in Muslim contexts."[10] In some cases, this has meant delaying baptism after a public confession of Christian faith and allowing new believers to delay changing their official religious affiliation on their identity card, given the significant social costs to conversion. All three groups have taken an invitational and cooperative approach to their Muslim neighbors, which may surprise those who are only familiar with news reports of interreligious violence in the Global South. After the December 2004 earthquake and tsunami that destroyed several Indian Ocean villages, Paulus Hartono, the founder of Mennonite Disaster Service in Indonesia, urged the local leader of Hezbollah, a Muslim paramilitary group in Indonesia, to collaborate at relief work in Aceh. Despite initial misgivings at working with an "infidel," the Hezbollah commander opened up to the opportunity and worked with Hartono and the MDS group. The commander later recounted, "He spoke to me about humility and about the earthquake in Aceh. I started to open my heart."[11] Despite notable breakthroughs, the Indonesian churches' reconciling work with their non-Christian neighbors has grown increasingly challenging in a climate of growing interreligious tension.

In recent years, Indonesian Mennonite church leaders like Charles Christano and Mesach Krisetya have taken on significant roles in Mennonite World Conference. However, in Indonesia, churches have typically called themselves simply Christian rather than emphasizing denominational differences. In recent decades, there has been increased interest in Anabaptist-Mennonite tradition, especially among the youth. As Anabaptist textbooks are increasingly used in seminaries and colleges, it is more common that an explicitly Mennonite identity is claimed, even though some Anabaptist traditions can be derived from Indonesian idioms and frameworks rather than Mennonite history. GITJ, for example, uses Indonesian art and cultural traditions to contextualize the Anabaptist view of peacemaking as an expression of *paseduluran*, a Javanese word for brotherhood. After the jointly hosted 2022 assembly of Mennonite World Conference in Indonesia, stronger relationships between the three Indonesian groups may lead to common partnerships in understanding what it means to embody Anabaptism in an Asian context.

Innovations and adaptations in India

Anabaptist groups in India have a rich history that dates to the nineteenth century (see ch. 8). Despite serious challenges, the Mennonite churches in India remain committed to their original mission of spreading the gospel and serving the people of India through social services and education.

As with all the earliest Asian Anabaptist groups, the character and direction of Indian Anabaptism changed significantly after World War II. The influx of missionaries into India stopped after the end of the war and Indian independence from the British Empire in 1947. As the framers drafted a new constitution for the independent nation, Indian Mennonite leader Rev. P. J. Malagar and missionary J. N. Kaufman were delegated to send letters to explain Mennonite faith and practice and "make petition on behalf of the Mennonite Church, asking for a provision in the new constitution guaranteeing to us, as well as to other religious groups holding views similar to our own, a degree of religious liberty." Several of the framers replied positively to the suggestion, and Mahatma Gandhi sent a handwritten note in reply to the letter writers, declaring, "Your letter, why worry? I am in the same boat with you."[12]

As support for the "missionaries bharat chodo" (missionaries leave India) movement gained strength throughout India, the government investigated foreign agencies and their work, granting fewer visas for missionaries. Sensing the shifting direction of the political winds, most foreign missionaries left India and handed the administration of the churches over to Indian believers. The postwar growth of the oldest conferences, therefore, was sown by the sacrifice and dedication of self-supported, Indian-led missions. As a result, the Indian churches have reflected Indian leadership and character for the last half of the twentieth century.

In 2020, the *Global Anabaptist Mennonite Encyclopedia Online* (*GAMEO*) identified thirteen Anabaptist groups in India, ranging in size from the 86 members of Church of God in Christ, Mennonite, to the 212,000 members of the Conference of the Mennonite Brethren Churches in India, the oldest and largest Indian Anabaptist conference. The following six conferences illustrate the range of the largest groups as of the 2020 report.

- *Bharatiya Mennonite Church in India ki Pratinidhi Sabha (Mennonite Church in India, or MCI).* The first missionaries arrived in 1899 and settled in Madhya Pradesh near Dhamtari, but MCI members have now spread throughout India. Mostly rural, some churches have declined in numbers as children of converts have moved to cities for work. The denomination has been self-administered since 1952. (3,912 members)[13]

- *Bharatiya General Conference Mennonite Church (BGCMC).* Initially begun by missionaries who arrived in 1899, BGCMC is now divided regionally between the older areas of Champa-Korba and Janjgir-Mauhadih and newer work in the southern region of Jagdishpur-Saraipali. This linguistic division has contributed to divisions in the church, which has seen new growth and missions, especially in urban industrialized areas. (5,073 members)

- *Bihar Mennonite Mandli (BMM).* In 1940, Ida and S. J. Hostetler, missionaries from the Mennonite Board of Missions, moved from Dhamtari to Chandwa to establish what would become Bihar Mennonite Mission. The church plant struggled to grow, but after they distributed free meals during a devastating famine in the late 1960s, the mission survived and grew; it became independent in 1972. A generation of new leadership has revitalized the mostly rural congregations with highly educated members in the state of Jharkhand. (1,175 members)

- *Brethren in Christ Church Society, or Bharatiya Khristiya Mandali (Brethren in Christ Churches in North Bihar).* This group was founded in the mountainous region of Upper Bihar along the Koshi River, which changes course every ten years, earning it the nickname "River of Sorrows." The difficult environment hampered the establishment of mission stations among the Hindi-speaking believers, but mission work among the Santali people quadrupled the membership thanks to the "each one win one" approach of witnessing among friends and relatives. (2,597 members)

- *Conference of the Mennonite Brethren Churches in India (CMBCI).* Missionaries arrived in the Telugu-speaking region in late 1899, and CMBCI became self-governing in 1958. With a focus on evangelism and mission, the conference has grown into the largest Anabaptist conference in India and the second largest in the world. In one survey, 95 percent of CMBCI respondents grew up in Mennonite homes, and most were second- or third-generation Mennonites. In addition to evangelism, the conference operates schools, hospitals, and the Mennonite Brethren Centenary Bible College in Shamshabad, which runs the Center for Peace and Conflict Resolution Studies in addition to offering several other degrees. (212,000 members)

- *Bharatiya Jukta Christa Prachar Mandali, or BJCPM (Indian United Christ Evangelical Church).* Planted by the United Missionary Church in North America, BJCPM is a member of Mennonite World Conference even though the North American United Missionary Church is not. Frances Matheson and Ruby Reeves of Aylmer, Ontario, worked for the Methodist Episcopal Church for thirteen years before their own church organized the United Missionary Society in 1921, at which time they transferred their efforts to their denominational mission work. Materials from the BJCPM's Calcutta Bible Institute have reached 150,000 students. BJCPM does not identify as a Mennonite church but is active in Mennonite World Conference and inter-Mennonite relief work in India. (4,310 members)

Indian Anabaptists mostly come from disadvantaged socioeconomic groups, like the Dalits, poor farm laborers, or tribal groups. Scholars who study northeast tribal groups suggest that the translation of Christianity into tribal languages and idioms was a means for members of tribal groups who converted to preserve elements of their traditional culture from the encroachment of India's major religions.[14] The postindependence constitution of India identifies marginalized Dalit groups as Scheduled Castes and grants them Reservation status

Fig. 12.2 Students at Dhamtari Christian Academy (later named Mennonite Higher Secondary School), date unknown. Photo reprinted with permission of Mennonite Church USA Archives, Elkhart, Indiana, Mennonite Board of Missions Photograph Collection, India MP, 1939–1963, IV-10-7.2, box 4, folder 23, photo #145.

guaranteeing political representation, education quotas, and other affirmative actions, but many continue to suffer from low social status. After converting, Christian Dalits continued to practice their traditional occupations and suffered the stigma of their social background. In response to the hardships of their members' lives, Dalit churches have increasingly explored Dalit Christian theology, which shares themes with Latin American liberation theology and Black liberation theology. Dalit theology thus emphasizes the solidarity of those who suffer and the Christian values of sacrifice, commitment, and care for others. "Dalit Theology," according to church historian I. P. Asheervadham, "affirms the identity of the Dalits before God as people among whom God is working against oppression, and many Dalit communities are beginning to feel empowered by claiming their Dalitness."[15]

Despite initial misgivings and resistance, some Indian Anabaptists have experience renewal through exposure to Pentecostal revivals. Shantkumar Kunjam, bishop in MCI, recounted how the Mennonites initially resisted Pentecostal influences, but "now the presence of Pentecostal churches and leaders are acknowledged and accepted. There is no more open rivalry between the two. In fact, the MCI has accepted changes in its own worship patterns. There is more singing in worship and people are invited to share what the Lord has been doing in their lives during the past week."[16]

Women have served the churches in India since their earliest days, but they have only recently been ordained for ministry—the Mennonite Brethren Church ordained its first twenty-six women in 2008. The year before, the church revised its constitution to allow women to serve in the administration and leadership of the church. Rev. Sarada Arnold was elected vice president of the Governing Council. With a more curtailed role, women in the BJCPM can pray in public, but they cannot preach from the pulpit. Church worker Cynthia Peacock and other women have worked to offer theological training and form an independent women's group, but their efforts have met resistance or non-cooperation from male leaders.[17] In BJCPM and BGCMC churches, women are ordained as deacons and can preach, though not from the pulpit. Notable exceptions include Margaret Devadasan, who sometimes preached in BJCPM churches, and Cynthia Peacock, an advocate for increased roles for women.

Leadership struggles

The growth of institutions and regional differences have divided Indian churches in recent decades. From 1991 to 2001, BGCMC churches split over tensions between the conference secretary and president, leading to a decades of disunity and confusion among members, and with each side filing police reports against the other. That dispute was reconciled in 2001, but church life declined significantly during the contentious decade. In August 2020, the International Community of Mennonite Brethren declared that it no longer recognized P. B. Arnold's leadership over the Mennonite Brethren (MB) conference, after years of correspondence in which it expressed concerns about abuse of power, misappropriation of resources, and the use of courts to settle disputes. Indian MBs have opposed Arnold's leadership and attempts to sell off church properties with fasting prayers, marches, and hunger strikes.[18] The dispute remains unsettled in the court system, making the denomination's organizational future uncertain. The historian I. P. Asheervadham has proposed that Bihar Mennonite Mandli (BMM) avoided the splits of other conferences because it lacks church-owned property, the control of which has been at the heart of some conference disputes.[19]

Anabaptist identity in a multireligious country

While India is officially a multifaith country, there have been recent flare-ups of religious animosity and even violence. In a climate of increasing religious tensions, Indian Anabaptists work to preserve their distinct traditions while wanting to participate fully in the surrounding society. Their innovations are unique among the global Mennonite church. For example, the Mennonite Brethren Conference leadership recently decided to adopt clerical dress for its ministers. When leadership introduced the idea at the conference's 150-year celebration in 2010, they intended it to serve as witness to longevity and stability in a multiethnic and multireligious India, not as a marker of status within the priesthood. Mennonite missionaries often rejected distinctive dress when they arrived in India, but some Indian groups have chosen to set themselves apart through their clothing.

The different practices and interpretations of baptism among Indian Anabaptists reflect how the varied traditions of the missionaries who planted the first churches shaped the different Anabaptist expressions and practices. For example, MCI baptizes new members by pouring and typically performs footwashing before communion. BGCMC, on the other hand, practices baptism by sprinkling, but not footwashing, whereas BMM baptizes through immersion and celebrates footwashing. In November 2022, Indian Mennonite leaders from seven conferences gathered virtually to study the theological significance of baptism and how it is practiced. Beyond the differing modes of baptism, understanding the complexities of baptism can be difficult. Nishant Sidh, a member of Mennonite Church Rajnandgaon, explained the complexity of baptism in India, as it intertwines church membership with institutional access and social expectations in ways reminiscent of villages in the Russian Mennonite commonwealth of the nineteenth century:

> "To many of the candidates seeking baptism, [it] is a legal, social and religious requirement and not much more than that." . . . Baptism, [Sidh] explained, allows one to become a member of a church and enjoy all the rights and privileges that come with it. Men cannot get married, unless they are baptized into the church. Baptism makes getting a job in a Christian institution easier. Yet because of these requirements, "many of the candidates are being baptized without the saving knowledge of Christ."[20]

Indian Anabaptists have also emphasized and taught the Anabaptist peace position to different degrees. Mennonite Church India has taught the separation of church and state and refusal to serve in the military or police force since its earliest days. Since independence, MCI members who have served in the armed forces have been excommunicated. The Center for Peace and Conflict Resolution Studies at Mennonite Brethren Centenary Bible College in Shamshabad has been a valuable resource for Indians who want to study reconciliation and the pursuit of peace in all human relations.

Recently, Christian and other minority groups in India have been intimidated and harassed by anti-Christian and anti-Muslim groups. In 2021, J. Nelson Kraybill, then the president of Mennonite World Conference, sent a letter of support to believers in India who have been pressured by the government to close churches and mosques in rural villages. Kraybill's pastoral letter quoted a letter from a Mennonite pastor in India, who recounted, "Last week, our church abruptly stopped its Sunday service due to threats from anti-religious groups."[21] Vigilantes had passed videos of the congregation to police to encourage them to shut the congregation down.

After the departure of foreign workers and funds in the 1950s and 1960s, Indian Anabaptists reexamined the divisions that they inherited from the missionaries' backgrounds, and differences in history and practice seemed less significant to Indians than they had been for the missionaries. In the 1960s, six conferences began cooperating with each other in the Mennonite Christian Service Fellowship of India (MCSFI). Led by bishop P. J. Malagar, MCSFI cooperated with the North American service organization Mennonite Central Committee in disaster relief, supporting voluntary service, strengthening inter-Mennonite fellowship, and promoting evangelism and peace education. Bishop Malagar, looking back on the founding of the Indian churches, lamented that the missionaries had not taught a stronger peace position. In light of what he saw as Indian Mennonite complacency about injustice and war, he wrote: "Possibly the Indian Mennonites need to develop their own genius in this field rather than just become too intelligent in Anabaptist history and theology."[22] The century-long story of Indian Anabaptists is, indeed, that of churches

Fig. 12.3 P. J. Malagar, MCSFI executive secretary, at his retirement, 1979.
Photo reprinted with permission of Mennonite Heritage Archives, Winnipeg, 280-50.0-004.

with a "genius" for discerning their identity as Anabaptist Christians in a multireligious society that has linked a holistic gospel of body and soul since their earliest days.

A peace church in Japan

After Japan's defeat and the end of World War II, many Japanese people grew disillusioned with the country's militarism and traditional religions, ushering in an era of openness to new religions. After the postwar government adopted a "peace constitution," four different Anabaptist-related groups sent missionaries to Japan, finding many people interested in a peaceable type of Christianity different from those of other missionary groups. Takashi Yamada, for example, secretly opposed the war while serving in the navy, and was spiritually exhausted when he began attending English classes taught by General Conference missionary Peter Voran. After deciding to follow Christ, Yamada joined the small church group that met in Voran's home and studied theology in Tokyo. Eventually, Yamada served as pastor in several congregations and as conference chair.[23] Describing his hopes for the Kirishima Christian Brotherhood in Kobayashi, Miyazaki Prefecture, Yamada wrote, "In our brotherhood we are interested in examining our religion, faith, ideas and lives in light of the Bible and our religious

Fig. 12.4 Takashi Yamada, pastor in Kobayashi, Japan, and vice-chair of the Asian Mennonite Conference.

Photo reprinted with permission of Mennonite Heritage Archives, Winnipeg.

Fig. 12.5 Worshipers at Kushiro Mennonite Church, Sunday morning, August 1954. Photo reprinted with permission of Mennonite Church USA Archives, Elkhart, Indiana, Mennonite Board of Missions Photograph Collection, Japan, 1950–1957, IV-10-7.2, box 5, folder 36, photo #7.

tradition, namely the spiritual legacy of 16th-century Anabaptists, and to carefully consider how our faith and practice can continue to take root and grow in the real world."[24]

Today, the primarily urban congregations of Japan Mennonite Brethren Churches (Nihon Menonaito Burezaren Kyodan) and Japan Brethren in Christ Church (Nihon Kirisuto Keiteidan) are located on the Japanese mainland of Honshu. The Japan Mennonite Christian Church Conference (Nihon Menonaito Kirisuto Kyokai Kyogikai) churches were planted by the Mennonite Church in mostly agricultural regions on the island of Hokkaido, north of Honshu. In addition to congregations in declining rural areas, there are now congregations in Hokkaido's cities. Most of the churches in the Japan Mennonite Christian Church Conference (Nihon Menonaito Kirisuto Kyokai Kaigi) are in cities on the Island of Kyushu, to the south of Honshu. A new conference of congregations in Tokyo was created in 1964, now known as the Tokyo Area Fellowship of Mennonite Churches (TAFMC). In 2020, there were sixty-eight congregations with 2,628 members.

Though few in number, the Japanese churches struggle with some of the same issues as Mennonites in other countries. In rural Hokkaido, young adults looking for greater opportunities are moving to cities, where they may not find a church community. Many Mennonite pastors study in seminaries from other denominations, where the theological training may not reinforce Anabaptist themes. The different Mennonite conferences are exploring how to cooperate with each other for greater effectiveness, but they do not always share a mutual understanding of what it means to be Anabaptist. As the churches develop, they are looking for new ways to share the gospel of peace in Japan to a new generation.[25]

Anabaptism in Asia: A complex story

Anabaptists are present in many other parts of Asia as well, including China, Vietnam, Myanmar, and Taiwan, making Asia home to some of the oldest, youngest, largest, and smallest global Anabaptist groups. While the cultural and socioeconomic difference between Anabaptists in industrialized Japan or South Korea and those to the south and west makes it difficult to sketch a collective portrait of Asian Anabaptists, all the Anabaptist groups are commonly countercultural. Discipleship and worship are expressed distinctively in areas where the great global religions of Islam, Buddhism, Confucianism, Hinduism, Shintoism, and Taoism have deep cultural and social roots.

Many Anabaptists look for ways to live out their faith in a manner that embraces the central teachings of the tradition while acknowledging and integrating traditional cultural patterns. For many Asian and African Christians, converting to Anabaptism can often mean discerning how they should live out the gospel message in cultures where deceased ancestors are commonly venerated. In Taiwan, for example, clan and folk religious practices are part of the social fabric, and joining the church can affect the convert's extended family's social standing. When a young man joined the Taiwanese Mennonite Church in 1981, "one of his parents was very angry and asked him, 'Will you let me be a starving ghost or provide food to me after my death?' Nobody in the family talked to him from that moment on, as if he were invisible."[26] Whether Christianity entails a total rejection of traditional religious practices will continue to be a key question for Asian Anabaptists in the future.

— THIRTEEN —

Migration and Mission

Latin American Anabaptists

The history of Christianity in Latin America begins with the arrival of Spanish and Portuguese conquistadores in the Western Hemisphere around 1500. They came to claim the land for their respective monarchies, and as they seized territories from Mexico to Chile, they conquered and colonized the region while disease devastated the Indigenous inhabitants of Mesoamerica and South America. To cultivate their plantations, the Europeans trafficked and enslaved people from Africa. Today, the Indigenous, African, and racially mixed people of Latin America reflect the history of colonized Mesoamerica and South America.

The Portuguese and Spanish rulers of Latin America used the Roman Catholic Church to administer their territories. This effort aimed to replace or suppress the traditional pre-Columbian cultures prevalent in the region, and over the next four centuries, the project mostly succeeded.[1] As a result, the first people to join Mennonite churches did not convert from other religions—they came seeking alternatives to Catholicism.

For centuries, the Catholic Church had worked with the Spanish and Portuguese authorities to govern the colonies. Because the Catholic Church was seen as the arm of repressive Spanish and Portuguese authorities, newly independent governments invited Protestant missionaries in order to appear more progressive. Early Mennonite missionaries were happy to be linked with other Protestant minorities, often modeling their mission efforts after those of mainstream Protestant organizations.

In his history of Latin American Mennonites, Jaime Prieto notes that the complex history of the church reflects the different ways it arrived in the region—through mission and migration. Like churches in Africa and Asia, many of the churches were established with support from North American mission agencies. Other Mennonites migrated to Latin America from Canada or Europe, resulting in a different type of separatist, German-speaking Mennonite community. Today, Mennonites are present in over twenty Latin American countries, and their churches are as diverse as the countries they live in. Latin America is the region where Anabaptism is growing the fastest, with 65 percent of its church members having converted since 1991. The stories in this chapter highlight themes common among the rich diversity of Mennonite communities in Latin America, including the Caribbean.

Missions

Argentina

In 1919, members of the Cavadore family gathered in the home of Mae and Tobias Hershey to worship with others who had converted after a series of recent evangelistic campaigns. That service in the Hershey family home in Pehuajó, Argentina, formed the nucleus of what would become the first Anabaptist church in Latin America, and the Cavadores became some of its early leaders. Within four years, work would begin on the construction of a new church for the believers, most of whom were Spanish and Italian immigrants or their children.

West of Pehuajó, in the town of Trenque Lauquen, Emma E. and Josephus W. Shank began their missionary work in 1920, mostly among English families who worked for the railroad. By November that year, Spanish-language services had begun. Evangelization work was taken up by Albano Luayza, the first Argentinian Mennonite pastor. Luayza led the church in Santa Rosa, which persevered despite resistance from local groups who refused to rent a house to the missionaries.

Another important leader in the early Argentinian church was Anita Cavadore, a member of the Italian immigrant family who joined the church in its earliest days, and whose leadership was critical to

Fig. 13.1 Trenque Laquan Church, Argentina. Photo reprinted with permission of Mennonite Church USA Archives, Elkhart, Indiana, Mennonite Board of Missions, Photographs, Argentina, 1942–1963, IV-10-7.2, box 1, folder 42, photo #13.

its survival. Originally from Pehuajó, Anita Cavadore worked as an assistant to the mission started by the Shanks in Trenque Lauquen. She was a "Bible reader" in the community, a worker who evangelized the community by going door to door. Along with Emma E. Shank, Cavadore visited thirty families a week and taught Sunday school as well. Cavadore's importance to the Mennonite church and those who joined it was acknowledged in 1930, when she was elected to serve on its national board of directors.

As the Mennonites expanded into mission fields across Argentina, they had to discern how to adapt to changing political contexts marked by repressive military regimes between 1930 and 1940. The missionaries counseled the churches to avoid making statements about the political situation or the socialist groups trying to organize workers in its opposition, but when Argentina grew more militarized in the interwar years, some began to speak out. As it appeared that the world was heading to a second global war, Mennonites debated their responses to the impending crisis. The missionary L. S. Weber encouraged Mennonites to put their energies into preparing for the next world rather than changing this one—he believed military disarmament was an unrealistic goal, and it was more likely that this was the beginning of the second coming of Christ.

Having recently emigrated from Spain and Italy, Argentinian Mennonites paid close attention to the Spanish Civil War and the rise of Benito Mussolini's Fascist government. They rejected Weber's

Fig. 13.2 Albano Luayza preaching at Ituzaingo Mennonite Church in Buenos Aires, Argentina, on September 11, 1970.
Photo reprinted with permission of Mennonite Church USA Archives, Elkhart, Indiana, Mennonite Board of Missions, 1882–2002, Photographs, 1899–2003, Argentina Mission Relief Work, 1960s–1970s, IV-10-07.2, box 1, folder 44.

Migration and Mission 289

theological advice out of a conviction that Mennonites should share the gospel of peace. At the 1934 congress of the Argentine League of Protestant Women, Felisa Cavadore presented a fiery message to the delegates to take Jesus' message seriously: "If Jesus promised to bless the peacemakers, it is because he wanted us to be peacemakers." Albano Luayza criticized Mussolini directly, writing, "Can Italy wage war in the aid of Christendom? No! No! War is anti-Christian. Jesus said, 'Love your enemies, Do good to those who hate you.' . . . Pray God that the group of faithful Christian grow, who are capable of dying for the ideal of peace, rather than carrying homicidal arms for the destruction of their fellow human beings!"[2] In the end, Argentina declared its traditional stance of neutrality, which it maintained despite political upheaval during World War II.

In 1943, Mennonite missionaries bought forty acres in Legua 17 to settle missionary families and begin their work among the Indigenous Toba people in the Argentinian Chaco. When Pentecostal meetings in the 1950s revived Protestant spiritual life throughout the country, the growing spiritual revival connected with the Toba, who were suffering from disease and tighter military control of the region. This revival of the Holy Spirit engaged their traditional religious sensibilities. Previously, only traditional shamans underwent spiritual transformation; now, spiritual experiences were available to everyone. In large revival meetings, over two hundred people would be baptized in response to the Holy Spirit's guidance.

During this time, the missionaries Albert and Lois (Litwiller) Buckwalter stressed the importance of spreading the gospel in the Toba language and accompanying rather than seeking to control the Indigenous churches that were developing. This enabled the Toba to assume leadership of their own churches—as pastor Aurelio López said, "I received a revelation. We wish to make our own aboriginal church. Let us stop following after the white people. When we establish this church I want to take the hand of an aboriginal to be pastor, to organize the church."[3] The Buckwalters worked alongside the new Toba churches, advocating for their churches' legal status at a time when the government was trying to exert its control over them.

Mennonite missionaries continued to work with the newly formed United Evangelical Church and other Indigenous churches in the

Fig. 13.3 (*Front row, left to right*) Albert Buckwalter with Mariano Naporichi, J. Sanchez, and A. Acre, members of the Saenz Pena community.
Photo courtesy of *Canadian Mennonite*/Mennonite Archives of Ontario, Conrad Grebel University College, Waterloo, 153.

Argentinian Chaco to collaborate in the translating of Scripture. From 1971 to 2010, Byrdaline and Willis Horst, for example, worked with the Indigenous leaders of the evangelical church Iglesia Evangélica Unida. To make Scripture accessible to nonreaders, Byrdaline Horst and Pilagá translators recorded dramatic presentations of the Gospels and Acts. This radical approach of walking alongside Indigenous Christians as companions rather than supervisors continued the standard set by Albert and Lois Buckwalter decades before.

After the end of the US mission and the creation of the Iglesia Evangélica Menonita Argentina (IEMA) in the 1950s, American missionaries collaborated with local pastors and lay leaders to enhance the church's economic self-sufficiency, with Argentinian leadership increasing steadily. Several charismatic movements influenced missionaries and leaders in the 1960s and 1970s. Looking back on four years of charismatic renewal, Raúl García, president of the IEMA, said, "The Lord with his Spirit blows where He wills, as He wills and when He wills. All that is left for us to know is how to adjust the sails of our vessels properly so that we don't block the blowing of the wind; nor should we ourselves try to blow more than the wind does, negating the free passage of the wind of God."[4] The church's membership was 650 in 1953; 2,000 by 1988; and 4,426 in 2022.[5]

Colombia and beyond

In the late 1940s, Mennonite Brethren (MB) and General Conference (GC) Mennonite Church mission work began in Colombia. The MB mission focused on the regions of el Chocó and del Valle near the Pacific coast, whereas the GC work was more inland, near Cachipay. Today's Iglesia Evangélica Menonita de Colombia is the successor to the GC mission work, and Iglesias Cristianas Hermanos Menonitas de Colombia the successor of the MB work.

The MB and GC Mennonite workers arrived at a time when the country was beginning to spiral into civil war. New believers were ostracized by their families and repressed by officials for their non-Catholic beliefs. To survive the repression, early converts formed tight-knit communities, where they worshiped, studied the Bible, and supported one another. As the repression relaxed in the 1950s and 1960s, members of the rural churches moved to cities, opening their witness to more people. They created welcoming networks for other newcomers and evangelized in underdeveloped urban areas.

From the 1980s to the first decade of the 2000s, Colombia's violent civil war escalated as Cold War tensions intensified the conflict between nationalist forces, drug cartels, and a leftist guerrilla movement. Despite the violence, the MB and GC churches maintained their nonviolent commitments, combining spiritual renewal and a concern for social justice to reach out to people displaced and marginalized by the growing crisis. The patterns of close community support they developed in the 1950s and 1960s served them well when civil war flared up again.

In response to the rising violence and injustice, Mennonites in Colombia founded the Justapaz ("a just peace") program in 1990 to promote nonviolence and peacebuilding. Longtime director Ricardo Esquivia promoted nonviolence among neighborhood organizations, even in the face of death threats from paramilitary groups. Working with other churches, Justapaz continues to work for peace at great personal risk to its members. Like many Central and South American

Fig. 13.4 The dedication service at the first Mennonite church in Bogota, Colombia, Iglesia Cristiana Menonita de Ciudad Berna, 1967. Photo courtesy of *Canadian Mennonite*/Mennonite Archives of Ontario, Conrad Grebel University College, Waterloo, 2.

Mennonites, Colombian Mennonites have lived out their faith amid political and economic difficulties.

After the 1972 Mennonite World Conference in Curitiba, Brazil, the Anabaptist Latin American Study Group presented a statement on justice and nonviolence that illustrates the close connection between charismatic revival and concern for social justice that characterizes much of Latin American Anabaptism. The statement condemned economic injustices in Paraguay and El Salvador; the murder of Indigenous people in Brazil, Colombia, and Paraguay; and the torture and repression by regimes in Argentina, Paraguay, Bolivia, Brazil, and Uruguay. Its authors called for "a new outbreak of the Holy Spirit, who can show us that being silent in the face of these injustices means that we accept them; . . . [may the Spirit] help us to open our eyes and see the oppressed, to identify ourselves with them, to work for their liberation, even if it costs us our privileges, while at the same time loving those who oppress."[6] The combination of spiritual revival with calls for social justice reflects a tradition among Anabaptists stretching back to the sixteenth century.

Women in leadership

When North American missionaries arrived in Latin America, they taught that women were to remain under the authority of men and be silent in worship, referring to 1 Corinthians 11:1–16 for scriptural support. Despite this instruction, women like Anita Cavadore were essential to the early growth and spread of the Mennonite churches, echoing the history of missions across the globe. As equal rights movements spread throughout Latin America in the 1960s and 1970s, they also affected Mennonite churches.

In 1984, at the annual Consulta Anabautista Menonita Centroamericana (CAMCA; Central American Anabaptist Mennonite Consultation) in Honduras, and the 1985 meeting in Costa Rica, attendees took up the themes of "the role of Christian women in the churches of Central America" and "the ministry of women," respectively. Presenters like Alba Elena Castillo and Leonor Méndez presented evidence from philosophy and the Bible to argue for greater participation of women in leadership. Examples of women judges in the Old Testament and Jesus' treatment of women were seen as support for their equality as Christians.

Mennonite women in Spanish-speaking and Indigenous churches increasingly serve in leadership roles. In Puerto Rico, they have served as pastors and deacons since the 1980s. The Colombian Mennonite Church affirmed the right of women to be ordained as pastors in 1989. María Rodríguez became the first female pastor in Costa Rica after years of serving in pastoral roles. Today, women's pastoral ministry is recognized in nearly all Mennonite and Brethren in Christ conferences, and women study theology at Mennonite seminaries in Colombia and Guatemala.[7]

Latin American women who attended the 2003 Mennonite World Conference in Bulawayo, Zimbabwe, were challenged by the African women theologians they met and formed the Movement of Latin American [Women] Theologians (Movimiento dé teólogas latinoamericanas) to reflect collectively on how to promote greater involvement and equality for women.[8] If the trend of increasing women in leadership continues, churches that embrace women in leadership will offer a unique Anabaptist witness in the region and a sharp contrast with the patriarchal structures of Low German–speaking Mennonite churches.

Low German Mennonite migration

In addition to mission and outreach, Anabaptism is a global phenomenon because of the migration of Low German–speaking Mennonites who have established communities across the Americas in their pursuit of political freedom and economic opportunity. Some have adapted to modern life and the surrounding culture, whereas others have perpetually sought new lands so they can separate themselves from society, even readopting horse-and-buggy lifestyles.

In 1916, when the provincial governments of Manitoba and Saskatchewan mandated compulsory public education and instruction in English, several thousand conservative Mennonites left for northern Mexico or the Chaco in Paraguay (see ch. 9). Six thousand Old Colony Mennonites, around half of those living in Canada, moved to Chihuahua, Mexico, in a caravan of steel-wheeled wagons. The early, drought-stricken years were difficult, and many families returned to Canada. However, those who stayed emphasized that they had moved for religious freedom rather than economic gain. Despite the hardships, in 1927 a letter reported, "Well, by now many a reader will wonder—what good can come from Mexico. It is this, that with regard to churches and schools we have complete religious freedom."[9] The Old Colony members saw their suffering as a natural consequence of their

Fig. 13.5 A group of Sommerfelder Mennonites leaving Altona, Manitoba, for Paraguay, 1926. Photo reprinted with permission of Mennonite Heritage Archives, Winnipeg, PP-Photo coll. 166-294.0.

pursuit of faithfulness, a price they were willing to pay to preserve their traditions in relative isolation.

While the Old Colony Mennonites were settling in Chihuahua, Sommerfelder and Bergthaler Mennonites—the two other groups that had settled in Manitoba in the 1870s—were making their way to a remote location in the Chaco jungle in Paraguay, where President Manuel Gondra's government promised them freedom of religion. After a difficult journey along the Paraguay River, they established Menno Colony in the inhospitable land of the Chaco. Letters back to Canada reported a grim reality, describing the "green hell": little food, children dying, and boils and other sores on the adults. Within a year, however, correspondents wrote of bountiful crops and the hope of many good years to come. "[We] are all looking forward with hope into the future. [We] have . . . good water and the fecundity with few exceptions is not wanting. . . . The people are enjoying the fruits of their labour."[10]

In the 1930s, Menno colonists were joined by two thousand Low German Mennonites, primarily from the Soviet Union, whom Mennonite Central Committee helped settle nearby in Fernheim Colony. Another 240 families settled in Curitiba, Brazil. The Mennonite Brethren, Mennonite Church, and Evangelical Mennonites who had fled the Soviet Union had to relearn religious and spiritual practices that had been lost during the years of Soviet repression. Some felt that they had been sold a false bill of goods about life in Paraguay. Fernheim struggled to prevent a third of their members from leaving to establish Friesland Colony in hopes of a better location in eastern Paraguay.

Distraught at the difficult life in the Chaco, many Fernheim colonists hoped that they would soon be able to return to Europe, particularly Germany. They saw Adolf Hitler's National Socialist government as a potential financial benefactor, as well as a bulwark against the Soviet Union. As several Mennonite leaders affirmed, "We know and give thanks that God created National Socialism in the time of the great Bolshevik danger for Western Europe. The almighty God has let Adolf Hitler be a great blessing to many nations, and we hope that He preserve our beloved homeland for many years."[11] Having suffered at the hands of the USSR for decades, they now looked to leaders who took a perceived Soviet threat seriously.

Fig. 13.6 Mennonite settlers in the village of Friedensfeld, Fernheim Colony, 1930. Photo reprinted with permission of Mennonite Heritage Archives, Winnipeg, 518-32.0.

Several influential leaders attempted to establish support for National Socialism through newspapers and youth organizations, despite fierce resistance from other Fernheimers. When three North American missionaries from Argentina arrived in Fernheim in April 1940, some of the colonists were celebrating Adolf Hitler's birthday. Shocked at what they found, the missionaries promoted pacifism and voluntary service and admonished the colonists to drop their support for a government that was waging war in Europe. Soon thereafter, North American missionaries visited the colony to teach North American Mennonite understandings of Anabaptism.

After World War II, forty-five hundred new Soviet Mennonite arrivals—mostly women and children—who had fled the Soviet Union through Poland and Germany organized the Volendam and Neuland Colonies in Paraguay. Others created colonies in Uruguay, Argentina, and Bolivia. Many of these settler families eventually left for what they hoped were easier lives in Canada or other parts of Latin America, but those who stayed grew more secure economically and religiously, and they soon established Spanish-speaking churches in Asunción and mission outreach to Indigenous groups.

Today, there are twenty-five thousand Indigenous Anabaptists in Paraguay, including members of the Enlhet, Nivaclé, Guaraní, and other Indigenous groups. The twenty-five hundred members of the Convención Evangélica Hermanos Menonitas Enlhet locate their origin in the baptisms of seven Enlhet men by Mennonite Brethren colonists in 1946. In 1948, two of the men traveled by oxcart for many days to preach the gospel to others, sowing the seeds of today's church.

Old Colony Mennonites continued to expand through migration in the perpetual pursuit of land where they could maintain the religion of their ancestors. In 1948, Kleine Gemeinde Mennonites from Canada started a settlement near the Old Colony settlement in Chihuahua. When the Mexican government implemented social security initiatives that threatened to bind the Mennonites closer to government intervention and support, Old Colony and Kleine Gemeinde delegates investigated new places to settle. As an English-speaking country under British control, British Honduras (now Belize) offered the Mennonites military exemption, freedom from the oath, the right to run private schools, and "protection of life and property."[12]

In Belize, many of these Old Colony Mennonites returned to a horse-and-buggy lifestyle. In their quest for land, other conservative Old Colony Mennonites left the settlement for Bolivia, Paraguay, Argentina, and other parts of Mexico. They continue to drive horse-drawn buggies, wear plain clothes, and worship in German. Many reject electricity and motorized vehicles in a desire to maintain older, simpler ways. As Old Colony member Anna Wiebe told interviewers, "Because everything was going to vehicles, and we wanted to keep things as we had them." They rejected modern conveniences because "our beliefs . . . taught us that vehicles are for worldly people and [that] horse-and-buggies are for us" and that "electricity [is] for the worldly people, and we are not worldly people."[13]

Economic and social integration in Paraguay
Under the influence of the Fernheim and Friesland Colonies and progressive leaders from Menno Colony, Paraguayan Mennonites moved from the margins into greater involvement in society. Through hard work, cooperative farming practices, and financial assistance from Mennonite Central Committee (MCC), the colonies flourished. Today, the colonies are an important part of the Paraguayan economy, producing 70 percent of the dairy, 20 percent of the grains, and almost

50 percent of the meat for the entire country. No longer marginalized, the colonies are wealthy and possess significant cultural capital.

When they arrived in the Chaco, the first Mennonites may not have realized the larger geopolitical implications of their settlements. The Paraguayan government had sold the land to establish its claim on territory that was in dispute with Bolivia. The land is the traditional territories of the Indigenous Enlhet and Nivaclé peoples, but their presence was not acknowledged by the governments or the Mennonites. Early Mennonite descriptions of the colonies described the Chaco as "primitive and unsettled" and "wilderness." The successful colonies, these accounts continued to assert, did what no one else had been able to accomplish during the four hundred years of European control. "Like Caesar," one author concluded, "[the Mennonite settlers] came, they saw, and they conquered—but peacefully."[14] The historian Peter Klassen recognized that "the good and peaceful Mennonites clearly disturbed the peace in . . . the Chaco."[15] Despite their desire to distance themselves from Paraguayan politics, the Mennonites' very presence in the Chaco was a political act.

In 1954, General Alfredo Stroessner enacted a military coup, beginning one of the longest periods of military dictatorship in Latin American history. Stroessner tightly controlled the country while opening its natural resources to foreign control. Many Mennonites continue to admire Stroessner for his favorable support of Mennonites and other Protestant groups and the completion of the Transchaco Highway, an economic lifeline that directly connected the once-isolated colonies to Asunción.[16] Together with Paraguayan Mennonites and Paraguayan soldiers, fifty MCC Pax workers (see ch. 14) constructed the highway, which in addition to its economic benefit, was a "project of internal colonial expansion and control."[17]

In 1989, a bloodless coup removed Stroessner from power after thirty-five years, returning Paraguay to an elected, civilian government. As the country moved into a period of democratization, Mennonites began to actively participate in the political affairs, shaping the 1992 constitution by successfully lobbying for the inclusion of protections that would allow them to continue to live out their values: separation of church and state, preservation of marriage and the family, religious freedom, and conscientious objection to military service.[18]

When the democratic government divided the country into provinces (departments), most Mennonites lived in the area of the country now called Boquerón. Mennonite Cornelius Sawatsky was soon elected as governor and Mennonite Heinz Ratzlaff as federal deputy. As one historian notes, Mennonites were now "forced to address new questions about political parties, campaign ethics, and the corrosive nature of corruption."[19] For years, Mennonites insisted that they wished to remain separate from Paraguayan politics—now, running for political office is relatively routine.

Today's Paraguayan Mennonites disagree about whether they should remain "the quiet in the land" or take responsibility for political life, but Mennonite participation in politics has grown. Nicanor Duarte Frutos was elected president in 2003 on an anti-corruption platform. Duarte's wife María Gloria Penayo de Duarte was a member of a Spanish-speaking Mennonite church in Asunción, which Duarte attended even though he remained Catholic. Despite criticisms from members of the public that a Mennonite president could not defend the country, Duarte appointed several Mennonites to key cabinet positions to help root out corruption. To overcome Mennonite reluctance to service, he asked them to take greater responsibility for the politics of the country, writing:

> Imagine trying to play soccer on a field that is littered with broken bottles, cement rubble, construction debris. For fifty years that's what politics in Paraguay has been like. It's impossible to participate without getting injured. We're not asking you Mennonites to play on this field. But up until now, you've just been sitting in the stands, watching from a safe distance. What I'm asking you to do is to get out of your seat and come down and help me clean up the field so that we can play in a safe, decent, and fair way.[20]

In pursuit of faithfulness in Latin America
The story of Mennonite migration to Latin America continues in two trajectories—separation or integration, each reflecting a diversity of experiences and responses to the world around them. The first migrants came to escape politics: Canadian policies, Soviet repression and civil war, and the destruction of World War II. The first Old Colony settlers in Chihuahua and the Chaco understood themselves to be participants in a narrative of suffering faithfulness that stretched from the biblical

exodus to the stories of the *Martyrs Mirror*. The Old Colonists continue to seek new lands where they can live in isolation and peace, whereas the Paraguayan Mennonites have become more integrated into surrounding society.

Old Colony Mennonites continue to move in search of affordable land and to preserve their traditional way of life. Moving to the margins or frontiers of society to maintain their separation from technology and distinctive culture, members of a "transnational" Mennonite family relocate between multiple countries like Mexico, Bolivia, and Paraguay, all the while retaining their Mexican or Canadian citizenship. Bolivia has seen the greatest growth in Old Colony Mennonite colonies in recent years, as the government regularly grants settlers the right to clear forests for agriculture.[21]

Meanwhile, the Mexican government has pressured Mennonites in southern Mexico to adopt more sustainable farming practices, as the state of Campeche has lost a fifth of its forest cover in the past two decades. While genetically modified crops and advanced weedkillers have made it easier for Old Colony Mennonites to support their families, the loss of forest threatens to be an ecological disaster. Mennonite and government working groups are seeking sustainable and profitable solutions. However, concerns about global climate change may increase tensions between Old Colony Mennonites and government officials.

The Paraguayan colonies, on the other hand, have grown more settled and stable after several decades of prosperity. Economic success has allowed the colonies to stabilize and thrive. They have planted new Spanish-speaking churches, and their colony schools offer more courses in Spanish. As their non-German churches grow, questions about the relationship between ethnicity and the gospel inevitably arise. According to historian Jaime Prieto, self-reflection has led to a rethinking of Mennonite identity. He writes, "As being 'Mennonite' was defined less and less in ethnic, cultural, and linguistic terms, the Mennonite church as a whole sought to define itself as a particular path of faith within the larger Christian community."[22] It is uncertain what lies ahead for redefining and creating equitable relationships with Latin American churches. For many Paraguayans, Mennonitism is still primarily viewed as an ethnicity rather than a faith. Altering this perception will require significant work and time.

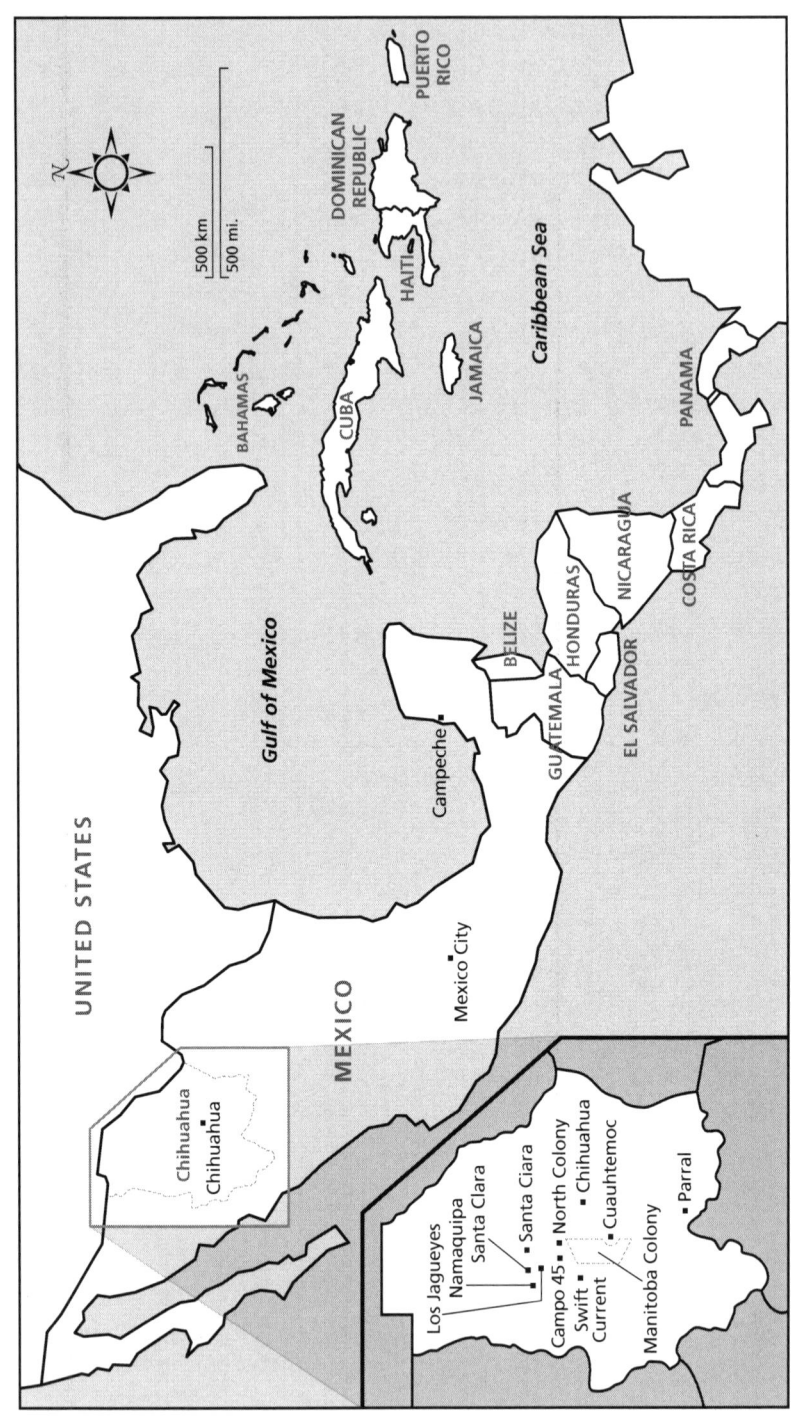

Questions for Latin American Anabaptists

Politics

Despite the cultural, racial, and economic diversity of Latin American Anabaptists, common questions arise for all who gather for worship in the region. Their history has been lived out in contexts of political repression, civil war, and economic pressure. Spanish-speaking and Indigenous Mennonites have explored liberation theology and the connection between poor and marginalized Latin Americans and the experience of sixteenth-century Anabaptists. Like the Paraguayan colonists, they also ask how involved they should be in politics, particularly to work for economic justice, human rights, or the protection of Indigenous people like the Kekchi of Guatemala who have been massacred and attacked by military forces.

Sometimes, Mennonite activism has moved through traditional corridors of power. In Nicaragua under the left-wing Sandinista regime, only pastors and theological students received conscientious objector status, but churches were generally able to live out their nonviolent faith. Colombian and Paraguayan Mennonites successfully lobbied for broader conscientious objector status. In other countries, grassroots movements work directly with those who suffer. For example, in the 1980s, the Honduran Evangelical Mennonite Church worked with several humanitarian organizations to serve Salvadoran refugees, often at great personal risk.

Charismatic Christianity

Since the 1970s, Pentecostalism and popular Pentecostal preachers revived many Latin American Protestant and Catholic Christians. These revivals have had a significant impact on Mennonite spiritual life, but the long-term impact of the Pentecostal and charismatic movement remains unclear. Colombian church leader Héctor Valencia remarked, "The influence came through congresses in which our pastors participated, of which meetings and movements of healing were particularly influential. I don't know if this has been positive or negative. The Pentecostals feel impelled to preach, to evangelize and share the word with others. But at times I see that this remains at the level of external rituals."[23]

The charismatic movement tends to minimize the importance of denominations and conferences in favor of experiences of the Holy

Spirit shared with anyone regardless of their church of origin, and its highly personal and individualistic nature can erode group cohesion. In the 1990s, a series of conflicts rocked the Puerto Rican Mennonite Conference (Conferencia de Iglesias Evangelicas Menonitas de Puerto Rico, or CIEMPR) when, among other issues, some congregations had come under the influence of Pentecostal preachers. In the end, Puerto Rican churches that favored Pentecostalism broke from CIEMPR to form the Evangelical Mennonite Mission of the Caribbean, Inc. (Misíon Evangélica Menonita del Caribe, Inc.).

According to historian Jaime Prieto, one of the "fundamental tasks facing Mennonite churches in Latin America today" is to embrace the sixteenth-century Anabaptists' combination of the Holy Spirit with biblical study, theological reflection, and pastoral care. If they should emphasize only the spiritual inheritance without the other elements, he writes, they will miss out on other aspects of the tradition, "such as a critical stance vis-à-vis the state, a theology and practice favoring the poor, a biblical hermeneutic of nonresistance, and toleration of various ways of understanding the profound mystery of God's work in the world."[24]

Mennonite mosaic

The diversity of Latin America is reflected in the members of the Mennonite church there. While many members have recently joined an Anabaptist church, Argentinian Mennonites commemorated the centenary anniversary of the first baptisms in 2019 and now send out missionaries of their own. Old Colony Mennonites continue to seek out marginal lands to clear and practice their faith, whereas many Paraguayan colony members are integrating into the politics and culture of their country. Some of these groups seek each other out for common conversation, but others run parallel courses, unaware of each other's existence.

— FOURTEEN —

Renewed Identities and New Realities in the West

War, historian Perry Bush has noted, forces pacifists to "sharpen their convictions."[1] The wars and revolutions of the first half of the twentieth century clarified Anabaptists' relation to the world around them and honed their nonresistant position. North American society had often been antagonistic to nonresistant nonconformists, but the age of total war forced Canadian and American Anabaptists to actively engage with authorities and articulate and justify the grounds for their special status. During the Second World War, the peace churches worked with the government to find alternatives to military service that contributed to society, yet many men in the United States and Canada joined the military when drafted, suggesting that the peace position needed considerable cultivation. European Mennonites, for the most part, fought for or supported their governments. Gradually, many reembraced the historic peace position after the war as they rebuilt their ravaged cities or fled their homes, displaced by the devastation. Anabaptists in Europe and North America realized that they needed to reexamine their identities and their relationships with each other.

In the years that followed, North American Mennonites moved away from the ethnic, separatist understandings of Anabaptist identity and increasingly articulated and expressed their Christian identity through service to the world. The young adults who had chosen alternative service to the war were inspired by their wartime experiences and found a "growing identity as a people of service."[2] With a strong sense of responsibility for the world around them, Mennonites began new social service institutions and programs. Inevitably, the sharp lines of cultural separation or geographic isolation began to blur as North American Mennonites engaged more fully with the world while also reinforcing their nonresistant convictions, leading Mennonites to live out their faith in new ways, ushering in the age of "servant activism" that has marked much of mainstream Anabaptist identity over the past century.[3]

Taking stock and rebuilding in Europe

One of the most pressing social needs for Mennonites in the second half of the twentieth century was rebuilding Europe from out of the rubble of war and aiding displaced Mennonites. When the tide of war turned against the Germans in 1943, Mennonites in Prussia and the Soviet Union joined the retreating German armies. Along with thousands of other refugees, Mennonites fled west during the harsh winter—many women and children died along the way. Around 35,000 Mennonites reached Germany, but when the Soviet armies arrived in Germany, they seized 23,000 Soviet Mennonites and forcibly returned them to the USSR. Twelve thousand others fled to the West, waiting in displaced person camps for their fates to be decided. Along with Dutch Mennonite leaders, Mennonite Central Committee (MCC) persuaded the authorities that the refugees had Dutch backgrounds, not German ones, thereby helping 6,000 refugees travel to Canada and another 6,000 to South America.[4]

As they rebuilt their devastated cities and reknit postwar society, European Mennonites also began rebuilding their Anabaptist identity—especially important work for German-speaking Mennonites. German Mennonites had not nurtured the peace position before the war nor seen it as an essential element of their religious identity.[5] After the Nazis came to power, most German Mennonites saw war as a necessary evil and military service as a positive obligation to the state. When he contemplated the wide range of Mennonite attitudes toward defenselessness and nonresistance in Europe (and North America), Harold S. Bender—historian and author of "The Anabaptist Vision"—wondered whether there was enough unity to accurately claim a global Mennonite community. However, he became encouraged by a growing reappreciation for the peace position among Dutch, French, Swiss, and German Mennonites following the war.⁶

Despite some members' concerns about making peace the core of the gospel message, German Mennonite representatives met with MCC at the Thomashof center near Karlsruhe to issue the "Thomashöfer Erklärung [Declaration]" in 1949, proclaiming that nonresistance was again "'an obligation' for the signatories due to the 'heritage of the fathers' and the 'testimony of biblical truth.'"⁷ In the decades that followed, German Mennonites would work with Dutch, Swiss, and French Anabaptists to provide a witness for the free peace church tradition in Europe.

Fig. 14.1 A young woman on the "Great Trek" of the thousands who retreated westward from the Soviet Union. Many were killed or died of disease along the way.
Photo courtesy of Heinz Hindorf/Mennonite Archives of Ontario, Conrad Grebel University College, Waterloo, 3070.

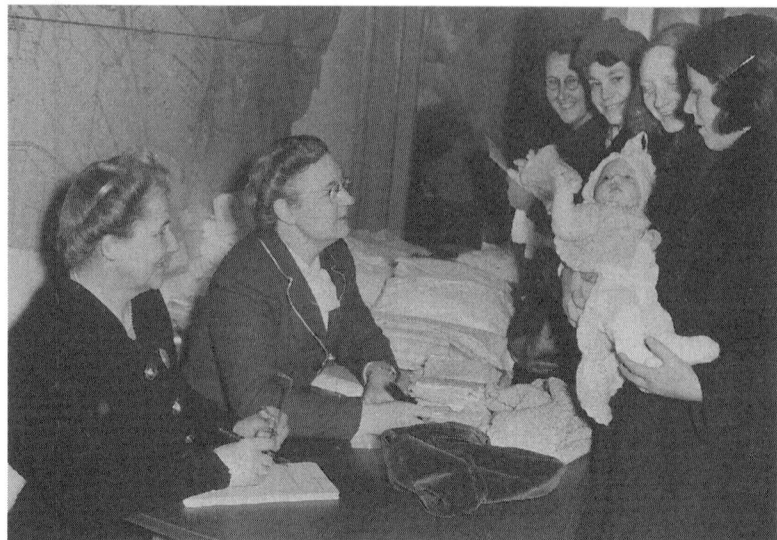

Fig. 14.2 Mennonite Central Committee worker Lulu Smith (*second from left*) checks in refugee women (names unknown) at a baby clothing distribution center in Rotterdam, the Netherlands, while another worker (name unknown) looks on, late 1940s. Photo courtesy of *Canadian Mennonite*/Mennonite Archives of Ontario, Conrad Grebel University College, Waterloo, 153.

Fig. 14.3 MCC worker Katherine Duerksen opens a bale of relief clothing. Photo courtesy of *Canadian Mennonite*/Mennonite Archives of Ontario, Conrad Grebel University College, Waterloo, 155.

For the Dutch Doopsgezinden, whose members had both aided and resisted the occupation, the wounds of the war lingered for decades. After their liberation, some Doopsgezinden, like other Dutch Christians, ostracized or punished neighbors who had collaborated with the occupying German forces. An unknown number of their members had joined the German army, and others had been informers or supported the pro-Nazi political party. A Doopsgezind man in Grijpskerk, for example, had agreed to report to the Germans if his preacher delivered anti-German sermons. While there were some collaborators, many more had died in bombings, under forced labor, or as part of the resistance movements. Dutch pastors, looking for paths for reconciliation, advocated for fair trials for collaborators and opposed the death penalty.[8]

New patterns in the Soviet Union

Mennonites who were unable or chose not to leave the Soviet Union after the war faced a harsh reality. In response to increased suppression, they developed a "Gulag theology" of God's continued presence amid suffering. Many men, including religious leaders, had died in the war or were imprisoned in the Gulag system, so women played a central role in continuing and organizing religious life under an officially atheist regime.

Yet despite decades of state education and thoroughgoing Russianization, Mennonite communities experienced a religious awakening in the 1950s. "Often post-war believers gathered and gave emotional testimonies at birthday parties, weddings, and funerals," writes historian Leonard G. Friesen. "Those with Bibles read from them, whereas others recalled Bible passages or hymns they had once sung. Communities of believers painstakingly wrote out entire hymnals or New Testaments and distributed them to communities which had nothing."[9] With the support of evangelical Baptists, Soviet Mennonites developed new patterns of faith and practice while they were cut off from Anabaptists in other countries. Many Mennonites, for example, gravitated toward Baptist institutions and connections, which became the primary religious affiliation over time.

When the Soviet system began to open and then unravel in the 1980s, people who could claim German heritage were able to leave the Soviet Union and settle in West Germany, resulting in the largest migrations of Anabaptists in history. Between 1987 and 1997, around one million Soviet Germans left the Soviet Union and its successor states, among whom were one hundred thousand Mennonites. By the time of the Soviet Union's collapse in 1991, there were almost no self-identified Mennonites in the USSR, ending the Russian Mennonite story and beginning a new one in Germany. The Soviet Germans joined around three million Ukrainians and Russians who emigrated to Europe and North America.[10]

Upon arriving in the West, however, Soviet Mennonites found themselves in an unfamiliar land, where Americanized, individualistic, and secularized German society felt foreign to them. After years of Soviet repression, Soviet Mennonites had become suspicious of the government and those around them, and many were uninterested in religious life. Those who were religious preserved their identity through separate dress and developing their own youth and educational organizations. Some of the members referred to themselves as Mennonite, some as Baptist, and some as evangelicals. Disillusioned with the lack of personal warmth and religious interest among West Germans, many of them found it difficult to integrate into German society. Today, the Soviet Mennonites form the largest Anabaptist group in Europe, but they still have unresolved questions and tensions about their historical and theological connection with other European Mennonites. The children of Soviet Mennonites born in the West will need to grapple with what it means to be German, Russian, and Mennonite.

North American horizons expand

Alternative service during World War II was an opportunity for Anabaptist men and women to serve alongside other Christians opposed to war and work for peace, exposing them to different ways of being a peace church. Many returning Civilian Public Service (CPS) men and women wanted to continue to serve people and society through new ministries. For example, during the war, over a thousand Mennonites had worked in large public psychiatric hospitals, where the sight of patients being mistreated was unsettling. In response to the stories that CPS workers shared when they returned to their congregations, Mennonite Central Committee started its own psychiatric institutions in Maryland, Kansas, California, Pennsylvania, and Indiana.

In the fifty years after World War II, North American Mennonites became more aware of their interconnectedness in global networks and systems. Historian Steven M. Nolt suggests that the process of globalization was partly because of Mennonites' efforts to distinguish themselves from Cold War attitudes around them and because of increased personal contact with the world beyond North America. This newfound sense of belonging to a global citizenship transformed how Mennonites ate, dressed, and even decorated their homes, including among those who never traveled outside Canada or the United States.[11]

Shortly after the war, Mennonite young men volunteered to travel to Europe to help rebuild homes and churches. To organize the growing number of volunteers, MCC created the Pax (Latin for "peace") program in 1950, which sent men and women abroad to work in cooperation with local leaders. Initially, the "Pax men" built houses for German refugees, but the program soon expanded into Jordan, where they built houses for Palestinians, and South Korea, to help rebuild after the Korean War. Active until 1975, the Pax program sent over eighteen hundred workers to countries throughout Asia and Africa, as well as to a few Latin American countries.

Additional international programs that fostered a globalized perspective included the Teachers Abroad Program (TAP), which sent volunteer teachers to Africa. In 1950, MCC established the International Voluntary Exchange Program (IVEP), bringing young adults from twenty-seven countries to North America to work and live with local Mennonite communities and families. For many young North American Mennonites, serving internationally in MCC's Serving and Learning Together (SALT) assignment or in the Intermenno exchange program to Europe was a common experience of their early adulthood. Hosting IVEPers and hearing stories from returning Pax and TAP program workers helped connect even rural Mennonite communities to the global world so that "virtually every Mennonite congregation and extended family included people who had lived overseas."[12] Combined with higher education and urbanization, the programs fostered a sense of belonging to a global community larger than any national allegiance could contain.

In the 1980s, Mennonites sponsored refugees from Southeast Asia, who were fleeing Vietnam, Laos, or Cambodia in deep desperation. Refugee advocacy became a key priority for Mennonites, many of whom had experienced dislocation and destitution themselves as refugees from Prussia or the Soviet Union after World War II. MCC Canada was the first organization to sign an agreement with the Canadian government to sponsor refugees. Like the community-led programs that sponsored Syrian refugees between 2019 and 2021, grassroots communities worked together to house and support refugee families. Some of the refugees joined Mennonite churches, further diversifying Mennonite denominations, especially in British Columbia and California.

In 1946, while traveling with her husband to Puerto Rico to visit CPS workers, Edna Ruth Miller Byler of Pennsylvania, met MCC workers Mary Hottenstein Lauver and Olga Reimer Martens, who were teaching sewing to a group of women so they could support their families. At the same time, Byler heard of a project run by Ruth Lederach, a nurse working with MCC in Bethlehem (at that time part of Jordan). Lederach employed refugee Palestinian women to embroider fabric for sale in Pennsylvania. Byler saw an opportunity to provide women with dignity and a means of income by linking these two initiatives. She began buying hand-embroidered fabrics at a fair price and selling them out of the trunk of her car when she returned to the United States. With the profits from the sales, Byler bought more fabric from the women, beginning a cycle of income opportunities for the women. Her project was straightforward: "I'm just a woman trying to help other women," she said.[13] MCC adopted Byler's program in 1962, renaming it the Overseas Needlework and Crafts Project. Considered by some to be one of the first global fair-trade programs, Byler's network expanded to include thirty countries as well as products made by men, providing opportunities for sustainable income many times over.[14]

Churches sold the needlework informally until Mennonite Central Committee opened its first SelfHelp Crafts of the World store in 1972. Soon, over one hundred SelfHelp stores had opened across Canada and the United States, even in rural Mennonite communities. The stores' inventory expanded beyond fabric to include jewelry and decorative art, which would have seemed out of place in Mennonite homes a generation earlier. Purchasing a piece of decorative wall art or a basket from woven banana stalks was now a way for Mennonites to demonstrate their global commitments through purchases made at a store selling products discovered by Mennonites seeking an alternative to military service.[15]

The new global mindset changed what Mennonites ate at the dinner table, as well. In response to news of a "world food crisis" in the 1970s, Doris Janzen Longacre posted requests in Mennonite periodicals, asking for suggestions for "how to eat better and consume less." Originally from Kansas, Longacre had served with MCC in Vietnam and Indonesia. Inspired by her international experience, she sought direction for how cooking and eating could be a type of Christian discipleship. Longacre sifted through thousands of recipes, combining five hundred of them with expert essays on food issues and overconsumption into the *More-with-Less Cookbook* in 1976. The authors of recipes from the Global South often included short notes on their origins during MCC service or through intercultural marriage. More than a recipe collection, the book offered its readers spiritual reflections and guides for further action. Joetta Handrich Schlabach continued Longacre's project in 1991 with *Extending the Table: A World Community Cookbook*, including recipes from Mennonites in ninety-three countries and extolling the pleasure of hospitality.

With nearly 800,000 copies sold, the *More-with-Less Cookbook* may be one of the most-read Anabaptist texts. Theologian Gayle Gerber

Fig. 14.4 Along with her daughter Cara Sue, Doris Janzen Longacre (*right*) demonstrates how to prepare a stir-fry at seminar for home economists held in Lancaster, Pennsylvania, 1972.
Photo reprinted with permission of Mennonite Church USA Archives, Elkhart, Indiana, Mennonite Central Committee Photograph Collection, Food, IX-13-2.8, box 2, folder 20.

Koontz noted, "If you consider the theological teaching and witness of [*More-with-Less*] cookbook, its impact far outweighs that of most Mennonite writings in theology and ethics."[16] Living and cooking "more with less" became a Mennonite practice associated with a new type of Anabaptist simplicity and separatism.

Relatively understudied are the global initiatives of the Plain or Old Order groups. David N. Troyer, a New Order Amish man from Berlin, Ohio, founded Christian Aid Ministries (CAM), the relief program of Conservative and Old Order Mennonite and Amish communities, in 1981. CAM started as a program for persecuted Christians, but its activities expanded to include shipping Bibles and food to Nicaragua, Haiti, and Liberia. The Beachy Amish, a group who broke off from the Old Order Amish, have established mission outposts on nearly every continent, leading some of them to raise questions about their role in globalization, despite their separation from Western society.[17]

Whether it is progressive Mennonites eating lentils and rice in addition to traditionally German and Russian Mennonite foods like zwieback or Beachy Amish authors wondering how their clothing contributes to poverty in distant countries, it is clear that Anabaptists have

Fig. 14.5 Edna Ruth Byler, founder of SelfHelp, unpacking a shipment of wooden crafts from Haiti. Photo reprinted with permission of Mennonite Heritage Archives, Winnipeg, MHC 280-196.0-009.

become more interwoven into global networks. Quite often, their programs were begun as part of their work to develop initiatives separate from the surrounding culture. During their international work and travel, Mennonites realized how far they had assimilated into North American culture—including taking on its prejudices and paternalism toward other cultures.

A new medley of Mennonite melodies

As Anabaptists engaged in urban social service efforts, pursued mission outreach, and migrated to new locations, they moved beyond their traditional rural patterns of life. These new contexts presented challenges and led to transformations in the community's understanding of faith and discipleship. When Anabaptists moved from rural areas to cities, they struggled to maintain the close social bonds they had assumed in their small-town congregations. In small towns, they would run into each other on the street or in stores, but in cities, they led more anonymous lives, making it difficult to enforce strict church discipline or create deep community. While worship and community life were deeply intertwined in rural areas, members in cities had to make a concerted effort to come together during the week or on Sundays. Despite these challenges, many congregations found that opening their doors to newcomers helped break down traditional barriers and brought new life to their communities. However, this influx of new members also presented new challenges, as Mennonites encountered issues around race, class, prejudice, and social injustice. As a result, Mennonite identity took a new path, one that was often rocky and led to several dead ends.

Latino outreach

The first outreach to Spanish-speaking communities arose not out of a planned church plant or a desire to increase diversity in the church but out of an organic need. In the 1920s, Ignacia and Manuel León, recent immigrants from Mexico, were impressed with the Bible instruction and warm welcome that their children were receiving from the Chicago Home Mission, an independent mission station started in 1893 to serve Mennonites living in Chicago, including several medical students. After several American missionaries returned from Argentina in 1932, they started a worship service in Spanish, and seventy families joined. The congregation called David Castillo, a Pentecostal leader, to be the first Latino American Mennonite minister after he agreed to study theology at Goshen College. Castillo would serve at Lawndale Mennonite Congregation, the first Mennonite congregation with a Hispanic minister. Lawndale nurtured several important Hispanic Mennonite leaders in the years to come; Grace and Neftali Torres, for example, led Lawndale Mennonite and Latino Mennonites across the United States until leaving for missionary work in Puerto Rico.[18]

The growth of Latino Mennonite congregations in the United States continued slowly through the 1940s and 1960s, with early church plants in Texas, Pennsylvania, New York, Ohio, and Iowa. Early converts had to negotiate multiple cultural barriers. While many rejected Roman Catholicism, they did not always wish to leave behind everything of their cultural heritage. According to historian Felipe Hinojosa, Texas converts resisted the missionaries' efforts to eradicate practices that were central to Mexican cultural life, such as "the dance, the bingo, the lottery, the dice, horse race, and whatnot."[19] Despite the missionaries' efforts to live out the gospel, their racism and prejudice would sometimes set back gains at welcoming new members and growth. In South Texas, for example, Mennonite Brethren and (Old) Mennonite missionaries assumed a cultural and religious superiority over the Hispanic population, rejecting traditional healing practices as superstition, and they restricted the ways that women could serve as leaders.[20]

From 1955 to 1999, the number of Hispanic Mennonite members in the United States grew from 185 members to 3,471—remarkable growth at a time when the North American churches grew at 1 percent overall. Hispanic Mennonite congregations and leaders have contributed significantly to the life and growth of North American Anabaptism. Their members come from all over the Spanish-speaking world and represent different levels of cultural assimilation. Some descend from Hispanic communities that have lived in the American Southwest since before the United States annexed the territory. Another group comprises the first generation of immigrants from Mexico or Puerto Rico, and for whom speaking Spanish is a way of maintaining their cultural identity. Their second- and third-generation descendants are culturally assimilated to the United States and prefer to speak a mix of

Spanish and English.²¹ Different countries of origin add to the mix of cultures and practices among Latino Mennonites.

Relations between Latino Mennonite congregations and the broader Mennonite churches can be unclear, despite Latino-serving denominational structures and important leaders in Anabaptist denominations. Missionaries "either did not have a distinctive Anabaptist theology or they did not see the usefulness of teaching it to the Latino/a converts," according to historian Juan Martínez.²² New members had a strong evangelical or Pentecostal identity, but they considered the term Mennonite to be indelibly associated with the ethnic groups, not the gospel. Mennonite leader Gilberto Flores has argued that Anabaptist theology potentially "creates a historical bridge," especially the parts of the Anabaptist tradition that emphasize spreading the gospel, the presence of the Holy Spirit, and the care for the marginalized. When Hispanic Anabaptist-Mennonites draw from the Anabaptist theological tradition, Flores suggests, they will likely do so along with other theological influences.²³ In his book *Reflections of an Hispanic Mennonite*, longtime leader José Ortíz reflected on how being a Latino/a Mennonite

Fig. 14.6 Hispanic Mennonite leaders José Ortiz (*center*) and Juan Ventura (*right*), 1973. Photo reprinted with permission of Mennonite Church USA Archives, Elkhart, Indiana, IV-10-007.3, drawer 3, folder 46.

in the United States requires the negotiation of three identities: Latino, Mennonite, and American.²⁴

Black and Mennonite

Few African Americans had joined the Mennonite Church by the middle of the twentieth century; by 1950 it was estimated that there were between 150 and 282 African American Mennonites.²⁵ James and Rowena Lark, early African American church leaders, joined the Mennonites in 1935. The Larks soon accepted further leadership roles with congregations around the United States with a vision for evangelism that spoke to social needs. James Lark, who became the first African American Mennonite bishop in 1954, advocated for Mennonites to spend their energy and money on mission work "at home," particularly to reach out to African Americans with the same commitment that they gave to international missions.²⁶

The Larks pushed the American Mennonite church to reach out to African American communities, but there remained in the church the

Fig. 14.7 Church leaders James and Rowena Lark, 1951. Photo reprinted with permission of Mennonite Church USA Archives, Elkhart, Indiana, LeRoy Bechler African American Mennonite Collection, 1947–2007, HM 4-367.

overt racism of some white Mennonites who opposed interracial marriage, used racial slurs, or refused to admit African Americans to parochial schools. Despite white Mennonites' efforts to reach out to Latino and African American communities, white Mennonites often shared similar prejudices and racism of the culture around them and drew from reactionary political thought that exacerbated racial tensions.[27] One white bishop, for example, supported the racial agenda of Alabama governor George Wallace in 1966, wondering, "Just how much is any Anabaptist going to become excited about the fact that Negroes can or cannot vote?"[28] The *Sword and Trumpet*, a journal aspiring to be an "uncompromising expression of Mennonite Conservatism,"[29] criticized "civil rights and antiwar protesters, condemned nonviolent civil disobedience as lawlessness and cast a generally disapproving eye on the cultural challenges of the 1960s."[30]

Despite the difficult struggle that would be required to push toward racial equality in a tradition with strong Euro-American ethnic identity, some congregations worked to integrate their membership, and some predominantly African American congregations were established that continue today, including in Los Angeles and Cleveland. After leaving the military in 1957, Leslie Walker Francisco II reconnected with Calvary Mennonite Church in Newport News, Virginia, and assumed leadership along with his wife Naomi in 1971. Guided by a desire to evangelize beyond the Mennonite church, Francisco and his sons led street and tent revivals to share the gospel. The church soon expanded to Hampton, merging with the Newport News congregation to become one of the largest Anabaptist churches in the United States, with numerous community service projects and mission outreach to Africa. Bishop L. W. Francisco III assumed pastoral leadership after his father, and he, in turn, has been followed in senior leadership by his daughter Lesley Francisco McClendon. Calvary Community, known today as C3 Hampton, and the Franciscos' leadership training ripples outward through training and mentoring of other leaders, including Glen Guyton, who has served as executive director of Mennonite Church USA.[31]

In 1968, the Mennonite Church (MC) formed the Urban Racial Council (URC) to systematically address the needs of African American and urban churches and create a stronger link between social justice and missions. URC leaders called on the Mennonite Church to address racial and economic justice concurrently. With the creation of the URC, Mexican and Puerto Rican Mennonites saw an opportunity to join their voices with African American Mennonites: "We want to have a say in everyday affairs of the church," wrote Lupe De León in the MC periodical the *Gospel Herald*. "Chicanos want to make decisions in the church. We want to have a say in everyday affairs of the church. We want to be leaders."[32] In 1970, the URC was reformed as the Minority Ministries Council (MMC), which became a means for Mexican, Puerto Rican, Native American, and African American Mennonites to create programs that combined social justice initiatives with the gospel. Some of the projects included music recordings by the Mennonaires, a gospel choir from Burnside Community Church, Columbus, Ohio; seminars for white Mennonites to listen to Mennonites of color tell stories of the pain of racism; and the Cross Cultural Youth Convention in 1972 to "provide minority youth with an opportunity to gain a sense of their identity and to help young people be proud to stick with the church."[33]

The Minority Ministries Council disbanded in 1973. The initiative was ahead of the denomination in considering civil rights and economic justice and different understandings and experiences of racism, as well as frustration from women who were kept out of leadership positions. While there were internal tensions among members of the group, the historian Felipe Hinojosa has argued that some white Mennonite leaders, uneasy with the growing prominence of Black and Brown leaders, had incrementally whittled down the group's power. Several MMC members left the Mennonite Church "frustrated by their experiences after they had given everything to the church they loved."[34]

Redefining Anabaptist identity

In the United States, Canada, and Europe, church plants continued to expand Anabaptist theology and practice into new domestic contexts to which the churches have had to adapt. After WWII, multiple North American mission boards sent workers to Europe to plant churches. The Anabaptist Network in the United Kingdom brought together individuals and groups from backgrounds with no direct connection to the historic Anabaptist churches, but who shared a sense of "coming home" when they discovered the Anabaptist tradition. At times, the multiplicity of North American mission agencies with competing agendas led European Mennonites to distrust the efforts. Over time, European Anabaptists from different countries worked alongside each other and North Americans in domestic missions. In France, for example, the Mission Mennonite Française (MMF, or French Mennonite Mission), jointly run between the Mennonite Board of Missions and Charities and French Mennonites, established a congregation in the Châtenay-Malabry suburb of Paris, and a multiracial congregation grew out of a student center in Paris in 1981.[35]

In both North America and Europe, new endeavors often led to new questions about identity. For example, in Europe, new congregations in countries with no historical Anabaptist presence (Austria, Belgium, England, Italy, Portugal, and Spain) led to questions about what it meant to be part of the global movement. "Were these churches Mennonite? If so, how were they to relate to other European Mennonite churches? Or were the newly planted churches evangelical, or generic 'free' churches, without a specific Anabaptist identity?"[36] In other words, to what extent did Anabaptist identity depend on direct connection to one of the historical, nationally organized churches?

Successful urban outreach in Europe and North America has created congregations with specific ethno-cultural identities. In Ontario, historian Marlene Epp identified "Hispanic, Laotian, Hmong, Korean, Ethiopian, and Punjabi"[37] congregations, which have diversified North American Anabaptism while their own identities remain tied to specific cultural identities. Whether these Anabaptists' Sunday worship will eventually grow more diverse, and the second or third generations will loosen their ethnic or linguistic traditions, remains unclear.

Women as leaders

In addition to serving as the leading edge of racial and cultural diversity, urban congregations and mission outreach were some of the earliest Anabaptist meetings where women served as pastors. In the Netherlands, Anna Mankes-Zernike became the first ordained Anabaptist woman in 1911. From 1919 to 1954, thirty-seven Canadian women, including nineteen single women, were ordained as missionaries. Emma Sommers Richard had been a missionary with her husband in Japan before her 1973 ordination in Lombard (IL) Mennonite Church, making her the first woman ordained in the North American Mennonite Church (MC). Marilyn Kauffman Miller became the first woman ordained in the General Conference (GC) Mennonite Church two years later. Ann Allebach had been ordained in the GC church in 1911, but never served in a Mennonite congregation, and Janet Douglas was licensed by the Mennonite Brethren in Christ denomination (now known as the Missionary Church in the United States and Evangelical Missionary Church in Canada) in 1882, but was never fully ordained. In Mennonite Church USA and Mennonite Church Canada today, women commonly serve in pastoral and denominational leadership roles.

Other Anabaptist churches, particularly those influenced by the evangelical movement, have continued to debate whether women can be ordained as ministers, even while allowing them to serve in other roles within the church. Among Canadian Mennonite Brethren, "no other issue has received this level of attention . . . during the second half of the 20th century."[38] While the conference recognized that women played "a significant role in the early church," women were not ordained for pastoral leadership until Mama Kadi Tshinyama's ordination by the Mennonite Brethren Church of Congo in 2003. Her ordination inspired the North American MB family to revisit the question, and in

Fig. 14.8 Portrait of Anne Mankes-Zernike by Jan Mankes.
Drawing by Jan Mankes, 1899–1920. Rijksmuseum, Amsterdam, RP-T-1980-88.

2006, individual congregations were permitted to ordain women. In 2008, Bev Peters and Grace Kim were ordained for ministry, the first two MB women ordained in North America.[39]

Coming together and drifting apart

Like those in many North American churches, Mennonites found themselves swept up in the political polarization of the 1960s. Young, educated Mennonites shifted leftwards politically, whereas others found themselves in alignment with the political and theological positions of the New Right and conservative evangelicalism. Both Mennonite worldviews appealed to the same tradition to support their position. On the right, the Mennonite tradition of living as "the quiet in the land" supported the admonition that Christians should not tell the government how to conduct its affairs. Young, educated Mennonites who leaned left appealed to the martyrs of the sixteenth century, who were willing to suffer for their radical beliefs. As one church leader noted after meeting several draft resisters, the young Mennonites were "taking their Mennonite tradition very seriously, the tradition that has been taught them by their elders in the church."[40] According to the historian Perry Bush, Mennonites remained together despite the political polarization of the 1960s because they still understood that they were part of the same religious tradition, making it easier to dialogue with one another.[41] But as the forces of acculturation continued to work through Mennonite communities, Mennonites found it increasingly difficult to keep a shared sense of a common identity intact.

As they have done throughout their history, Anabaptist groups reassessed their relationships to each other during the twentieth century. Sometimes this was done to seek greater unity, and sometimes the process was painfully divisive. From the martyrologies that listed Dutch and Swiss martyrs together to the creation of Mennonite World Conference, Anabaptists had long nurtured relationships that transcended national borders. But the transnational unity that Hans de Ries's martyrology had kindled four centuries earlier unraveled in the twentieth and twenty-first centuries. In 2002, the largest Mennonite conferences, the historically predominately Swiss Mennonite Church (MC) and historically predominately Russian Mennonite General

Conference (GC) Mennonite Church, both of which were binational conferences, merged to form Mennonite Church USA and Mennonite Church Canada. The merger was facilitated by the 1995 Confession of Faith in a Mennonite Perspective, which was intended to "build a foundation for unity within and among churches." The original hope had been to create one conference, but the discernment process brought national differences to the surface, so two national church bodies were formed. The differences between the Swiss/German and Dutch/Russian traditions were easier to bridge than the national border. The North American Mennonite Brethren Church likewise divided into separate US and Canadian organizations in 1999.

In the following years, the GC-MC merger in MC USA and MC Canada did not live up to its hopeful promise of Christian unity. Differences in polity, theology, and practice soon rose to the foreground. The structure of the Mennonite Church had given greater authority to centralized conferences, whereas the General Conference congregations had greater autonomy. The differences in polity exacerbated theological differences between progressive and conservative Anabaptists. Several conferences and congregations left MC USA, including Lancaster Mennonite Conference (LMC), the largest conference in the denomination, in 2017. As a result, MC USA gradually declined from 114,000 members in 2003 to around 60,000 in 2023.[42]

The divisions centered around topics of gender and sexuality that have roiled and polarized public discourse throughout North America. Mennonites had discussed whether to welcome LGBTQ+ individuals since the 1980s, but the legalization of same-sex marriage and changing cultural norms in the early decades of the twenty-first century brought divisions to the surface. Mennonites who understood Scripture and the 1995 confession to restrict marriage to between a man and a woman grew concerned when conferences and national structures did not discipline those who believed that God's love, as revealed in the Bible, supports an inclusive church. While the flashpoints have crystallized around sexuality, it is likely that other cultural and socioeconomic fault lines lie underneath the divisions.

Increasingly, congregations and conferences sought new connections that matched their theological orientation rather than geographic location. Congregations from Florida and California, for example, joined Mosaic Mennonite Conference, which was formed by the reconciliation of Franconia and Eastern District Conferences in 2019, healing a split from 1864 about who could receive communion. After it was expelled from the US Conference of Mennonite Brethren Churches (USMB), a congregation in Fresno, California, joined MC USA in 2022. In August 2018, forty leaders of six evangelical Anabaptist groups—LMC, CMC (formerly Conservative Mennonite Conference), USMB, Brethren in Christ US, Brethren Church, and Evana—gathered at Rosedale Bible College in Ohio to meet one another and discern whether there were opportunities for future collaboration. How the moving pieces of this period of transformation will settle into place remains unclear, and it remains to be seen who will consider themselves part of the same Anabaptist story.

What's in a name?

In 2023, CMC announced that it would now be known as the Rosedale Network of Churches, with the tagline "A Global Family of Churches." This came five years after changing its name from the Conservative Mennonite Conference, concerned that "Conservative" would remind people of Republican politics or Plain Anabaptists and that "Mennonite" led to confusion with the liberal Anabaptism of MC USA. CMC had been founded as the Conservative Amish Mennonite Conference in 1910 and had dropped "Amish" in 1957. The 2023 name reflects the conference's institutional location at Rosedale Bible College and Rosedale International, which carries out its mission work.

Like the Anabaptists of the seventeenth century who strategically chose names like Mennonite, Doopsgezind, or Brethren, contemporary Anabaptist groups have rebranded themselves to differentiate from other groups or to be more appealing to outsiders. For example, the Lancaster Mennonite Conference changed its name to LMC: A Fellowship of Anabaptist Churches in 2018 to represent the geographic spread of its congregations.

Individual congregations have also increasingly chosen to drop "Mennonite" from their names. According to a study, 85 percent of churches belonging to the US Conference of Mennonite Brethren Churches no longer call themselves Mennonite but still hold to Mennonite Brethren fellowship and theology.[43] Many churches feel that "Mennonite" creates barriers to growth because of its association with cultural Mennonites, either the Russian Mennonites of the conference's origins or the Amish, the most visibly recognizable Anabaptists in the United States. These congregations have reported significant growth since rebranding. It is unclear, however, whether the name changes facilitate a move away from Anabaptist convictions over time.

Mainstream North American Mennonites increasingly refer to themselves as Anabaptist Mennonites, Anabaptist Christians, or simply Anabaptists to distance themselves from the cultural connotations of the term Mennonite. However, the situation becomes more complicated when considering the global church. According to the Global Anabaptist Profile, churches in the Global South are more likely to identify as Mennonite, whereas Europeans and North Americans are more likely to claim an Anabaptist identity. Yet the broader term Anabaptist may more accurately describe many members of Mennonite World Conference—Zimbabwean Anabaptists are Brethren in Christ, and Indonesian synods do not have the word Mennonite or Anabaptist in their names, nor do members of the Meserete Kristos Church.

Looking forward and looking back

In the twentieth century, Anabaptists in Europe and North America experienced tremendous changes that have challenged their core identity. As they moved from rural agricultural contexts to urbanized professional ones, they engaged with the social and cultural transformations that were changing the world around them, like feminism, civil rights, ecumenism, and LGBTQ+ inclusion. There has not been a unified response to these cultural changes; some have been resisted and some have been adopted by the acculturated groups that claim an Anabaptist identity depending on whether they lean toward the Anabaptist/social justice or the evangelical end of the spectrum. Anabaptists in the twenty-first century will determine for themselves whether the challenges they face will draw them closer together or continue to push them further apart.

— FIFTEEN —

Faith in Changing Times

Evangelism, Anabaptism, and the Old Orders in the Twentieth Century

After World War II, the pace with which North American Anabaptists of all types engaged with society and culture quickened. Men and women returning from CPS camps were energized by their wartime experiences to continue to put their faith into action. Seeking new work and educational opportunities, many Mennonites left the rural, relatively isolated farm life for urban and suburban professional opportunities, and others found work in the trades or in factories. In these new contexts, they worked and studied alongside people from very different backgrounds and learned new ways of being in the world. After work, they would return home to listen to their radios or even watch television, which increasingly drew them into surrounding cultural and political patterns, but some found that modern media offered new sources for religious revival or opportunities to spread the gospel.

As a result, nearly all North American Anabaptists sensed a potential drift in their collective identity. The rapid pace of change heightened the sense of uncontrollable threats to traditional patterns of worship and standards for discipleship. Just as nineteenth-century Mennonites and Amish responded to cultural changes by either embracing new practices or drawing Old Order lines, twentieth-century Anabaptists responded to quickening change with a variety of responses. Historians Royden Loewen and Steven M. Nolt have identified three approaches that Anabaptists took in response to this cultural transformation: evangelical renewal, Anabaptist recovery, and Old Orders.[1] All three responses equipped Anabaptists with tools to either separate from or embrace the surrounding cultures, leading to the development of new programs, institutions, and religious expression.

Evangelicalism

After attending a mission conference in the summer of 1950, a young Amish woman, Anna Beiler, described her "hilltop experience" at the event in a letter to a friend. The conference speakers had exhorted attendees to be mindful of their duty to go "in the valley and work for the Lord whatever He leads us to do." "When one gives himself up to testify for Christ," she wrote, "it brings unspeakable joy to the heart." As Anna Beiler discerned God's will for her life in response to her emotional exhilaration at this exhortation—and the possibility that it might take her from her home and family—she committed to "praise His Holy name and be ever thankful for the love, grace, and mercy He daily showers upon us."[2] Beiler's joyful spiritual awakening at a revival-type meeting, which led her out of her Amish community, was common among Anabaptists shaped by the new evangelical revivals of the mid-twentieth century.

Evangelicalism, a movement within Protestant Christianity, emphasizes personal conversion and faith in Jesus Christ as the way to salvation. Historian of evangelicalism David Bebbington has proposed a quadrilateral of priorities that all evangelicals share, despite the diversity among evangelical movements:

1. Biblicism: Evangelicals believe in the authority of the Bible as the inspired word of God and the source of religious authority.

2. Crucicentrism: Evangelicals emphasize the centrality of the death and resurrection of Jesus Christ as the means of salvation.

3. Conversionism: Evangelicals believe in the importance of personal conversion or a "born again" experience, in which an individual repents of their sins and puts their faith in Jesus Christ.

4. Activism: Evangelicals are often involved in evangelism, missionary work, or social activism, seeking to share the gospel and make a social impact.[3]

Although it is helpful for identifying evangelicals' basic shared assumptions, Bebbington's quadrilateral offers only a minimal description of the varied contours of evangelicalism, which now dominates Christian expression in the United States and, to a lesser extent, Canada. Even though many Hispanic and Black American Christians identify as evangelical, the positions and practices of white evangelicals dominate the public perception. Some scholars have suggested that evangelicals are defined as much by their cultural consumption—what they buy, read, and listen to—as they are by a set of religious convictions or practices.[4] For example, white evangelical Anabaptists likely read books from the evangelical parachurch group Focus on the Family or listen to evangelical contemporary Christian music. As a result, evangelical Anabaptists may have more in common culturally with other North American evangelicals than with other Mennonite groups. As it spread from the United States into Canada, evangelicalism has come to dominate much of North American Christian expression in the twentieth and twenty-first centuries, and its influence increasingly shapes the global church. The various churches within the global Anabaptist tradition are no exception.

Evangelical renewal

After the conflicts between the modernists and fundamentalists in the 1910s and 1920s about the authority of the Bible and how to reconcile science and faith, among other things, North American evangelicals withdrew from the public sphere. Their reemergence in the 1930s and 1940s was facilitated through modern means—especially radio evangelism and mass revivals. As they built new organizations, schools, and media, such as the flagship evangelical magazine *Christianity Today*, evangelicals desired to be less divisively rigid and to tackle social issues from a more liberal mindset. For example, the renowned evangelist

Billy Graham intended *Christianity Today* to "plant the evangelical flag in the middle of the road, taking the conservative theological position but a definite liberal approach to social problems."[5] In this new evangelicalism, many Mennonites and Brethren in Christ found a path to integrate into society and shed what they saw as the dead spirituality and ethnic dimension of Anabaptism. Others, however, worried that hitching Mennonite wagons to the rising evangelical star might lead to a corruption of core Anabaptist principles.

Billy Graham's ability to attract followers from outside of typical evangelical circles in his large, multiday revival meetings offered a new model to some Anabaptist leaders for renewing their members' spiritual life and perhaps gaining new members. In June 1951, Mennonite evangelists and brothers George R. Brunk II and Lawrence Brunk held a revival meeting in Lancaster County, Pennsylvania, in a tent that held twenty-five hundred people. The message and media of the Brunks' meetings were so successful that the revival lasted seven weeks. Later that summer, the Brunks held a revival where fifteen thousand people, mostly Mennonites, attended. In the coming years, the Brunk Brothers

Fig. 15.1 Audience at a Brunk Revival Campaign meeting in Abbotsford, British Columbia, 1958. Photo courtesy of Mennonite Archives of Ontario, Conrad Grebel University College, Waterloo, XV-19.3-2001-14-205.

Fig. 15.2 George Brunk II speaking at a meeting in Waterloo, Ontario, 1952.
Photo courtesy of David L. Hunsberger/Mennonite Archives of Ontario, Conrad Grebel University College, Waterloo, 10.28-DH-140.

Revival Campaign accepted invitations from across Canada and the United States to hold revivals, where attendees were encouraged to accept Christ for the first time or renew their commitment to the church and faith.

In the 1940s and 1950s, evangelicalism appealed especially to urban, entrepreneurial Mennonites and Brethren in Christ who were open to experimenting with contemporary worship styles and modern means of spreading the faith. Evangelicalism's focus on individual conversion and one's personal relationship with God weakened the role of church authorities and "sanctified the individual initiative and authority that was at the heart of agribusiness and entrepreneurship, providing a potent combination of faith and enterprise."[6] Mennonite business leaders in southern Manitoba, for example, promoted modern media as a way to spread the revival project by allowing individual Mennonites to broaden their styles of worship and preaching without leaving their home congregations. In Lancaster County, Pennsylvania, in deference to the bishops' resistance to new media, the management of the Christian radio station WDAC "bought and distributed several thousand fixed-tuned radios which could pull in only WDAC's 94.5 FM signal," thereby eliminating the possibility that curious Anabaptist listeners might scan the dial for other programming.[7] The commercial radio station aired hymns and preaching, including the nationally syndicated *Back to the Bible*, featuring the Mennonite radio evangelist Theodore H. Epp broadcasting from Lincoln, Nebraska.

For Euro-American Anabaptists shedding their ethnic identity and leaving behind traditional rural economic patterns, revivalism and evangelicalism provided a potential means to integrate into mainstream culture and invite others to join their ranks. In 1952, the Kleine Gemeinde congregation in Steinbach, Manitoba, changed its name to the Evangelical Mennonite Church and discontinued practices like shunning in favor of a more open and positive expression of Christian life. In 1957, they joined with other Mennonite-affiliated congregations in Steinbach in inviting American evangelist George R. Brunk II to come to Manitoba to "light 'revival' fire in members' hearts."[8] Evangelicals' revival meetings, radio broadcasts, and devotional material broadened and deepened many Mennonites' devotional lives. This was particularly true for homemakers and those living in rural communities, for whom gospel radio hours and traveling tent revivals opened up new spiritual possibilities.

Evangelicalism's personal message also empowered those new to the faith to leave the traditions in which they were raised. In South Texas, the evangelism that Yolanda Villareal learned from Mennonite Brethren (MB) missionary Annie Dyck led her to convert to Mennonitism and work with white MB missionaries in building the church. According to historian Felipe Hinojosa, who interviewed Villareal, Mennonite evangelism in South Texas had both social and personal dimensions. Along with other women, Villareal sewed quilts and distributed clothing in the local community. The women's group (*la femenil*), Villareal noted, gave women a place to "worship God and help each other with needs that we had."[9] "Aside from challenging cultural tradition and providing moral guidance," Hinojosa notes, "the newly established churches inadvertently provided a space for women to gather and support one another."[10] In rural communities without strong social support outside of families, evangelical mission plants provided physical as well as spiritual support.

Over the next decades, evangelicalism continued to influence the spirituality and theology of Anabaptists who saw the movement as either a spiritual resource or a danger. As historian Steven M. Nolt has observed, even though they have different "emphases and inclinations," Anabaptism and evangelicalism "share an activist impulse—a desire to convert their Christian convictions into lived religion and a refusal to regard faith as private or merely otherworldly."[11]

In the nineteenth century, many Anabaptists defined themselves against evangelical-style initiatives; the Old Order Amish, Old Order Mennonites, and Old German Baptist Brethren adopted nonconformist identities to distinguish themselves from groups that they perceived to be sliding recklessly headfirst down the slippery slope of assimilation. In the twentieth century, some Anabaptist leaders were concerned with how evangelicals appeared to separate conversion from discipleship and for how revival meetings seemed to manipulate attendees.

Some Mennonite leaders worried that the evangelical revivals, while offering spiritual renewal and commitment, emphasized individual conversion and emotional experiences at the expense of traditional Anabaptist teachings of discipleship, humility, and submission. In a 1953 editorial in the Mennonite Church (MC) periodical *Gospel Herald*, Paul Erb worried that the search for truth as found in Scripture was "something very different from a revivalistic intoxication that sends the addict reeling from one evangelistic meeting to another."[12] Evangelism, Erb pointed out, was practiced by the early Anabaptist movement; however, they did not preach a "facile and flabby pietism"; they called on members to take up one's cross and follow Jesus.[13] "Full discipleship (Nachfolge Christi) became one of the cardinal doctrines of the Anabaptist faith, and one of the chief requirements for membership in the 'gathered church' of the [sixteenth-century Anabaptists]."[14]

In the General Conference periodical *The Mennonite*, W. F. Unruh exhorted his readers not to separate the great commission's command to teach and baptize from its call to make disciples: "Too often evangelists urge upon people to believe in Jesus and accept Him as Savior and leave it at that, believing that when decision is made all is well, then they are saved and God will do the rest." Those who decide to follow Christ, Unruh wrote, "are to be taught to obey all the commands of Christ."[15]

Erb's and Unruh's criticisms of evangelism may have stemmed from memories of the fundamentalist-modernist disputes decades earlier or from a desire to protect the new institutions that mainstream denominations were building. In the mid-twentieth-century period, many Mennonite groups were developing new institutions and programs, which may have also led to some caution by establishment leaders who worried about potentially centripetal influences on their denominations. Historian John D. Roth suggests that "as the Mennonite church developed more rationalized forms of church polity, the defenders of these new, centralized structures looked askance at any form of renewal that promoted congregational autonomy and encouraged division."[16]

Despite warnings about the burgeoning revivalist movement's potential for superficial discipleship, most Anabaptists would not have seen the calls for faith renewal or a spirituality that spoke to one's emotional dimensions to be antithetical to discipleship. Rather, these provided a spiritual support for believers as they followed Christ in their lives. Historian Devin Manzullo-Thomas argues that an evangelical identity eased Brethren in Christ members out of their ethnic isolation into greater involvement with American society while they simultaneously advocated Anabaptist principles of simplicity and humility and articulated a critique of Christian participation in war in national evangelical circles.[17]

While the Brethren in Christ successfully managed to graft evangelical elements into their Anabaptist identity, the growth of evangelical-minded Mennonites in other streams has led to divisions—especially since the 1980s, as evangelical Anabaptists coalesced around more conservative theological and social positions while other Mennonites have taken more liberal stances. In 1983, a group of ministers and leaders from Ohio formed the Association of Evangelical Mennonites in response to a concern about "the damaging liberal drift in theology and the consequent erosion of faith and of our Anabaptist biblical orthodoxy in the Mennonite Church, Conferences, and Institutions." Their eight-point doctrinal statement included, in addition to a witness against abortion, statements in favor of masculine pronouns for God, the state's right to use capital punishment, congregational autonomy, heterosexual marriage, and the priesthood of all believers.[18] In 2002, the Evangelical Anabaptist Fellowship formed a new network, the Alliance of Mennonite Evangelical Congregations, in response to the merger of the General Conference and Mennonite Churches into Mennonite Church USA and the new confession of faith's "departure from Biblical orthodoxy."[19] In 2015, congregations critical of Mennonite Church USA's lack of clarity on LGBTQ+ inclusion formed the Evana (Evangelical and Anabaptist) Network. In these new networks, evangelically oriented Anabaptists from different historical Mennonite streams found new connections with one another. In 2017, Evana, which comprised mostly MC congregations, formed a fraternal relationship with Tabor College, a college with a strong Mennonite identity founded by Russian Mennonite Brethren and Krimmer Mennonite Brethren living in Kansas.[20]

Positions on sexuality and gender were often identified as the wedge issues dividing evangelical and other Anabaptists, but other social and cultural identities also likely shaped the realignments of North American Anabaptist identities and loyalties. Studies of non-Anabaptist evangelicals have shown that ethnic and social location determine political and social attitudes more than specific evangelical teachings. In other words, evangelical teachings often reinforce positions held by most community members, even those outside the church.[21] It is likely that the same would be true of liberal churches in urban communities. In this way, the religious splits and realignments of the previous century largely reflect the shifting social locations of Anabaptists since the Second World War.

Evangelicalism's influence on North American religion has been broad and deep. Perhaps one-quarter of the United States population now identifies as "evangelical or born again," making it the largest Protestant movement in that country.[22] A 2017 survey of Mennonite World Conference Churches found that members of the Evangelical Mennonite Conference (Canada) and BIC Canada were more likely to describe their religious beliefs as evangelical than Anabaptist (69 percent evangelical versus 47 percent Anabaptist among EMC, and 54 percent versus 42 percent among BIC Canada). Among members of the US Conference of Mennonite Brethren Churches, respondents were just as likely to describe themselves as Anabaptist as evangelical (53 percent each), and in the Brethren in Christ US, members were slightly more likely to describe themselves as Anabaptist (73 percent) than evangelical (63 percent).[23] According to historian George M. Marsden, the fundamentals of evangelical teachings on salvation, Scripture, and the deity of Christ "have spread remarkably throughout the majority of the world and have become the most typical Protestant expressions of burgeoning world Christianity, far outnumbering those in the West."[24]

The Anabaptist Vision and the revival of historical identity

On December 29, 1943, Harold S. Bender, history professor at Goshen College in Indiana, delivered the presidential address at the annual gathering of the American Society of Church History. Presented to an eminent academic organization, Bender's hastily written speech, "The Anabaptist Vision," was built on decades of his research on the history of sixteenth-century Anabaptism. (The speech, mentioned in earlier chapters, was eventually published in the *Mennonite Quarterly Review* and as a subsequent booklet.) Warmly received by the scholars that evening, Bender's vision of Anabaptist origins would go on to become an important source of religious renewal and the normative understanding of Anabaptist identity and history for decades to come.

Bender depicted Anabaptism as a theologically rich tradition, not the marginal movement of fanatics and rebels as Martin Luther and others had characterized it since the sixteenth century. Whereas centuries of theologians and historians had brushed Anabaptists into the dustbin of history, Bender argued that the biblically inspired

Fig. 15.3 Historians Harold S. Bender (*right*) and Cornelius J. Dyck at the Institute for Mennonite Studies at the Mennonite seminary in Elkhart, Indiana. Photo courtesy of *Canadian Mennonite*/Mennonite Archives of Ontario, Conrad Grebel University College, Waterloo, 297.

discipleship and voluntary church membership of the Swiss and Dutch Anabaptists was the fulfillment of the Reformation and the restoration of the New Testament church. The Mennonites, he added, had maintained that radically faithful tradition into the twentieth century. In their unwillingness to compromise their beliefs for political expediency, Anabaptists took Luther's and Zwingli's reforming ideas to their logical conclusions. Bender identified three guiding principles of "genuine Anabaptism":

- Discipleship: The essence of Christianity is following Jesus in daily life.
- Community: A voluntary church that is separated from the world, often persecuted, and practices mutual aid.
- Ethic of love and nonresistance: The "complete abandonment of all warfare, strife, and violence, and the taking of human life."[25]

Bender's clearly argued analysis offered a generation of Mennonites a religious identity that they could take pride in as many of them left their rural communities. Taught at Mennonite colleges and packed in the luggage of Mennonite Central Committee workers helping to rebuild postwar Europe, Bender's pamphlet linked the religious identity of twentieth-century Mennonites to the story and vision of Anabaptists in the cities and universities of sixteenth-century Europe. The model of faithfulness found in the early Anabaptists helped mainstream Mennonites engage surrounding society while maintaining a separate communal identity. In his "Vision," Bender tried to sail a third way through the theological shoals of liberalism and fundamentalism while rejuvenating the Anabaptist commitment to peace. The historian Paul Toews has emphasized the importance of Bender's "Anabaptist Vision" on Mennonite identity: "For Mennonite scholarship and self-understanding, it was a *kairos* moment, a moment of breakthrough. No other single event or piece of historical writing has filtered so deeply into Mennonite thinking. The phrase 'the Anabaptist Vision' became the identifying incantation of North American Mennonites like no other set of words."[26]

Through a prolific output of theological writings, American Mennonite theologian John Howard Yoder greatly shaped Mennonite thinking in the second half of the twentieth century. According to

Yoder, Jesus' teachings on nonviolence, discipleship, and the kingdom of God were not simply lofty ideals; Christians were to live them out publicly and embody them in the church. The church, according to Yoder and those whom he influenced, was where Christian ethics were lived out. Later revelations of Yoder's sexual harassment and sexual abuse of women have significantly tarnished his legacy. Mennonite theologians who have drawn from Yoder's thought have had to reexamine the connection between his life and his theology. Scholars, especially women theologians and ethicists, have initiated conversations about alternate methods and sources for Anabaptist theology, identity, gender justice, and peace ethics.[27]

In the 1960s and 1970s, Mennonites who urged the church to join civil rights movements or resist the militarism of the Vietnam War held up the Radical Reformers as models for the church to follow. Increasingly, the traditional doctrine of nonresistance, or defenselessness, felt too passive for activist Mennonites, and they advocated for creative and active peacemaking instead. The younger generation pushed the church to engage more proactively on behalf of others, expanding the scope of Mennonite and Brethren in Christ political advocacy on behalf of their own conscientious objectors in the World Wars. The Anabaptist model and wartime alternative service programs facilitated the theological shift from nonresistance to active peacemaking as well as increased sociocultural acculturation.[28] The Anabaptist tradition of linguistic, cultural, or physical separation had been transformed into a philosophical or theological separation from others.

By the 1990s, Bender's "Anabaptist Vision" continued to inform Mennonite identity, but its power had weakened. Historians in the 1970s critiqued Bender's historical scholarship for selectivity and idealization. In holding up Zürich as the original hearth of "evangelical and constructive Anabaptism," Bender minimized revolutionary, Spiritualist, and violent Anabaptists, even within the Swiss stream.[29] In addition, Mennonite institutions and authorities had lost some of their authority. More urban and educated than their parents and grandparents, acculturated Mennonites had developed more complex identities with a greater variety of influences on their lives.

Some critiqued a perceived chasm between the Anabaptist radicals of the sixteenth century and the structures and practices of twentieth-century Mennonite reality.³⁰ At the 1962 Mennonite World Conference (MWC) in Kitchener, Ontario, the African American Mennonite civil rights activist Vincent Harding called on white Mennonites to become more actively involved in the civil rights movements and to integrate their congregations. Harding appealed to Anabaptist history when he called on Mennonites to follow the example of "our persecuted Anabaptist forefathers" to seek racial justice, reminding them of the persecution of their predecessors. "But," Harding said, "we have forgotten, forgotten what it means to be a persecuted minority, forgotten what it is to rejoice in suffering for Christ's sake, forgotten our comradeship with the outcasts, forgotten how it was to be fools for Christ's sake."³¹ At the Amsterdam MWC conference five years later, Harding delivered two powerful speeches calling on Mennonites to listen to and join contemporary revolutionary movements, arguing that Mennonites who were true to their traditions of nonconformity and discipleship should join the protests and marches growing across the world.³² By the time of the 1967 MWC gathering, Harding had left Mennonite circles.

More recent critiques of the Anabaptist Vision include scholar Dorothy Yoder Nyce's argument that Bender's vision did not equip the modern church to interpret those parts of the Bible like 1 Corinthians 14:34–35 that were used to restrict women's participation in the life of the church.³³ Other writers have accused those who followed Bender of teaching a discipleship that lacked the spiritual resources and grace that Bender (and the early Anabaptists) may have taken for granted, thereby failing to provide the spiritual practices for a life of following Christ in discipleship.³⁴

While many Mennonites hoped to move beyond Bender's Anabaptist Vision, the neo-Anabaptist movement of the late twentieth century attempted to take Anabaptist thought beyond the boundaries of the historic Anabaptist churches, often using contemporary theological and philosophical approaches to do so, drawing from John Howard Yoder's thought as well as from scholars like Stanley Hauerwas and James McClendon.³⁵

Neo-Anabaptist scholars and pastors concerned about increasing nationalism in some Christian movements, as well as those who see Western society as an increasingly post-Christian reality, draw from Anabaptists' long-standing rejection of an alliance between church and the state, centrality of community, and focus on Jesus-centered discipleship. Authors like Greg Boyd, who was concerned with political partisanship among mainstream evangelicals, or Stuart Murray, a leader in the Anabaptist Network in the United Kingdom, spoke for movements that have remained separate from the historic Mennonites, yet many theologians and congregations in the traditional Anabaptist groups have found neo-Anabaptist thought a helpful resource for their own identity and revival. In 2015, the Herald Press imprint of Mennonite Church USA and Mennonite Church Canada publishing arm, MennoMedia, published a revised edition of Stuart Murray's *Naked Anabaptist* for North American Mennonite readers, to aid in their discernment of materialism, individualism, and nationalism in the North American context.

Old Order and separatist options among the Amish and Low German Mennonites

Since 2000, young, unmarried women from conservative Anabaptist groups in the United States and Canada have traveled to Mexico to teach in Old Colony Mennonite parochial schools. Sent by a board in the United States, the teachers from Old Order Amish, New Order Amish, and Old Order Mennonite churches hope to reform the Old Colony curriculum. As Amish teacher Mary Stoltzfus reflected, the teachers hope to "nurtur[e] the school toward orderliness and teaching good values and study habits."[36] The project is remarkable in its allowance for women to assume leadership positions within this new context, and for how it highlights a sense of shared identity among the Plain groups. Although the American and Low German Mexican groups have quite different histories, they share a common spirituality: all dress differently from the surrounding culture, often speak a dialect of German, and maintain parochial schools for educating their children.

Among Old Order groups, who were not as influenced by the Anabaptist Vision's historical guideposts and the evangelical revivals, faithfulness means choosing to draw visible lines of demarcation from the surrounding culture to maintain communal and familial ties. All faith is expressed through culture; the question for them is what culture to adopt and what to reject. While acculturated Anabaptists were debating levels of political engagement to resist the Vietnam draft or advocate for the poor, separatist churches debated whether to connect their homes to public sewer systems or which language to use in their parochial schools.

As they puzzled out how to practice faithful discipleship, separatist groups arrived at a kaleidoscope of answers, but they shared a surprisingly similar spirituality. Old Older spirituality emphasizes the communal elements of faith; from their early childhood, members learn to yield their will to God and the community. Through church discipline, churches strengthen members' relation to God and each other. A church's Ordnung—the discipline and widespread practice of the congregation—helps members follow God's will through the church. According to Amish historian Joseph F. Beiler, those who have "learned to love and live" the Ordnung have been given "freedom of heart, peace of mind, and a clear conscience." An Old Order Anabaptist living within the Ordnung, Beiler writes, "actually has more freedom, more liberty, and more privilege than those who are bound to the outside."[37]

Old Order Amish

The largest Anabaptist group in North America is the Amish, and there are "more people, in more places, calling themselves Amish than ever before."[38] Between 1992 and 2007, Amish districts (congregations) increased from 930 to 1,615 and expanded from twenty-two states and the province of Ontario into twenty-seven states and Ontario. The growth and geographic expansion of the Amish, as well as the decentralized nature of Amish religious practice, has increased the diversity found within the constellation of Amish groups.

Some Amish live intentionally austere, plain lives separated as much as possible from the modern world and surrounding society, but others live near suburbs, work in factories, and shop at big box stores. Most Amish champion parochial schooling as a vital element of their efforts to maintain their distinct identity, whereas Amish in places like Holmes County, Ohio, and LaGrange County, Indiana, send their children to public schools. There are additional differences among the Amish in their attitudes toward evangelical theology, the use of the Pennsylvania German dialect, disciplinary practices, and acceptable use of technology, including computers and cell phones.[39] According to

Fig. 15.4 Old Order Amish women and man at an auction in the Kitchener-Waterloo region. Photo courtesy of David L. Hunsberger/Mennonite Archives of Ontario, Conrad Grebel University College, Waterloo, 53.

historian Steven M. Nolt, the differences can be attributed to migration histories, understandings of Ordnung, and whether the Amish were in Swiss Amish or Pennsylvania German settlements, which has shaped the Amish in different local and regional contexts.[40]

In the 1950s and 1960s, Old Order Amish and Mennonites in the United States came into conflict with local and state authorities over requirements for children to attend public high school or for parochial schools and teachers to meet state standards. Fearing that their children would be led astray by teachers outside of the faith or trained for careers that would lead children outside of the community, Amish parents resisted state mandates and closures. Photos of Amish parents and their children resisting the authorities gained sympathetic attention in the national presses, further heightening the tension. In 1971, the United States Supreme Court settled the conflict by ruling that Amish parents could not be denied the right to decide when their children could stop school, because doing so did not create social or economic burdens on society.[41]

Low German Mennonites

At various points in the twentieth century, conservative groups from the Dutch-Russian tradition found it too difficult to practice their faith in light of the decadence of the surrounding culture. As described in earlier chapters, they instead developed a transnational identity of pilgrims and strangers passing through this world, making migration and a diasporic community a key component of their spiritual understanding. As the corrupt world encroached on them, they migrated to stave off assimilation that they saw happening among other Mennonites.

In the 1920s and 1940s, Mennonites left Manitoba and Saskatchewan for Mexico and Paraguay in response to stricter school legislation. Reflecting on the 1922 migration, Old Colony bishop Isaak M. Dyck worried that the legislation would produce "an inextinguishable enthusiasm for the art of war" and encourage nationalism in its members. The Mennonites were being faithful to the Anabaptist call to "walk in all humility and lowliness" and follow the examples of suffering discipleship found in the *Martyrs Mirror*.[42] These groups would continue to migrate in search of greater isolation or economic opportunity (see ch. 13). Many Low German Mennonites returned to southern Ontario to find seasonal agricultural work, often living in communities with large numbers of Old Order Mennonites. While they maintain their Canadian citizenship, the Low German Mennonites' primary loyalty is to their transcontinental Mennonite community.[43]

In their internal conversations, these churches primarily discerned their identities from different starting presuppositions than those of more acculturated Anabaptists, yet they, too, drew from historical memory or evangelical influences at times. The New Order Amish separated from the Old Order in the 1960s to emphasize the formation of an individual's spirituality, using Sunday school materials to raise their children in the faith. Echoing influences from the evangelical stream, they emphasize an "assurance of salvation" and undertake missionary work. Influenced by Mennonite revival meetings, Beachy Amish and Amish Mennonite groups in the 1950s and 1960s found a new zeal for evangelization and mission, including church plants across the globe.[44]

Searching for the center in changing times

Mennonites, Amish, and other Anabaptists continued to embrace new ways of reviving or reimagining their faith as the social and religious changes of the twentieth century continued into the twenty-first. In 2006, just over a tenth of American Mennonites lived on farms, down from a third of Mennonites who did so in the early 1970s. With significant populations in the cities of Winnipeg, Vancouver, and Kitchener-Waterloo, Canadian Mennonites became more urbanized earlier in their history. In both countries, the Brethren in Christ (the Canadian denomination is now called Be In Christ Church of Canada) also migrated to the cities, leading to similar questions about maintaining religious identity in new cosmopolitan contexts.

Often connected to an increasing participation in higher education and increased exposure to the surrounding culture, Anabaptists in urban contexts have found new sources for religious renewal. Some congregations introduced more liturgical forms of worship, and many churches now include a praise band in their Sunday service, as one would find in many evangelical churches. Trained in seminaries, Mennonite ministers and theologians have found spiritual inspiration in liberation theology and the womanist theology of Black American (and other) writers like Monica Coleman and Jacquelyn Grant, who emphasize God's empathy and compassion rather than the focus on suffering found in the Anabaptist tradition. Whether these new waves of renewal will tell a new global Anabaptist story or whether the centrifugal forces are too great to overcome depends on those within the movement that began with the radical act of adult baptism in houses, barns, and attics five centuries before.

Conclusion

The Ties That Bind a Global Movement

Historians are trained to understand the past, but we are often tempted to look forward, using the past to predict the future. Anabaptism's remarkable transformation from a sixteenth-century reforming movement to an ethnoreligious community to a global phenomenon should serve as a warning to historians that predicting the future is a fool's errand. While I am tempted to prognosticate on the future of Anabaptism, I find myself needing to refrain. As a historian trained to understand early modern history, interpreting the developments of the past sixty or so years feels like looking at current events that are "too early to tell" in how they will shape trends and conclusions.

Anabaptists have increasingly complicated reactions to telling their history—this goes beyond the complexity of crafting a clear narrative. As Anabaptists approach the fifth century of their movement, some wish to commemorate rather than celebrate Anabaptism, which began as an acrimonious division in the body of Christ. Other Anabaptists do not see the need to look back at the past at all—they believe that the Bible and the Holy Spirit are the only authorities needed for Christian identity.

There are also those who want a usable and inspirational past to craft their contemporary identities. The tales of faithful martyrs, entrepreneurial missionaries, or heartbreaking migrations provide hooks and models to which they can appeal; there is something comforting about belonging to a larger story. However, as Anabaptism has become more diverse, with new languages, histories, and traditions folded in, there is an appreciation that telling the story of a heroic heritage can exclude those who have joined the movement or belittle other Christians with whom Anabaptists are trying to reconcile.

This book has tried to tell a complicated history of the Anabaptists—one that does not cover up or explain away moments of hypocrisy, failure, or conflict. Rather than self-flagellation, these stories are intended to inspire and instruct in a way that I hope can be usable to those who see themselves as part of the tradition. The history of Christianity is filled with stories of Christians who fail to live up to their own standards. Even Peter and the other disciples appear to have misunderstood Jesus' message in the final days of his ministry. Anabaptists might take comfort in embracing both the accounts of their imperfections and the stories of steadfast perseverance and growth.

Historians who treat sources carefully and make their conclusions cautiously have had epistemological humility instilled in them as part of their professional development. Times of drifting, isolation, or unfaithfulness should similarly provide Anabaptists with the gift of humility as they look back over their past. By embracing a history that celebrates the good and repents the regrettable, Anabaptists may renew the traditional Anabaptist value of humility, especially at a time when the ties that bind Anabaptists to one another feel worn down by political polarization, economic disparity, and distance. If the past illustrates anything, it is that the future is not ours to control.

When they gather for worship, community meals, or Mennonite World Conference assemblies, Anabaptists share testimonies with one another, hold each other accountable, and look for ways to share one another's burdens. They create a common community with an agreed-upon story that new members write themselves into; others may choose to edit themselves out. Seventeenth-century Dutch martyrologies created a sense of transnational Anabaptism out of previously separated groups of adult baptizers, and Anabaptism persists as a movement because its members believe that such unity exists and act as if it its story is true.[1] A global church without an authoritative center may feel like a shaky foundation to those seeking clarity, unanimity, and distinct lines of relationships. The remarkable endurance and transformation of Anabaptism recounted in this book suggest that the story of Anabaptism is powerful enough to be told in different languages and practiced in different ways for many years to come.

Notes

Chapter 1
1. Benrath, *Wegbereiter der Reformation*, 236–39; translation in Lindberg, *European Reformations*, 9.
2. Snyder, *Life and Thought of Michael Sattler*.
3. Benedict, *Rule of St. Benedict in English*, ch. 23, 310, quoted in Snyder, *Life and Thought of Michael Sattler*, 241.
4. John Howard Yoder, *Schleitheim Confession*, 10.
5. Eire, *Reformations: Early Modern World*, 27–30.
6. Scribner and Dixon, *German Reformation*, 11–12.
7. Hendrix, *Recultivating the Vineyard*, 17.
8. *Deutsche Reichstagsakten unter Kaiser Sigmund*, 1:56, quoted in Strauss, "Ideas of Reformation and Renovation," 21–22.
9. Whitford, *Companion to Reformation Theology*, 389.
10. Luther, *Career of the Reformer IV*, 336–37.
11. Although the story of Luther nailing his theses to the church door is an iconic moment in church history, there is little evidence that he ever hammered them in himself. For a summary of the debate, see Dixon, *Contesting the Reformation*, 205–7.
12. Luther, *Career of the Reformer II*, 112–13.
13. Kim, "Anabaptism in Korea," 311–14.

Chapter 2
1. Packull, "Origins of Swiss Anabaptism," 38.
2. Quoted in Roth, "Recent Currents in the Historiography," 525.
3. Snyder, "Swiss Anabaptism," 48–49.
4. Quoted in Goertz, *The Anabaptists*, 8.
5. In Harder, *Sources of Swiss Anabaptism*, 202.
6. Quoted in Snyder, "Swiss Anabaptism," 50.
7. Quoted in Snyder, 54.
8. Quoted in Stayer, *Anabaptists and the Sword*, 98.
9. In Estep, *Anabaptist Beginnings* 31–37.
10. For a range of historian interpretations of the radicals' view of the church at this important stage, see Snyder, "Birth and Evolution of Swiss Anabaptism," 522–23.

11 In Harder, *Sources of Swiss Anabaptism*, 333–35.
12 In Harder, 335–36
13 In Harder, 343.
14 In Harder, 345.
15 Blickle, *Communal Reformation*; Blickle, *Revolution of 1525*.
16 Stayer, *Peasants' War and Anabaptist Community of Goods*.
17 Snyder and Hecht, *Profiles of Anabaptist Women*, 47.
18 Neff and Bender, "Manz, Felix (ca. 1498–1527)."
19 John Howard Yoder, *Legacy of Michael Sattler*, 71.
20 John Howard Yoder, 73.
21 John Howard Yoder, 79.
22 Stayer, *Peasants' War and Anabaptist Community of Goods*.
23 Quoted in Snyder and Hecht, *Profiles of Anabaptist Women*, 64–66.
24 Quoted in Wenger and Kreider, "Dress."
25 Lutheran-Mennonite-Roman Catholic Trilateral Dialogue Commission, "Baptism and Incorporation into the Church."

Chapter 3
1 Snyder, *Sources of South German/Austrian Anabaptism*, 149.
2 Snyder, 140.
3 Snyder-Penner, Russel. "Hans Nadler's Oral Exposition," 398–400.
4 Bender, "The Anabaptist Vision," 3–24. The essay was originally delivered as an address to American Society of Church History in 1943 and was later published in booklet form by Herald Press.
5 Quoted in Snyder, *Anabaptist History and Theology*, 194.
6 Quoted in Stayer, "Swiss-South German Anabaptism," 99.
7 Oyer, "Anabaptist Women Leaders in Augsburg," 88–91.
8 Quoted in Oyer, *They Harry the Good People*, 38–41.
9 Quoted in Stayer, "Swiss-South German Anabaptism," 104.
10 For a summary of Marpeck's theology, see Roth, "Marpeck and the Later Swiss Brethren," 360–63.
11 Hecht, "Women and Religious Change," 59–61.
12 Snyder and Hecht, *Profiles of Anabaptist Women*, 140–55.
13 Quoted in Rothkegel, "Anabaptism in Moravia and Silesia," 169.
14 Quoted in Stayer, "Swiss-South German Anabaptism," 110.
15 Hutterian Brethren, *Chronicle of the Hutterian Brethren*, 1:80–81.
16 Quoted in Bossert and Stayer, "Reublin, Wilhelm."
17 Quoted in Bossert and Stayer.
18 Hans Jakob Christoph Grimmelshausen, *Der Abenteurerliche Simplicissimus*, quoted in Snyder and Hecht, *Profiles of Anabaptist Women*, 204.
19 Dipple, "Spiritualist Anabaptists," 151–67.
20 Stayer, "Community of Goods and Economics," 321–38.

Chapter 4
1. Moss, "Your Sons and Daughters Shall Prophesy."
2. Philips, "A Confession," in Williams and Mergal, *Spiritualist and Anabaptist Writers*, 214.
3. Klötzer, "Melchiorites and Münster," 234.
4. Translation of the *Amsterdam Chronicle*, quoted in Mellink, *Documenta Anabaptistica Neerlandica*, 28.
5. Visser, "Mennonites and Doopsgezinden in the Netherlands," 301–2.
6. Quoted in Snyder and Hecht, *Profiles of Anabaptist Women*, 339–40.
7. Quoted in Waite, "David Joris and Dutch Anabaptism," 136.
8. For recent scholarship on David Joris, see Waite, "David Joris (ca. 1501–1556)."
9. Menno Simons, "Reply to Gellius Faber," in *The Complete Writings of Menno Simons*, 671.
10. Waite, "David Joris (ca. 1501–1556)."
11. Goertz, *The Anabaptists*, 160.
12. Gregory, *Salvation at Stake*, 90.
13. Driedger, "Anabaptists and the Early Modern State," 515.
14. Weaver-Zercher, *Martyrs Mirror: A Social History*, 16.
15. Fabri, *Von dem Ayd Schwören*, sigs. E3v–E4, quoted in Gregory, *Salvation at Stake*, 16–17.
16. Gregory, *Salvation at Stake*, 212.
17. Friedmann, "Ausbund."
18. Quoted in Gregory, *Salvation at Stake*, 203.
19. Gregory, 227.
20. Translation of *Dit boec wort genoe[m]t: Het offer des Heeren*, 30v–31r.
21. Geraerts, "Prosecution of Anabaptists in Holland," 47.
22. Geraerts, 29–30.
23. Oyer, *They Harry the Good People*, 42.
24. Moore, *Bearing Witness*, xiv.
25. Kahsay Tewoldebirhan, "Eritrean Pastor from Banned Religion Denied Burial," April 19, 2023, https://www.bbc.com/news/live/world-africa-64439326/page/5.

Chapter 5
1. Translation of Langendijk, "De Zwitsersche eenvoudigheid," 68.
2. Translation of Langendijk, 71.
3. Dop, "Terwyl in de Kalkwyk veele dier Doopsgezinden woonen," 114; Lowry, *Documents of Brotherly Love*, 2:1097, 1103.
4. Stayer, "Passing of the Radical Moment," 147–52.
5. Van Braght, *Martyrs Mirror*, 1136.
6. Driedger, *Obedient Heretics*, 117–19.
7. See Mary S. Sprunger, "Limits of Faith."

8   Urry, *Mennonites, Politics, and Peoplehood*, 46–48.
9   Quoted in Jantzen, *Mennonite German Soldiers*, 28–29.
10 Jantzen, 50–54.
11 Leonard G. Friesen, *Mennonites in Russian Empire and Soviet Union*, 84.
12 Kuiper, "Mennonites and Politics in Friesland."
13 Groenveld, "Doopsgezinden in Tal En Last," 99–102; Kaplan, "Intimate Negotiations," 225–47.
14 Voolstra, "Mennonite Faith in the Netherlands," 277–78.
15 See Koop, *Anabaptist-Mennonite Confessions of Faith*.
16 Bangs, *Letters on Toleration*, 174.
17 Bangs, 92–93.
18 Furner, "Lay Casuistry and Survival of Later Anabaptists," 429–70.
19 Lowry, *Documents of Brotherly Love*, 1:79.
20 "Members of the Menonist Church, Petition," reproduced in MacMaster, *Land, Piety, Peoplehood*, 77.
21 MacMaster, 61–78.
22 MacMaster, 67.
23 MacMaster, 71.
24 Translated in MacMaster, *Conscience in Crisis*, 84–85.
25 MacMaster, 265.
26 In Eby and Reesor, *Letters to the Mennonite Community*.
27 Eby and Reesor, 23.
28 Eby and Reesor, 29.

Chapter 6

1   Quoted in Roth, "Pietism and the Anabaptist Soul," 28.
2   Roth, 26–34.
3   Quoted in Hein, "Palatinate."
4   Van Braght, *Martyrs Mirror*, 9–10.
5   The material on early worship patterns comes from John Rempel, "Mennonites," 545–59.
6   Elias Schad, "Anabaptist Meeting in a Forest," 294.
7   Kaplan, "Fictions of Privacy," 1031–64.
8   John Rempel, "Mennonites," 552.
9   Roth, "Marpeck and the Later Swiss Brethren," 370–72.
10 Visser, "Mennonites and Doopsgezinden in the Netherlands," 328.
11 von Schlachta, "Anabaptists and Pietists," 117.
12 Quoted in Von Schlachta, 117.
13 Von Schlachta, 117.
14 Quoted in Roth, "Pietism and the Anabaptist Soul," 34.
15 Driedger, "Article Missing from *Mennonite Encyclopedia*," 105.
16 Hamm, "Improving Mennonites in an Age of Revolution," 45, 46.
17 Driedger, "Article Missing from *Mennonite Encyclopedia*," 110.

18 De Vries, "Een staaltje Feliciaanse diplomatie."
19 Driedger, "Article Missing from *Mennonite Encyclopedia*"; Voolstra, "'The Hymn to Freedom,'" 192–93. Many Doopsgezinden continued to be active in the Nut through the nineteenth century. The Nut and the Teylers Foundation exist to this day.
20 Quoted in Nolt, *History of the Amish*, 27.
21 John Howard Yoder, *Schleitheim Confession*, 11–13.
22 "Dordrecht Confession of Faith (Mennonite, 1632)."
23 In Roth and Springer, *Letters of the Amish Division*, 38.
24 Lowry, *Documents of Brotherly Love*, 2:1135.
25 Roth and Springer, *Letters of the Amish Division*.
26 Quoted in Nolt, *History of the Amish*, 47.
27 Driedger, "Article Missing from *Mennonite Encyclopedia*," 115.

Chapter 7

1 Leonard G. Friesen, *Mennonites in Russian Empire and Soviet Union*, 105–22, 136–40.
2 Quoted in Loewen and Nolt, *Seeking Places of Peace*, 58.
3 "From Germany," *Herald of Truth* 7, no. 4 (April 1870): 56.
4 Schlabach, *Peace, Faith, Nation*, 88–95. Quotation on page 88.
5 Klassen, "Mennonites in Russia and Their Migration."
6 Reimer, "The Spirit Says Go!," 31–44.
7 Quoted in Schlabach, *Peace, Faith, Nation*, 212.
8 Quoted in Nolt, *History of the Amish*, 167.
9 Quoted in Schlabach, *Peace, Faith, Nation*, 213–14.
10 Quoted in Nolt, *History of the Amish*, 170.
11 The Egly Amish became the Defenseless Mennonite Church from 1908–1948, the Evangelical Mennonite Church from 1948–2003, and are now known as the Fellowship of Evangelical Churches.
12 In Hostetler, *Amish Roots*, 85–86.
13 Nolt, *History of the Amish*, 201.
14 The Mennonite Church of the Swiss and South German immigrants was often unofficially called the "Old" Mennonite Church to differentiate it from the "new" groups that broke away. The term was still used in the 1980s.
15 Nolt, *History of the Amish*, 215–16.
16 Lehman and Nolt, *Mennonites, Amish, and American Civil War*, 31.
17 Lehman and Nolt, 3.
18 Quoted in Lehman and Nolt, 226.
19 Quoted in Lehman and Nolt, 16.
20 Quoted in Klassen, "Mennonites in Russia and Their Migration," 199.
21 Klassen, 229–32.
22 Schlabach, "Reveille for *Die Stillen im Lande*," 213–26.

23 Quoted in Schlabach, 219.
24 Quoted in Keith Sprunger, "Bethel College."
25 Quoted in Schlabach, 217.
26 Giesbrecht, "Metis, Mennonites and the 'Unsettled Prairie,'" 103–11.
27 Braun, "Potentially Disputed Land in Colombia."
28 Quoted in Sharp, "Mennonites and Native Americans."
29 Mennonite Church General Assembly, "On Observing 1992," 35.
30 Stuckey-Kauffman, "A Woman's Ministry."

Chapter 8
1 "Die Stillen im Lande," or "the quiet in the land," likely originates from Psalm 35:20.
2 Dharma, "Mennonite Churches of Indonesia," 32–34.
3 Dharma, 41.
4 Dharma, 77.
5 Dharma, 85.
6 Asheervadham, "Churches of India," 158.
7 Asheervadham.
8 Quoted in Juhnke, *Vision, Doctrine, War*, 143.
9 Quoted in Juhnke, 139.
10 Hinz-Penner, *Searching for Sacred Ground*; Hinz-Penner, "Hart, Lawrence Homer (1933–2022).
11 Unrau, "Shoulderblade, Julia Yellow Horse (1913–1973)."
12 Neufeldt, "Settler Colonial Conscripts," 508–26; Rempel Petkau, "How Complicit Are Mennonites?"

Chapter 9
1 Baerg, *Diary of Anna Baerg, 1916–1924*, 4.
2 Quoted in Al Reimer, "*Sanitätsdienst* and *Selbstschutz*," 136.
3 Baerg, *Diary of Anna Baerg, 1916–1924*, 19.
4 Neufeld, *Russian Dance of Death*, 26.
5 Graber and Shelly quoted in Homan, *American Mennonites and the Great War*, 42.
6 As quoted in Juhnke, *Vision, Doctrine, War*, 211.
7 As quoted in Juhnke, 210.
8 Bush, "Mennonites and the Great War," 95.
9 Juhnke, *Vision, Doctrine, War*, 239–40.
10 As quoted in Juhnke, 226.
11 Quoted in Bush, "Mennonites and the Great War," 98–99.
12 Quoted in Juhnke, *Vision, Doctrine, War*, 245.
13 Quoted in Krahn and Sawatzky, "Old Colony Mennonites."
14 Homan, *American Mennonites and the Great War*, 180–81.
15 Bender, "The Anabaptist Vision."

16 Stayer, Packull, and Deppermann, "From Monogenesis to Polygenesis," 83–121.
17 Quoted in Fehr and Lichdi, "Mennonites in Germany," 125.
18 Redekop, "Nazi Support among Mennonites," 81–95.
19 Quoted in Fehr and Lichdi, "Mennonites in Germany," 129.
20 Quoted in Fehr and Lichdi, 130.
21 Quoted in Dharma, "Mennonite Churches of Indonesia," 52.
22 Weidemann, "Identity and Complicity."
23 Quoted in Regehr, *Mennonites in Canada, 1939–1970*, 37.
24 Loewen and Nolt, *Seeking Places of Peace*, 180–81.

Chapter 10
1 Quoted in Williams, "Delegates Embrace New Identity."
2 Quoted in Setiawan, "Assembly Small but Full of Joy."
3 Setiawan.
4 Mennonite World Conference, "Membership, Map and Statistics."
5 Quoted in Myers and Malembe, "Mennonites Celebrate Women's Ordinations."
6 LGBTQ+ is an acronym for lesbian, gay, bisexual, transgender, queer, and more. In Canada, the acronym 2SLGBTQ+ is extended to include "Two Spirit," a term used within some Indigenous communities that reflects complex understandings of gender.
7 Jenkins, *The Next Christendom*; Sanneh and Carpenter, *Changing Face of Christianity*.
8 Sanneh, *Disciples of All Nations*, xix–xx.
9 Pew Research Center, *Global Christianity*, 9.
10 The five volumes are *Anabaptist Songs in African Hearts*, edited by Lapp and Synder; *Testing Faith and Tradition*, edited by Jecker and Hoekema; *Mission and Migration*, by Prieto; *Churches Engage Asian Traditions*, edited by Lapp and Synder; and *Seeking Places of Peace*, by Loewen and Nolt.
11 Prieto, *Mission and Migration*.
12 Roth, *Cloud of Witnesses*, 17–19.
13 Robert, "American Society of Missiology," 13–15; Whiteman, "Contextualization," 2–7.
14 Between 1850 and 1944, European and North American Mennonites founded 25 missions. Between 1950 and 1979, they founded 101. Fifty-two of those were founded between 1945 and 1959 alone. Shenk, "Mission and Service and Globalization," 9.
15 Kisare, *Kisare, a Mennonite of Kiseru*, 103, quoted in Stoner-Eby, "Building a Church," 26.
16 Loewen and Nolt, *Seeking Places of Peace*, 108–9.
17 Roth, *Cloud of Witnesses*, 126–31.
18 Miller, Traore, and Hollinger-Janzen, "Mennonites in Sidi, Burkina Faso."

19 Quoted in Kraybill, "Peacebuilding Depends on Biblical Foundations."
20 Quoted in Kraybill.
21 Quoted in Kanagy, Miller, and Roth, *Global Anabaptist Profile*, 89.
22 Benner, "Wiens: Rising Political Star in Paraguay."
23 Mennonite World Conference, "Living Out the Gospel."
24 Kanagy, Miller, and Roth, *Global Anabaptist Profile*, 24–25.
25 In North America, Old Order Amish can come into conflict with authorities on issues of zoning, buggy safety, or education. Weaver-Zercher, *Martyrs Mirror: A Social History*, 325–26.
26 Quoted in Miller, "Following Jesus into Prison," 13.
27 Lee was released on July 30, 2015, several months earlier than planned. Birky, "South Korean CO Asks: 'Can I Kill?'"
28 Djojodihardjo, "An Experience in My Life," 29.
29 Djojodihardjo, 32.
30 Over 50 percent of Latin American Mennonites interviewed experienced healing, compared to 24–41 percent of people from other regions. Kanagy, Miller, and Roth, *Global Anabaptist Profile*, 23.
31 Nolt, "Contemporary Anabaptists in North America," 573.
32 Roth, *Cloud of Witnesses*, 22–23.
33 Old Order groups are often included under the Anabaptist umbrella, even though members of the more conservative expressions of the tradition do not necessarily see themselves connected to more worldly streams.

Chapter 11

1 Schrag, "Together in Faith,"
2 Esposito, "Lutherans Ask Forgiveness."
3 Unless otherwise noted, information in this section is taken from Tshimika and Dube, "Churches in Africa," 1–13.
4 Tshimika and Dube, 5.
5 Tshimika and Dube, 2.
6 Walls, "Crowther, Samuel Ajayi (A)."
7 Kisare, *Kisare, a Mennonite of Kiseru*, 102, quoted in Stoner-Eby, "Building a Church," 29.
8 Tshimika and Dube, "Churches in Africa," 10.
9 Unless otherwise indicated, information in this section is from Dube, Dube, and Nkala, "Brethren in Christ Churches in Southern Africa," 97–188.
10 Quoted in Dube, Dube, and Nkala, 102–3.
11 Sibanda, "Voices from the Hills," 197–222.
12 Sider, "Davidson, Hannah Frances (1860–1935)."
13 Kanagy, Miller, and Roth, *Global Anabaptist Profile*, 39.
14 Kanagy, Miller, and Roth, 35.

15 Kumedisa, "Mennonite Churches in Central Africa," 49–51. Unless otherwise noted, the analysis in this section comes from Kumedisa's work.
16 Bertsche, "I Just Did What Jesus Said," 7–9.
17 Kumedisa, "Mennonite Churches in Central Africa," 59.
18 Quoted in Kumedisa, 71.
19 Fast, "Lord's Work May Be Furthered," 470.
20 Chimbalanga, "Mathieu Kazadi and New Evangelical Mennonite Church," 119–21.
21 Kumedisa, "Mennonite Churches in Central Africa," 85.
22 Mulebo Ndandula, Chimbalanga, Beleji, Bertsche, and Schellenberg, *The Jesus Tribe*, 72.
23 Tshidimu, "Mennonites in Congo," xv.
24 Checole, "Mennonite Churches in Eastern Africa," 207.
25 Quoted in Checole, 206.
26 MacMaster and Jacobs, *Gentle Wind of God*, 135.
27 Quoted in Maxwell, "Partnership and Persecution."
28 Roth, *Stories:* 190–91.
29 AICs are sometimes also referred to as African Indigenous Churches, African Instituted Churches, or African Independent Churches.
30 Quoted in Braun, "No Safe Area under the Sky."
31 Checole, "Mennonite Churches in Eastern Africa," 253.

Chapter 12
1 Kim, "Anabaptism in Korea," 311.
2 Bock Ki Kim, quoted in Mennonite World Conference, "Movement Flourishing in South Korea."
3 Kim, "Anabaptism in Korea," 314.
4 Recently, scholars have made significant contributions to the history of the Indonesian churches, including Dharma, "Mennonite Churches of Indonesia"; Soekotjo and Yoder, *Gospel in the World of Java*; Lawrence M. Yoder, *Muria Story*; and Roth, *Cloud of Witnesses*.
5 Roth, *Cloud of Witnesses*, 121.
6 Soekotjo and Yoder, *Gospel in the World of Java*, 305.
7 The most accessible history of the JKI is found in Roth, *Cloud of Witnesses*, 133–54, which draws on unpublished doctoral dissertations by Adi Sutanto and Rony Chandra Kristanto.
8 Roth, 136–37.
9 Sutanto, "Strategy for Planting Churches in Java," 79, quoted in Roth, *Cloud of Witnesses*, 143.
10 Roth, *Cloud of Witnesses*, 159.
11 Quoted in Setiawan, "A Good Kind of Infidel." Hezbollah means "party of God"; thus many Muslim groups use this name but are not necessarily related to one another.

12 Asheervadham, "Churches of India," 163.
13 All membership numbers are from the 2020 update to the *Global Anabaptist Mennonite Encyclopedia Online*. Malagar, Thiessen, and Bender, "India."
14 Asheervadham, "Churches of India," 133–34. Unless otherwise noted, this section draws from Asheervadham's data and interpretations.
15 Asheervadham, 154.
16 Quoted in Setiawan, "Together Proclaim the 'Manifold Wisdom of God.'"
17 Moss, "Overcoming Barriers and Building Empowerment."
18 Huber, "India MB Conference Faces Turmoil."
19 Asheervadham, "Churches of India," 190.
20 Quoted in Duerksen, "Discerning Why Baptism Matters."
21 Kraybill, "Pastoral Letter to Anabaptist-Mennonites in India."
22 Quoted in Asheervadham, "Churches of India," 215.
23 Yamada, "Anabaptist Mennonite Churches in Japan," 289–90.
24 Yamada, 307.
25 These themes are identified in Yamada, 308–10.
26 Pan, "Mennonite Churches in Chinese-Speaking Areas," 249.

Chapter 13

1 Prieto, *Mission and Migration*, 3. The analysis and much of the content of this chapter relies on Prieto's scholarship.
2 Both quotations are found in Prieto, 13–14.
3 Quoted in Prieto, 23.
4 Quoted in Prieto, 96.
5 Shank, Snyder, and García, "Iglesia Evangélica Menonita, Argentina."
6 Quoted in Prieto, *Mission and Migration*, 127–28.
7 Prieto, 335–39.
8 Prieto, 337–38.
9 Quoted in Loewen, "To the Ends of the Earth," 441.
10 Quoted in Prieto, *Mission and Migration*, 443.
11 Quoted in Prieto, 45.
12 Loewen, "To the Ends of the Earth," 446.
13 Quoted in Loewen, *Horse-and-Buggy Genius*, 84.
14 Quoted in Weaver, *Service and the Ministry of Reconciliation*, 33.
15 As quoted in Prieto, *Mission and Migration*, 39.
16 Prieto, 49.
17 Weaver, *Service and the Ministry of Reconciliation*, 34.
18 Prieto, *Mission and Migration*, 328.
19 Roth, *Stories*, 200. The analysis of Mennonite participation in politics comes from Roth's work.
20 Quoted in Roth, 200.

21 Giesbrecht, *Strangers and Pilgrims*.
22 Prieto, *Mission and Migration*, 120.
23 Quoted in Prieto, 330.
24 Prieto, 331–32.

Chapter 14
1 Bush, "Mennonites and the Great War," 87.
2 Bush, "Flexibility of the Center," 201.
3 Toews, *Mennonites in American Society*, 182–83.
4 Homan, "We Have Come to Love Them," 39–59.
5 Jantzen, *Mennonite German Soldiers*.
6 von Schlachta, "Hands under the Cross," 63–64.
7 von Schlachta, "Hands under the Cross," 68.
8 Verbeek and Hoekema, "Mennonites in the Netherlands," 84–86.
9 Leonard G. Friesen, *Mennonites in Russian Empire and Soviet Union*, 257.
10 Friesen, 273.
11 Nolt, "Globalizing a Separate People," 487–506. The argument in this section comes from Nolt's analysis.
12 Shenk, "Mission and Service and Globalization," 494.
13 Ten Thousand Villages, "Just a Woman Trying to Help."
14 Bondarenko, "Fair Trade"; Ten Thousand Villages, "Just a Woman Trying to Help."
15 Nolt, "Globalizing a Separate People," 501–2.
16 Quoted in Byler, "Earmarks of a Bestseller," 17.
17 Cory Anderson, *Amish-Mennonites across the Globe*.
18 Hinojosa, *Latino Mennonites*, 42–47.
19 Southern District Conference Minutes, Oct. 20–24, 1945, Buhler, Kansas, Hillsboro, KS, Center for Mennonite Brethren Studies, quoted in Hinojosa, "Texas-Mexico Border, Part 1."
20 Hinojosa, "Borderlands in the Mennonite Imagination," 188–91.
21 Flores, "Hispanic Mennonites in North America."
22 Martínez, "Toward a Latino/a Mennonite History," 40.
23 Flores, "Hispanic Mennonites in North America"; Roth, *Stories*, 182.
24 Ortíz, *Reflections of an Hispanic Mennonite*; Hinojosa, *Latino Mennonites*, 183–91.
25 Bechler, *Black Mennonite Church in North America*, 172; Shearer, "Conflicting Identities," 273.
26 Bechler, *Black Mennonite Church in North America*, 48.
27 Shearer, "Conflicting Identities."
28 Stanford G. Shetler, quoted in Bush, "The Flexibility of the Center."
29 Quoted in Bender, "Sword and Trumpet."
30 Bush, "Flexibility of the Center," 194.
31 Mennonite Church USA, "Glen Guyton."

32 Quoted in Hinojosa, *Latino Mennonites*, 89.
33 Heinzekehr, "Legacy of Minority Ministries Council."
34 Hinojosa, "Freedom Dreams."
35 Blough, "Mission Efforts in Europe," 239–41.
36 Blough, 252.
37 Epp, *Mennonites in Ontario*, 28.
38 Heidebrecht, *Women in Ministry Leadership*, 1.
39 Kalmar, "Ordination of Two Women Revives Discussion."
40 As cited in Bush, "Flexibility of the Center," 196.
41 Bush, "Flexibility of the Center."
42 In Canada, the national Mennonite Church also lost members, but their decline was not as severe. Instead, the greater challenge to national unity has been decreasing funds and diminished loyalty to the national church. As a result there has been a greater emphasis on loyalty to provincial denominations.
43 Janae Rempel, "What's in a Name?"

Chapter 15
1 The analysis in this section comes from Loewen and Nolt, *Seeking Places of Peace*, 107–64.
2 Quoted in Loewen and Nolt, 144.
3 Drawn from Bebbington, *Evangelicalism in Modern Britain*, 2–17.
4 Du Mez, *Jesus and John Wayne*.
5 Marsden, *Reforming Fundamentalism*, 158.
6 Nolt, "Activist Impulses across Time," 32.
7 Quoted in Loewen and Nolt, *Seeking Places of Peace*, 151.
8 Loewen and Nolt, 148.
9 Quoted in Hinojosa, "Texas-Mexico Border, Part 2," 168.
10 Hinojosa, 168.
11 Nolt, "Activist Impulses across Time," 12–13.
12 Erb, "Evangelism for Full Discipleship," 555.
13 Erb, 439–40.
14 Erb, 539.
15 Unruh, "Great Commission as Watchword of Evangelism," 340.
16 Roth, "Anabaptism and Evangelicalism Revisited," 51.
17 Manzullo-Thomas, "Born-Again Brethren in Christ," 203–38.
18 Dyck and Steiner, "Association of Evangelical Mennonites."
19 Gerhart, "Alliance of Mennonite Evangelical Congregations."
20 Tabor College, "Tabor Signs Partnership with Evana Network."
21 Marsden, *Fundamentalism and American Culture*, 331.
22 Marsden, 325.
23 Kanagy, Miller, and Roth, *Global Anabaptist Profile*.
24 Marsden, *Fundamentalism and American Culture*, 325.

25 Bender, "The Anabaptist Vision," 21.
26 Toews, *Mennonites in American Society, 1930–1970*, 84.
27 Krall, "Anger and Anabaptist Feminist Hermeneutic," 145–63; Albrecht and Stephens, *Liberating the Politics of Jesus*; Roberts, Martens, and Penner, *Recovering from the Anabaptist Vision*. A comprehensive account of John Howard Yoder's sexual abuse and responses to it appears in Goossen, "Defanging the Beast."
28 Bush, *Two Kingdoms, Two Loyalties*. Bush argues that Guy F. Hershberger's mainstream theology started the movement toward active peacemaking.
29 Bender, "The Anabaptist Vision," 8.
30 E.g., John Howard Yoder, "Anabaptist Vision and Mennonite Reality."
31 Harding, "The Christian and the Race Question," 524–25.
32 Harding, "Voices of Revolution," 590–93.
33 Nyce, "The Anabaptist Vision," 309–19.
34 Dintaman, "Spiritual Poverty of the Anabaptist Vision," 205–8.
35 Fitch, "Neo-Anabaptism among Contemporary Christians," 582.
36 Quoted in Janzen, "Old Order Teachers Write Home from Mexico," 244.
37 From a 1974 treatise by Amish historian Joseph F. Beiler quoted in Hostetler, *Amish Roots*, 85; Loewen and Nolt, *Seeking Places of Peace*, 159–60.
38 Nolt, "Who Are the Real Amish?," 378.
39 Ems, *Virtually Amish*.
40 Nolt, "Who Are the Real Amish?," 378, 380–81.
41 Nolt, *History of the Amish*, 309–19.
42 Quoted in Loewen, "To the Ends of the Earth," 433–34.
43 See Loewen, *Village among Nations*.
44 Cory Anderson, "Twentieth-Century 'Amish Mennonite,'" 361–411; Cory Anderson, *Amish-Mennonites across the Globe*.

Conclusion
1 In *Imagined Communities*, the scholar Benedict Anderson described the origins of nationalism as a similar agreed-upon story.

Bibliography

Albrecht, Elizabeth Soto, and Darryl W. Stephens, eds. *Liberating the Politics of Jesus: Renewing Peace Theology through the Wisdom of Women*. T&T Clark Studies in Anabaptist Theology and Ethics. New York: T&T Clark, 2020.

Anderson, Benedict. *Imagined Communities: Reflections on the Origin and Spread of Nationalism*. 2nd ed. New York: Verso, 2006.

Anderson, Cory. *The Amish-Mennonites across the Globe*. Amish-Mennonite Heritage Series 2. Millersburg, OH: Acorn Publishing, 2019.

———. "Retracing the Blurred Boundaries of Twentieth-Century 'Amish Mennonite' Identity." *Mennonite Quarterly Review* 85, no. 3 (July 2011): 361–411.

Asheervadham, I. P. "The Mennonite and Brethren in Christ Churches of India." In Lapp and Snyder, *Churches Engage Asian Traditions*, 125–219.

Baerg, Anna. *Diary of Anna Baerg, 1916–1924*. Translated by Gerald Peters. Winnipeg: CMBC Publications, 1985.

Bangs, Jeremy Dupertuis. *Letters on Toleration: Dutch Aid to Persecuted Swiss and Palatine Mennonites, 1615–1699*. Rockport, ME: Picton Press, 2004.

Bebbington, David. *Evangelicalism in Modern Britain: A History from the 1730s to the 1980s*. London: Unwin Hyman, 1989.

Bechler, Le Roy. *The Black Mennonite Church in North America, 1886–1986*. Scottdale, PA: Herald Press, 1986.

Bender, Harold S. "The Anabaptist Vision." *Church History* 13, no. 1 (1944): 3–24.

———. "Sword and Trumpet, The." In *Global Anabaptist Mennonite Encyclopedia Online* [hereafter *GAMEO*]. Herald Press, 1959; online ed. last modified August 26, 2016. https://gameo.org/index.php?title=Sword_and_Trumpet,_The.

Benedict. *The Rule of St. Benedict in English*. Collegeville, MN: Liturgical Press, 1982.

Benner, Dick. "Wiens: Rising Political Star in Paraguay." *Canadian Mennonite*, June 22, 2012. https://canadianmennonite.org/articles/wiens-rising-political-star-paraguay.

Benrath, Gustav Adolf, ed. *Wegbereiter der Reformation*. Klassiker des Protestantismus. Bremen: Schünemann, 1967.

Bertsche, Jim. "I Just Did What Jesus Said." In Mulebo Ndandula, Chimbalanga, Beleji, Bertsche, and Eidse Schellenberg, *The Jesus Tribe*, 7–9.

Birky, Madeline. "South Korean CO Asks: 'Can I Kill?'" Mennonite World Conference, January 28, 2016. https://mwc-cmm.org/young-anabaptists-yabs/stories/south-korean-co-asks-can-i-kill.

Blickle, Peter. *Communal Reformation: The Quest for Salvation in Sixteenth-Century Germany*. New Jersey: Humanities Press, 1992.

———. *The Revolution of 1525: The German Peasants' War from a New Perspective*. Baltimore: Johns Hopkins University Press, 1985.

Blough, Neal. "Mission Efforts in Europe: New Congregations, New Questions." In Jecker and Hoekema, *Testing Faith and Tradition*, 233–54.

Bondarenko, Peter. "Fair Trade." Accessed April 22, 2023. https://www.britannica.com/topic/fair-trade.

Bossert, Gustav, Jr., and James M. Stayer. "Reublin, Wilhelm (1480/84–after 1559)." In *GAMEO*. Herald Press, 1989, online ed. accessed November 1, 2023. https://gameo.org/index.php?title=Reublin,_Wilhelm_(1480/84-after_1559).

Braun, Will. "Potentially Disputed Land in Colombia Attracts Low German Mennonites." *Canadian Mennonite*, September 17, 2017. https://anabaptistworld.org/legally-disputed-land-in-colombia-attracts-low-german-mennonites/.

———. "'We Have No Safe Area under the Sky.'" *Canadian Mennonite*, August 31, 2022. https://canadianmennonite.org/stories/we-have-no-safe-area-under-sky.

Brewer, Brian C., ed. *T&T Clark Handbook of Anabaptism*. New York: Bloomsbury Academic, 2022.

Burkholder, Jared S., and David C. Cramer, eds. *Activist Impulse: Essays on the Intersection of Evangelicalism and Anabaptism*. Eugene, OR: Wipf and Stock, 2012.

Bush, Perry. "The Flexibility of the Center: Mennonite Church Conflict in the 1960s." *Mennonite Quarterly Review* 72, no. 2 (April 1998): 189–206.

———. "Mennonites and the Great War." In *American Churches and the First World War*, edited by Gordon L. Heath. McMaster Divinity College General Series 7. Eugene, OR: Pickwick, 2016.

_____. *Two Kingdoms, Two Loyalties: Mennonite Pacifism in Modern America.* Baltimore: Johns Hopkins University Press, 1998.

Byler, J. Daryl. "Earmarks of a Bestseller: After 25 Years *More-with-Less Cookbook* Is Still Changing Eating Habits and Lives." *A Common Place*, November 2000.

Checole, Alemu. "Mennonite Churches in Eastern Africa." In Lapp and Snyder, *Anabaptist Songs in African Hearts*, 191–253.

Chimbalanga, Jean Felix. "Mathieu Kazadi and the New Evangelical Mennonite Church." In Mulebo Ndandula, Chimbalanga, Beleji, Bertsche, and Eidse Schellenberg, *The Jesus Tribe*, 119–21.

Deutsche Reichstagsakten unter Kaiser Sigmund. Vol. 1. 2nd ed. Göttingen: n.p., 1956.

de Vries, Marleen. "Een staaltje Feliciaanse diplomatie: Het departement letterkunde van Felix Meritis tijdens en na de patriottentijd (1779–1795)." *Skript. Historisch Tijdschrift* 13, no. 3 (1991): 131–39.

Dharma, Adhi. "The Mennonite Churches of Indonesia." In Lapp and Snyder, *Churches Engage Asian Traditions*, 21–123.

Dintaman, Stephen F. "The Spiritual Poverty of the Anabaptist Vision." *Conrad Grebel Review* 10, no. 2 (Spring 1992): 205–8.

Dipple, Geoffrey. "Spiritualist Anabaptists." In Brewer, *Handbook of Anabaptism*, 151–67.

Dit boec wort genoe[m]t: Het offer des Heeren, om het inhout van sommighe opgeofferde kinderen Gods [. . .]. [Netherlands], 1578.

Dixon, C. Scott. *Contesting the Reformation.* Malden, MA: Wiley, 2012.

Djojodihardjo, S[oehadiweko]. "An Experience in My Life." *Concern, a Pamphlet Series*, no. 15 (July 1967): 25–35.

Dop, Bert. "'Terwyl in de Kalkwyk veele dier Doopsgezinden Woonen': Doopsgezinden in een Groninger veenkolonie in de achttiende eeuw." *Doopsgezinde Bijdragen* 21 (1995): 97–132.

"Dordrecht Confession of Faith (Mennonite, 1632)." In *GAMEO*. Online ed. accessed September 2, 2023. https://gameo.org/index.php?title=Dordrecht_Confession_of_Faith_(Mennonite,_1632).

Driedger, Michael. "Anabaptists and the Early Modern State: A Long-Term View." In Roth and Stayer, *Companion to Anabaptism and Spiritualism*, 507–44.

_____. "An Article Missing from the *Mennonite Encyclopedia*: 'The Enlightenment in the Netherlands.'" In *Commoners and Community: Essays in Honour of Werner O. Packull*, edited by C. Arnold Snyder, 101–20. Kitchener, ON: Pandora Press, 2002.

———. *Obedient Heretics: Mennonite Identities in Lutheran Hamburg and Altona during the Confessional Age*. Burlington, ON: Ashgate, 2002.

Dube, Bekithemba, Doris Dube, and Barbara Nkala. "Brethren in Christ Churches in Southern Africa." In Lapp and Synder, *Anabaptist Songs in African Hearts*, 97–188.

Duerksen, Travis. "Webinar Continues Legacy of Discerning Why Baptism Matters." Mennonite Mission Network, January 25, 2023. https://www.mennonitemission.net/news/4835/Webinar-continues-legacy-of-discerning-why-baptism-matters.

Du Mez, Kristin Kobes. *Jesus and John Wayne: How White Evangelicals Corrupted a Faith and Fractured a Nation*. New York: Liveright, 2020.

Dyck, Cornelius J., and Samuel J. Steiner. "Association of Evangelical Mennonites." In *GAMEO*. Herald Press, 1995; online ed. accessed November 16, 2023. https://gameo.org/index.php?title=Association_of_Evangelical_Mennonites.

Eby, Heinrich, and Thomas Reesor. *Letters to the Mennonite Community in Upper Canada: With an Addition, Berlin, (Upper Canada), Printed by Henry Eby, 1840*. Pickering, ON: Thomas Reesor, 1939.

Eire, Carlos M. N. *Reformations: The Early Modern World, 1450–1650*. New Haven: Yale University Press, 2016.

Ems, Lindsay. *Virtually Amish: Preserving Community at the Internet's Margins*. Acting with Technology. Cambridge: MIT Press, 2022.

Epp, Marlene. *Mennonites in Ontario*. Rev. ed. Waterloo, ON: Mennonite Historical Society of Ontario, 2012.

Erb, Paul. "Evangelism for Full Discipleship." *Gospel Herald* 46 (June 9, 1953): 539–40, 555.

Esposito, Nicolas. "Lutherans Ask Forgiveness from Mennonites." Ecumenical News, July 23 2010. https://www.ecumenicalnews.com/article/lutherans-seek-to-reconcile-with-mennonites-1076/.

Estep, William Roscoe, ed. *Anabaptist Beginnings (1523–1533): A Source Book*. Bibliotheca Humanistica et Reformatorica 16. Nieuwkoop: B. de Graaf, 1976.

Fabri, Johannes von Heilbronn. *Von dem Ayd Schwören: Auch von der Widertauffer Marter, vnd wo her entspring, das sie also fröhlich unnd getröst die peyn des tods leyden . . .* [Ingolstadt?], 1550.

Fast, Anicka. "'Let Us 'Also Work with Our Hands, So That the Lord's Work May Be Furthered': A Disruptive Ecclesial Economy at Kafumba, 1922–1943." *Mennonite Quarterly Review* 93, no. 4 (October 2019): 437–71.

Fehr, James Jakob, and Dieter Götz Lichdi. "Mennonites in Germany." In

Jecker and Hoekema, *Testing Faith and Tradition*, 97–152.

Fitch, David E. "Neo-Anabaptism among Contemporary Christians." In Brewer, *Handbook of Anabaptism*, 579–94.

Flores, Gilberto. "Hispanic Mennonites in North America." *Mennonite Life* 56, no. 3 (September 2001).

Friedmann, Robert. "Ausbund." In *The Mennonite Encyclopedia*, 1:191–92. Kitchener, ON: Mennonite Publishing House, 1955.

Friesen, Aileen. "A Portrait of Khortytsya/Zaporizhzhia under Occupation." In *European Mennonites and the Holocaust*, edited by John D. Thiesen and Mark Jantzen, 229–49. Transnational Mennonite Studies. Toronto: University of Toronto Press, 2020.

Friesen, Leonard G. *Mennonites in the Russian Empire and the Soviet Union: Through Much Tribulation*. Tsarist and Soviet Mennonite Studies. Toronto: University of Toronto Press, 2022.

Furner, Mark. "Lay Casuistry and the Survival of Later Anabaptists in Bern." *Mennonite Quarterly Review* 75, no. 4 (October 1, 2001): 429–70.

Geraerts, Jaap. "The Prosecution of Anabaptists in Holland, 1530–1566." *Mennonite Quarterly Review* 86, no. 1 (January 2012): 5–47.

Gerhart, Robert W. "Alliance of Mennonite Evangelical Congregations." In *GAMEO*. Article published October 2010. https://gameo.org/index.php?title=Alliance_of_Mennonite_Evangelical_Congregations.

Giesbrecht, Donovan. "Metis, Mennonites and the 'Unsettled Prairie,' 1874–1896." *Journal of Mennonite Studies* 19 (2001): 103–11.

Giesbrecht, Kennert. *Strangers and Pilgrims: How Mennonites Are Changing Landscapes in Latin America*. Vol. 2. Steinbach, MB: Die Mennonitische Post, 2018.

Goertz, Hans-Jurgen. *The Anabaptists*. Milton Park: Routledge, 2013.

Goossen, Rachel Waltner. "'Defanging the Beast': Mennonite Responses to John Howard Yoder's Sexual Abuse." *Mennonite Quarterly Review* 89, no. 1 (2015): 7–60.

Gregory, Brad. *Salvation at Stake: Christian Martyrdom in Early Modern Europe*. Cambridge: Harvard University Press, 1999.

Groenveld, S. "Doopsgezinden in tal en last: Nieuwe historische methoden en de getalsvermindering der Doopsgezinden, ca. 1700–ca. 1850." *Doopsgezinde Bijdragen (Nieuwe Reeks)* 1 (1975): 81–110.

Hamm, Ernst. "Improving Mennonites in an Age of Revolution." *Conrad Grebel Review* 30, no. 1 (Winter 2012): 24–51.

Harder, Leland, ed. *The Sources of Swiss Anabaptism: The Grebel Letters and Related Documents*. Classics of the Radical Reformation 4. Scottdale, PA: Herald Press, 1985.

Harding, Vincent. "The Christian and the Race Question." In *The Lordship of Christ: Proceedings of the Seventh Mennonite World Conference, Kitchener, Ontario, Canada, August 1–7, 1962*, edited by Cornelius J. Dyck, 520–27. Elkhart, IN: Mennonite World Conference, 1963.

———. "Voices of Revolution." *Mennonite Life* 82, no. 32 (October 3, 1967): 590–93.

Hecht, Linda A. Huebert. "Women and Religious Change: The Significance of Anabaptist Women in the Tirol, 1527–1529." *Studies in Religion* 21 (1992): 57–66.

Heidebrecht, Doug. *Women in Ministry Leadership: The Journey of the Mennonite Brethren 1954–2010*. Winnipeg: Kindred Productions, 2019.

Hein, Gerhard. "Palatinate." In *The Mennonite Encyclopedia*, 4:111. Kitchener, ON: Mennonite Publishing House, 1955.

Heinzekehr, Hannah. "The Legacy of the Minority Ministries Council." *Anabaptist World*, January 31, 2017. https://anabaptistworld.org/legacy-minority-ministries-council/.

Hendrix, Scott H. *Recultivating the Vineyard: The Reformation Agendas of Christianization*. Louisville: Westminster John Knox Press, 2004.

Hinojosa, Felipe. "Freedom Dreams: On the Legacy of the Minority Ministries Council." *Anabaptist Historians* (blog), April 24, 2017. https://anabaptisthistorians.org/2017/04/24/freedom-dreams-on-the-legacy-of-the-minority-ministries-council/.

———. *Latino Mennonites: Civil Rights, Faith, and Evangelical Culture*. Young Center Books in Anabaptist and Pietist Studies. Baltimore: Johns Hopkins University Press, 2014.

———. "Race, Gender, and Mennonite Brethren Religious Identity Along the Texas-Mexico Border, Part 1." *Direction* 34, no. 2 (Fall 2005): 145–58.

———. "Race, Gender, and Mennonite Brethren Religious Identity Along the Texas-Mexico Border, Part 2." *Direction* 35, no. 1 (Spring 2006): 162–75.

———. "The US/Mexico Borderlands in the Mennonite Imagination." *Anabaptist Witness* 7, no. 2 (October 2020): 183–91.

Hinz-Penner, Raylene. "Hart, Lawrence Homer (1933–2022)." In *GAMEO*. Article published June 2023. https://gameo.org/index.php?title=Hart,_Lawrence_Homer_(1933–2022).

———. *Searching for Sacred Ground: The Journey of Chief Lawrence Hart, Mennonite*. Telford, PA: Cascadia, 2007.

Homan, Gerlof D. *American Mennonites and the Great War, 1914–1918*. Studies in Anabaptist and Mennonite History 34. Scottdale, PA: Herald Press, 1994.

———. "'We Have Come to Love Them': Russian Mennonite Refugees in the Netherlands, 1945–1947." *Journal of Mennonite Studies* 25 (2007): 39–59.

Hostetler, John A. *Amish Roots: A Treasury of History, Wisdom, and Lore*. Baltimore: Johns Hopkins University Press, 1989.

Huber, Tim. "India MB Conference Faces Turmoil." *Anabaptist World*, October 27, 2020. https://anabaptistworld.org/india-mb-conference-faces-turmoil/.

Hutterian Brethren, trans. and ed. *Chronicle of the Hutterian Brethren*. Vol. 1. Rifton, NY: Plough.

Jantzen, Mark. *Mennonite German Soldiers: Nation, Religion, and Family in the Prussian East, 1772–1880*. Notre Dame: University of Notre Dame Press, 2010.

Janzen, Rebecca. "American Old Order Teachers Write Home from Mexico: Reflections on Gender, Religion and Caregiving." *Journal of Mennonite Studies* 36 (July 1, 2018): 237–58.

Jecker, Hanspeter, and Alle Hoekema, eds. *Testing Faith and Tradition: A Global Mennonite History*. Intercourse, PA: Good Books; Kitchener, ON: Pandora Press, 2006.

Jenkins, Philip. *The Next Christendom: The Coming of Global Christianity*. Oxford: Oxford University Press, 2002.

Juhnke, James C. *Vision, Doctrine, War: Mennonite Identity and Organization in America, 1890–1930*. Scottdale, PA: Herald Press, 1989.

Kalmar, Laura. "Ordination of Two Women Revives Discussion." *Mennonite Brethren Herald*, May 1, 2008. https://mbherald.com/ordination-of-two-women-revives-discussion/.

Kanagy, Conrad, Elizabeth Miller, and John D. Roth. *Global Anabaptist Profile: Belief and Practice in 24 Mennonite World Conference Churches*. Goshen, IN: Institute for the Study of Global Anabaptism, 2017.

Kaplan, Benjamin J. "Fictions of Privacy: House Chapels and the Spatial Accommodation of Religious Dissent in Early Modern Europe." *American Historical Review* 107, no. 4 (2002): 1031–64.

———. "Intimate Negotiations: Husbands and Wives of Opposing Faiths in Eighteenth-Century Holland." In *Living with Religious Diversity in Early-Modern Europe*, edited by C. Scott Dixon, Dagmar Freist, and Mark Greengrass, 225–47. Farnham: Ashgate, 2009.

Kim, Kyong-Jung. "Anabaptism in Korea." In Lapp and Synder, *Churches Engage Asian Traditions*, 311–14.

Kisare, Z. Marwa. *Kisare, a Mennonite of Kiseru: An Autobiography*. Salunga, PA: Eastern Mennonite Board of Missions and Charities, 1984.

Klassen, John N. "Mennonites in Russia and Their Migration." In Jecker and Hoekema, *Testing Faith and Tradition*, 182–232.

Klötzer, Ralf. "The Melchiorites and Münster." In Roth and Stayer, *Companion to Anabaptism and Spiritualism*, 217–56.

Koop, Karl. *Anabaptist-Mennonite Confessions of Faith: The Development of a Tradition*. Kitchener, ON: Pandora Press, 2004.

Krahn, Cornelius, and H. Leonard Sawatzky. "Old Colony Mennonites." In *GAMEO*. Herald Press, 1990, online ed. accessed November 2, 2023. https://gameo.org/index.php?title=Old_Colony_Mennonites.

Krall, Ruth E. "Anger and an Anabaptist Feminist Hermeneutic." *Conrad Grebel Review* 14, no. 2 (1996): 145–63.

Kraybill, J. Nelson. "Anabaptist Peacebuilding Depends on Biblical Foundations." Mennonite World Conference, July 24, 2019. https://mwc-cmm.org/stories/anabaptist-peacebuilding-depends-biblical-foundations.

———. "A Pastoral Letter to Anabaptist-Mennonites in India." Mennonite World Conference, August 27, 2021. https://mwc-cmm.org/stories/pastoral-letter-anabaptist-mennonites-india.

Kuiper, Yme. "Mennonites and Politics in Late Eighteenth-Century Friesland." In *Religious Minorities and Cultural Diversity in the Dutch Republic: Studies Presented to Piet Visser on the Occasion of His 65th Birthday*, edited by August den Hollander, Mirjam van Veen, Anna Voolstra, and Alex Noord. Boston: Brill, 2014.

Kumedisa, Erik. "Mennonite Churches in Central Africa." In Lapp and Synder, *Anabaptist Songs in African Hearts*, 45–94.

Langendijk, Pieter. *De gedichten van Pieter Langendijk*. Vol. 1. Amsterdam: Wed. van B. Visscher, 1721.

Lapp, John A., and C. Arnold Synder, eds. *Anabaptist Songs in African Hearts: A Global Mennonite History*. Global Mennonite History Series. Kitchener, ON: Pandora Press; Intercourse, PA: Good Books; 2006.

———. *Churches Engage Asian Traditions: A Global Mennonite History*. Global Mennonite History Series. Kitchener, ON: Pandora Press; Intercourse, PA: Good Books, 2011.

Lehman, James O., and Steven M. Nolt. *Mennonites, Amish, and the American Civil War*. Baltimore: Johns Hopkins University Press, 2007.

Lindberg, Carter. *The European Reformations Sourcebook*. Malden, MA: Blackwell Publishers, 2000.

Loewen, Royden. *Horse-and-Buggy Genius: Listening to Mennonites Contest the Modern World*. Winnipeg: University of Manitoba Press, 2016.

———. "To the Ends of the Earth: An Introduction to the Conservative Low German Mennonites in the Americas." *Mennonite Quarterly Review* 82, no. 3 (July 2008): 427–48.

———. *Village among Nations: "Canadian" Mennonites in a Transnational World, 1916–2006*. Toronto: University of Toronto Press, 2013.

Loewen, Royden, and Steven M. Nolt. *Seeking Places of Peace: A Global Mennonite History*. Intercourse, PA: Good Books, 2012.

Lowry, James W., ed. *Documents of Brotherly Love: Dutch Mennonite Aid to Swiss Anabaptists*. Vol. 1. Millersburg, OH: Ohio Amish Library, 2007.

———. *Documents of Brotherly Love: Dutch Mennonite Aid to Swiss Anabaptists*. Vol. 2. Millersburg, OH: Ohio Amish Library, 2015.

Luther, Martin. *Career of the Reformer II*. Luther's Works 32. Saint Louis: Concordia, 1958.

———. *Career of the Reformer IV*. Edited by Lewis W. Spitz. Luther's Works 34. Philadelphia: Muhlenberg Press, 1960.

Lutheran-Mennonite-Roman Catholic Trilateral Dialogue Commission. "Baptism and Incorporation into the Body of Christ, the Church: Lutheran-Mennonite-Roman Catholic Trilateral Conversations 2012–2017." *Mennonite Quarterly Review* 95, no. 1 (2021): 9–94.

MacMaster, Richard K. *Conscience in Crisis: Mennonites and Other Peace Churches in America, 1739–1789: Interpretation and Documents*. Scottdale, PA: Herald Press, 1979.

———. *Land, Piety, Peoplehood: The Establishment of Mennonite Communities in America, 1683–1790*. Mennonite Experience in America 1. Scottdale, PA: Herald Press, 1985.

MacMaster, Richard K., and Donald R. Jacobs. *A Gentle Wind of God: The Influence of the East Africa Revival*. Scottdale, PA; Herald Press, 2006.

Malagar, Pyarelal J., John Thiessen, and Harold S. Bender. "India." In *GAMEO*. Article published May 2014; online ed. accessed December 10, 2022. https://gameo.org/index.php?title=India.

Manzullo-Thomas, Devin C. "Born-Again Brethren in Christ: Anabaptism, Evangelicalism, and the Cultural Transformation of a Plain People." *Mennonite Quarterly Review* 90, no. 2 (April 1, 2016): 203–38.

Marsden, George M. *Fundamentalism and American Culture*. 3rd ed. New York: Oxford University Press, 2022.

———. *Reforming Fundamentalism: Fuller Seminary and the New Evangelicalism*. Grand Rapids: Eerdmans, 1987.

Martínez, Juan. "Toward a Latino/a Mennonite History [State of the Art of North American Mennonite History Conference 2004]." *Journal of Mennonite Studies* 23 (2005): 38–46.

Maxwell, Joyce. "Partnership and Persecution: Ethiopia's Meserete Kristos Church." Mennonite Central Committee Canada, December 23, 2019. https://mcccanada.ca/centennial/100-stories/partnership-persecution-ethiopias-meserete-kristos-church.

Mellink, A. F., ed. *Documenta Anabaptistica Neerlandica.* Vol. 5. *Amsterdam (1531–1536).* Leiden: Brill, 1985.

"Members of the Menonist Church: Petition," December 10, 1785. Legislative Petitions of the General Assembly, 1776–1865, no. 36121, box 291, folder 76. Library of Virginia, Richmond. Available online at http://rosetta.virginiamemory.com:1801/delivery/DeliveryManagerServlet?dps_pid=IE2817254.

Menno Simons. *The Complete Writings of Menno Simons.* Edited by J. C. Wenger. Translated by Leonard Verduin. Scottdale, PA: Herald Press, 1956.

Mennonite Church General Assembly. "On Observing 1992." August 3, 1991, Eugene, OR. Text available at https://www.anabaptistwiki.org/mediawiki/index.php/On_Observing_1992_(Mennonite_Church,_1991).

Mennonite Church USA. "Glen Guyton." Last modified August 30, 2023. https://www.mennoniteusa.org/who-are-mennonites/church-structure/executive-board-staff/glen-guyton/.

Mennonite Encyclopedia, The. Vol. 1. Scottdale, PA: Mennonite Publishing House, 1955.

Mennonite World Conference. "Anabaptist Movement Flourishing in South Korea." MWC, February 15, 2016. https://mwc-cmm.org/stories/anabaptist-movement-flourishing-south-korea.

———. "Living Out the Gospel as Received." MWC, August 3, 2022. https://mwc-cmm.org/stories/living-out-gospel-received.

———. "Membership, Map and Statistics." MWC, July 29, 2019. https://mwc-cmm.org/membership-map-and-statistics.

Miller, Elizabeth. "Following Jesus into Prison." *The Mennonite*, October 2014, 12–15.

Miller, Elizabeth, Siaka Traore, and Rod Hollinger-Janzen. "Mennonites in Sidi, Burkina Faso." *Bearing Witness Stories Project* (blog), June 15, 2015. https://martyrstories.org/sidi-burkina-faso/.

Moore, Charles E., ed. *Bearing Witness: Stories of Martyrdom and Costly Discipleship.* Walden, NY: Plough, 2016.

Moss, Christina. "'Overcoming Barriers and Building Empowerment: Stories of Anabaptist Women in India' by Cynthia Peacock." *Anabaptist Historians* (blog), June 24, 2017. https://anabaptisthistorians.org/2017/06/24/overcoming-barriers-and-building-empowerment

-stories-of-anabaptist-women-in-india-by-cynthia-peacock/.

———. "'Your Sons and Daughters Shall Prophesy': Visions, Apocalypticism, and Gender in Strasbourg, 1522–1539." PhD diss., University of Waterloo, 2019. http://hdl.handle.net/10012/14513.

Mulebo Ndandula, Vincent, Jean Felix Chimbalanga, Jackson Beleji, Jim Bertsche, and Charity Eidse Schellenberg. *The Jesus Tribe: Grace Stories from Congo's Mennonites 1912–2012: A Project of Africa Inter-Mennonite Mission.* Edited by Rod Hollinger-Janzen, Nancy J. Myers, and Jim Bertsche. Elkhart, IN: Institute of Mennonite Studies, 2012.

Myers, Nancy J., and Charlie Malembe. "Congo Mennonites Celebrate Women's Ordinations." Mennonite World Conference, July 3, 2014. https://mwc-cmm.org/vi/node/243.

Neff, Christian, and Harold S. Bender. "Manz, Felix (ca. 1498–1527)." In *GAMEO*. Herald Press, 1957; online ed. accessed November 1, 2023. https://gameo.org/index.php?title=Manz,_Felix_(ca._1498-1527).

Neufeld, Dietrich. *A Russian Dance of Death: Revolution and Civil War in the Ukraine.* Edited by Al Reimer. Winnipeg: Hyperion Press, for the Mennonite Literary Society and the University of Winnipeg, 1977.

Neufeldt, Reina C. "Settler Colonial Conscripts: Mennonite Reserves and the Enfolding of Implicated Subjects." *Postcolonial Studies* 25, no. 4 (2022): 508–26.

Nolt, Steven M. "Activist Impulses across Time: North American Evangelicalism and Anabaptism as Conversation Partners." In Burkholder and Cramer, *Activist Impulse*, 11–44.

———. "Contemporary Anabaptists in North America." In Brewer, *Handbook of Anabaptism*, 561–78.

———. "Globalizing a Separate People: World Christianity and North American Mennonites, 1940–1990." *Mennonite Quarterly Review* 84, no. 4 (2010): 487–506.

———. *A History of the Amish.* 3rd edition. New York: Good Books, 2015.

———. "Who Are the Real Amish? Rethinking Diversity and Identity among a Separate People." *Mennonite Quarterly Review* 82, no. 3 (July 2008): 377–94.

Nyce, Dorothy Yoder. "The Anabaptist Vision: Was It Visionary Enough for Women?" *Conrad Grebel Review* 12, no. 3 (1994): 309–19.

Ortíz, José M. *Reflections of an Hispanic Mennonite.* Intercourse, PA: Good Books, 1989.

Oyer, John S. *They Harry the Good People Out of the Land: Essays on the Persecution, Survival and Flourishing of Anabaptists and Mennonites.* Edited by John D. Roth. Goshen, IN: Mennonite Historical Society, 2000.

———. "Anabaptist Women Leaders of Augsburg August 1527 to April 1528." In Hecht and Snyder, *Profiles of Anabaptist Women*, 82–105.

Packull, Werner O. "The Origins of Swiss Anabaptism in the Context of the Reformation of the Common Man." *Journal of Mennonite Studies* 3, no. 1 (January 1, 1985): 36–59.

Pan, Chiou-Lang. "The Mennonite Churches in Chinese-Speaking Areas." In Lapp and Synder, *Churches Engage Asian Traditions*, 221–57.

Pew Research Center. *Global Christianity: A Report on the Size and Distribution of the World's Christian Population*. Washington, DC: Pew Research Center, 2011.

Philips, Obbe. "A Confession." In *Spiritualist and Anabaptist Writers*, edited by George H. Williams and Angel M. Mergal. Library of Christian Classics. Philadelphia: Westminster Press, 1957.

Prieto, Jaime. *Mission and Migration: A Global Mennonite History*. Translated and edited by C. Arnold Synder. Global Mennonite History Series: Latin America. Intercourse, PA: Good Books, 2010.

Redekop, John. "The Roots of Nazi Support among Mennonites, 1930 to 1939: A Case Study Based on a Major Mennonite Paper." *Journal of Mennonite Studies* 14 (January 1, 1996): 81–95.

Regehr, T. D. *Mennonites in Canada, 1939–1970: A People Transformed*. Toronto: University of Toronto Press, 1996.

Reimer, Al. "*Sanitätsdienst* and *Selbstschutz*: Russian-Mennonite Nonresistance in World War I and Its Aftermath." *Journal of Mennonite Studies* 11 (1993): 135–48.

Reimer, Johannes. "The Spirit Says Go! Mission and Early Charismatic Expressions among Russian Mennonite Brethren." *Anabaptist Witness* 4, no. 1 (April 2017): 31–44.

Rempel, Janae. "What's in a Name?" *Christian Leader*, July 1, 2020. https://christianleadermag.com/whats-in-a-name-2/.

Rempel, John. "Mennonites." In *The Oxford History of Christian Worship*, edited by Geoffrey Wainwright and Karen B. Westerfield Tucker, 545–59. New York: Oxford University Press, 2006.

Rempel Petkau, Evelyn. "How Complicit Are Mennonites in Residential School Abuse?" *Canadian Mennonite*, August 26, 2010. https://canadianmennonite.org/articles/how-complicit-are-mennonites-residential-school-abuse.

Robert, Dana L. "Forty Years of the American Society of Missiology: Retrospect and Prospect." *Missiology* 42, no. 1 (January 1, 2014): 6–25.

Roberts, Laura Schmidt, Paul Martens, and Myron A. Penner, eds. *Recovering from the Anabaptist Vision: New Essays in Anabaptist Identity and*

Theological Method. New York: T&T Clark, 2020.

Roth, John D. "Anabaptism and Evangelicalism Revisited: Healing a Contentious Relationship?" In Burkholder and Cramer, *Activist Impulse*, 45–73.

———. *A Cloud of Witnesses: Celebrating Indonesian Mennonites.* Harrisonburg, VA: Herald Press, 2021.

———. "Marpeck and the Later Swiss Brethren." In Roth and Stayer, *Companion to Anabaptism and Spiritualism*, 347–88.

———. "Pietism and the Anabaptist Soul." In *The Dilemma of Anabaptist Piety: Strengthening or Straining the Bonds of Community?*, edited by Stephen L. Longenecker, 17–34. Bridgewater, VA: Forum for Religious Studies, 1997.

———. "Recent Currents in the Historiography of the Radical Reformation." *Church History* 71, no. 3 (September 1, 2002): 523–35.

———. *Stories: How Mennonites Came to Be.* Scottdale, PA: Herald Press, 2006.

Roth, John D., and James M. Stayer, eds. *A Companion to Anabaptism and Spiritualism, 1521–1700.* Brill's Companions to the Christian Tradition 6. Boston: Brill, 2007.

Roth, John D., and Joe Springer, eds. *Letters of the Amish Division: A Sourcebook.* 2nd ed. Goshen, IN: Mennonite Historical Society, 2002.

Rothkegel, Martin, "Anabaptism in Moravia and Silesia." In Roth and Stayer, *Companion to Anabaptism and Spiritualism*, 163–216.

Sanneh, Lamin O. *Disciples of All Nations: Pillars of World Christianity.* Oxford Studies in World Christianity. New York: Oxford University Press, 2008.

Sanneh, Lamin O., and Joel A. Carpenter. *The Changing Face of Christianity: Africa, the West, and the World.* New York: Oxford University Press, 2005.

Schad, M[aster] Elias. "True Account of Anabaptist Meeting in a Forest and a Debate Held with Them." *Mennonite Quarterly Review* 58, no. 3 (July 1984): 292–95.

Schlabach, Theron F. *Peace, Faith, Nation: Mennonites and Amish in Nineteenth-Century America.* Scottdale, PA: Herald Press, 1988.

———. "Reveille for *Die Stillen im Lande*: A Stir among Mennonites in the Late Nineteenth Century: Awakening or Quickening, Revival or Acculturation?" *Mennonite Quarterly Review* 51, no. 3 (July 1, 1977): 213–26.

Schrag, Paul. "Together in Faith." *Anabaptist World*, August 18, 2009. https://anabaptistworld.org/together-faith/.

Scribner, R. W., and C. Scott Dixon. *The German Reformation*. 2nd ed. Studies in European History. London: Red Globe Press, 2003.

Setiawan, Stephanie. "Assembly Small but Full of Joy." Mennonite World Conference, July 27, 2022. https://mwc-cmm.org/stories/assembly-small-full-joy.

———. "A Good Kind of Infidel." Mennonite World Conference, November 21, 2022. https://mwc-cmm.org/stories/good-kind-infidel.

———. "Together Proclaim the 'Manifold Wisdom of God.'" Mennonite World Conference, September 16, 2022. https://mwc-cmm.org/stories/together-proclaim-manifold-wisdom-god.

Shank, J. W., Elven V. Snyder, and Raul O. García. "Iglesia Evangélica Menonita, Argentina." In *GAMEO*. Herald Press, 1987, online ed. accessed November 15, 2023. https://gameo.org/index.php?title=Iglesia_Evangélica_Menonita,_Argentina.

Sharp, John E. "Mennonites and Native Americans: A Reconciliation?" *Mennonite Life* 61, no. 2 (June 2006). https://mla.bethelks.edu/ml-archive/2006June/sharp.php.

Shearer, Tobin Miller. "Conflicting Identities: White Racial Formation among Mennonites, 1960–1985." *Identities* 19, no. 3 (May 2012): 268–84.

Shenk, Wilbert R. "Mission and Service and the Globalization of North American Mennonites." *Mennonite Quarterly Review* 70, no. 1 (January 1996): 7–22.

Sibanda, Eliakim. "Voices from the Hills vs. Words from the Missionary: Competing Rural Cultures in Southwestern Zimbabwe." *Journal of Mennonite Studies* 35 (2017): 197–222.

Sider, E. Morris. "Davidson, Hannah Frances (1860–1935)." In *GAMEO*. Herald Press, 1988, online ed. accessed November 6, 2022. https://gameo.org/index.php?title=Davidson,_Hannah_Frances_(1860-1935).

Snyder, C. Arnold. *Anabaptist History and Theology*. Kitchener, Ont.: Pandora Press, 1997.

———. "The Birth and Evolution of Swiss Anabaptism (1520–1530)." *Mennonite Quarterly Review* 80, no. 4 (October 1, 2006): 501–645.

———. *The Life and Thought of Michael Sattler*. Studies in Anabaptist and Mennonite History 27. Scottdale, PA: Herald Press, 1984.

———, ed. *Sources of South German/Austrian Anabaptism*. Translated by Walter Klaassen, Werner O. Packull, and Frank Friesen. Classics of the Radical Reformation 10. Kitchener, ON: Pandora Press, 2001.

———. "Swiss Anabaptism: The Beginnings, 1523–1525." In Roth and Stayer, *Companion to Anabaptism and Spiritualism*, 45–81.

Snyder, C. Arnold, and Linda A. Huebert Hecht, eds. *Profiles of Anabaptist Women: Sixteenth-Century Reforming Pioneers*. Studies in Women and Religion 3. Waterloo, ON: Canadian Corporation for Studies in Religion, 1996.

Snyder-Penner, Russel. "Hans Nadler's Oral Exposition of the Lord's Prayer." *Mennonite Quarterly Review* 65, no. 4 (October 1991): 393–406.

Soekotjo, S. H., and Lawrence M. Yoder. *The Way of the Gospel in the World of Java: A History of the Muria Javanese Mennonite Church GITJ*. Edited by John D. Roth. First English edition. Goshen, IN: Institute for the Study of Global Anabaptism, 2020.

Sprunger, Keith. "Bethel College (North Newton, Kansas, USA)." GAMEO. 2013; online ed. accessed December 21, 2023. https://gameo.org/index.php?title=Bethel_College_(North_Newton%2C_Kansas%2C_USA).

Sprunger, Mary S. "The Limits of Faith in a Maritime Empire: Mennonites, Trade and Politics in the Dutch Golden Age." In *The Limits of Empire: European Imperial Formations in Early Modern World History : Essays in Honor of Geoffrey Parker*, edited by Tonio Andrade and William Reger, 59–77. Burlington: Ashgate, 2012.

Stayer, James M. *Anabaptists and the Sword*. Lawrence, KS: Coronado Press, 1972.

———. "Community of Goods and Economics." In Brewer, *Handbook of Anabaptism*, 321–38.

———. *The German Peasants' War and the Anabaptist Community of Goods*. McGill-Queen's Studies in the History of Religion 6. Montreal: McGill-Queen's University Press, 1991.

———. "The Passing of the Radical Moment in the Radical Reformation." *Mennonite Quarterly Review* 71, no. 1 (January 1, 1997): 147–52.

———. "Swiss-South German Anabaptism, 1526–1540." In Roth and Stayer, *Companion to Anabaptism and Spiritualism*, 83–117.

Stayer, James M., Werner O. Packull, and Klaus Deppermann. "From Monogenesis to Polygenesis: The Historical Discussion of Anabaptist Origins." *Mennonite Quarterly Review* 49, no. 2 (April 1975): 83–121.

Stoner-Eby, Anne Marie. "Building a Church Locally and Globally: The Ministry of Zedekiah Marwa Kisare, First African Bishop of the Tanzanian Mennonite Church." *Journal of African Christian Biography* 7, no. 2/3 (July 2022): 23–32.

Strauss, Gerald. "Ideas of Reformation and Renovation from the Middle Ages to the Reformation." In *Handbook of European History: 1400–1600*, edited by Thomas A. Brady Jr., Heiko A. Oberman, and James D. Tracy, 2:1–28. Grand Rapids, MI: Eerdmans, 1996.

Stuckey-Kauffman, Priscilla. "A Woman's Ministry: Clara Brubaker Shank, 1869–1958." *Mennonite Quarterly Review* 60, no. 3 (July 1986): 404–28.

Sutanto, Adi. "A Strategy for Planting Churches in Java through the Sangkakala Mission with Special Emphasis on the Javanese and Chinese People." DMiss, Fuller Theological Seminary, School of World Mission, 1986.

Tabor College. "Tabor Signs Partnership with Evana Network." February 10, 2017. https://tabor.edu/tabor-signs-partnership-evana-network/.

Ten Thousand Villages. "'I'm Just a Woman Trying to Help Other Women.' —Edna Ruth Byler." Accessed April 22, 2023. https://www.tenthousandvillages.com/history.

Tewoldebirhan, Kahsay. "Eritrean Pastor from Banned Religion Denied Burial," April 19, 2023. https://www.bbc.com/news/live/world-africa-64393826/page/5.

Toews, Paul. *Mennonites in American Society, 1930–1970: Modernity and the Persistence of Religious Community*. Vol. 4. Scottdale, PA: Herald Press, 1996.

Tshidimu, François. "Mennonites in Congo: Looking toward the Second Century." Foreword to Mulebo Ndandula, Chimbalanga, Beleji, Bertsche, and Schellenberg, *The Jesus Tribe*, xi–xvi.

Tshimika, Pakisa, and Doris Dube. "Introduction to Mennonite and Brethren in Christ Churches in Africa." In Lapp and Synder, *Anabaptist Songs in African Hearts*, 1–13.

Unrau, Ruth. "Shoulderblade, Julia Yellow Horse (1913–1973)." In *GAMEO*. Herald Press, 1989; online ed. accessed September 2, 2023. https://gameo.org/index.php?title=Shoulderblade,_Julia_Yellow_Horse_(1913-1973).

Unruh, W. F. "The Great Commission as the Watchword of Evangelism." *The Mennonite* 68, no. 22 (June 2, 1953): 340.

Urry, James. *Mennonites, Politics, and Peoplehood: 1525 to 1980*. Winnipeg: University of Manitoba Press, 2006.

van Braght, Thieleman J. *The Bloody Theatre, or Martyrs Mirror of the Defenceless Christians Who Baptized Only upon Confession of Faith, and Who Suffered and Died for the Testimony of Jesus, Their Savior, from the Time of Christ to the Year A.D. 1600*. 10th ed. Scottdale, PA: Herald Press, 1975.

Verbeek, Annelies, and Alle Hoekema. "Mennonites in the Netherlands." In Jecker and Hoekema, *Testing Faith and Tradition*, 57–96.

Visser, Piet. "Mennonites and Doopsgezinden in the Netherlands, 1535–1700." In Roth and Stayer, *Companion to Anabaptism and Spiritualism*, 299–345.

von Schlachta, Astrid. "Anabaptists and Pietists: Influences, Contacts, and Relations." In *A Companion to German Pietism, 1660–1800*, edited by Douglas Shantz, 116–38. Boston: Brill, 2014.

———. "Hands under the Cross: MCC and the Post-War Construction of German Mennonite Peace Identity." *Intersections: MCC Theory & Practice Quarterly* 9, no. 4 (Fall 2021): 63–68.

Voolstra, Sjouke. "The Hymn to Freedom." In *From Martyr to Muppy (Mennonite Urban Professionals): A Historical Introduction to Cultural Assimilation Processes of a Religious Minority in the Netherlands, the Mennonites*, edited by Alastair Hamilton, Sjouke Voolstra, and Piet Visser, 187–202. Amsterdam: Amsterdam University Press, 1994.

———. "Mennonite Faith in the Netherlands: A Mirror of Assimilation." *Conrad Grebel Review* 9, no. 3 (Fall 1991): 277–92.

Waite, Gary K. *David Joris and Dutch Anabaptism, 1524–1543*. Waterloo, ON: Wilfrid Laurier University Press, 1990.

———. "David Joris (ca. 1501–1556)." In *GAMEO*. Article published February 2020. https://gameo.org/index.php?title=David_Joris_(ca._1501–1556)#1990_Article.

Walls, Andrew F. "Crowther, Samuel Ajayi (A)." Dictionary of African Christian Biography, accessed November 16, 2023. https://dacb.org/stories/nigeria/legacy-crowther/. Reproduced from *Mission Legacies: Biographical Studies of Leaders of the Modern Missionary Movement*, edited by G. H. Anderson, R. T. Coote, N. A. Horner, and J. M. Phillips. Maryknoll, NY: Orbis, 1994.

Weaver, Alain Epp. *Service and the Ministry of Reconciliation: A Missiological History of Mennonite Central Committee*. Cornelius H. Wedel Historical Series 21. North Newton, KS: Bethel College, 2020.

Weaver-Zercher, David L. *Martyrs Mirror: A Social History*. Baltimore: Johns Hopkins University Press, 2016.

Weidemann, Erika. "Identity and Complicity: The Post-Second World War Emigration of Chortitza Mennonites." In *European Mennonites and the Holocaust*, edited by John D. Thiesen and Mark Jantzen, 269–89. Transnational Mennonite Studies. Toronto: University of Toronto Press, 2020.

Wenger, John C., and Robert S. Kreider. "Dress." In *GAMEO*. Herald Press, 1989, online ed. accessed August 29, 2023. https://gameo.org/index.php?title=Dress.

Whiteman, Darrell L. "Contextualization: The Theory, the Gap, the Challenge." *International Bulletin of Missionary Research* 21, no. 1 (January 1, 1997): 2–7. https://doi.org/10.1177/239693939702100101.

Whitford, David M. *T&T Clark Companion to Reformation Theology*. New York: Bloomsbury, 2014.

Williams, Lisa. "MCEC Delegates Embrace New Identity and Priority Statements." Mennonite Church Eastern Canada, May 4, 2022. https://mcec.ca/article/18917-mcec-delegates-embrace-new-identity-and-priority-statements.

Yamada, Masakazu. "The Anabaptist Mennonite Churches in Japan." In Lapp and Synder, *Churches Engage Asian Traditions*, 277–310.

Yoder, John Howard. "Anabaptist Vision and Mennonite Reality." In *Consultation on Anabaptist-Mennonite Theology*, edited by A. J. Klassen. Fresno: Council of Mennonite Seminaries, 1970.

———, trans. and ed. *The Legacy of Michael Sattler*. Classics of the Radical Reformation 1. Scottdale, PA: Herald Press, 1973.

———, trans. and ed. *The Schleitheim Confession*. Scottdale, PA: Herald Press, 1977.

Yoder, Lawrence M. *The Muria Story: A History of the Chinese Mennonite Churches in Indonesia*. Kitchener, ON: Pandora Press, 2006.

Index

Present-day locations for many place-names are included in parentheses.

Abbotsford, British Columbia, 330
Abebe, Desalegn, 261
Aceh (Indonesia), 273
Acre, A., 291
Adams County, Indiana, 161–62
Address to the Christian Nobility of the Germans, An (Luther), 39
Adi, Sri Padmawati, 271–72
Affair of the Sausages, 45–46
Africa Inter-Mennonite Mission (AIMM; formerly Congo Inland Mission), 252
African American Mennonites, 318–20
African Initiated Churches, 260
Agape Mennonite Church (Hong Kong), 230
Agricultural Union (Ukraine), 153–54
Ahlefeldt, Bartholomäus von, 111
Akron, Pennsylvania, 312
Alabama, 191
Alberli, Heinrich (Heini), 42
Albrecht of Brandenburg, 36
Alexander II (tsar of Russia), 155
Alexandertal (Alt-Samara), 118
Allebach, Ann, 322
Alliance of Mennonite Evangelical Congregations, 334
Alsace, 71, 125–26, 142, 199
alternative service, 200, 212, 338
Alternative Service Work (ASW) program, 224–25
Altona. *See* Hamburg
Alt-Samara, 118

AmaNdebele people, 248–49, 251
American Mennonite Brethren Mission, 252
American Revolution, 113, 128, 164
Amish, 144–49, 156, 325–26, 328. *See also* Amish Mennonites; Beachy Amish; Egly Amish; Old Order Amish; Stuckey Amish
Amish Mennonites, 162–63, 206, 343
Amman, Jacob, 144–49
Amsterdam
   Bernese Anabaptists, 107
   Bij 't Lam, 137
   Melchiorites, 82, 87, 91
   Mennonite World Conference, 339
   Pietism, 139
   during World War II, 219
Amstutz, Daniel, 267
Am Trakt colony, 118
Anabaptist Network (UK), 320–21, 340
Anabaptist Vision (concept), 337, 339–340
"Anabaptist Vision, The" (Bender), 9, 62, 214–15, 307, 336–39
ancestor veneration, 188–89, 244, 284
Antwerp, 96
apocalypticism
   in the Low Countries, 84–86
   medieval, 33–34
   in South Germany, 62, 66–67, 71, 75

Argentina, 153, 286–92, 296–97
Argentine League of Protestant Women, 290
Arnold, P. B., 279
Arnold, Sarada, 278
Ascherham, Gabriel, 76
Asheervadham, I. P., 278–79
Association of Evangelical Mennonites, 334
Augsburg, 64, 67–68
Ausbund, 76, 103, 136, 157
Auspitz (Czech Republic), 76, 78
Austerlitz (Czech Republic), 76
Austerlitz Brethren, 71, 76–78
Australia, 273
Austria, 62, 66, 321
Avignon (France), 29
Aylmer, Ontario, 277

Babylonian Captivity of the Church, The (Luther), 39
Back to the Bible (radio program), 331
Bader, Augustin, 71
Badibanga, Valentin, 253
Baerg, Anna, 197, 202
Baker, Newton D., 207
Bali (Indonesia), 236
Balodgahan (India), 185
Bandung (Indonesia), 271
baptism, 134, 136–37, 237
  implications of, 101
  in India, 280
  in Indonesia, 182, 267
  in the Low Countries, 62–63, 82
  and Marpeck, Pilgram, 71
  medieval, 22
  and Mennonite Brethren split, 157–58
  in Nikolsburg, 74
  in Zürich, 52, 59
  See also Tau, the
Basel (Switzerland), 64, 96
Batam (Indonesia), 236
Batavian Revolution, 120
Batenburgers, 93
Batenburg, Jan van, 93

Batonga people, 249
Bavaria, 129
Beachy Amish, 191, 314, 343
Bearinger, Noah, 223–24
Bebbington, David, 328
Behem, Hans, 17–19, 27
Beiler, Anna, 328
Beiler, David, 159
Beiler, Joseph, 341
Bekele, Felekech, 259
Bekjen, Pieter Pietersz, 135
Belgium, 165, 321
Belize, 153, 297
Bender, Harold S., 9, 44, 62, 214–15, 307, 336–39
Benedict of Nursia, Saint, 20–21
Bergthaler Mennonites, 296
Berlin, Ohio, 314
Bern (Switzerland), 107
Bethel (KS) College, 169
Bethlehem (Palestine), 312
Beutelsbach (Germany), 58
Beyene, Tewodros, 238
Bharatiya General Conference Mennonite Kalisiya, 185–87, 275
Bharatiya Jukta Christa Prachar Mandali (Indian United Christ Evangelical Church), 276–77
Bharatiya Mennonite Church in India ki Pratinidhi Sabha. *See* Mennonite Church in India (MIC)
BIC. *See* Brethren in Christ
BIC Mpingo Wa Abale Mwa Kristu, 251
Bidloo, Govert, 120
Bihar Mennonite Mandli, 276, 279
Birai, Naftali, 250
Birch Tree, Missouri, 173–74
bishops (Catholic), 19–20
Blaurock, George, 51, 59, 73, 103, 134
Bluffton (OH) College, 214
Bluffton, Ohio, 162, 166, 209
Bocholt (Germany), 94
Bögli, Maria, 107
Bohemia, 29, 33, 71

Boissevain-van Lennep, Minette
"Mies," 219
Bolivia, 119, 153, 235, 301
Bondo (Indonesia), 181
Bontreger, John E., 159
Boquerón (Paraguay), 300
Botschafter, 200
Botswana, 251
Bouwens, Lenaert, 98–99
Boyd, Greg, 340
Braght, Thieleman J. van, 132–33. See also *Martyrs Mirror*
Brazil, 209, 235, 293
Brenkenhofswalde congregation (Prussia), 129
Brenneman, John M., 165
Brethren Church, 325
Brethren Churches (Nihon Menonaito Burezaren Kyodan), 283
Brethren in Christ (BIC)
  and evangelicalism, 325, 330, 334–35
  and Mennonite World Conference, 215, 326
  missions, 172, 191, 251, 276
  Old Order split, 161
  in southern Africa, 248–51
  urban, 344
  during World War I, 206
  during World War II, 225
Brethren in Christ Church (Nihon Kirisuto Keiteidan), 283
Brethren in Christ Church of Zambia (Mbungano Yabunyina Muli Kristo), 243, 250
Brethren in Christ Church of Zimbabwe (Ibandla Labazalwane KuKristu eZimbabwe), 243–44
Brethren in Christ Church Society, or Bharatiya Khristiya Mandali (Brethren of Christ Churches in North Bihar), 276
British Columbia, 210
British Honduras (Belize), 153, 297
Brothers and Sisters of the Common Life, 32

Brötli, Johannes (Hans), 47, 51, 54
Brubaker, Clara, 173–74
Bruderhöfe, 79–80
Brunk, George R., 213
Brunk, George R., II, 329–32
Brunk, Lawrence, 330
Bruppacher, Barbara, 124
Bucer, Martin, 64, 71
Buckwalter, Albert, 290–91
Buckwalter, Lois (Litwiller), 290–91
Budget, The, 208
Bulawayo (Zimbabwe), 249, 294
Bünderlin, Hans, 71
Burkholder, Christian, 139
Burkino Faso, 237–38
Burning Bush Forest Church, 229
Burnside Community Church, 320
Bush, Perry, 305, 323
Byler, Edna Ruth Miller, 312

Calcutta Bible Institute, 277
California, 324
Calvadore, Anita, 287–88
Calvary Mennonite Church, 319
Cambodia, 312
Canada, 262, 306
  and evangelicalism, 331
  and Indigenous relations, 170
  and migrants to Mexico, 295–96, 298
  nationalism, 164
  and National Socialism, 216
  and Pietists, 139
  politics, 239
  post-World War II, 310–11
  privilegia, 112
  Russian Mennonites in, 119, 155–56, 209–10
  urban, 343
  during World War I, 204–8
  during World War II, 223–26
cardinals (Catholic), 19, 38
Castelberger, Andreas, 42–44, 49
Castillo, Alba Elena, 294
Castillo, David, 173, 316
Cattepoel, Dirk, 218
Caucasus region, 119, 222

Cavadore, Anita, 287–88, 294
Cavadore, Felisa, 290
Celebes (Indonesia), 236
celestial flesh doctrine, 84, 88, 100
Central Illinois Mennonite Conference, 252
Centre Béthésda Mennonite de Québec, 229
Chaco, the (Argentina), 171
Champa (India), 185
Champa-Korba (India), 275
Chandwa (India), 276
charismatic movement, 291
Charles V (Holy Roman Emperor), 39, 100
Chelčický, Petr, 33
Chibwana, Sani Selemani, 251
Chicago Home Mission, 173, 315
Chihuahua (Mexico), 210–11, 295–96
China, 187–89, 194, 230, 235
Chin Christian Church (Ontario), 230
Chinese Mennonite Christian Church, 183. *See also* Gereja Kristen Muria Indonesia (GKMI)
Choi, Jeremiah, 230
Chortitza colony, 117–18, 155, 210–11
Christano, Charles, 274
Christendom, 101
  corpus Christianum, 27
  pre-Reformation, 19–24
Christian Aid Ministries (CAM), 314
Christian and Missionary Alliance, 173
Christian Church Gospel Association (Ji Du Jiao Fu Yin Hui), 187
Christianity Today, 329–30
Christianization, 19
Christiano, Charles, 270
Christlicher Bundesbote, 205
Christlicher Gemeinde-Kalendar, 200
church discipline, 54, 74
Church of the Brethren, 140, 161, 212

Civilian Public Service (CPS), 224–25, 310–11, 327
Civil War, American, 159, 165
Clement V (pope), 29
clergy, medieval, 17–18
Clinton Frame Mennonite Church, 163
Coleman, Monica, 344
Colombia, 171, 292–94, 303
Columbus, Christopher, 171
Communauté des Églises de Frères Mennonites au Congo (Mennonite Brethren Church of Congo), 129, 231, 240, 254, 322–23
Communauté Évangélique Mennonite (Evangelical Mennonite Church of Congo), 231, 254
Communauté Mennonite au Congo (Mennonite Church of Congo), 231, 240, 254
communion
  in late medieval piety, 22–23
  and Nikolsburg, 74
  and Nürnberg, 63
  and Sattler, Michael, 56
  in the sixteenth century, 134, 136
  and transubstantiation, 23–24, 96
  and Zürich, 51–52
community of goods
  among Austerlitz Brethren, 76
  among Batenburgers, 93
  in Münster, 91
  and mutual aid, 81
  in Nikolsburg, 75
  in the Schleitheim Confession, 57
conciliarism, 29–30
Concordance (Concondanzt vnd zyger), 138
Conference of the Mennonite Brethren Churches in India, 276
confession, 24
Congo, 130, 162, 176, 231, 240, 252–56, 260
Congo Inland Mission (Africa Inter-Mennonite Mission, AIMM), 252

Conservative Amish Mennonite Church. *See* Rosedale Network of Churches
Conservative Mennonite Church. *See* Rosedale Network of Churches
Constantine (emperor), 9, 19
Consulta Anabautista Menonita Centroamericana, 294
Convención Evangélica Hermanos Menonitas Enlhet, 297
Cornies, Johann, 153–54
Costa Rica, 294
Council of Constance, 29–30, 33
Crimea, 119, 222
Crimean War, 155
Cross Cultural Youth Convention, 320
Crowther, Samuel Ajayi, 246
Cuba, 188
Curitaba, Brazil, 293, 296–300
Czech Republic. *See* Bohemia

Dalit, 149, 183–84, 277–78
Danzig (Poland), 115, 199, 215, 218
Davidjorists, 94, 98
Davidson, Hannah Frances, 248–49
Debose, Aster, 259
Defenseless Mennonite Conference, 252
defenselessness. *See* nonresistance
Deken, Agatha, 120
Deknatel, Johannes, 131, 139, 149
dekulakization, 211
Delchumie, Kedir, 259
De León, Lupe, 320
del Valle (Colombia), 292
Democratic Republic of the Congo, 228. *See also* Congo
Denck, Hans, 63–66, 70–71
Der Bote, 216
Derg (dictatorship), 258–59
devotio moderna, 32
Dhaje, Nikanor, 257
Dhamtari (India), 185–186, 275
Dhamtari Christian Academy, 277

Diener-Versammlung (ministers' meeting), 159–61
Diet of Speyer, 89, 100
Diet of Worms, 39–40
Dirks, Heinrich, 179
discipleship
 and "Anabaptist Vision, The," 62, 215, 337–38
 in Asia, 284
 and evangelicalism, 333–34
 in Indonesia, 182
 and martyrdom, 105
 and Pietism, 132–33, 139
 and service, 234, 237–39
discipline, 341
 Flemish/Frisian split over, 100
 in Hamburg, 114
 and shunning, 99–100, 144–46
 in Wismar Articles, 99
Disi, Ephraim, 251
Diyoyo, Ngaga, 253
Djojodihardjo, Sardjoe, 220–21
Djojodihardjo, Soehadiweko, 240–41, 269–70
Djoko Punda (Congo), 252, 254
Doctrine of Discovery, 170, 172
Donner, Heinrich, 116
Doopsgezinden, 100, 111, 120–21, 325
 Flemish/Frisian split, 100
 in the nineteenth century, 151–52
 seminary, 135
 and transnationalism, 215
 Waterlanders, 99, 138
 during World War II, 219–20, 306, 309
 See also Flemish Mennonites; Frisian Mennonites
Dordrecht Confession, 144–46, 162
Doucher, Susanna, 69
Douglas, Janet, 322
Driedger, Michael, 148–49
Duarte Frutos, Nicanor, 300
Dube, Doris, 244, 248–49
Duerksen, Katherine, 307
Dung, Le Thi Phu, 239
Durango (Mexico), 210–11

Dutch East Indies. *See* Indonesia
Dutch Republic, 80, 100, 107–10, 129, 139, 141–42, 148
Dyck, Annie, 332
Dyck, Cornelius J., 336
Dyck, Isaak M., 343
Dyck, Johann Jakob, 203

East African Revival, 256–58
Eastern District Conference, 324–25
Eastern Mennonite Missions, 239
East Kasai (Congo), 254
Eby, Benjamin, 128
Eby, Gordon, 227
Eckhardt, Meister, 32
education
 criticisms of, 164, 342
 international, 311, 340
 in the nineteenth century, 168–69
 in North America, 162
 in the Russian Empire, 153
 seminary, 135, 344
Église de Dieu Réparateur des Brèches, 229
Église Mennonite Agape, 229
Egly Amish, 161–62
Egly, Henry, 161–62
Ehrenpreis, Andreas, 79–80
Einsatzgruppen, 218, 222
Elbing (Poland), 115
el Chocó (Colombia), 292
Elisabeth (1549 martyr), 103–4
Elkhart, Indiana, 168, 209, 336
El Salvador, 293
Emden (Germany), 86, 99
England, 251, 320–21
Engle, Elizabeth, 248
Engle, Jesse, 248
Enlhet people, 298–99
Enlightenment, the, 111–13, 141–42
Enoch (prophet of the end times), 10, 88
Entfelder, Christian, 71
Epp, David H., 199–200
Epp, Gerhard, 218
Epp, Marlene, 321

Epp, Theodore, H., 331
Erasmus of Rotterdam, 30–32, 86, 105
Erb, Paul, 333
Eritrea, 105–6, 229
Esquivia, Ricardo, 292–93
Esslingen (Germany), 67, 70
Ethiopia, 229–30, 244, 257
Evana (Evangelical and Anabaptist) Network, 325, 334–35
Evangelical Anabaptist Fellowship, 334
evangelicalism, 323, 327–35
Evangelical Mennonites, 296
Evangelical Mennonite Brethren, 187
Evangelical Mennonite Church of Burkina Faso (Eglise Evangélique du Burkina Faso), 237–38
Evangelical Mennonite Church (Vietnam), 239
Evangelical Mennonite Conference (EMC), 335. *See also* Kleine Gemeinde
Evangelical Mennonite Mission of the Caribbean, Inc. (Misíon Evangélica Menonita del Caribe, Inc.), 304
Evangelical Missionary Church. *See* Missionary Church
evangelism. *See* missions
Extending the Table: A World Community Cookbook (Schlabach), 313

Fairview, Michigan, 208
Fast, Anicka, 254
Fast, Ed, 239
Fast, Ivan, 222
Fast, Jacob, 222
Felix Meritis, 141–43
Fellowship of Evangelical Churches (Defenseless Mennonite Conference), 252
Ferdinand I (Holy Roman Emperor), 78
Fernheim Colony (Paraguay), 296–300

Flemish Mennonites, 100, 149
Flores, Gilberto, 317
Florida, 324
Focus on the Family, 329
Foundation for Missions and Charities (PIPKA), 236, 270
Foundation of Christian Learning, The (*Dat Fundament des christelyken leers*) (Menno), 96–98
France, 120, 230
Francisco, Leslie Walker, II, 319
Francisco, L. W., III, 319
Francisco, Naomi, 319
Franconia Conference, 324–25
Frankenhausen (Germany), 66
Frederick the Wise of Saxony, 34, 40
Freedom of a Christian, The (Luther), 39
French Revolution, 113, 128, 164–65
Freyburg, Helena von, 73
friars, 21–22
Friedrich II (king of Prussia), 115–16
Friedrichstadt (Germany), 129
Friedrich Wilhelm II (king of Prussia), 116
Friesen, Leonard G., 309
Friesland Colony (Paraguay), 296
Frisian Mennonites, 100, 149
Froschauer, Christoph, 45
Fujian Province, 189
fundamentals, 193–94, 213–14, 329
Funk, John F., 168–69

Gabrielites, 76, 78
Gale (Nyumbane, Zimbabwe), 249
Gandhi, Mahatma, 275
García, Raúl, 291–92
Gasmair, Michael, 73
Gasser, Anna, 74
Gelagle, Tigist Tesfaye, 230
Gelassenheit (submission), 32, 63, 67
and Hutterites, 79
General Conference Mennonite Church
in China, 187
in Colombia, 292
conference session, 192
historiography of, 214
in India, 184–86
merger with (Old) Mennonite Church, 323–24, 334
in the nineteenth century, 167
ordination of women, 322
during World War I, 206, 209, 212
during World War II, 225
General Mennonite Conference (Algemene Doopsgezinde Sociëteit), 152
Gereja Injili di Tanah Jawa (GITJ, or Evangelical Church of Java), 181, 265, 267–70
Gereja Kristen Muria Indonesia (GKMI, or Muria Christian Church of Indonesia), 183, 236, 265, 270
Germany, 137, 198–99, 205, 216–18, 306, 310
Ghana, 260
Ghost Dance, 189–91
Global Mennonite History Series, 15, 233, 244
Golden Apples in Silver Bowls (*Güldene Aepffel in Silbern Schalen*), 138
Good News Theological Seminary (Ghana), 260
Goshen (IN) College, 213–14, 316
Goshen, Indiana, 163
Goshen Mennonite Church (Ottawa, ON), 229
Gospel Herald, 205–6, 214, 320
Gottshall, W. S., 209
government and rulers
and Conservative Amish Mennonite Conference, 162
in India, 280
in Latin America, 303
and Marpeck, Pilgram, 70–71
in Nikolsburg, 75
in the nineteenth century, 164–66
in Paraguay, 299

and *privilegia*, 112
and Revolution, American, 127
and Schleitheim Confession, 55
during World War II, 306
Graber, C. L., 205
Grace Lao Mennonite Church, 230
Graham, Billy, 329–30
Grant, Jacquelyn, 344
Great Schism, 29
Great Terror, 211–12
Grebel, Conrad, 45–46, 51–52, 59, 77, 134
Gregory, Brad S., 101
Gregory the Great (pope), 23
Gregory XI (pope), 29
Greiner, Blasius, 104
Grijpskerk (Netherlands), 309
Gross, Jakob, 70
Grubb, Silas, 208
G30S, 268–69
Guaraní people, 171, 297
Guatemala, 303
Gulag theology, 309
Guyton, Glen, 319

Haarlem (Netherlands), 141
Haigh, Lawrence, 252
Haigh, Rose, 252
Haiti, 314
Hakka Mennonite Brethren Conference, 187
halbtäufer (half-Anabaptists), 144–49
Haldemann, Salomé, 230
Hamburg (Germany), 113–15, 129, 139
Händiges, Emil, 216
Harding, Vincent, 339
Harlingen (Netherlands), 99
Hart, Homer, 191
Hart, John Peak, 191
Hart, Lawrence, 171, 191, 192
Hartono, Paulus, 273
Hartzler, Jesse, 207
Hauerwas, Stanley, 339
Haury, Samuel Schmidt, 189
Haury, Susanna Hirschler, 189
Hayalume, Léonie Kelendende Kadi, 255

Hecht, Linda Huebert, 74
Hechuan (China), 187
Heisey, Alice, 248–49
Hellwart, Margaret, 58
Herald of Truth, 156, 169
Herald Press, 340
Herold der Wahrheit, 169
Herr, Jon, 166
Hershey, Mae, 286
Hershey, Tobias, 286
Herzogenbuchsee (Switzerland), 107
Hezbollah, 273
Hiebert, Martha, 253
Hillsboro, Kansas, 209
Himmler, Heinrich, 223
Hinojosa, Felipe, 316, 320, 332
historiography, 336–40
   awakening, or quickening, in nineteenth century, 167
   during early twentieth century, 214–15
   end of "golden age," 104–5
   Gemeindechristentum, 214
   late medieval church, 27
   multiple origins of, 62
   normative Anabaptism, 44
History of the Martyrs, or Genuine Witnesses of Jesus Christ (Ries), 122
Hitler, Adolf, 216, 219, 296–97
HIV/AIDS, 251
Hoa, Tran Minh, 239
Hochrütiner, Lorenz, 42, 47
Hofer, David, 207
Hofer, Joseph, 207
Hofer, Michael, 207
Hoffman, Melchior, 70, 84–87, 95–96, 100
Hội Thánh Mennonite Việt Nam (Vietnam Mennonite Church), 239
Hokkaido (Japan), 283–84
Holmes County, Ohio, 10, 341
Holy Spirit, 54, 97, 157
   in Argentina, 290–92
   Denck's perspective on, 64–66
   in Ethiopia, 260

in Indonesia, 271–72
guidance of, 48, 53–54, 345
in Latin America, 293, 304
and Latino Mennonites, 317
and Pentecostalism, 241
and Rebstock, Barbara, 95
in South Germany, 80–81
and Spiritualism, 71–73
and women in leadership, 53–54, 86
Homan, Gerlof, 220
Honduran Evangelical Mennonite Church, 303
Honduras, 239, 294
Höngg (Switzerland), 47
Hong Kong, 230, 237
Höningen (Germany), 131
Honshu (Japan), 283
Horseroads, Thomas, 192
Horst, Byrdaline, 291
Horst, Willis, 291
Hostetler, Ida, 276
Hostetler, S. J., 276
Hottinger, Claus, 42, 47
Hottinger, Jacob, 51
Hottinger, Margret, 53, 74
Houten, Samuel van, 152
Houttuyn, Martinus, 141, 149
Hubmaier, Balthasar, 53–55, 64, 74, 76
Hügeline, Elsbeth, 74, 76
Hulst, Pieter Teyler van der, 141
humanism, 64
    Italian, 30
    Northern, 30
Hurst, Simeon, 248
Hus, Jan, 29, 33
Hussites, 33
Hut, Hans, 66–67
    and apocalypticism, 100
    baptism by Denck, 64
    and Esslingen, 70
    gospel of all creatures, 67
    hymns, 103
    in Nikolsburg, 75
    on the sword, 68–69
    and the Peasants' War, 53

Hutterites, 57, 74, 78–80, 122, 129, 156, 174, 207
Hutter, Jacob, 76, 78
Hützny, Elisabeth, 125
Hylkema, Cornelis Bonnes, 219

Ibandla Labazalwane KuKristu eZimbabwe (Brethren in Christ Church in Zimbabwe), 243–44
iconoclasm, 47, 74
Iglesia Cristiana Menonita de Ciudad Berna, 293
Iglesia Evangélica Menonita Argentina, 291
Iglesia Evangélica Menonita de Colombia, 292
Iglesias Cristianas Hermanos Menonitas de Colombia, 292
India, 149, 183–87, 264, 274–82
Indiana, 159, 161, 170, 235
Indigenous peoples in North America, 170–72, 189–192, 354n
Indigenous relations, 170–72, 189–91, 196, 293, 297, 299
Indonesia, 81, 178–83, 326. *See also* Java; Sumatra
indulgences, 24, 36
Ininger, Wolf, 42
Inola, Oklahoma, 208
Institute for the Global Study of Anabaptism, 241
Intermenno (exchange program), 311
Iowa, 316
Isaka, Ruth, 176
Italy, 321

Jagdishpur (India), 185, 275
Jakarta, 271
Janjgir (India), 185, 275
Jans, Anna, 94–95
Jansz, Pieter, 178–79, 265
Jansz, Pieter Anthonie, 181
Jansz van der Lint, Arent, 94
Janzen, Aaron, 252–53
Janzen, Ernestina, 253
Japan, 220–21, 264–67, 282–84, 322

Japan Mennonite Christian Church Conference (Nihon Menonaito Kirisuto Kyokai Kaigi), 283
Japan Mennonite Christian Church Conference (Nihon Menonaito Kirisuto Kyokai Kyogikai), 283
Java, 178–83, 220, 230, 236
Jemaat Kristen Indonesia (JKI, or Indonesia Christian Congregation), 81, 230, 266, 271–73
Jenkins, Philip, 232
Jepara (Indonesia), 267, 271
Jesus Village Church, 40–41, 262
Jews, 26, 218–20, 227
Jharkhand (India), 276
Jonathan, Chrismanto, 270
Joris, David, 93–96, 98
Jost, Lienhard, 85–86, 95
Jost, Ursula, 85–86
June Protocol of 1865, 157–58
Justapaz (peace organization), 241, 292–93

Kafumba (Congo), 252, 254
Kai Chow (China), 187
Kanadier, 203, 210
Kanisa la Mennonite Tanzania, 257
Kansas, 156, 170, 209, 214
Karlstadt, Andreas von, 49, 63
Kasai region (Congo), 228
Kassa, Alphonse Kisubi, 130
Kauffman, Daniel, 193, 205–6, 214
Kauffman, Hans Jacob, 126
Kaufman, J. N., 274–75
Kautz, Jakob, 71
Kazadi, Mathieu, 254
Kekchi people, 303
Kelet congregation (Indonesia), 266
Keluarga Sangkakala movement, 271
Kemp, François Adriaan van der, 120, 122–23
Kempis, Thomas à, 32
Kenya, 256–57
Kessler, Johannes, 56
Kikandji (Congo), 252
Kikunga, Mbonza, 250

Kim, Grace, 323
Kinshasa, 255
Kirishima Christian Brotherhood, 282–83
Kisare, Zedekiah Marwa, 235, 247, 256
Kitamba, Daniel, 176–77
Kitchener, 128, 339, 344
Kituba language, 253
Klassen, Arli, 229
Klassen, Peter, 299
Kleine Gemeinde, 156, 164, 206, 297, 332
Klinkert, Hillebrandus, 178
Kobayashi, Miyazaki Prefecture (Japan), 282–83
Kohm, Mathilde, 162
Konferensi Pelayan Ladang Tuhan, 271
Koontz, Gayle Gerber, 313–14
Korba (India), 185
Korea Anabaptist Center, 262
Korean War, 311
Kratz, Clayton, 209
Kraybill, J. Nelson, 280–81
Krefeld (Germany), 139
Krehbiel, Charles, 165–66
Krehbiel, Henry J., 212
Kreler, Laux, 69
Krimmer Mennonite Brethren, 187, 206, 335
Krisetya, Mesach, 270, 274
Krüsi, Hans, 64
Kubala, Djimbo, 253
Kudus (Indonesia), 182–83, 267, 271
Kuiper, Frits, 219
Kunjam, Shantkumar, 278
Kushiro Mennonite Church, 283
Kyushu (Japan), 283

LaGrange County, Indiana, 341
Lancaster County, Pennsylvania, 159, 165, 331
Lancaster Mennonite Conference (LMC), 212–13, 256–58, 261, 324–25

Landis, Hans, 59, 125
Langendijk, Pieter, 107–9
Lao Mennonite Fellowship of Canada, 229–30
Laos, 312
Lark, James, 318
Lark, Rowena, 318
Latino Mennonites, 173, 315–19
Lauver, Mary Hottenstein, 312
Lawndale Mennonite Congregation, 316
Lederach, Ruth, 312
Lee, SangMin, 240
Legua 17 (Argentina), 290
Leiden, Jan van, 89, 91–92, 101
Leiden University, 120
León, Ignacia, 173, 315
León, Manuel, 173, 315
Leopold II (king of Belgium), 252
Leo X (pope), 36
LGBTQ+ inclusion, 232, 324, 326, 334
Lichti, Diane, 29
Liechtenstein
  family, 74
  Leonhart, 74
Linck, Agnes, 53
LMC. *See* Lancaster Mennonite Conference
Loewen, Royden, 328
Lombard (IL) Mennonite Church, 322
Longacre, Doris Janzen, 313–14
López, Aurelio, 290
Lord's Supper. *See* communion
Low German, 156, 171, 235, 294, 295
Low German Mennonites, 171, 295–96, 340, 343
Luayza, Albana, 287, 290
Luba people, 254
Lulua people, 252
Lutheran World Federation, 59, 243–44
Luther, Martin
  in "The Anabaptist Vision," 215, 336–37

  bowling, 38
  career, 34–40
  correspondence from Anabaptists, 49
  and humanists, 37–38
  and the Low Countries, 86
  and Menno, 96
  ninety-five theses, 36
  sola scriptura, 62, 105

Maatschappij tot Nut van 't Algemeen (Society for Public Welfare), 142
Macha (chief), 249
Macha Mission Station (Zambia), 249
Mack, Alexander, 140
Madhya Pradesh (India), 184–85, 275
Mahlabathini (Zimbabwe), 249
Makhno, Nestor, 201–2, 204
Makura, Rebeka, 257
Malagar, P. J., 274–75, 281
Malawi, 251
Malaysia, 264
Manchuria, 221
Manitoba, 156, 170, 191, 210, 295–96, 343
Mankes-Zernike, Anna, 321–22
Manual of Bible Doctrines (Kauffman, Daniel), 193–94
Manz, Felix
  and baptism, 50–51, 134
  disputation in Zürich, 50, 52
  hymns, 103
  martyrdom of, 56, 58–59, 100, 103
  nonresistance, 54
  protests, rural, 49
  and Reublin, 77
  and Zwingli, 45
Manzullo-Thomas, Devin, 334
Maphane (Zimbabwe), 249
Markham Christian Worship Centre, 230
Marpeck, Pilgram, 70–71, 73–74
Marsden, George M., 335

Martens, Olga Reimer, 312
Martínez, Juan, 317
Martin, Sheldon, 225
Martyrs Mirror, 112, 122, 126, 157–58, 169, 215, 301, 343
Massy, Aaron, 186
Matopo Mission, 249
Matthijs, Jan, 88–91
Mauhadih (India), 185
Maust, Erma, 258
Mbungano Yabunyina Muli Kristo (Brethren in Christ Church of Zambia), 243, 250
McClendon, James, 339
McClendon, Lesley Francisco, 319
MCC. *See* Mennonite Central Committee
MDS. *See* Mennonite Disaster Service
meetinghouses, 133–34, 161, 163
Meeting Place, The, 229
Meheret Evangelical Church, 229
Mekonnen, Daniel, 258
Melchiorites, 88–89, 93–95
Menadij (Indonesia), 220
Méndez, Leonor, 294
Menno Colony, Paraguay, 235–36, 296–97
Mennonite Brethren
 baptism by immersion, 137
 in China, 187
 in Colombia, 292
 in Congo, 252
 divisions, 324–25
 and evangelicalism, 335
 in India, 279
 migration to North America, 156
 missions, 172
 missions in Texas, 316, 332
 name, 325–26
 ordination of women, 231, 322–23
 origins, 157–58
 in Paraguay, 296–97
 USMB (US Conference of Mennonite Brethren Churches), 325, 335
 during World War I, 206
Mennonite Brethren Centenary Bible College (India), 276, 280
Mennonite Brethren in Christ. *See* Missionary Church
Mennonite Central Committee (MCC), 209, 234, 270, 296–300, 307–8, 311–12, 337
Mennonite Christian Service Fellowship of India, 281
Mennonite Church Canada (MC Canada), 322, 324
Mennonite Church Eastern Canada, 229–30, 236
Mennonite Church in India (MCI, or Bharatiya Mennonite Church in India ki Pratinidhi Sabha), 184–86, 275
Mennonite Church in Vietnam. *See* Evangelical Mennonite Church (Vietnam)
Mennonite Church (MC). *See* (Old) Mennonite Church
Mennonite Church Rajnandgaon (India), 280
Mennonite Church USA (MC USA), 322, 324, 325, 334
Mennonite Disaster Service (MDS), 234, 273
Mennonite Edict of 1789, 116
Mennonite Mission Network, 260
Mennonite Quarterly Review, 336
Mennonite, The, 208, 333
Mennonite Voluntary Service (MVS), 234
Mennonite World Conference (MWC), 14, 130
 assemblies, 229–31, 233, 243–44, 268, 293, 294, 339
 and Bharatiya Jukta Christa Prachar Mandali, or BJCPM (Indian United Christ Evangelical Church), 276
 in India, 274
 mutual aid, 130
 origins, 215–16
 and remembering rightly, 59
 transnationalism, 323

Mennonitische Blätter, 216
Menno Simons. See Simons, Menno.
Menominee (Potawatomi chief), 170–71
Meserete Kristos Church, 105–6, 231, 238, 258–61, 326
Métis people, 170
Mexico
 colony model, 119, 153
 and immigration in North America, 315–16
 and Low German Mennonites, 171, 210–11, 295–96, 298, 301, 343
 parochial schools, 340
Mifflin County, Pennsylvania, 159
Miller Brown, Henry J., 187
Miller Brown, Maria, 187
Miller, Marilyn Kauffman, 322
Miller, Orie, 209
Minnesota, 156
Minority Ministries Council (MMC), 320
Missionary Church, 322
Missionary Church Association, 187
Mission Mennonite Française (French Mennonite Mission), 321
missions
 in Africa, 244–46
 in China, 187–189
 Egly Amish, 162
 Hispanic Mennonite, 316
 in India, 183–87, 275–77
 among Indigenous North Americans, 189–91
 modern, 177–79
 in the nineteenth century, 167, 172–75
 post-World War II, 234–35
 shifting identity, 193–95
 in the sixteenth century, 53, 73
Missouri, 173–74
Molotschna, 117–18, 153, 164, 201, 209, 211, 222
monasticism, 20–22
Mongolia, 237, 270

Montana, 191
Montreal River Camp, 224
Moravia, 62, 71, 74–75
Moravian church, 265
More-with-Less Cookbook (Longacre), 313–14
Mosemann, John H., 212–13
Moseman, Ruth, 247
Mount Muria, 178
Moyo, Mlobeki, 249
Moyo, Ndabambi, 249
Mozambique, 251
Mtshabezi (Zimbabwe), 249
Muganda, Ezekiel, 248
Mugango (Tanzania), 256
Mühlhausen, 66
Muller, Samuel, 152
Münster, 83, 88–92, 101, 111, 120
Münsterites, 93, 96
Müntzer, Thomas, 49, 63, 65–66, 70
Muria Javanese Church. See Gereja Injili di Tanah Jawa (GITJ)
Murray, Stuart, 340
music, 136, 138, 191, 260, 278, 309, 329
Muslims, 26
Mussolini, Benito, 288, 290
Mutombo (Congolese evangelist), 253
mutual aid, 215
 Dutch aid to Swiss, 81
 post-World War II, 81
 during Russian Revolution, 81
MWC. See Mennonite World Conference
mwena Yesu (Jesus person), 253
mysticism, late medieval, 32–33

Nadler, Han, 61–62
Nagenda, William, 258
Naked Anabaptist, The (Murray), 340
names
 baptism-minded (*Taufgesinnten*), 51, 111
 Brethren (*Brüder*), 51

Doopsgezinden, 99–100, 111, 124
Mennonites, 100
in twentieth and twenty-first centuries, 325–26
Waterlanders, 99
Napoleon (emperor of the French), 113, 128, 164
Naporichi, Mariano, 291
Nationaal-Socialistische Beweging (Dutch Fascist party), 219
National Institutes of Health, 225
National Socialism, 216, 296–97, 306
Native Americans. *See* Indigenous peoples in North America
Ndjoko, Charlotte Djimbo, 231
Ndlovu, Danisa, 243–44
Ndlovu, Stephen, 250–51
Nebraska, 156, 209
Neff, Christian, 215
neo-Anabaptism, 339–40
Netherlands, 150–51, 164, 178, 219–20, 273. *See also* Dutch Republic
Newcomer, John, 127
New Jerusalem, 82, 84, 89, 93, 95
New Order Amish, 314, 340, 343
Newport News, Virginia, 319
Newton, Isaac, 141
New York, 316
Niagara Peninsula, 127
Nicaragua, 303
Nicodemism, 94, 104
Nieuwuenhuyzen, Jan, 142
Niger, 246
Nijmegen (Netherlands), 219
Niklashausen (Germany), 17–19
Nikolsburg (Moravia), 67, 74–75
Nivaclé people, 297, 299
Noko, Ishmael, 243–44
Nolt, Steven M., 311, 328, 332, 342
nonconformity, 213, 305
nonresistance
 during the American Civil War, 165–66
 in "Anabaptist Vision, The," 62, 214–15, 336–38
 in Congo, 260
 in the Dutch Republic, 120
 in Indonesia, 183, 267
 in Latin America, 304
 in *Martyrs Mirror*, 133
 Menno's perspective on, 98
 post-World War II, 238–39, 305
 recanters, 70
 in the Schleitheim Confession, 55–56, 58
 in South Korea, 262
 during World War I, 198
  in North America, 204–8
  in Russia, 200
 during World War II
  in Germany, 216
  in Netherlands, 219
  in North America, 224
nonviolence. *See* nonresistance
Northern Rhodesia (Zambia), 249
Nürnberg (Germany), 63
Nyabasi (Tanzania), 256
Nyanga mission (Congo), 176, 178
Nyce, Dorothy Yoder, 339

Obbenites, 93
Ockenfuss, Hans, 42
Oesada (Indonesia), 220
Ogwada, Wilson, 257
Ohio, 165–66, 316, 325
Oklahoma, 189
Old Colony Mennonites, 156, 210–11, 295–98, 301, 340–41
Oldeklooster (Netherlands), 96
Old German Baptist Brethren, 333
(Old) Mennonite Church
 African American churches, 319
 Amish Mennonite merger with, 163
 and evangelicalism, 333–34
 and fundamentalism, 214
 fundamentals, 193, 214
 merger with General Conference, 323, 334
 missions in India, 184–85
 missions in Texas, 316
 in the nineteenth century, 167–70

missions, rural, 173
and women leaders, 322
during World War I, 205–6
Old Order Amish, 158–64, 208, 333, 340–42
Old Order Mennonites, 161, 206–8, 333, 340, 343
Ontario
  Amish Mennonites, 163
  congregational identities, ethnic, 321
  Low German Mennonites, 343
  migration to, 127
  Old Orders, 161, 341
  Russländer, 210
  transnationalism, 129
  during World War I, 206
  during World War II, 223–24
On the Christian Baptism of Believers (Hubmaier), 54
Ordnung, 158–59, 174, 341
Organización Cristiana Amor Viviente, 239
Ortíz, José, 317
Ottoman Empire, 33–34, 71
Oyer, John, 69

pacifism. *See* nonresistance
Palatinate, 76, 122, 125–26, 129, 131–32, 139, 148
Palestine, 311
papacy and popes, 19, 26, 29–30
Paraguay
  colony model, 119, 153
  government of, 171, 239, 293
  Indigenous relations in, 171
  migration to, 209–10, 235, 343
  and National Socialism, 216, 296
  privilegia, 112
  prosperity in, 301
Paris, France, 321
paseduluran (brotherhood), 274
Passau (Germany), 76, 102
Pati (Indonesia), 240, 266–67
Pax program, 234, 299, 311
peacemaking, 238–39, 274, 290, 338

Peacock, Cynthia, 278
Peasants' War of 1525, 52, 54–55, 66–67, 101, 111
Pehuajó, Argentina, 286
Pel-de Groot, Geertje, 219
Penayo de Duarte, María Gloria, 300
Pennsylvania, 125–29, 139–40, 156, 161, 330
Pentecostalism, 237, 240–41, 254, 278, 290, 303–4, 316–17
persecution
  in Congo, 255
  of Denck, Hans, 63
  in Ethiopia, 258–59
  in the sixteenth century, 100–104, 135
  in Switzerland, 56, 125
  in Tyrol, 73
  in Vietnam, 239–40
Peters, Bev, 323
Pfister, Barlime, 42
Philipites, 76, 78
Philippines, 189, 237, 264–65
Philips, Dirk, 93, 96, 99, 115
Philips, Obbe, 87, 93
Philpott, Jane, 239
Phumula Mission (Zimbabwe), 251
Pietism, 132, 138–40, 148–49, 157, 265
Pilagá people, 291
Pingjum (Netherlands), 96
PIPKA. *See* Foundation for Missions and Charities
Plener, Philip, 76
Poland, 112, 115–17
Portugal, 321
Prieto, Jaime, 233, 286, 301, 304
printing press, 30
privilegia, 112, 116, 153, 210–11
Prussia
  Am Trakt colony, 118
  early modern, 115–16, 122
  and migration to North America, 169
  nationalism, 164
  post-World War II, 306, 312

394 *Radicals & Reformers*

transnationalism, 128–29
  during World War I, 199
  during World War II, 216
Puentes para la Paz (Bridges for Peace), 238
Puerto Rican Mennonite Conference (Conferencia de Iglesias Evangelicas Menonitas de Puerto Rico), 304
Puerto Rico, 294, 304, 312, 316
purgatory, 23–25, 36–37

Qing-Feng Lee, 188
Quakers, 140, 209, 212

radio, 331–32
Ratzlaff, Heinz, 300
Ravensbrück (Nazi concentration camp), 219
Rebstock, Barbara, 85, 95
Reesor-Keller, Leah, 230
Reeves, Ruby, 277
Reflections of an Hispanic Mennonite (Ortíz), 317
Reformed church, 59
regeneration, 62, 71–73, 84, 97–98
Reimer, Klaas, 164
Reist, Hans, 144–49
Reistians, 144–49
Ressler, Jacob Andrew, 185–86
Return to the Earth project, 171
Reublin, Wilhelm, 47, 52–53, 70, 77
revival, 309, 332, 343
revivals, 157–58
  early Anabaptist, 51
  in the nineteenth century, 157–57, 179
  in the twentieth century, 222, 256–58, 271–72, 290, 319, 32, 330–34
Rhineland, 76
Rhodes, Cecil John, 248
Rhodesia. *See* Zimbabwe
Richard, Emma Sommers, 321–22
Ries, Hans de, 122
rightly remembering, 59–60, 105

Rinck, Melchior, 53
Rodríguez, María, 294
Romania, 80
Roosen, Gerrit, 114, 149–50
Rosedale Bible College, 325
Rosedale Network of Churches, 162–63, 325
Roth, John D., 233, 260, 273, 334
Rothmann, Berhard, 88–89, 92
Rotterdam, 95, 219, 307
Rule of Saint Benedict, 21
Rumyantsev (Russian count and general), 80
Russia, 280
  alternative service, 166–67
  and Flemish/Frisian split, 100
  Mennonite Brethren, 137
  and migration to North America, 169
  migration to, 116–19, 126, 129
  nationalism, 164
  in the nineteenth century, 153–56. *See also* Soviet Union
  privilegia, 112
  Ukraine, 2022 invasion of, 261
  during World War I, 200–204
Russian civil war, 201–4
Russländer, 203, 210
Rustiman (grandson of Tunggul Wulung), 181
Rutgers, Swaen, 99
Rwanda, 256

Sacramentarians, 86
sacraments, 22–24
Sacrifice of the Lord, The (Het offer des Heeren), 103
Sacrosancta, 29–30
Saenz Pena community (Argentina), 291
saints, 26
Salatiga (Indonesia), 230
Saltzman, Vinora Weaver, 195
Salvation Army, 182
Sampurnowati, Endang, 181
Samyandi (Indonesia), 220
Sanchez, J., 291

Sanneh, Lamin, 232
Santali people, 276
Santa Rosa (Argentina), 287
Saskatchewan, 210–11, 295, 343
Sattler, Marguerita, 56–57
Sattler, Michael, 56–57, 64, 70, 77, 103
Saxony, 34
Schad, Elias, 134
Schauenburg, Count of, 114
Schellenberg, Abraham, 205
Schiemer, Leonhard, 67, 73
Schlabach, Joetta Handrich, 313
Schlabach, Theron, 157
Schlaffer, Hans, 67, 73
Schleitheim Confession, 21, 55–56, 68, 75, 144–46
Schmidt Bartel, Henry C., 187
Schmidt Bartel, Nellie, 187
Schmucker, Isaac, 159
Schneck, Abraham ("Krieg Schneck"), 166
Schoulderblade, Julia Yellow Horse, 191
Schröder, Agnetha, 179
Schumacher, Fridli, 51
Schwarzenau Brethren, 140
Schwertler (sword-bearers), 75
Selassie, Haile (emperor of Ethiopia), 258
Selbstschutz, 201–2
Selective Service and Training Act, 212
SelfHelp, 312–13, 314
Semarang, 230
Seoul, 262
separatism, 73, 98, 142, 146–49
service, 305
Serving and Learning Together (SALT), 311
Setiawan, Andres, 270
Seventh-day Adventists, 182
Shamshabad (India), 276, 280
Shank, Emma E., 286, 288
Shank, Josephus W., 286
Sheela, Phoebe (later Solomon), 186
Shelly, Wilmer, 205

Shik, Lee Yoon, 40–41, 262
Shirati (Tanzania), 256–57
shrines, 26
shunning, 332
Sibanda, Gono, 249
Siberia, 119
Sidh, Nishant, 280
Sie Djoen Nio, 181–83, 237
Sie Giok Gian, 183
Sigismund (king), 29
Silesia (Czech Republic), 76, 78
Silobi (Zimbabwe), 249
Simons, Menno, 96–99, 111, 115, 124, 157
simplicity, 133, 334
Singapore, 237, 270
Sitting Bull (Tȟatȟáŋka Íyotake), 189
Slagel, Arthur, 209
Slagel, Vesta Zook, 195
slavery, 165
Slovakia, 79, 122
Smissen, Carl Justus van der, 129, 205
Smith, C. Henry, 214
Smith, Lulu, 307
Soeyono (Indonesia), 220
sola scriptura, 45, 62, 105
Solomon, Phoebe (née Sheela), 186
Solomon, Stephen, 186
Sommerfelder Mennonites, 296
South Africa, 251
South Dakota, 209
South Korea, 40–41, 241, 262–64, 311
South Tapanuli (Indonesia), 178
Soviet Union, 202, 209, 211–12, 216, 235, 296–300, 306–7, 309–10, 312
Spain, 321
Spanish-American War, 173, 188
Spanish Civil War, 288
Spiritualism, 71, 94, 97–98, 338
spirituality, 138, 157–58. *See also* Pietism
Stäbler (staff-bearers), 75–76
Standing Elk, Eugene, 192

Stauffer, Elam, 247, 256
Stauffer, Elizabeth, 247
Stehman, Jacob, 208
Steinbach, Manitoba, 332
Steiner, Menno S., 173, 188
Stevens, Thaddeus (US representative), 165
St. Gallen (Switzerland), 52, 64
Stinstra-Braam, Anna, 120
Stoltzfus, Mary, 340
Strasbourg, 64, 67, 70, 84–86, 91, 95
Stroessner, Alfredo (Paraguayan leader), 299
Stuckey Amish, 162
Stuckey, Joseph, 162
Stumpf, Simon, 45, 47–48
Stutthof concentration camp, 218
submission. See *Gelassenheit*
Sumatra, 179
Sunday schools, 161, 169, 172–73
Sutanto, Adi, 270–72
Sutjipta, Adi, 270
Swaab, Marion, 219
Swiss Brethren
  in Esslingen, 70
  and half-Anabaptists, 143–49
  music, 136
  mutual aid, 77
  persecution, 122–25
  spirituality, 138
  transnationalism, 108–9, 128–30
Switzerland
  Amish division in, 143–49
  Marpeck in, 71
  and Mennonite World Conference, 268
  persecution in, 74–75, 100, 124–26
  reforms, 46, 62
  transnationalism, 128–29
Sword and Trumpet, 213–14, 319
Syria, 312

Tabor College (Hillsboro, KS), 335
Taiwan, 284
Taiwanese Mennonite Church, 284
Tanganyika. *See* Tanzania
Tan Hao An (Herman), 268, 270
Tan King Ien, 268
Tanzania, 235, 247, 256–58
Tanzanian Mennonite Church, 235
Tau, the, 66, 88–89, 95
Tauler, Johannes, 32
Tayu (Indonesia), 220, 266
Teachers Abroad Program (TAP), 311
Tee Siem Tat, 181–83, 237, 265, 268
Test Acts, 127–28
Tetzel, Johann, 36
Texas, 316, 332
Teylers Foundation, 141
Theologica Deutsch, 32
Thiessen, Gerhard "Gerry," 226
Thirty Years' War, 79
Thomashöfer Erklärung, 307
Tigray region (Ethiopia), 260
tithes, 46–47
Toba people, 290
Tokyo, 283
Tokyo Area Fellowship of Mennonite Churches, 283
toleration, 111, 114, 119, 122
Torres, Grace, 316
Torres, Katherine, 238
Torres, Neftali, 316
Tot Leerzaam Vermaak (For Instructive Pleasure), 141
Transchaco Highway, 299
Trenque Lauquen, 286
treuherzige (true-hearted). See *halbtäufer* (half-Anabaptists)
Troyer, David N., 314
Troyer, Jonas D., 159
Tsao Hsien (China), 187
Tsese-Ma'heone-Nemeotötse (*Cheyenne Spiritual Songs*), 191
Tshiama, Adolphine, 228
Tshidimu, François, 255
Tshimika, Pakisa K., 244, 248
Tshinyama, Mama Kadi, 322–23
Tunggul Wulung, Ibrahim, 179–83, 237, 265

Twelve Articles of Memmingen, 55
Tyrol (Austria), 54–55, 71, 73, 75–76

Uganda, 256
Ukraine
  Associated Mennonite Brethren Churches, 130
  colonization of, 170
  colony model, 254
  famine, 209
  and Mennonite Brethren, 157
  migration from, 210–11
  migration to, 117–19
  in the nineteenth century, 153–56
  Russian 2022 invasion of, 130, 230, 261
  during World War I, 200–204
  during World War II, 222
  See also Soviet Union
Union of Bohemian Brethren (Unitas Fratrum), 33
United Evangelical Church (Argentina), 290
United Kingdom, 340
United Missionary Church, 276–77
United Native Ministries Council, 172
United States of America, 80, 155–56, 164–65, 204–8, 271, 273, 311
Unruh, W. F., 333
Upper Bihar (India), 276
Urban Racial Council, 319
Urban VI (pope), 29
Uruguay, 235, 293
Useful and Edifying Address to the Youth (Burkholder), 139

Vallecillo, Reynaldo, 239
Vancouver (BC), 344
Vatican, 59
Ventura, Juan, 317
Vietnam, 312
Vietnam War, 338
Villareal, Yolanda, 332
Virginia, 140, 161, 169, 214

Visser, Piet, 138
Vistula Delta, 115–17
Vlissingen (Netherlands), 219
Volksdeutsche, 221–22
Vorwärts, 205
Voth, Heinrich R., 189–91

Waldeck, Franz von (prince-bishop of Münster), 89
Waldshut (Germany), 54
Wallace, George (governor of Alabama), 319
Wanezji Mission (Zimbabwe), 251
Wang Hsuen Ch'en, 187
War of the Lamb, 122
Washington, George, 127
Waterland, 99
Waterlanders, 99, 138, 149
Waterloo, 344
Wayindama, Emmanuel, 255
Weaver, Vinora (later Saltzman), 195
Weber, L. S., 288
Weber, Peter, 131, 139
Wedel, Cornelius H., 214
Weierhof (Germany), 215
Welahan (Indonesia), 183
West Germany. *See* Germany
West Kasai (Congo), 254
Wetseh, Abraham, 250
Widjaja, Albert, 270
Wiebe, Anna, 297
Wiebe, Isebrand, 128
Wiebe, Johan, 156
Wiedemann, Jakob, 76–78
Wiens, Arnoldo, 239
William III (king of England, stadholder of Holland), 120
Wilmot (Ontario), 163
Winnipeg, 344
Witikon (Switzerland), 47
Witmarsum (Netherlands), 96
Wittenberg, 34, 49
women
  in Congo, 231, 255
  in early Anabaptism, 53–54, 57–58, 69, 74
  in Ethiopia, 259

in India, 278
in Latin America, 294–95
leaders, 316, 321–23
in Münster, 91
persecution of, 104
in Texas, 332
World War I
in Germany, 198–99
in North America, 204–8
in Russia, 200–201
World War II, 297, 305, 310–11, 320, 327, 335
in China, 221–22
in Germany, 215–18
in Indonesia, 220–21, 266–67
in the Netherlands, 219–20
in North America, 223–26
in the Soviet Union, 222–23
Writs, Willem, 141–42
Württemberg (Germany), 76, 104
Wüst, Eduard, 157
Wüstenfelde (Germany), 111
Wycliff, John, 29

Yamada, Takashi, 282–83
Yayasan Keluarga Sangkakala (Trumpet Family Foundation), 271–72
Yoder, John Howard, 337–39
Yoder, Mahala, 162
Yoder, Paton, 163
Yoder, Phebe, 257
Yogyakarta (Indonesia), 271
Yorubaland (West Africa), 246
Yosep (Indonesia), 220

Zaandam (Netherlands), 152, 219
Zaire. *See* Democratic Republic of the Congo
Zambia, 249
Zaporizhzhia, 222
Zimbabwe, 248–51, 326
Zollikon (Switzerland), 49–51, 55, 134
Zook, Vesta (later Weaver), 195
Zürich, 13, 55, 58, 100, 125, 134, 338
  Affair of the Sausages, 45–46
  Castelberger circle, 42–44, 49
  disputation of January 17, 1525, 50, 52
  disputation of October 26, 1523, 48
Zwingli, Ulrich, 44–45, 215, 337

The Author

Troy Osborne is associate professor of history and theological studies at Conrad Grebel University College in Waterloo, Ontario, where he teaches courses on the Reformation and Mennonite history. He has a PhD from the University of Minnesota and degrees from Goshen College and Anabaptist Mennonite Biblical Seminary. His articles have appeared in the *Mennonite Quarterly Review*, *Archive for Reformation History*, and *Church History and Religious Culture*.

Looking back,
LIVING FORWARD

Celebrate the five hundredth anniversary of Anabaptism in 2025 with these amazing resources from MennoMedia. Each resource in the Anabaptism at 500 suite offers spiritual inspiration, connection, education, and invitation to the Anabaptist community and to the broader Christian church.

Anabaptism at 500 resources include the following:

- *Anabaptist Community Bible*
- *Faith in Full Color: A Tapestry of Anabaptist Stories* compiled and written by Jeanne Zimmerly Jantzi
- Devotionals
  - *Footsteps of Faith: A Global Anabaptist Devotional*
  - *Drawing Near: A Devotional Journey with Art, Poetry, and Reflection*
- Children's books engaging Anabaptist traditions and themes
  - *Sparking Peace* by Teresa Kim Pecinovsky and Hannah Martin
  - *Stitched Together* by Aimee Reid
  - *A Light to Share: Stories of Spreading Love and Changing the World* by Natalie Frisk

Learn more about these resources at AnabaptismAt500.com.